# Interpartner Dynamics in Strategic Alliances

A volume in
*Research in Strategic Alliances*
T. K. Das, *Series Editor*

# RESEARCH IN STRATEGIC ALLIANCES

T. K. Das, *Series Editor*

**Published**

*Researching Strategic Alliances: Emerging Perspectives*
Edited by T. K. Das

*Strategic Alliances in a Globalizing World*
Edited by T. K. Das

*Behavioral Perspectives on Strategic Alliances*
Edited by T. K. Das

*Strategic Alliances for Value Creation*
Edited by T. K. Das

*Management Dynamics in Strategic Alliances*
Edited by T. K. Das

*Managing Knowledge in Strategic Alliances*
Edited by T. K. Das

*Interpartner Dynamics in Strategic Alliances*
Edited by T. K. Das

**Forthcoming volumes**

*Managing Public–Private Strategic Alliances*
Edited by T. K. Das

*Strategic Alliances for Innovation and R&D*
Edited by T. K. Das

*Managing Resources and Risks in Strategic Alliances*
by T. K. Das

# Interpartner Dynamics in Strategic Alliances

*edited by*

**T. K. Das**

*City University of New York*

INFORMATION AGE PUBLISHING, INC.
Charlotte, NC • www.infoagepub.com

**Library of Congress Cataloging-in-Publication Data**

A CIP record for this book is available from the Library of Congress
http://www.loc.gov

ISBN: 978-1-62396-135-0 (Paperback)
  978-1-62396-136-7 (Hardcover)
  978-1-62396-137-4 (ebook)

Copyright © 2013 Information Age Publishing Inc.

All rights reserved. No part of this publication may be reproduced, stored in a retrieval system, or transmitted, in any form or by any means, electronic, mechanical, photocopying, microfilming, recording or otherwise, without written permission from the publisher.

Printed in the United States of America

# CONTENTS

Foreword to the Series ........................................................................... vii

About the Series ..................................................................................... ix

1 Alliance Competence: From Conceptualization
  to Implementation, With Implications for the Alliance Manager ..... 1
  *Robert Edward Spekman*

2 Operating Routines, Cultural Alignment, and Relational
  Mechanisms in Alliances ................................................................... 27
  *Poonam Khanna, Dovev Lavie, and Pamela R. Haunschild*

3 The Roles of Third Parties in Strategic Alliance Governance .......... 55
  *Rosalinde Klein Woolthuis, Bart Nooteboom, Gjalt de Jong,
  and Dries Faems*

4 A Natural-Resource-Based Examination of Strategic Alliance
  Formation............................................................................................ 73
  *Anne Norheim-Hansen*

5 A Circumplex Approach to Interpartner Dynamics
  in Strategic Alliances ......................................................................... 97
  *Olivier Furrer, Brian Tjemkes, Pepijn Vos, Carmen Boymans,
  and Marit Ubachs*

6 Multilevel Embeddedness in Multilateral Alliances:
  A Conceptual Framework ................................................................ 131
  *Sveinn Vidar Gudmundsson, Christian Lechner,
  and Hans van Kranenburg*

7  Interpartner Dynamics in Asymmetric Strategic Alliances: The Role of Interpersonal Networks.................................................. 149
   *Annabelle Jaouen, Olivier Meier, and Audrey Missonier*

8  Dynamic Evolution of Equity Joint Venture Relationships: Role of the Parent Companies and Joint Venture Control............. 163
   *Pieter E. Kamminga and Jeltje van der Meer-Kooistra*

9  Managing Conflict in International Strategic Alliances................ 187
   *Saleema Kauser*

10 Accounting for Partners That Are Worth Trusting ........................ 211
   *Morten Jakobsen*

11 Quality of Partner Relations in International Construction Alliances....................................................................................................... 233
   *Beliz Ozorhon and David Arditi*

12 Power as a Management Tool for Strategic Alliances: A Study of Russian Agri-Food Business ............................................ 255
   *Vera Belaya and Jon Henrich Hanf*

13 Impact of Interpartner Diversity on the Performance of Global Strategic Alliances ............................................................. 279
   *Hiroshi Yasuda*

   About the Contributors........................................................................ 301

# FOREWORD TO THE SERIES

Relationships have been important to commercial activity and economic transactions for thousands of years. Yet the development of a global competitive landscape has substantially enhanced the importance of partnerships between economic entities. These partnerships, referred to as strategic alliances, provide access to resources and capabilities that allow firms to gain economies of scope and to increase their productivity and innovation. The economies, productivity, and innovations are necessary to at least maintain competitive parity and especially to achieve a competitive advantage in the often highly competitive global markets. Strategic alliances have also become a prominent means of entering new markets, especially foreign markets. Therefore, alliances and the networks of firms of which they are a part have become essential for the conduct of business for all types of firms, large, small, established, and new.

Because of their growing importance, research on strategic alliances has increased markedly in the last two decades, yet there is need for an authoritative compendium of strategic alliance research and knowledge. This book series on *Research in Strategic Alliances* fills this critically important gap in our field. It provides a thorough examination of significant topics that provide complete and up-to-date knowledge on strategic alliances. This book series will serve as a catalyst for more effective management of strategic alliances and will guide future research on them. I commend it to you.

—Michael A. Hitt
Distinguished Professor and Joe B. Foster Chair in Business Leadership at Texas A&M University, and Past President of the Academy of Management and the Strategic Management Society

# ABOUT THE SERIES

The globalization of markets has led to increased interdependence among business firms, leading to an explosion in the number of strategic alliances. Strategic alliances, briefly, are cooperative arrangements aimed at achieving the strategic objectives of two or more partner firms. These interfirm arrangements can range from joint R&D to equity-based joint ventures. However, the scholarship relating to strategic alliances remains largely dispersed in the literatures of traditional academic disciplines such as strategic management, marketing, economics, and sociology. This book series on strategic alliances will cover the essential progress made thus far in the literature and elaborate upon fruitful streams of scholarship. More importantly, the book series will focus on providing a robust and comprehensive forum for new scholarship in the field of strategic alliances. In particular, the books in the series will cover new views of interdisciplinary theoretical frameworks and models (dealing with resources, risk, trust, control, cooperation, learning, opportunism, governance, developmental stages, performance, etc.); significant practical problems of alliance organization and management (such as alliance capability, interpartner conflict, internal tensions, use of information technology); and emerging areas of inquiry. The series will also include comprehensive empirical studies of selected segments of business—economic, industrial, government, and nonprofit activities—with wide prevalence of strategic alliances. Through the ongoing release of focused topical titles, this book series will seek to disseminate theoretical insights and practical management information that will enable interested professionals to gain a rigorous and comprehensive understanding of the field of strategic alliances.

# CHAPTER 1

# ALLIANCE COMPETENCE

## From Conceptualization to Implementation, With Implications for the Alliance Manager

**Robert Edward Spekman**

### ABSTRACT

Many companies face the challenge of competing on the global stage, and alliances have been touted as one approach to gain competitive advantage. Over the last 20 years, the number of alliances has grown almost exponentially, but the rate of failure still holds at about 60%. A command-and-control approach will not work in today's world, yet to managers whose traditional way of doing business resists collaboration, an alliance mindset does not come naturally. This chapter examines why managers haven't gotten better at alliance management. We are interested in understanding why some firms are more successful at alliance management and which skills result in a higher rate of success. The construct of alliance competence is explored and its various elements defined. Also articulated are different strategies a firm might employ to develop these skills and capabilities in its alliance managers, including organizational structures and processes. Alliances are about people, so we emphasize the interpersonal dynamics of alliance competence.

## INTRODUCTION

To say that alliances are pervasive throughout the corporate landscape almost seems to trivialize their true impact on the conduct of global business. My coauthors and I made that statement over ten years ago in the preface to our book on alliance competence (Spekman, Isabella, & MacAvoy, 2000). Since we wrote that book, alliances have continued to grow in importance and have become part of the corporate strategic landscape, a way for global firms to achieve a competitive advantage. In fact, firms have relied on alliances to enhance their power in the marketplace (Kogut, 1991), access new markets and/or new technology (e.g., Rothaermel & Boeker, 2008), and improve profitability as well as shareholder performance (e.g., Swaminathan & Moorman, 2009). Yet despite all the advantages gained from alliances, they fail at the rate of 60% to 70% (Spekman et al., 2000), and the rate of failure has not decreased significantly in 20 years. As suggested by Kale and Singh (2009), such mixed results present a paradox: firms need alliances to compete effectively in the global economy, but their track record is not very encouraging.

Given that the number of alliances has grown almost exponentially in the last 20 years and the rate of success has not increased, it makes sense to revisit the question: Why haven't managers gotten better at alliance management? The best way to address this question is to step back and ask a more fundamental question: Which management skills determine alliance success?

Alliances require a change in how managers think and act and how they relate to their partners. Friedman (2005) argues that collaborative skills are essential in the flat world, but such skills do not come naturally to managers who came of age in the command-and-control world of the past and are uncomfortable with anything else. Since it is impossible to control what one does not own, these managers face profound challenges that cut to the heart of how they have done business. What if we could raise the rate of alliance success through a better understanding of the specific skills they need to acquire or improve?

## RELEVANT LITERATURE

Firms share resources to achieve mutually beneficial goals that neither partner can achieve alone (Lambe, Spekman, & Hunt, 2002). *Resources* are defined as any tangible or intangible entity available to the firm to compete in the marketplace and include both physical assets and capabilities held by personnel. When partner firms combine complementary resources, alliances are more likely to succeed. One firm may have local market access, the other a brand and tacit knowledge of the brand in other markets. As partners, each with access to the resources and knowledge of the other, they can expedite the success of the brand in the new market.

To acquire and utilize a diverse set of capabilities, firms develop alliance strategies that help integrate different disciplines and bodies of knowledge; provide access to technologies, markets, and customers that might not be easily reached otherwise; enable the acquisition of R&D; and employ innovations that might otherwise be too costly to implement and allow one technology or set of standards to dominate another. Strategic alliance thinking represents the integration of economic and social theories and, to firms adept at its practice, can provide a sustainable competitive advantage.

Firms that lack alliance competence, meanwhile, tend to be relegated to second-class positions in the markets they serve. Because alliances typically require that a company change some of its attitudes and behaviors, old rules may no longer apply. To some firms, ownership and control are imperative; other firms are loath to rely on a partner to help them achieve their goals. Yet trust is the mortar that binds partners together. To the cautious, a contract might provide a degree of protection, but trust is both the key to successful collaboration and, as it happens, a firm's best protection against opportunistic behavior.

What does it mean to be alliance-competent? Competence is a multidimensional concept about the attitudes and behaviors that lead to success, so alliance competence suggests that a firm understands the process of developing, nurturing, and managing an alliance. Firms that are widely recognized as being competent are sought out as partners, are selective in their choice of partners, and have a well-honed approach to alliance management. They embrace the tenets of collaborative behavior and are better equipped to leverage the full potential of their partners for the benefit of the alliance.

A sustainable competitive advantage is a function of the partners' collective resources and their alliance competence. Three elements must be understood if a firm is to be alliance-competent. First is that alliances are about relationships, and relationships are about people. The second is that knowledge and information are assets to be shared and that its free and open flow benefits all parties. The third is that certain processes, systems, and structural factors guide and enable alliance-like behavior, the objective being to improve collaboration and integration across units and across boundaries and thus bring value to the marketplace.

## CONCEPTUAL FRAMEWORKS UTILIZED

Much of the work done in the area of alliances has evolved out of three research traditions: transaction cost economics, social exchange theory, and resource dependency. Each is described briefly below. These traditions have provided scholars with cultural frameworks on which to develop theories about alliance formation, governance choice, maintenance, and termination.

## Transaction Cost Economics (TCE)

The major body of work by Williamson (1975, 1991) states that contractual mechanisms break down under conditions of high uncertainty or asymmetry of information. When this occurs, there is a probability one partner will act opportunistically to the detriment of the other. Opportunism endangers the performance of the alliance, because each partner will act in its own self-interest; one partner may withhold information and/or resources from the other, for instance, to protect its own assets or competencies.

This tendency is held in check by trust and other relational norms in which partners acknowledge their interdependence. In addition, it is possible that *equity alliances*, in which partners take an ownership stake in the alliance, reduce the threat of opportunism. Also, it is possible to encourage contractual safeguards in which there are penalties assessed to a partner that violates a provision of the alliance contract. These safeguards could be in the form of "poison pills," in which the rules of the game are spelled out clearly and in detail. Such actions often reduce transaction costs and make positive outcomes more likely.

## Social Exchange Theory

If one views alliances as derived from social networks and based on socially constructed behaviors, it is not surprising to find that *social exchange* is a condition in which the actions of one party provide the rewards and incentives for the actions of another party over a period of repeated interaction (Homans, 1961). The importance of social exchange can be traced to notions of relational contracting (Macneil, 1980), social embeddedness (Granovetter, 1985), and game theory (Axelrod, 1984) as approaches to understanding the nature of alliance partners' interaction. It is believed that interfirm exchange and coordination processes should enhance ties among partners and should promote more equitable exchanges. In addition, mutual commitment and trust should result in better alliance outcomes. For example, mutual commitment of resources reduces uncertainty. Trust can be viewed as confidence in a party's expectations about another's fairness, behavior, and goodwill (Ring & Van de Ven, 1992). Trust develops over time as partners work together and is the positive reputation for non-opportunistic behavior. Trust increases the scope of the relationship, enhances learning, improves communications between partners, enhances a number of collaborative behaviors, facilitates greater joint planning, and leads to better outcomes (Muthusamy, White, & Carr, 2007).

A subfield within a social exchange framework is a *network* view. At its core, a network perspective argues that all firms are interconnected in that they collaborate with other firms to create value for the marketplace (Granovetter, 1985). The network view is a process view in which partners agree to exchange goods over a period of time. Weaker partners are at a disadvantage due to asymmetries caused by size, relative dependency, and transaction-specific investments that are made. Chen and Chen (2002) examined alliances between emerging economies (Taiwan) and developed countries and found that emerging economies tend to partner with larger firms as a vehicle for improving their reputation and credibility. The network paradigm focuses on the contingent nature of the relationship and reinforces the importance of alliances as a means to exchange goods and services. Network thinking has been the hallmark of the IPM Group and has been the guiding paradigm for many of the studies it has authored. The argument for a network approach stems from the belief that firms are inextricably linked and their patterns of interaction are guided by the network connections they have.

## Resource Dependency (RD)

Few firms are self-sufficient. *Resource dependency* is based on the notion that resource control determines success, so firms compete for those resources, inevitably creating dynamics of power and dependence as well as uncertainty in decision making. Alliances are one mechanism to deal with these issues. Heide (1994) stated that dependence and uncertainty are key antecedents to the formation of any interfirm relationship, positing that TCE parallels RD in viewing nonmarket governance as a response to environmental uncertainty and dependence. To the extent these approaches explain the rise of strategic alliances, they might be considered complementary theories and not competing ones.

The fundamental thesis of the *resource-based view* (RBV) of the firm is that firm resources are both significantly heterogeneous and imperfectly mobile (Wernerfelt, 1984). Resource heterogeneity suggests that each organization has an assortment of resources (e.g., specialized knowledge, distribution networks, and R&D skills) that are unique and imperfectly mobile, therefore not easily transferred to other firms. To the extent they are deemed valuable, rare, durable, and inimitable (Barney, 1991), these resources are a source of competitive advantage. In fact, RBV suggests that when a firm possesses all four of these attributes, it will attain a sustainable competitive advantage because it will provide higher value for its customers than its competitors.

A complementary explanation of alliance success, *competence-based theory*, provides a linkage between resources and strategy (Lewis & Gregory, 1996). From this perspective, a *competence* is a firm's ability to use both tangible and intangible resources to compete in its marketplace (Sanchez, Heene, & Thomas, 1996). In fact, work by Hamel and Prahalad (1994) argues that competences might be considered resources, although intangible, because they contribute to a firm's ability to compete successfully.

## Competence Defined

A *competence* may be defined as any valuable resource or capability that makes a firm more attractive for acquisition or alliance. In either case, the target firm is chosen so that the other firm might have access to these resources and/or capabilities.

Specific to each successful company is a *core* competence, or unique grouping of skills, resources, technologies, people, and so on, that makes a company a leader in a certain field. These competences comprise intangible assets that allow a firm to successfully compete and to differentiate itself from its competition (Prahalad & Hamel, 1990). Examples of intangible assets are (1) company reputation, (2) product reputation, (3) employee know-how, (4) networks, (5) supplier know-how, (6) distribution know-how, and (7) databases (Valentino, 1992).

Consistent with the notion of networks is the concept of the strategic center of the network without which the network lacks a sense of direction (Lorenzoni & Baden-Fuller, 1995). The *strategic center* is the firm that engages the partners in such a way that the network benefits and that one partner does not gain at the other's expense. In many ways, the strategic center is the moral compass of the network by encouraging members to be not merely doers but innovators and problem solvers. These firms force network members to share their expertise with other network members, borrow ideas from others which are then exploited and developed, and, finally, recognize that the network is as strong as its weakest member (Lorenzoni & Baden-Fuller, 1995). A company at the strategic center is an advocate for a new view of the competitive dynamics and sees competition not at the firm level but at the network level.

Although the notion of a strategic center implies an unfettered sharing of knowledge and experience across a network, such an expectation would be unrealistic; issues such as partner incompatibility, cultural distance, and positional embeddedness can create barriers to the transfer of knowledge (Kiessling & Richey, 2005). *Partner incompatibility* refers to the lack of alignment between partners across a number of dimensions such as trust and other relational attributes. *Cultural distance* is based on how far apart the firms are regarding such issues as researched by Hofstede (1980) in his seminal study of cultural dimensions. The differences between U.S. and Asian firms were most pronounced, which might account for the poor track record of alliances across the Pacific. *Positional embeddedness* captures the impact of the positions organizations occupy within the overall structure of the network. A firm at the center of a network has access to information about other network members that firms on the periphery do not (Gulati & Gargiulo, 1999). More centralized firms have an ability to control information, and information bestows power.

Based on the above, it is possible to expand the discussion to classify assets that add value to the firm's competences. The first class of assets would be *idiosyncratic resources* possessed by the firm. These resources tend to lead to short-term effects, because the individual might leave the firm, or the explicit knowledge might be easily acquired by a competitor. One need only examine the Zantac case and witness how Glaxo designed around Smith-Kline's patents for Tagamet to remove a part of a molecule that caused certain side effects, resulting in Zantac's meteoric rise to become a billion-dollar-plus star in Glaxo's portfolio. Yet it is the tacit knowledge that is often more difficult to imitate, especially if such knowledge is woven into the genetic structure of the firm. Apple's ability to anticipate market needs and create products that capture its customers' imagination has certainly given the firm a sustainable competitive advantage. The question that remains is whether this ability will continue with the passing of Steve Jobs.

A second value-adding class of assets would be a firm's technical capabilities: the routines a firm has in place for doing what the firm does on a daily basis. There are the systems that the firm cannot describe or transfer adequately but together enable R&D, manufacturing, marketing, and sales to add value. Sharing these competencies requires the highest level of trustworthiness among partners and can be facilitated through an equity relationship, which may promote non-opportunistic behavior (Tallman, 1999). The leadership of a firm can determine its willingness to trust. For instance, the firm's reward/compensation system can set a tone for the level of trust held by its employees. In the auto industry, GM has been trusted much less by its supply base than has Honda and Toyota. While the relationship has been more adversarial with GM and its suppliers than with both Honda and Toyota, part of the reason can be attributed to the culture of the firms as well as the larger societal cultural in Japan. Norm-based trust (Zucker, 1986) might be a reflection of larger societal cultural issues (Hofstede, Neuijen, Ohayv, & Sanders, 1990).

A third class of assets would be *managerial competencies*, the skills and resources that the firm leverages in the present and uses to develop newer skills and resources for the future. Organizational structure can impact both the firm's ability to leverage its extant alliances and its ability to develop new skills for the future. In alliances, bureaucracy can stifle the firm's ability to innovate due to the rigid rules that standardization and centralization manifest. On the other hand, in an adhocracy, its structure encourages the expression of communication, discussion, and information sharing that, in turn, promotes a climate in which alliances are more likely to succeed. Here, the notion of competence as a tool to leverage and create new capabilities is bound to lead to better alliance performance.

## Learning as a Competency

Kale and Singh (2009) have developed the notion of *alliance learning processes*, which involve the articulation, codification, sharing, and internalization of alliance management know-how. They demonstrate that, by leveraging this know-how, a firm is able to enhance its alliance success rates and that these learning processes partially mediate a firm's overall alliance performance. Their argument represents a confluence of three separate streams of research: (1) knowledge-based view (KBV) of the firm (e.g., Kogut & Zander, 1992), (2) organizational learning (e.g., Huber, 1991), and (3) dynamic capabilities (e.g., Winter, 2003). Grant (1996) advocated that the KBV of the firm approach identified knowledge as central to the firm, not only because of its quantitative importance to value added but also because of its strategic importance. Grant further stated that knowledge possesses the characteristics most relevant to gaining a sustainable competitive advantage: It is scarce, costly to imitate, and difficult to transfer. The KBV of the firm is based on two fundamental assumptions: that no two firms possess the same knowledge and that knowledge is hard to transfer from firm to firm.

Regarding organizational learning, Cohen and Levinthal (1990) demonstrated that firms learn at different rates, depending on *absorptive capacity*, or the ability to recognize the value of new information, assimilate it, and apply it. They argue that absorptive capacity depends greatly on one's prior related knowledge and diversity of background. The greater one's knowledge and the more diverse one's background, the more one is able to seek and appreciate the value of new external knowledge. Research has demonstrated that alliance partners that do not have any understanding of each other's R&D are more likely to have a hard time combining their diverse backgrounds. Some understanding of or an appreciation of the other's technology is more likely to result in alliance success. Often firms are constrained in their abilities to develop new technology either through path dependency or organizational inertia (Cyert & March, 1963).

*Dynamic capabilities* refer to the capability of an organization to purposefully create, extend, or modify its resource base (Anand, Oriani, & Vassolo, 2010). Unlike the previous discussion, the key question addressed here is how a firm develops the skills that allow it to compete and gain an enduring competitive advantage. Their results suggest that firms with a stronger advantage in an emerging technology are more likely to enter that technology through internal development, whereas those with weaker capabilities are more likely to enter that technology through alliances in which they hope to leverage the skills of their partners (Anand et al., 2010). One question that is not addressed is whether a firm with excellent partnering skills but without a technological advantage can be as successful in the emerging technology as a firm that possesses that expertise.

If the answer is yes, then alliance formation can help a firm break out of a technology gap. Yet there is the problem of absorptive capacity. That is, if a firm lacks core capabilities, its complementary capabilities should theoretically serve as a means of acquiring the external capabilities via alliances. While Anand and his colleagues suggested that such an approach might yield positive results, they cautioned the reader that their results do not address the issue of whether the firm is able to internalize the technology after the alliance is formed (Anand et al., 2010). Not only must knowledge flow across the boundaries of the firm; it also must be receptive to the knowledge it obtains.

## Knowledge Transfer as a Competency

Whether stated or not, the goal of most alliances is to acquire knowledge by learning from one's partners. Khamseh and Jolly (2008) attempted to categorize the factors that affect a firm's ability to transfer knowledge in alliances. It is one thing to learn from one's partner; it is quite another to transfer that knowledge to your organization. The kind of knowledge will affect the degree to which it is absorbed and certain characteristics of the partners can impact the degree to which the flow of information is either facilitated or hindered.

The first factor in the transferability of knowledge is the nature of the knowledge to be shared. *Explicit* knowledge is codified and is more easily transferred. *Tacit* knowledge is often embodied in the individual and more challenging to articulate, so knowledge transfer is slower and often more tedious. Knowledge also can vary in degree of complexity, which can make some hard to understand; knowledge that is hard to understand is also hard to communicate, so it may require special mechanisms to transfer (Khamseh & Jolly, 2008). Also important is the role the knowledge plays. A firm's core knowledge lies at the heart of its competitive advantage and would be very difficult to share. Not all tacit knowledge is core, but core knowledge is likely to be tacit. On the other hand, some knowledge may be complementary in that it does not overlap but bolsters each partner. When such synergies exist, the knowledge is more easily transferred.

The second factor is the absorptive capacity of partners. A prior relationship among partners and/or similarity in the bases of knowledge is likely to result in a higher rate of knowledge transfer. A prior relationship between partners often leads to trust, which facilitates knowledge transfer, and similar bases of knowledge result in better understanding the needs of one's partner, which also affects the transfer of knowledge.

The third factor is partner behavior. Increased interaction between partners increases the probability that knowledge will flow between partners. The more protective partners are of the knowledge they possess, the less effective its transfer is. Trust is an essential ingredient in any attempt to transfer knowledge because it acts as a counterpoint to any opportunistic behavior. As Inkpen (2000) suggested, trust is the currency that determines knowledge accessibility.

The fourth factor is the extent to which firm activity relies on knowledge transfer. *Exploitative* activities involve the efficient application of information that the firm currently has, so the need for additional knowledge is minimal. *Exploratory* activities focus more on innovation and knowledge creation, for which the free flow of information is critical.

## ANTECEDENTS OF ALLIANCE COMPETENCE

There are two streams of alliance research, one on what comprises alliance competence and the other on the mechanisms that facilitate it. Within the first, scholars have focused on either a given firm's portfolio of alliances or what might contribute to a better understanding of those competencies. I focus on the latter.

Alliance management requires particular skills, and different skill sets affect an alliance in different ways. Alliance managers play a critical role in how an alliance performs from day to day and are responsible for interaction among partners. Spekman et al. (2000) describe the alliance manager's role as shouldering the responsibility for sustaining the alliance, ensuring that the alliance follows a prescribed path, maintaining relationships that are critical to alliance success and maintaining the alliance's momentum.

Schreiner, Kale, and Corsten (2009) provided a theoretical account of the cognitive, behavioral, and organizational skills that enable a firm to effectively manage any given alliance. Building on work by Mohr and Spekman (1994), Schreiner et al. (2009) empirically address three main aspects in managing a given alliance: coordination, communication, and bonding.

In addition, they examine how firms develop alliance capability. Simonin (1997) and Zollo, Reuer, and Singh (2002) suggest that experience leads to higher levels of alliance competence. This finding is intuitive in that practice makes perfect, yet how much experience does one require? Work by Draulans, deMan, and Volberda (2003) suggests that after six alliances, there are diminishing returns: alliance performance still improves, but at a decreasing rate.

In addition to experience, having a dedicated alliance function helps to build alliance competence because it both facilitates the coordination of alliance-related activity and serves as a repository for building alliance management know-how (Kale, Dyer, & Singh, 2002). This last point is subject to some debate; it is not clear whether a dedicated alliance function is superior to inculcating alliance tenets and principles as part of the corporate culture. It would be difficult, however, to envision a dedicated alliance function without an alliance culture that supported it. At the same time, a dedicated alliance function might also depend on senior management's support of alliance-related thinking within the firm. Experience suggests that if the tenets and principles of alliance-like behavior are not supported by senior management, it is unlikely that a firm will develop any alliance capabilities. That said, the argument in favor of a dedicated function has face validity.

Since the problems facing an alliance vary over its lifespan, it stands to reason that another aspect of alliance competence is the ability to manage an alliance over time. As with any process, there are a number of stages through which the development of an alliance must pass, each of which requires different kinds of decisions, has a different outcome, and often requires different skills and/or capabilities. Figure 1.1 summarizes one view of the different phases through which a typical alliance might travel as it matures and reaches its end point. Whether the process is three phases or seven is not the point; of interest here is how problems are addressed and how the skills of the alliance manager change over the different phases. During the formulation phase, potential partners look for strategic fit, complementarities, shared goals, and vision. This is often referred to as due diligence and gives the potential partners an opportunity to move the alliance from an idea to a concrete reality.

Each phase addresses both business and relationship issues. In the early phases, managers begin an assessment of their needs and motivations for the alliance. Focus is given to the anticipated outcomes and what the alliance hopes to accomplish. Often a more senior member of the management team envisions a unique solution to a problem facing the firm. The solution often involves forming an alliance. Here the analysis is mostly driven by questions that seek to specify the reason for the alliance and attempt to identify candidates who qualify as potential partners. As part of its due diligence, a firm will determine its goals for the proposed alliance and

| Anticipation | Engagement | Valuation | Coordination | Investment | Stabilization | Termination |
|---|---|---|---|---|---|---|
| Begin assessment of needs and motivations | Look for complement, congruence, and potential | Making the business case and negotiating the deal | Operational focus, integration, and coordination | Committing resources and people | Managing over time | One of the options as the alliance reaches its endpoint |

**Figure 1.1** Phases of the alliance life cycle. *Source:* Adapted from Spekman, Isabella, MacAvoy, and Forbes (1996).

the skill set needed to fulfill the goals. Partner selection criteria must align with those determinations. Engagement occurs when the firm meets with prospective partners to share their vision, articulate the business case, and ascertain interest and fit in operational issues, strategic issues, and culture.

*Valuing* is the process by which parties assess the exchange rate and value each party brings to the alliance. Negotiations have begun, for the most part, and firms are beginning to calculate the contribution of each so that, if indicated, an equity arrangement can be determined. For instance, during the early stages of the alliance between Renault and Volvo, the two firms agreed that, although Renault was five times the size of Volvo, Volvo would be given an equal voice in the alliance. This gesture signaled that Volvo's contribution to the success of the alliance was deemed equal to that of Renault. Certainly, Volvo's reputation for safety and engineering and its access to the U.S. market weighed heavily in that decision.

During the process, terms and conditions must be negotiated, sources of known conflict eliminated, performance metrics agreed to, and formal governance established. There are several cautionary points to be made here:

- Avoid "country club" alliances, where CEOs form the outline for an alliance, then have their people focus on the details. Experience suggests that this approach is a recipe for disaster. Senior management buy-in is critical, but a hand-off from a senior manager to an operational manager rarely goes well. This failure occurs because senior managers tend to work at an abstract level with few details, and such vagueness does not provide adequate direction.
- Because they must live with the outcome of the negotiations, the people who will run the alliance should be directly involved. Often the early work is done by the business development people, who hand off the alliance to the alliance managers, who must live and die by an alliance they played no part in forming.
- Be wary of attorney input during the formation phase of the alliance. Lawyers tend to write contracts that are untenable, given the business case; their top priority is protecting the firm, so they often write contracts to that end, at the expense of viability. Nevertheless, they should be involved in the process, because the contract is the living document that describes what the alliance partners have agreed upon.
- Once the contract is written, put it away and resist referring to it constantly. If the contract is pulled and examined, larger problems often surface. I believe that contracts play an essential role, but when they move into the foreground, the spirit of the alliance suffers, and more rigid, contract-like thinking, which is more hierarchical and counter to the alliance process, tends to take over.

An important consideration in the early phases of alliance formation is how negotiations ought to proceed. Issues will require conflict resolution; they need not be rooted in opportunism. When ambiguity, uncertainty, and tension endanger trust, good conflict resolution techniques can mitigate such negative effects. Problem solving as an approach leads to more productive outcomes than either contention or yielding to partner demands; its implicit focus on information exchange and a win–win philosophy is likely to result in an integrative solution. Das and Kumar (2009) refer to interpartner harmony driven by *commitment*, the desire to sustain the alliance, and *forbearance*, which implies partner interaction based on and conducive to long-term confidence in the alliance. One hopes that partners are open, flexible, and responsive to each other and that they avoid attributing partner behaviors and motivations to anything other than their commitment to the alliance's success.

Coordinating and investing tend to occur during the normal life of the alliance as parties learn how to align better and work together. *Investing* is the process by which partners strengthen bonds so that the alliance endures. Lambe et al. (2002) speak of a virtuous cycle in which partners recommit to the alliance. Each dedicates resources to the alliance, thereby forging a closer, more permanent relationship. They go on to argue that alliance-competent firms are better able to leverage complementary resources and understand the skills and capabilities of their partners. Only through integrative processes and other means of sharing knowledge can the alliance achieve its goals.

When problems arise during the management of the alliance, partners often refer to the exit clauses that accompany the formal alliance agreement. I am troubled when termination so quickly becomes the default option. If the alliance is important to both parties, exit as an option is less than satisfactory. I would rather the partners rely on a no-blame review (NBR) (Spekman et al., 2000), which seeks to understand the root cause of the problems, not to place blame. Effort is dedicated to discussing problems and resolving conflicts that have come to negatively affect alliance performance. An NBR may recommend termination, but it is not the default option; partners instead might redefine the alliance, change its course, or resume its existing trajectory.

Based on notions derived from the book by Fisher and Ury (1981), *Getting to Yes*, the intent of the NBR is to reach a mutually satisfactory solution to issues and not finger point. In fact, data from Spekman et al. (2000) suggest that conflict resolution skills are more relevant than negotiation skills.

Alliance management is far more complicated and complex than one might imagine, and the person chosen to manage an alliance becomes a very strategic asset. In fact, a weak alliance manager can ruin a strong alliance. The person chosen for the role, though quite capable otherwise, is often ill-equipped to handle the interpersonal dynamics involved. I believe that the alliance manager is a critical linchpin in building those relationships and in balancing the needs of the business and the partnership. Table 1.1 depicts the different roles played by an alliance manager and summarizes some of the responsibilities associated with them.

As can be seen from Table 1.1, the skills and capabilities needed to be an effective alliance manager are quite diverse, requiring a person who is flexible and adaptive to the stage of the alliance and its requisite roles and who has characteristics that enhance the alliance's mission. The alliance

**TABLE 1.1  Alliance Management Roles and Responsibilities**

| Primary Management Roles | Role Responsibilities (Illustrative) |
|---|---|
| Visionary | • Serves as the driving force behind the alliance's creation<br>• Maintains a broad perspective spanning inside and outside the company<br>• Understands the compatibility of strategic intents<br>• Has a vision of the possibilities the alliance creates |
| Strategic Sponsor | • Sells the concept of strategic alliances inside the company and out<br>• Has the authority to commit people and resources to the alliance<br>• Is part of the alliance, not peripheral to it<br>• Builds an organization with dedicated resources<br>• Encourages social development for alliance growth<br>• Spans many boundaries and layers |
| Advocate | • Sells the value of the relationship to the alliance participants<br>• Sells the value of the specific alliance in question<br>• Develops support for the alliance<br>• Actively owns the day-to-day alliance<br>• Broadcasts its successes and achievements<br>• Makes a significant emotional investment<br>• Pushes the vision of the alliance forward |
| Networker | • Relies on contacts to expedite alliance business<br>• Knows who to ask for help and when to ask<br>• Puts the right people together<br>• Expends effort to cultivate trust in key relationships<br>• Sees interpersonal relationships a key |
| Facilitator | • Encourages open and honest communication among all parties<br>• Facilitates effective reviews of the state of the alliance<br>• Resolves conflict immediately<br>• Is sensitive to the needs of all parties |
| Manager | • Shoulders responsibility for sustaining the alliance<br>• Ensures that the alliance stays on course<br>• Maintains and builds critical relationships<br>• Maintains the alliance's momentum |

*Source:* Adapted from Spekman et al. (2000).

manager is a unique individual who has skills that go beyond the traditional capabilities of a line manager. Line managers tend to operate in functional silos, their position of responsibility typically gained through depth of knowledge. Alliance managers, on the other hand, cross many boundaries and may be considered boundaryless; by virtue of the broad range of strategic and operational issues that must be addressed, they operate simultaneously on three levels: across two or more parent firms, within the parent company, and within the alliance. They must balance the needs and desires of the parent companies, the needs and desires of their home companies, and the day-to-day management of the alliance. On an interpersonal level, alliance managers maintain relationships with superiors, peers, and subordinates both in the alliance and the parent organizations.

## TEACHABLE VERSUS UNTEACHABLE ALLIANCE COMPETENCIES

Merely describing all the touch points makes the job seem almost superhuman. The degree to which the alliance manager must deal with higher-level strategy yet work at the tactical level contemporaneously is not for the faint of heart. Add to that the complexity the different cultures, agendas, and languages that exist in global alliances and one can see why the role of the alliance manager is difficult to articulate. That said, there are a number of competencies that can be taught and others that cannot be taught but can be developed. Teachable skills can be observed and are similar to explicit knowledge in that they are fairly easy to describe and are readily observed. Unteachable skills are more tacit in nature and often address how one thinks and sees the world.

Table 1.2 compares teachable and unteachable competencies. The two differ substantially, though this may not be immediately apparent. Teachable skills can be developed through formal schooling, on-the-job training, or other means. Functional competencies relate to the actual business, its products and technology. Strong alliance managers have both breadth and depth of knowledge, and their past experiences tends to foster an enterprise-wide perspective. As a result, they have an appreciation for the core business and an understanding of adjacent markets. Such a background is very useful if the alliance crosses different technologies or functional skills.

In addition, strong alliance managers tend to work in wide, complicated networks, operating from information nodes where they can influence the flow of information. In fact, their operating philosophy is to leverage their networks to accomplish the goals of their alliances. Along the way, it is important that they be perceived by others as honest brokers working hard on behalf of their alliances and do not push their own agenda. Also,

**TABLE 1.2  Comparisons between Teachable and Unteachable Alliance Competencies**

| Teachable Competencies | Unteachable Competencies |
|---|---|
| 1. Functional competencies<br>   Line/staff skills<br>   Education<br>   Functional expertise/experience<br>   General business knowledge | • Simultaneously sees multiple points of view<br>• Learns from the past but is not constrained by it<br>• Thinks across time |
| 2. Earned competencies<br>   Credibility and respect<br>   Extensive networks | • Sees patterns in chaos<br>• Is clever, creative and constantly curious |
| 3. Interpersonal competencies<br>   Social skills<br>   Communication skills<br>   Tact/sensitivity<br>   Cross-cultural awareness<br>   Process skills | • Possesses true wisdom<br>• Engages diplomatically<br>• Oriented towards learning |

*Source:* Adapted from Spekman et al. (2000).

since alliances are so heavily dependent on relationships between people, interpersonal skills are essential. Although it seems trite to speak about the need for interpersonal savvy, it cannot be emphasized enough. Related to the importance of interpersonal skills are communication skills. Strong alliance managers mirror the actions, tonal quality, and gestures of their counterparts. This skill is especially important in cross-cultural alliances, where it serves to decrease the distance between partners. Also important is cross-cultural sensitivity, which can be defined simply as showing respect for the culture of one's partner.

Unteachable alliance competencies, like tacit knowledge, are thought to be hard-wired into the alliance manager. More often than not, it is hard to develop these skills in a person; nevertheless, the effort must be made to identify unteachable alliance competencies and provide mentoring assistance. These competencies could be considered part of an alliance manager's thought process and how the alliance manager relates to the world around him or her. By seeing multiple points of view, a strong alliance manager shows an ability to take the other's perspective and can better develop a solution that is not viewed as biased or one-sided. Letting the past inform, but not direct, one's actions is an attribute based on the notion that there are no reliable alliance templates to help one address problems as they arise. While I hesitate to say that each alliance is unique, there are enough differences among alliances to give pause to a predetermined solution. The interpersonal dynamics that drive alliance behavior are different enough that a strong alliance manager takes past information and experience and adapts it to the current situation.

It is difficult to describe one's ability to think across time, but the notion is captured by the strong alliance manager who understands what is (the current state), imagines what is possible (the future), and can bridge the gap between the two. Strong alliance managers are unique in their ability to see patterns in chaos and transcend the linear thought progressions of many managers. They get their energy from the uncommon and the atypical. They are curious, clever, and creative, and look forward to issues that challenge the status quo; that requires flexibility in thought and action. They live in a world where they are comfortable working on fuzzy problems—that is, problems that cross disciplines and functions. They possess wisdom in that they are comfortable knowing that they don't have all the answers. Strong alliance managers have a learning mindset and a strong sense of personal engagement.

It should be clear from the above discussion that possession of teachable skills is a necessary but not sufficient condition for a strong alliance manager; unteachable competencies are what truly distinguish them. The problem facing most companies is how to develop a broader base of alliance managers. That is, most senior executives that I have spoken with say they would engage in more alliances if they had more alliance managers.

## BUILDING AN ALLIANCE COMPETENCE AT THE FIRM LEVEL

Firms need to know what will support and facilitate its ability to develop alliance management capabilities (Kale & Singh, 2009). Spekman et al. (2000) have documented five attributes that enable a firm to better support alliance managers.

1. *Know-how* is important throughout the entire alliance management process and relates to the expertise that is captured by the firm. As stated earlier, experience leads to greater alliance success. In fact, research by Anand and Khanna (2000) demonstrates that the stock market reacts more positively to firms with more alliance experience, because the belief is that these firms are more capable.
2. *Supportive process and structure* are the mechanisms that facilitate the sharing of alliance knowledge among partners as well as within the firm. Kale and Singh (2009) argue that a mechanism for enhancing a firm's alliance competence is to create a separate alliance function that is responsible for coordinating and managing a firm's overall alliance activity. One benefit is that this function serves as the repository of alliance-related experiences, captures best practices, and leverages this knowledge throughout the organization. This dedicated function permits greater coordination of alliance activity across the

entire range of the firm's alliances. Another benefit derived from the dedicated alliance function is that is demonstrates commitment on the part of senior management. A third benefit is that such a function can monitor alliance performance, identify problems, and remediate them when they arise. A fourth benefit is that it provides legitimacy and credibility for an alliance, which can result in the provision of additional resources (Kale & Singh, 2009).

If alliance partners establish reward systems, it is important that they be equitable, or the alliance will suffer. In addition, data taken from supply chain partners show that metrics that reward only cost reduction tend to sub-optimize; more successful supply chains reward performance metrics that look at end-use customer satisfaction (Spekman, Kamauff, & Myhr, 1998). This observation is consistent with the notion of leveraging the skills of one's partner to achieve system- or enterprise-wide goals.

3. *Mindset* relates to those relational variables (e.g., trust, commitment, communication) that enhance a firm's ability to partner. These characteristics engender a positive feeling among potential alliance partners and lower their resistance. In fact, one's reputation as a good alliance partner can lower the specter of opportunism and positively affect the other's alliance-like behavior. An alliance mindset reflects the attitude of the manager and captures the notion of whether managers think in I's or we's, or whether they attend meeting with their entire legal department. Thus, mindset (much like technology) facilitates a more open and honest flow of communication among partners.

4. *Bench depth* is simply the depth of talent that a firm has that is alliance-facile and can easily assume the role of alliance manager. Bench depth is directly related to transferring alliance-related knowledge to others within the firm.

5. *Learning* addresses the institutional mechanism by which alliance skills are recognized, taught, and institutionalized. Kale and Singh (2009) refer to learning as the codification of processes that foster alliance competence. Given that the individual manager is the repository of alliance knowledge, the issue becomes what might help that manager better capture and disseminate his or her knowledge to others in the firm. One way to accomplish this task is through the use of templates and forms that force others to ask questions and collect information that they might not otherwise do. These forms and templates serve to circulate best practices among others in the firm. A second approach might be to hold meetings and information sessions to expose others in the firm to best-of-breed examples. A third approach is to hold training sessions or attend meetings in

which others can share their alliance experiences. For instance, the Association of Strategic Alliance Professionals (ASAP) holds annual summits where alliances managers from a broad range of industries gather to exchange ideas and best practices. In fact, ASAP has recently begun a certification program for alliance managers.

Senior managers acknowledge the importance of alliances, but they do not have any formal programs to train, nurture, and develop alliance competences among their managers. Few companies do, and fewer companies have managers whose title is alliance manager. Herein lies the problem.

## IMPLICATIONS FOR MANAGERS

Alliance management is critical to the future of global businesses, and firms that are not alliance-competent will be relegated to second-class positions in the markets they serve. The cost of market entry, technology development, and access to new customers is too expensive and fraught with too much uncertainty and risk to attempt a go-it-alone strategy. Managers understand the magnitude of the problem, but few have attempted to address it. Alliance management is slowing being recognized as a legitimate activity, and the title of alliance manager is more common than it was five years ago.

Some companies and some industries have come to rely on alliances as a way to do business. Biotechnology stands out as a business sector that, to a large degree, owes its success to alliances. Yet much of the knowledge gained from these successes has been slow to disseminate to the wider business environment. This chapter has attempted to help managers crack the code. Alliance-like thinking has existed for decades, but for firms whose management has not wavered from a bureaucratic, command-and-control mentality, the road to alliance-like thinking has been a challenge at best.

Rule and Keown (1998) presented findings regarding high-performing alliances that are still valid today. They cited three major dimensions of competency that explained much of the variance between high- and low-performing alliances. The first dimension encompassed trust, commitment, and cultural compatibility. The second dimension captured the notion of a clear strategic vision and the existence of functional expertise that was dedicated to the alliance, as well as a clearly articulated governance structure. The third dimension emphasized open communication and the technology that facilitated the flow of information between partners. Their point is that successful alliances do not happen by accident.

Alliances are fragile organizational forms that pose a set of challenges for managers. This is especially true when alliances are viewed as a vehicle for learning. One challenge is the tension surrounding cooperation versus competition, what gets shared and at what level. Senior managers must develop processes that simultaneously allow information to flow across boundaries while protecting the unintentional leakage of information. In fact, there is a ratio of unintended information to intended information, and it is desirable that the ratio be less than one. A second challenge is to ensure that learning happens at all three levels (the firm, the alliance, and the individual level) so as to maximize the value gained through the alliance. The third challenge is to have permeable boundaries that encourage the free flow of information but limits the unintentional leakage of information. Yet the real concern is how to deal with those who violate the norms and act as "pirates in a partner suit" and willfully expropriate non-alliance-specific information. Adding to this problem is the fact that partners do not learn at the same rate; such asymmetry might result in one partner feeling disadvantaged.

These challenges can be mollified by reducing the threat of opportunism through better partner selection, negotiating an appropriate contract, or setting a suitable governance contract that will lessen the opportunistic intent of the partner firm. Saebi (2011) developed three indices that are consistent with previously discussed alliance mechanism, which are summarized in Table 1.3.

**TABLE 1.3 Indices of Alliance Processes and Infrastructure that Enhance Alliance Performance**

| | |
|---|---|
| Knowledge Mechanisms | 1. Competence framework |
| | 2. Cultural Program |
| | 3. Intercultural Training |
| | 4. In-house knowledge |
| | 5. Alliance Management development program |
| | 6. Best practices |
| | 7. External alliance training |
| | 8. In-house alliance training |
| Infrastructure | 1. Alliance department |
| | 2. Alliance managers |
| | 3. Alliance specialists |
| | 4. Rewards for alliance managers |
| | 5. Experts in finance and legal |
| Processes | 1. Individual evaluations |
| | 2. Cross-alliance evaluation |
| | 3. Alliance metrics |
| | 4. Alliance handbook |
| | 5. Partner selection program |
| | 6. Alliance databases |
| | 7. Joint business planning |
| | 8. Partner portal |

*Source:* Adapted from Saebi (2011).

As an index, more is better, and the ability to use more of each dimension should result in a higher level of alliance competence. There is no consensus as to the definition of alliance competence, but the activities presented above shed light on the range of formal and informal processes that can codify aspects of alliance competence. The list of items presented in Table 1.3 is very consistent with earlier discussions on knowledge transfer and learning, which are fundamental to the development of alliance management skills. The point is that there is convergence among the different authors on the need for certain structural and process-related attributes.

Building alliance competence among one's management team is important. Whether there is a dedicated alliance function or whether these requisite skills are inculcated as part of the firm's genetic structure is not the point. The point is that a firm must be able to learn, then disseminate that learning so that it is retained as a competitive advantage.

## REFERENCES

Anand, B. N., & Khanna, T. (2000). Do firms learn to create value? The case of alliances. [Special issue]. *Strategic Management Journal, 21*, 295–315.

Anand, J., Oriani, R., & Vassolo, R. S. (2010). Alliance activity as a dynamic capability in the face of a discontinuous technological change. *Organization Science, 21*, 1213–1232.

Axelrod, R. M. (1984). *The evolution of cooperation.* New York, NY: Basic Books.

Barney, J. B. (1991). Firm resources and sustained competitive advantage. *Journal of Management, 17*, 99–120.

Chen, H., & Chen, T.-Y. (2002). Asymmetric strategic alliances: A network view. *Journal of Business Research, 55*, 1007–1013.

Cohen, W. M., & Levinthal, D. A. (1990). Absorptive capacity: A new perspective on learning and innovation. *Administrative Science Quarterly, 35*, 128–152.

Cyert, R. M., & March, J. G. (1963). *A behavioral theory of the firm.* Englewood Cliffs, NJ: Prentice-Hall.

Das, T. K., & Kumar, R. (2009). Interpartner harmony in strategic alliances: Managing commitment and forbearance. *International Journal of Strategic Business Alliances, 1*, 24–52.

Draulans, J., de Man, A., & Volberda, H. W. (2003). Building alliance capability: Management techniques for superior alliance performance. *Long Range Planning, 36*, 151–166.

Fisher, R., & Ury, W. (1981). *Getting to yes: Negotiating agreement without giving in.* Boston, MA: Houghton Mifflin.

Friedman, T. L. (2005). *The world is flat: A brief history of the twenty-first century.* New York, NY: Farrar, Straus and Giroux.

Granovetter, M. (1985). Economic action and social structure: The problem of embeddedness. *American Journal of Sociology, 91*, 481–510.

Grant, R. (1996). Towards a knowledge-based theory of the firm. *Strategic Management Journal, 17,* 109–122.

Gulati, R., & Gargiulo, M. (1999). Where do interorganizational networks come from? *American Journal of Sociology, 105,* 1439–1493.

Hamel, G., & Prahalad, C. K. (1994). Competing for the future. *Harvard Business Review, 72*(4), 122–128.

Heide, J. B. (1994). Interorganizational governance in marketing channels. *Journal of Marketing, 58*(1), 71–85.

Hofstede, G. (1980). *Culture's consequences: International difference in work-related values.* Beverly Hills, CA: Sage.

Hofstede, G., Neuijen, B., Ohayv, D. D., & Sanders, G. (1990). Measuring organizational cultures: A qualitative and quantitative study across twenty cases. *Administrative Science Quarterly, 35,* 286–316.

Homans, G. C. (1961). *Social behavior: Its elementary form.* New York, NY: Harcourt, Brace and World.

Huber, G. P. (1991). Organizational learning: The contributing processes and the literatures. *Organization Science, 2,* 88–115.

Inkpen, A. C. (2000). Learning through joint ventures: A framework for knowledge acquisition. *Journal of Management Studies, 37,* 1019–1043.

Kale, P., Dyer, J. H., & Singh, H. (2002). Alliance capability, stock market response and long-term alliance success: The role of the alliance function. *Strategic Management Journal, 23,* 747–767.

Kale, P., & Singh, H. (2009). Managing strategic alliances: What do we know now, and where do we go from here? *Academy of Management Perspectives, 23*(3), 45–62.

Khamseh, H. M., & Jolly, D. R. (2008). Knowledge transfer in alliances: Determinant factors. *Journal of Knowledge Management, 12*(1), 37–50.

Kiessling, T. S., & Richey, R. G. (2005). International acquisitions from a network perspective and market based competencies. *Journal of Business Strategies, 22*(1), 1–20.

Kogut, B. (1991). Joint ventures and the option to expand and acquire. *Management Science, 37,* 19–33.

Kogut, B., & Zander, U. (1992). Knowledge of the firm, combinative capabilities and the replication of technology. *Organization Science, 3,* 383–396.

Lambe, C. J., Spekman, R. E., & Hunt, S. D. (2002). Alliance competence, resources, and alliance success: Conceptualization, measurement, and initial test. *Journal of the Academy of Marketing Science, 30,* 141–158.

Lewis, M. A., & Gregory, M. J. (1996). Developing and applying a process approach to competence analysis. In R. Sanchez, A. Heene, & H. Thomas (Eds.), *Dynamics of competence-based competition: Theory and practice in the new strategic management* (pp. 141–164). London, UK: Elsevier.

Lorenzoni, G., & Baden-Fuller, C. (1995). Creating a strategic center to manage a web of partners. *California Management Review, 37*(3), 146–163.

Macneil, I. R. (1980). *The new social contract: An inquiry into modern contractual relations.* New Haven, CT: Yale University Press.

Mohr, J., & Spekman, R. E. (1994). Characteristics of partnership success: Partnership attributes, communication behavior, and conflict resolution techniques. *Strategic Management Journal, 15*, 135–152.

Muthusamy, S. K., White, M. A., & Carr, A. (2007). An empirical examination of the role of social exchanges in alliance performance. *Journal of Managerial Issues, 19*, 53–75.

Prahalad, C. K. & Hamel, G. (1990). The core competences of the corporation. *Harvard Business Review, 68*(3), 79–91.

Ring, P. S., & Van de Ven, A. H. (1992). Structuring cooperative relationships between organizations. *Strategic Management Journal, 13*, 483–498.

Rothaermel, F. T., & Boeker, W. (2008). Old technology meets new technology: Complementarities, similarities and alliance formation. *Strategic Management Journal, 29*, 47–77.

Rule, E., & Keown, S. (1998). Competences of high-performing strategic alliances. *Strategy & Leadership, 26*(4), 36–37.

Saebi, T. (2011). *Successfully managing alliance portfolios: An alliance capability view.* Published doctoral dissertation, Maastricht University, Netherlands: Academic Publications Online (ARNO) (ISBN: 9789461590619).

Sanchez, R., Heene, A., & Thomas, H. (1996). Introduction: towards the theory and practice of competence-based competition. In R. Sanchez, A. Heene, & H. Thomas (Eds.), *Dynamics of competence-based competition: Theory and practice in the new strategic management* (pp. 1–35). London, UK: Elsevier.

Schreiner, M., Kale, P., & Corsten, D. (2009). What really is alliance management capability and how does it impact alliance outcomes and success? *Strategic Management Journal, 30*, 1395–1419.

Simonin, B. L. (1997). The importance of collaborative know-how: An empirical test of the learning organization. *Academy of Management Journal, 40*, 1150–1174.

Spekman, R. E., Isabella, L. A., & MacAvoy, T. C. (2000). *Alliance competence: Maximizing the value of your partners.* New York, NY: Wiley.

Spekman, R. E., Isabella, L. A., MacAvoy, T. C., & Forbes, T., III. (1996). Creating strategic alliances which endure. *Long Range Planning, 29*, 346–357.

Spekman, R. E., Kamauff, K. W., Jr., & Myhr, N. (1998). An empirical investigation into supply chain management: A perspective on partnerships. *Supply Chain Management, 3*(2), 53–67.

Swaminathan, V., & Moorman, C. (2009). Marketing alliances, firm networks, and firm value creation. *Journal of Marketing, 73*(5), 52–69.

Tallman, S. (1999). The multiple roles of alliances in competency-based multinational strategies. *Management International Review, 39*(2), 65–81.

Valentino, D. (1992). Do more of what you do best. *Across the Board, 29*(11), 54–55.

Wernerfelt, B. (1984). A resource-based view of the firm. *Strategic Management Journal, 5*, 171–180.

Williamson, O. E. (1975). *Markets and hierarchies: Analysis and antitrust implications.* New York, NY: Free Press.

Williamson, O. E. (1991). Comparative economic organization: The analysis of discrete structural alternatives. *Administrative Science Quarterly, 36*, 269–296.

Winter, S. G. (2003). Understanding dynamic capabilities. *Strategic Management Journal, 24*, 991–995.

Zollo, M., Reuer, J. J., & Singh, H. (2002). Interorganizational routines and performance in strategic alliances. *Organization Science, 13*, 701–713.

Zucker, L. G. (1986). Production of trust: Institutional sources of economic structure, 1840–1920. In B. M. Staw & L. L. Cummings (Eds.), *Research in Organizational Behavior, 8* (pp. 53–111). Greenwich, CT: JAI Press.

CHAPTER 2

# OPERATING ROUTINES, CULTURAL ALIGNMENT, AND RELATIONAL MECHANISMS IN ALLIANCES

Poonam Khanna, Dovev Lavie, and Pamela R. Haunschild

## ABSTRACT

Established research suggests that the success of alliances depends in part on the strategic and cultural fit between alliance partners. We argue that while cultural fit is critical in equity alliances such as joint ventures, in the case of nonequity alliances, the more important aspect of fit between partners lies in the compatibility of their operating routines. Relying on survey results from the information technology sector, we demonstrate that an alliance formed between partners with different internal task routines and management styles is less likely to develop relational mechanisms such as trust, embeddedness, and commitment, which are essential for the performance of the alliance. Differences in operating routines are more critical than cultural differences in nonequity alliances, especially when they relate to latent aspects of the partners' internal organizations as opposed to externally visible activities. We contribute to research on alliances by studying the negative performance implications of differences in partners' cultures and operating routines. We also reveal how the detrimental effects of such differences can be minimized when partners recognize their organizational differences and take necessary action to reconcile them. We identify prospective areas for future research and offer guidance for managers involved in partner selection and alliance management.

## INTRODUCTION

Strategic alliances have proliferated in recent years. These voluntary arrangements between firms facilitate exchange or sharing of resources for the co-development or provision of products, services, or technologies. Alliances may take the form of joint ventures that entail investments by the partners in a jointly established organization or of nonequity alliances that maintain the partners' independence and tend to have narrower scope and a shorter lifespan. Alliances are a useful vehicle for firms to access new markets, lower costs, reduce time-to-market, share risks, and swiftly adjust to changing market conditions. Nevertheless, nearly half of all alliances fail to meet their objectives, terminate prematurely, or perform unsatisfactorily (Kale, Dyer, & Singh, 2002; Spekman, Forbes, Isabella, & MacAvoy, 1998). Consequently, scholars have been very interested in identifying the factors that enable some firms to increase the success rates of their alliances.

One of the factors found to boost alliance performance is partner fit in terms of available complementary resources, compatible business models, and alignment of strategic objectives (Das & Teng, 1997; Kale, Singh, & Perlmutter, 2000). Such consistency between alliance partners is referred to as strategic fit. Besides strategic fit, cultural fit has also been identified as an important precursor to alliance success. Cultural fit refers to the successful integration of the partners' cultures or accommodation of each other's culture in a mutually acceptable manner (Child, Faulkner, & Tallman, 2005). Cultural fit can be difficult to achieve when partners continue to rely on their own distinct frames of reference. This leads to miscommunication and misunderstandings, which in turn have a negative effect on the success of the alliance (Cui, Ball, & Coyne, 2002).

These conclusions regarding the effects of strategic and cultural fit between partners on alliance success are based primarily on research on joint ventures and other equity arrangements in which partners seek to overcome their organizational differences (Weber, 2000). Although in many industries nonequity alliances are far more common than equity alliances, it has been assumed that the effects of strategic and cultural fit similarly apply to all types of alliances. We draw attention to the fact that there are fundamental differences between equity and nonequity alliances. Equity alliances such as joint ventures are often substantial combinations that create a unified organizational entity requiring integration of the partners' activities. In contrast, nonequity alliances are transient, limited in scope, and require coordination instead of integration of the partners' operations. We argue and demonstrate empirically that in light of these differences, it is unreasonable to expect the success factors in joint ventures or other equity arrangements to impact the outcomes of nonequity alliances in a similar manner. Moreover, a review of prior research on alliance success reveals that it has focused either on the implications of organizational differences between partners or on the effects of relational mechanisms such as trust and relational embeddedness (Lui & Ngo, 2005; Madhok & Tallman, 1998) on alliance performance. The joint effects of these factors have not been considered. Therefore, we further argue that in order to more fully understand the determinants of alliance success, it is essential to study the interplay of these two sets of success factors.

Additionally, while research on organizational differences has concentrated on the implications of cultural differences between partners (de Man & Duysters, 2002; Stahl & Voigt, 2008), we still know very little about how such differences affect alliance performance. Organizational culture refers to a complex set of values, beliefs, assumptions, and symbols, which can shape the firm's operations (Barney, 1986). Despite the richness of this construct, research on cultural differences has either tended to investigate narrower, unidimensional aspects of culture or has based conclusions on anecdotal evidence. In fact, prior research has not distinguished cultural differences from operational differences. We argue that while cultural and operational differences may be related, they are distinct concepts. Cultural differences refer to distinctive values, attitudes, and widely held beliefs regarding organizational systems, actions, and priorities (O'Reilly, Chatman, & Caldwell, 1991), while differences in partners' operating routines represent differences in persistent patterns of organizational behavior (Nelson & Winter, 1982). Distinguishing cultural aspects from operational aspects is critical for fully understanding the implications of organizational differences for the success of alliances. Accordingly, we offer a typology of organizational differences (see Figure 2.1) that encompasses both cultural and operational differences.

Our study advances research on interpartner dynamics in alliances on several fronts. First, by focusing on the implications of organizational differences in the context of nonequity alliances, which have been largely neglected in prior research, we build a better understanding of success factors for nonequity alliances. Specifically, we demonstrate that in nonequity alliances, differences in partners' operating routines, especially those that concern internal procedures not easily observable by the partners, are very important for success. This is because such differences interfere with the partners' ability to nurture mutual trust, build socially embedded relationships, and make

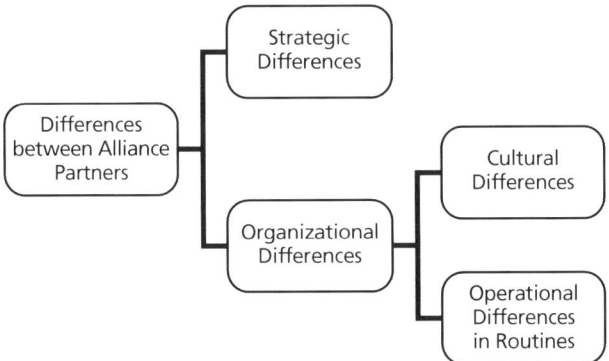

**Figure 2.1** A typology of differences between alliance partners.

mutual commitments. We find that differences in partners' management styles also undermine partners' ability to build mutual trust.

Second, we demonstrate that differences in partners' operating routines affect the success of nonequity alliances more than their cultural differences do. Since nonequity alliances are typically narrow in scope and short-term, the partners are unlikely to adapt their routines in an effort to align them with their partners' routines. Such behavior deviates from the advocated cultural integration in equity alliances. We argue that in addition to cultural differences, persistent operational differences in partners' approaches to performing ordinary tasks may also impede alliance relationships and thus should receive more attention.

Third, we uncover the association between organizational differences and relational mechanisms in alliances by showing that when the characteristics of alliance partners are aligned at the outset, effective relational mechanisms, such as trust, are more likely to emerge. Previous research has assumed that relational mechanisms evolve naturally in alliances. In contrast, our findings show that firms can also facilitate the evolution of relational mechanisms in their alliances by selecting partners that have operating routines and management styles similar to their own. Finally, we demonstrate that even when interpartner differences exist, their negative effects on relational mechanisms can be minimized by proactively identifying such differences.

## RELATIONAL MECHANISMS AND ALLIANCE PERFORMANCE

Relational mechanisms refer to the dynamics of partners' behavior and interaction over the course of their alliance. Research on alliances (Dyer & Singh, 1998; Saxton, 1997; Uzzi, 1996) has found that in successful alliances, partners' interactions are typically characterized by the presence of mutual trust, relational embeddedness, and relational commitment (Kale et al., 2000; Sarkar, Echambadi, Cavusgil, & Aulakh, 2001). We argue that these relational mechanisms promote coordination, conflict resolution, knowledge sharing, and resource investment, which in turn make collaboration more effective and ultimately improve alliance performance.

**Mutual Trust**

Mutual trust is the confidence that each party will behave as expected and fulfill obligations (Ring & Van De Ven, 1992). Mutual trust allows partners to share information and resources with reduced fear of opportunistic behavior or knowledge leakage. Moreover, the mutually oriented actions of trusting partners establish goodwill, which enhances their flexibility and improves the effectiveness of collaboration by reducing friction (Madhok, 1995). Trust in alliances also enables partners to ask for adaptations to new contingencies because such demands are not considered unreasonable. Moreover, trusting partners are more accommodating and willing to offer concessions. Thus, not only does mutual trust reduce the potential for conflict, it also reduces the need for expensive formal contracts between alliance partners. Accordingly, mutual trust can enhance alliance performance.

**Relational Embeddedness**

Relational embeddedness refers to the degree to which social attachment and interpersonal ties drive economic exchange (Granovetter, 1985). Relational embeddedness tends to evolve over time as the partners' employees interact during the course of the alliance. Unlike arm's-length transactions, socially embedded alliances typically involve frequent, face-to-face interactions between partners' employees. By enabling the exchange of knowledge and fine-grained information (Uzzi, 1996), facilitating the development of specialized knowledge and fostering intimate interaction among individuals engaged in coordinated tasks, relational embeddedness helps the partners realize opportunities that may not have otherwise materialized, thereby contributing to alliance performance.

**Relational Commitment**

Relational commitment refers to the partners' intent to establish enduring, reciprocal obligations in their alliance (Madhok, 1995). In an equity alliance, the partners' obligations are ensured by means of financial investments and formal contracts. Such formal mechanisms rarely exist in the case of nonequity alliances. Nevertheless, besides agreeing to pool and exchange needed resources, making long-term investments in relation-specific assets is critical for the performance of nonequity alliances. Committed partners are more likely to consider their alliance a mutually beneficial relationship and forgo short-term alternatives in favor of their ongoing relationship. The partners' motivation to protect their investments in the relationship increases over time as their investments accumulate. Therefore, the partners' reinforced commitment contributes to the success of the alliance.

In sum, we expect the relational mechanisms—mutual trust, relational embeddedness, and relational commitment—to enhance the performance of nonequity alliances.

**Hypothesis 1:** *The performance of a nonequity alliance will be positively related to the strength of relational mechanisms in the alliance.*

## ORGANIZATIONAL DIFFERENCES BETWEEN PARTNERS

Prior research has assumed that relational mechanisms evolve naturally in alliances. In contrast, we argue that the evolution of such mechanisms is facilitated by organizational similarity between partners. Specifically, we contend that the presence of organizational differences in an alliance is likely to weaken the collaborative relationship. For example, mutual trust is less likely to emerge in an alliance if one partner is open about information sharing while the other is not. Thus, the effects of organizational differences play out via the partners' evolving interaction during the course of their alliance. We expect that organizational differences between partners will weaken relational mechanisms, which will in turn be detrimental to the performance of their alliance.

### Dimensions of Organizational Differences

The concept of organizational differences has been underdeveloped in prior research. In order to refine this concept, we conducted a preliminary study involving interviews with alliance managers and executives in several companies. Based on this field research, we conceptualize organizational differences as encompassing both cultural and operational differences. We identified two specific dimensions of organizational differences. The intersection of these dimensions defines four domains of organizational

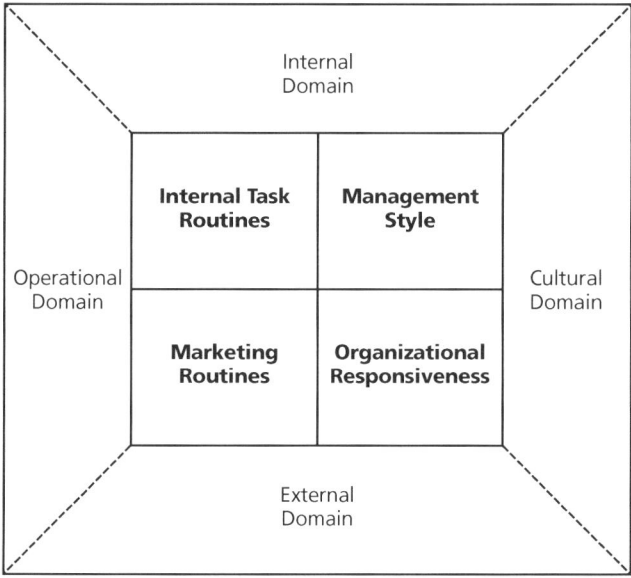

**Figure 2.2** The organizational differences matrix.

differences: management style, organizational responsiveness, internal task routines, and marketing routines (Figure 2.2).

The first dimension of organizational differences that we identified distinguishes operating routines from culture, where differences in operating routines correspond to unique yet internally consistent patterns of organizational behavior in partners' internal task routines and marketing routines (Nelson & Winter, 1982). Operating routines emerge over time as a result of repeated behavior. While enhancing operating efficiency and reliability, these routines become path-dependent and thus are difficult to change. Cultural differences, in turn, represent distinctive values, attitudes, and widely held beliefs concerning organizational systems, actions, and priorities. Much like routines, culture is resilient to change because of the stable nature of values, attitudes, and beliefs. Our second dimension distinguishes processes in the internal domain from those oriented toward the external environment. The internal domain here includes differences in management style and organizational procedures used by employees to conduct the organization's internal tasks. In contrast, the external domain captures differences in firms' attitudes toward outsiders such as customers, suppliers, and partners as well as in the marketing routines that they use. We argue that differences in these four domains inhibit relational mechanisms and consequently undermine alliance performance.

*Management Style*

A firm's management style is defined by its unique managerial approach, decision-making style, control systems, and communication modes (Datta, 1991). Differences in management style may be evident, for example, in firms' tendencies to rely on the decisions made by the most senior manager as opposed to involving multiple managers in a democratic fashion. Firms also differ with respect to their number of managerial layers, how strictly they follow bureaucratic procedures, and the extent to which they require formal contracts and documentation. For instance, some firms prefer informal, bullet-point type presentations while others require lengthy written reports.

*Organizational Responsiveness*

Organizational responsiveness refers to firms' attitudes toward their external environment, which guide their responses to external entities and events. Firms may differ in their attitudes in several ways. For example, some firms are open-minded towards external stakeholders and are willing to develop closer relationships with certain outsiders, while others tend to keep all external actors at arm's length. Similarly, some firms may willingly share information about future product introductions or allow outsiders to visit customer sites, while others may be circumspect in dealing with outsiders. Firms can also differ in their responses to changes in the external environment by being either reactive or proactive as well as in the expediency with which they respond to events in their environment.

*Internal Task Routines*

Internal task routines refer to the procedures that firms' employees follow to perform ordinary day-to-day tasks. Differences in internal task routines may be reflected in, for example, differing levels of discretion used by partners' employees in routine operations or variation in the degree of effort exerted when developing organizational skills for performing tasks (Cartwright & Cooper, 1993). Similarly, firms' internal task routines may also differ with respect to the extent to which employees coordinate their efforts and support teamwork when performing ordinary tasks (Rodriguez, 2005).

*Marketing Routines*

Marketing routines, which define the procedures that firms follow to learn about customer needs and devise plans for serving those needs, also differ considerably across firms (Kohli & Jaworski, 1990). For example, when it comes to marketing their products, some firms focus on users who are mostly interested in the technical adequacy of products, while others target senior executives concerned with implementation and service offerings. Similarly, firms also differ in the degree to which they focus on market requirements and the technology or product features when they communicate with customers. Further, some firms offer solutions that are the most appropriate for customer needs while others try to force-fit their own proprietary solutions.

## ORGANIZATIONAL DIFFERENCES AND RELATIONAL MECHANISMS

### Differences in Management Style

On entering into an alliance, partners typically try to set up appropriate communication lines and develop mutually acceptable control systems and processes for joint decision making. However, both organizational culture and operational routines are highly resistant to change, especially in the short term. At the same time, the relatively short-term orientation and peripheral nature of nonequity alliances serve as a disincentive to partners to attempt such changes. Therefore, partners tend to impose their own management styles on their alliances regardless of their partners' management styles. In fact, even when alliances are managed by a dedicated alliance function, they are considered an integral element of the firm's organization (Kale et al., 2002) and tend to reflect the firm's management style.

The resulting management style of the alliance can therefore take one of three forms: it may (a) remain undetermined, also referred to as "cultural ambiguity" (Buono, Bowditch, & Lewis, 1985), (b) reflect a compromise between the conflicting styles, or (c) be biased towards the dominant partner's management style. Under the first scenario, the partners avoid explicit definition of their alliance's decision-making processes and communication lines. Consequently, there is no opportunity for them to articulate their expectations from each other. The impact of such cultural ambiguity is that the partners' actions remain uncoordinated, with each partner essentially pursuing its own objectives independently. This lack of coordination between the partners creates the potential for misunderstandings, conflict, and distrust. At the same time, it also limits personal interaction and opportunities for bonding between the partners' personnel due to which they are unable to develop trusting relationships. Moreover, the absence of alliance-specific control systems and safeguards makes the partners vulnerable to opportunistic behavior from the other partner, which further undermines their mutual trust and relation-specific investments. Thus, cultural ambiguity prevents the development of relational mechanisms in the alliance.

The second scenario refers to an emerging management style that serves as a compromise. Since any hybrid management style will necessarily be different, to some degree, from each partner's own internal management style, the process of its development will be arduous and tense, resulting in potential miscommunication and conflict. Neither partner is likely to fully accept this management style because of the inertial organizational pressures they face. Consequently, organizational support and relation-specific investments in the alliance will be lacking. Moreover, for reasons discussed previously, in a nonequity alliance, partners' motivation to modify their management styles would be limited, rendering such ad hoc governance arrangements fragile. The partners will likely continue to function in a distinctive fashion. Nevertheless, this continued deviation from the agreed-upon hybrid management style may lead to misunderstandings, conflict, self-interested behavior, and mistrust.

In the third scenario, the dominant partner in the alliance imposes its own management style on the other partner. This approach is also unlikely to foster cooperation. The partner that is expected to adopt the management style of its counterpart would find it difficult to do so because this style would be in conflict with its own management style. Adopting the partner's management style would involve making concessions with respect to fundamental values, beliefs, and symbols, and would likely cause resentment toward the dominant partner. Imposition of one partner's management style is therefore likely to undermine relational commitment and bonding. In sum, regardless of the approach adopted, partners with substantially different management styles will find it difficult to nurture effective relational mechanisms in their alliance.

**Hypothesis 2:** *The greater the differences in the alliance partners' management styles, the weaker will be the relational mechanisms in their nonequity alliance.*

### Differences in Organizational Responsiveness

Differences in partners' ways of responding to the external environment carry both direct and indirect implications for the alliance. First, from each firm's perspective, its partner is an external stakeholder and is thus directly affected by the firm's responsiveness. Thus, differences in the partners' attitudes to outsiders are likely to weaken relational mechanisms in the alliance. For example, some firms are open-minded and trusting of outsiders, while suspicion or pretention is evident in other firms' dealings. When the former type of firm forms an alliance with the latter, the partners may fail to develop trust or reciprocity, and their mutual expectations are unlikely to be met. Partners may also have different attitudes towards sharing information or being receptive to the ideas of outsiders. Again, the outcome of such differences would be distrust and a focus on one's own self-interest. Thus the development of relational mechanisms such as trust, embeddedness, and commitment is likely to suffer in such circumstances.

There are also likely to be indirect effects of differences in organizational responsiveness on relational mechanisms. For instance, differences in partners' attitudes towards joint stakeholders may cause these stakeholders to doubt the viability of the alliance. Given that firms often have contractual commitments to their stakeholders such as suppliers, in such a situation, they may prefer to sacrifice the temporal alliance, which does not involve a contractual commitment, in favor of the long-term relationship with the stakeholder. Similarly, conflicts and misunderstandings are also likely to arise when one partner is faster than the other in responding to emerging events because unsynchronized reactions generate frustration and distrust, as well as foster opportunistic behavior. When the partners do not expect their counterparts to respond to market developments in the desired manner, they may deliberately withhold commitment and act independently to protect their own interests. Differences in partners' organizational responsiveness will thus weaken relational mechanisms.

**Hypothesis 3:** *The greater the differences in the alliance partners' organizational responsiveness, the weaker will be the relational mechanisms in their nonequity alliance.*

## Differences in Internal Task Routines

Differences in the routines followed by the partners for performing their internal organizational tasks can also impede relational mechanisms. For example, differences in the degree of discretion afforded by the partners' internal task routines may interfere with the development of effective relational mechanisms. Alliance managers with greater levels of discretion may expect their counterparts to implement activities at the same speed as they do themselves. They are likely to lose patience and resort to operating independently while their partners who do not enjoy a similar level of discretion are forced to wait for approval from higher levels in the organization. Thus, inconsistency in partners' internal task routines may create a vicious cycle of self-interested actions, minimal interaction between the employees, and an inability to build trusting relationships.

Similarly, differences in partners' routines in terms of task-related effort or cooperative procedures are also likely to preclude the establishment of effective relational mechanisms. Specifically, a mismatch in the quality or amount of effort exerted by employees of partner firms in pursuing joint objectives may impede the development of mutual trust. Employees of the firm whose routines place less emphasis on effort are likely to be seen as free-riding by the employees of its partner. Such a perception can lead to distrust and resentment at both the interpersonal and interorganizational levels (Zaheer, McEvily, & Perrone, 1998). Divergent emphases on cooperation and teamwork are also likely to lead to a similar outcome. While the employees of the firm that emphasizes cooperation are likely to perceive their counterparts as being uncooperative, the latter would likely feel that their partner's employees are dominating. Thus, differences in internal task routines result in failure to meet both partners' expectations about desirable modes of behavior in alliances, which weakens the alliance relationship and reduces partners' mutual trust. Such operational differences also reduce their interaction and limit their commitment to the alliance, which further undermines relational mechanisms.

**Hypothesis 4:** *The greater the differences in the alliance partners' internal task routines, the weaker will be the relational mechanisms in their nonequity alliance.*

## Differences in Marketing Routines

Finally, differences in marketing routines may also obstruct the development of relational mechanisms in alliance relationships regardless of whether the alliance involves collaborative marketing activities. For instance, joint customers may be perplexed by the partners' different value propositions associated with their different emphases of market needs versus technology. Such differences are likely to lead to a loss of customer confidence as well as to conflict between the partners as to the best way to approach their joint customers. Each partner's trained salespeople are likely to continue to follow their own marketing routines rather than adopting their partners' routines when approaching joint customers. Conflicts may also arise with respect to leadership roles in customer accounts. Similarly, different levels of diligence in addressing customer needs or attempts by one partner to force-fit its proprietary solution are also likely to lead to disagreements. Thus, despite the common interests of alliance partners, their divergent marketing routines are likely to lead to a mutual loss of confidence and to the pursuit of their own routines to protect their interests (Khanna, Gulati, & Nohria, 1998).

**Hypothesis 5:** *The greater the differences in the alliance partners' marketing routines, the weaker will be the relational mechanisms in their nonequity alliance.*

## Recognizing Organizational Differences

The extent to which organizational differences interfere with the development of relational mechanisms and ultimately undermine alliance performance may depend on the partners' efforts to acknowledge and resolve those differences. Partners that invest in their relationship early in the life of the alliance can create a foundation for norms of reciprocity and trust that facilitate coordination and mitigate conflicts over the course of the alliance (Madhok & Tallman, 1998). In order to counter the negative effects of organizational differences, it is important for the partners to openly discuss their differences and arrive at a shared perception of their relationship. Such openness can enhance the partners' ability to distinguish between real disagreements and misunderstandings, as well as to avoid ambiguity and uncertainty, which may lead to cultural clashes and conflicts (Cartwright & Cooper, 1993). Even though it is unlikely that one partner will adopt the other's culture or practices, the ability to recognize that organizational differences exist may nevertheless encourage partners to invest in relational mechanisms. On discovering differences in routines, partners may be able to agree on a mutually acceptable approach. They may also be able to reward alliance personnel in a manner that is consistent with the objectives of the alliance.

In turn, when partners are unaware of their organizational differences, they may incorrectly attribute their counterparts' behavior to self-interest, untrustworthiness, lack of long-term commitment to the alliance, or simply to an uncooperative attitude or incompetence, whereas it is in fact a function of the partner's distinct operating routines or management style. Such misattribution interferes with the evolution of effective relational mechanisms, ultimately endangering the success of the alliance. Therefore, once they have identified their organizational differences, each firms can more easily understand its partners' deviation from expected behavior, so that relational mechanisms evolve without interruption and contribute to alliance performance. Recognizing organizational differences can also help partners adjust their interpretations of one another's actions and take appropriate measures to foster relational mechanisms in their joint alliance. Consequently, partners that acknowledge their organizational differences can attenuate the negative implications of those differences.

**Hypothesis 6:** *Recognition of organizational differences between alliance partners will attenuate the negative association between organizational differences and the strength of relational mechanisms in their nonequity alliance.*

## RESEARCH DESIGN

### Sample and Questionnaire

Our sample includes three representative publicly traded firms in the U.S. information technology industry. Each of these firms operates a corporate alliance function and manages a sufficiently large number of alliances. These firms are: (1) Cadence Design, a provider of electronic design automation technologies and engineering services; (2) National Instruments (NI), a provider of virtual instrumentation solutions for the design, prototype, and deployment of systems for measurement, automation, and embedded applications; and (3) Vignette, a provider of content-management applications that enable customer interactions using multiple online channels.

In order to offer a valid representation of organizational differences, we derived our framework empirically while integrating important domains proposed by prior research (Cameron & Quinn, 1999). We used data from our preliminary field interviews to refine our variables and concentrated on characteristics that emerged in our field observations. Given the limited prior empirical research and inconsistent findings concerning organizational differences (Weber, 2000), we systematically derived scale items based on prior studies. We used feedback from our interviews with a select group of executives, alliance managers, and their supervisors in each of the sampled firms to refine the questions and instructions provided in the questionnaire. We then pretested the questionnaire with several alliance managers from each firm and incorporated their feedback by modifying questions that were unclear and phrasing them in a way that reduces potential perceptual biases.

### Survey of Alliance Managers

We sampled nonequity alliances in the three firms participating in our study. We then invited the managers of our initial sample of 964 alliances to complete an online survey. Alliance managers are the most qualified respondents for our purposes since they represent their firms in the alliance, are responsible for the day-to-day operation of the alliance and are thus familiar with the partners' cultural and operational attributes, and can assess the performance of alliances. Overall, we received 420 completed questionnaires (a response rate of 44%) including 66 from Cadence (out of 233 alliances), 330 from NI (out of 658 alliances), and 24 from Vignette (out of 73 alliances). We found that the probability of an alliance being selected into our sample was higher if it was important to the firm or involved foreign partners. Therefore, we control for these variables in our analysis. Most survey items are measured with a 7-point Likert-type scale ranging from 1 (*strongly disagree*) to 7 (*strongly agree*).

## Measures

*Dependent Variable*

*Alliance performance.* We measure alliance performance using survey items such as the extent to which the alliance produces the expected results, generates revenues, reduces time to market, and can potentially evolve into a long-term relationship. We combined these items using principal components factor analysis, which yields a single factor that serves as our performance measure.

*Independent and Moderating Variables*

*Relational mechanisms.* We measure relational mechanisms with a latent variable based on mutual trust, relational embeddedness, and relational commitment, which in turn are derived using principal components factor analysis (see Figure 2.3 for a list of items used for each relational mechanism).

*Organizational differences.* We measure *management style, internal task routines, marketing routines,* and *organizational responsiveness* using multiple items (see Figure 2.4 for a list of items used). For each variable, respondents separately assessed the organizational characteristics of their firms and the respective partners. Organizational differences were then measured as the

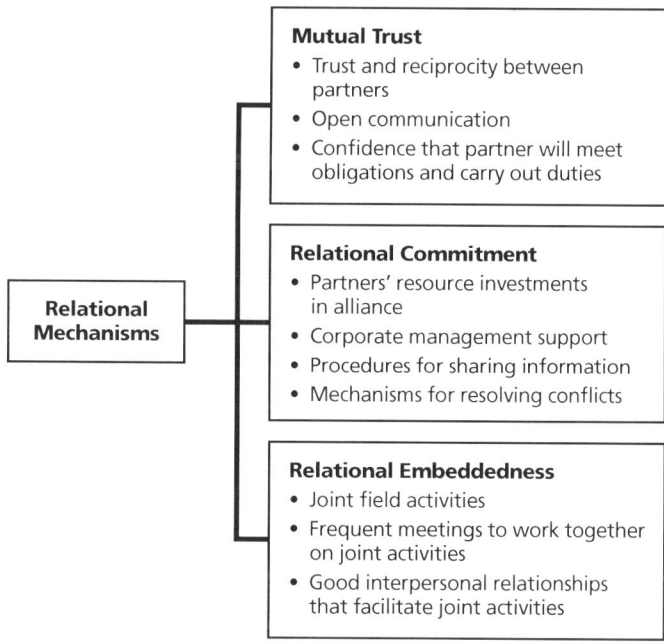

**Figure 2.3** Measuring relational mechanisms.

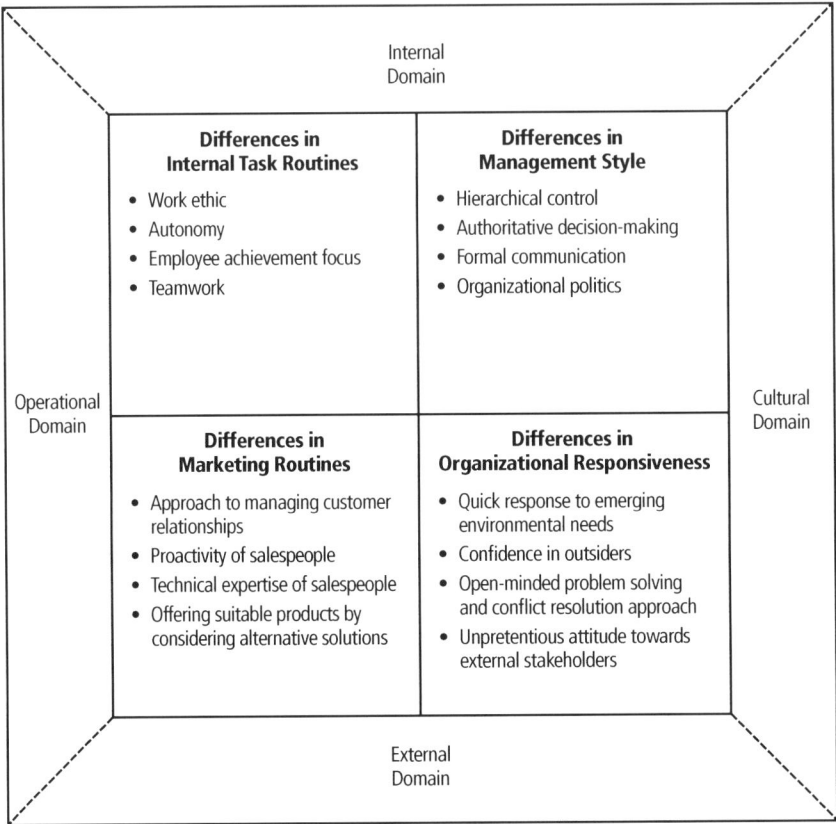

**Figure 2.4** Measuring organizational differences.

absolute value of the difference between the firm's and the partner's scores on each organizational characteristic. We then calculated the average difference across corresponding items (Rodriguez, 2005).

*Recognizing organizational differences.* We used factor analysis for constructing a multi-item scale to measure whether organizational differences were identified in the alliance. This measure served as the moderator of the association between organizational differences and relational mechanisms.

### Control Variables

When assessing the impact of organizational differences on relational mechanisms we control for potential predictors of relational mechanisms and alliance performance. Specifically, we control for *strategic fit* between the firm and its partners, distinguish organizational differences from cross-national differences by controlling for the *partner's country of origin*, account for *organizational size similarity* between the firm and its partners, and finally control for *lifecycle concurrence* between the firm and its partner.

Relational mechanisms evolve as partners become more familiar with each other. Thus, partners with previous joint partnering experience enjoy greater relational embeddedness and relational commitment. Therefore, we account for the partners' *prior joint partnering experience*. We also control for *alliance complexity* since the need for alliance-specific commitments and trust-based embedded relationships increases with the need for coordination. Because relational mechanisms may vary by the value chain function of the alliance, we control for the *type of alliance*. Further, we control for *market conditions* that may reflect on the quality of the relationship. Finally, we include *firm fixed effects* to control for unobserved interfirm heterogeneity.

When testing the impact of relational mechanisms on alliance performance, we account for *alliance complexity*, *type of alliance*, and *market conditions*, which may also directly impact alliance performance. We also control for *indirect competition* between the firm and its partner, for the *partner's global reach*, and for the *partner's importance* to the firm's alliance program. Finally, we use *firm fixed effects* to account for any remaining firm-level heterogeneity in alliance performance.

## Analysis

After accounting for missing data, our effective sample size includes 403 alliances. As detailed by Lavie, Haunschild, and Khanna (2012), we conducted the necessary tests to establish the construct validity of our measures. We test our model (see Figure 2.5) using structural equation modeling (SEM), which supports the testing of multiple relationships simultaneously, with relational mechanisms serving as a latent variable (see Tables 2.1 and 2.2). To uncover some nuanced effects, however, we also ran a model incorporating the three relational mechanisms separately. The detailed results of this analysis are reported in Lavie et al. (2012). The model fit indexes suggest that our model provides sufficient fit to the data.

## RESULTS

Table 2.1 reports the estimated coefficients for predictors of alliance performance and Table 2.2 reports the estimated coefficients for predictors of relational mechanisms. These tables also report $R^2$, which indicates the proportion of observed variance in the dependent variable that the model can predict. Our models explain 78% of the variance in alliance performance and relational mechanisms.

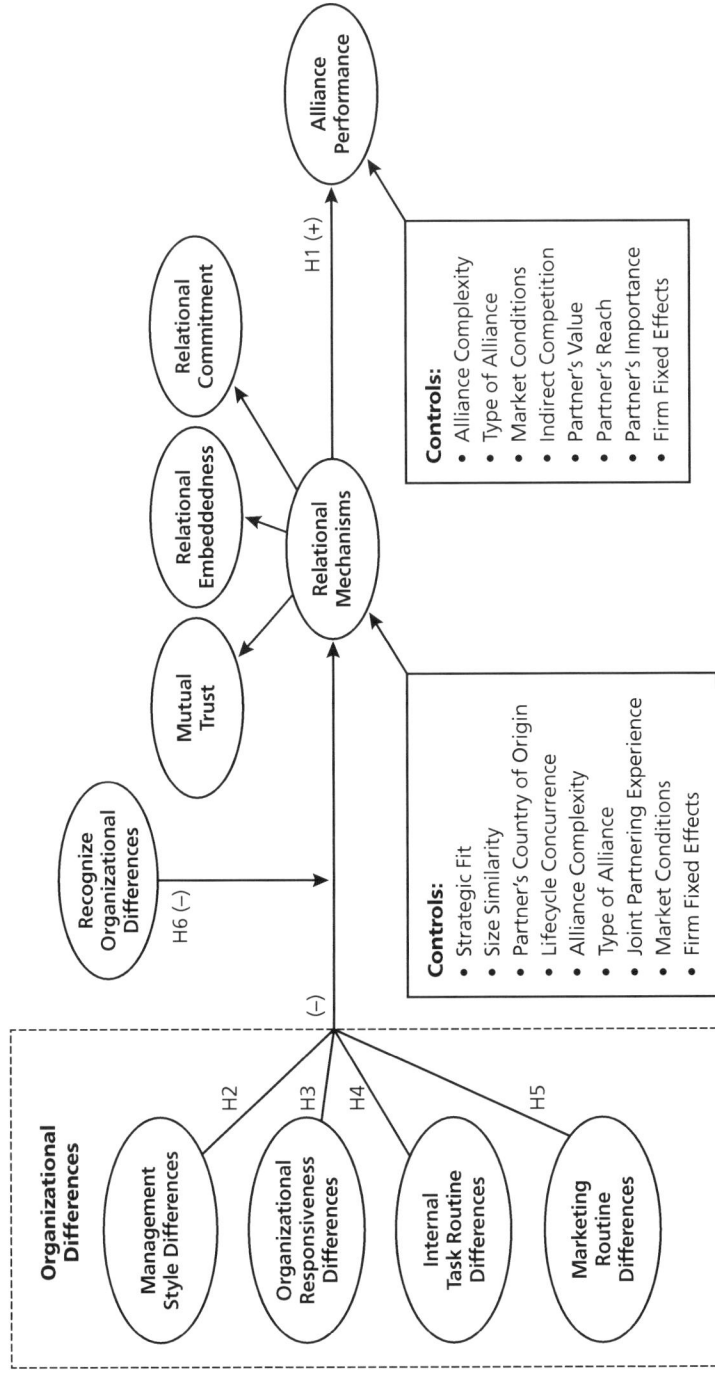

**Figure 2.5** A conceptual model of organizational differences and alliance performance.

**TABLE 2.1  Simultaneous Effects of Relational Mechanisms on Alliance Performance**[a,b]

| Variable | Alliance Performance |
|---|---|
| **Control Variables:** | |
| Alliance complexity | 0.00 |
| Alliance type | −0.07[†] |
| Market conditions | 0.07[†] |
| Indirect competition | −0.05[†] |
| Partner's value proposition | 0.09[*] |
| Partner's global reach | 0.08[*] |
| Partner's importance | 0.07[**] |
| Firm A | −0.01 |
| Firm B | −0.09[†] |
| **Independent Variable:** | |
| Relational mechanisms | 0.92[***] |
| **Model Statistics:** | |
| Measurement error | 0.29[***] |
| $N$ | 403 |
| $R^2$ | 0.78 |

| | Exogenous Variables | | |
|---|---|---|---|
| Variable | Mutual Trust | Relational Embeddedness | Relational Commitment |
| **Endogenous Variable:** | | | |
| Relational mechanisms | 1.05[***] | 0.99[***] | 1.06[***] |
| **Model Statistics:** | | | |
| Measurement error | 0.22[*] | 0.36[***] | 0.26[***] |
| $N$ | 403 | 403 | 403 |
| $R^2$ | 0.71 | 0.64 | 0.74 |

[a] Unstandardized coefficients are reported;
[b] Significance levels: [†] $p < 0.1$, [*] $p < 0.05$, [**] $p < 0.01$, [***] $p < 0.001$

As Table 2.1 shows, we find that alliance performance improves with the partner's value proposition, its global reach, and its importance to the firm. Further, consistent with Hypothesis 1, we find that relational mechanisms are positively related to alliance performance. According to Table 2.2, strategic fit is the main predictor of relational mechanisms, followed by favorable market conditions, while the partners' joint partnering experience contributes marginally to enhancing relational mechanisms.

When considering the impact of organizational differences on relational mechanisms, as shown in Table 2.2, our study does not reveal an overall

**TABLE 2.2 Simultaneous Effects of Organizational Differences on Relational Mechanisms**[a,b]

| Variable | Relational Mechanisms |
| --- | --- |
| **Control Variables:** | |
| Strategic fit | 0.56*** |
| Organizational size similarity | –0.01 |
| Partner's country of origin | 0.02 |
| Lifecycle concurrence | 0.01 |
| Alliance complexity | –0.01 |
| Alliance type | 0.06† |
| Prior joint partnering experience | 0.05† |
| Market conditions | 0.10** |
| Firm A | 0.20*** |
| Firm B | 0.17*** |
| **Independent Variables:** | |
| Management style differences | –0.02 |
| Organizational responsiveness differences | –0.05† |
| Internal task routine differences | –0.14*** |
| Marketing routine differences | 0.04 |
| Recognizing differences | 0.04 |
| Recognizing differences × Management style differences | –0.05 |
| Recognizing differences × Organizational responsiveness differences | –0.02 |
| Recognizing differences × Internal task routine differences | 0.25*** |
| Recognizing differences × Marketing routine differences | –0.16** |
| **Model Statistics:** | |
| Measurement error | 0.14 |
| $N$ | 403 |
| $R^2$ | 0.78 |

[a] Unstandardized coefficients are reported;
[b] Significance levels: †$p < 0.1$, *$p < 0.05$, **$p < 0.01$, ***$p < 0.001$

effect of differences in management style on relational mechanisms as predicted by Hypothesis 2. Support for Hypothesis 3, which predicted that differences in organizational responsiveness will have a detrimental effect on relational mechanisms, is weak. However, we find strong support for Hypothesis 4, which predicted that differences in internal task routines will undermine relational mechanisms. We find no support for Hypothesis 5 on the effect of differences in marketing routines on relational mechanisms. Finally, we find partial support for Hypothesis 6 regarding the moderating effect of recognizing organizational differences on the strength of the relationship between organizational differences and relational mechanisms. As a result of partners recognizing organizational differences, the effect of differences in internal task routines becomes positive, the effect of differences in marketing routines becomes negative while differences in management style and organizational responsiveness have no effect.

We conducted auxiliary analyses in order to gain further understanding of these results. Our analyses show that the effects of organizational differences in the internal domain (management style and internal task routines) are considerably stronger than those of differences in the external domain (organizational responsiveness and marketing routines). Further, our analyses show that the effects of operational differences in internal task routines are stronger than the effects of cultural differences in management style. Detailed results of auxiliary analyses are available in Lavie et al. (2012).

## CONCLUSION

Research on alliance performance has concluded that besides strategic fit, cultural fit between partners is key to alliance success. Thus, alliance performance is expected to improve when partners either modify their own culture to fit the partner's culture, or establish a common culture together. A closer look at this research shows that this conclusion may not be equally applicable to all types of alliances. This is because most of this research has focused on mergers and joint ventures, which involve the formation of a separate organizational entity. Nonequity alliances, which do not involve equity participation, have received limited attention. This distinction matters because while equity alliances typically entail integration of the partners' organizations, which necessitate cultural compatibility, nonequity alliances involve mainly coordination of activities between partners, making cultural similarity less important. Accordingly, in our study, we show that the success of nonequity alliances depends on similarity in the partners' operating routines, that is, organizational procedures that serve to perform ordinary tasks. Therefore, we show that some nonequity alliances may fail because of operational differences in the partners' operating routines and not as a result of inconsistent business objectives or different cultural legacies of the partners, as suggested by prior research.

Our study contributes to research on interpartner dynamics in alliances in several ways. Our most important finding is that in nonequity alliances, the ability of partners to nurture mutual trust, build embedded ties, and solicit commitments depends in large part on the extent of similarity in the partners' operating routines. This is particularly true of routines relating to internal tasks that are not clearly visible to partners. Our study shows that when partners rely on routines that they have developed independently in their regular operations, alliance performance may suffer to the extent that such routines are dissimilar. Our field interviews provided several illustrations of how relational mechanisms such as trust suffer when one partner's routines foster, say, coordination in carrying out internal tasks, whereas the other partner's employees pursue such tasks independently. Moreover, such differences in the alliance partners' operational routines are unlikely to be eliminated over time because of their path-dependent nature which precludes their subsequent change. In fact, each partner's own routines are even more likely to persist in the case of nonequity alliances because of the peripheral and transient nature of these alliances. The motivation of partners in nonequity alliances to change their established routines is even lower than in equity alliances because such change means sacrificing their efficiency with little gain in value. However, since nonequity alliances entail coordination of the partners' activities and interaction of employees, persistent differences in operating routines are likely to prove detrimental to collaboration, despite the partners' goodwill.

Our findings further suggest that trust between partners suffers when there are differences in their management styles. When partners rely on different management styles such as distinct decision-making processes or use of hierarchical governance, the expectation that each party will behave appropriately and fulfill its obligations is questioned. Interestingly, we also find that differences in the external domain, which includes marketing routines and responsiveness to outsiders, do not affect alliance success as much as differences in internal task routines. This may be because such differences are easier to spot prior to alliance formation and may lead firms to not enter into alliances with such potential partners in the first place. It is also possible that differences in routines in the external domain do not affect alliance performance because the partners are able to build on such differences in an effort to complement each other's endeavors.

Finally, we demonstrate that alliance partners can minimize the negative effects of differences in internal task routines by identifying such differences in a timely manner. A lack of awareness about differences between their organizations can lead firms to misattribute their partners' unexpected behavior to self-interest, untrustworthiness, a lack of long-term commitment to the alliance, uncooperative attitude, or incompetence. The mere understanding that partners have different routines to perform similar tasks can assist in resolving conflict, building trust, making commitments, and eventually enhancing alliance performance. The implication of this finding is that by actively looking for differences in prospective partners' operating routines as part of the partner selection and due diligence processes, a firm can not only select more suitable partners but also build effective relational mechanisms to facilitate reconciliation of any operational differences that may emerge during the course of the alliance. Paradoxically, recognizing differences in routines relating to marketing activities seems to have the opposite effect. We conclude that because such differences are often explicit, perhaps the differences that surface following alliance formation are those that remained latent at the outset but are important enough to offset the synergies enabled by complementary marketing routines.

In sum, our study advances alliance research by offering a more comprehensive account of the implications of organizational differences between alliance partners. We conclude that relational mechanisms such as trust, relational embeddedness, and relational commitment do not simply emerge during the course of the alliance, but that they are partially prompted by initial conditions relating to organizational similarity between the partners at the time of alliance formation. In addition, we demonstrate that besides strategic fit, other organizational similarities matter to alliance success. Our study extends emerging research that relates alliance formation to partner similarity (Rosenkopf & Padula, 2008) by demonstrating that partner similarity can also enhance alliance performance. Moreover, in contrast to prior research that has highlighted the role of cultural fit, we show that such fit between partners has limited effects in nonequity alliances and that operational consistency, particularly between the partners' internal operating routines, is at least as critical to relational mechanisms and ultimately to alliance performance.

**Directions for Future Research**

Our study offers several promising directions for future research. The notions of culture and operating routines encompass a broad set of values, beliefs, and behaviors (Ashkanasy, Broadfoot, & Falkus, 2000). We examine the implications of organizational differences along only certain domains. Future research should more systematically examine a comprehensive set of cultural and operational differences between alliance partners. Moreover, we demonstrate that alignment of partners' internal task routines is critical for alliances in the information technology sector. Future research may examine these implications in other industries and environmental conditions in an effort to identify the types of routines that are important in these contexts. Such research may also identify particular domains of cultural fit that matter in equity alliances. Cultural fit is not essential for the success of nonequity alliances due to their transient nature and limited scope, which enables the partners to maintain their independence. Yet cultural fit is likely important for equity alliances that require the creation of a unified organizational entity. Future research may advance understanding of success factors in alliances by comparing the implications of cultural and operational differences across both equity and nonequity alliances. Scholars may also consider the implications of organizational differences under various environmental and organizational contingencies. They may also further develop our notion of relational mechanisms by investigating how organizational differences affect opportunistic behavior, joint problem solving, and knowledge exchange in alliances (Dyer & Singh, 1998; Parkhe, 1993; Uzzi, 1996).

Moreover, while our findings suggest that acknowledging organizational differences can help reduce their negative implications, we do not explain how firms actually cope with such differences once they are uncovered. Future research may usefully investigate the approaches firms use to bridge their organizational differences. For instance, partners may design alliance-specific routines or even adjust their operating routines by leveraging their alliance capabilities (Kale et al., 2002). Partners may also attempt to bridge their differences at the interpersonal level, that is, by developing strong interpersonal relationships between employees of the partner firms.

Overall, we still have a lot to learn about why some firms can better manage their alliances. Prior research has related the varying alliance success rates to firms' alliance capabilities, which are developed based on prior experience with alliances. At the same time, however, research on learning suggests that experience alone is often not sufficient for effective learning and that deliberate learning is required. One mechanism that has been used to formalize processes for articulating, codifying, sharing, and internalizing the knowhow gained through experience is the use of a dedicated alliance function. A dedicated alliance function often helps firms build their alliance capability (Kale et al., 2002) by acting as a central point for learning how to manage alliances and measuring their performance. However, prior research also shows that the extent to which an alliance function leads to learning and contributes to a firm's alliance management capability depends entirely on the processes used to acquire, accumulate and leverage alliance management knowhow. In this regard, future research should explore specifically whether and how firms learn to identify organizational differences, both prior to alliance formation and during the course of the alliance. Such learning may be an essential element of firms' alliance capabilities. Moreover, the implications of acknowledging organizational differences early versus late in the alliance lifecycle would also be of interest to future research since early recognition may enable partners to more effectively enhance their relational mechanisms.

## Managerial Implications

Our study offers several important lessons for managers involved in selecting partners and managing alliances. When seeking partners, firms often look for strategic fit while paying less attention to their organizational differences, which may ultimately harm alliance performance. Managers can undertake a number of initiatives in order to counter these detrimental effects. An obvious way to minimize the negative effect of organizational differences would be to select partners that have internal task routines and managerial styles that are similar to the firm's own. This would require managers to spend considerable time and effort on conducting a more thorough due diligence prior to selecting an alliance partner.

To the extent that firms can successfully assess organizational fit in addition to strategic fit when selecting alliance partners, the subsequent management of alliances may become easier because of the selected partners' organizational similarity. Nevertheless, managers must attempt to actively identify any further differences once collaboration commences. Identifying such differences would require alliance managers to invest in learning about their partners' businesses as well as their organizations. Internal routines that remain latent following alliance formation may be the most critical for nurturing relational mechanisms—and eventually for alliance performance. Given the path dependence of organizational culture and routines and the limited scope and longevity of nonequity alliances, managers should not attempt to impose their procedures on the partner or modify the partner's organization as a way of reconciling the differences. Instead, they should acknowledge organizational differences and develop alliance-specific routines that do not run counter to either partner's established procedures. When this approach seems impossible, forming an equity alliance may allow for better alignment of distinctive organizational cultures. Alternatively, managers may also attempt to bridge these differences at the interpersonal level—that is, by developing strong personal ties between employees of the two organizations. At the minimum, even simply acknowledging that partners have distinctive operating routines can minimize misunderstandings and disagreements that may otherwise undermine collaboration.

Another important lesson from our study is that it is worthwhile for firms to invest in building their alliance capability, which encompasses their ability to select the appropriate partners, create the appropriate governance mechanisms for the alliance, and manage the relationship. Building such a capability requires creating formal mechanisms within the firm that enable the articulation and codification of experience gained through participation in alliances.

We caution here that, given limited resources, some tradeoffs may be necessary between the amount of effort spent on partner search and selection on the one hand and alliance relationship management on the other. For example, at a given point in time, a firm may be able to focus on developing the ability to select appropriate partners or to manage alliance relationships, but not both. In this situation, it may be advisable for the firm to proceed sequentially, focusing first on developing the ability to select appropriate partners by identifying differences in internal routines and management style. As it gathers experience in selecting partners, the firm should attempt to routinize this ability. Once partner selection routines are well established, the firm may shift its focus to developing the ability to manage relationships with partners that are organizationally different. Firms that have developed superior alliance management capabilities may be able to more successfully manage alliances with partners that are significantly different in terms of their internal task routines and management styles, thus increasing the likelihood of alliance success.

## ACKNOWLEDGMENTS

This chapter is based on Lavie, D., Haunschild, P. R., & Khanna, P. (in press), "Organizational Differences, Relational Mechanisms and Alliance Performance," *Strategic Management Journal*. We appreciate the feedback received from Brian Boyd, Israel Drori, Jim Fredrickson, Andy Henderson, Michael Jacobides and Dave Jemison in addition to the cooperation of our primary industry contacts: Jack Barber, Mark Belles, and Jan Willis. Helpful comments were received from seminar participants at the London Business School, the University of Texas at Austin, Politecnico di Bari, Haifa University, and the Technion. This study was presented at the 2008 Academy of Management Meeting in Anaheim; the 2009 Strategic Management Society Conference in Washington, DC; and the 2010 Israel Strategy Conference in Haifa. We appreciate the financial support received from the Office of the Vice President for Research at The University of Texas at Austin and a Research Excellence Grant received from the McCombs School of Business at The University of Texas at Austin. This research was also supported by the Israel Science Foundation (grant No. 917/07).

## REFERENCES

Ashkanasy, N. M., Broadfoot, L. E., & Falkus, S. (2000). Questionnaire measures of organizational culture. In N. M. Ashkanasy, C. P. M. Wilderon, & M. F. Peterson (Eds.), *Handbook of culture & climate* (pp. 131–145). Thousand Oaks, CA: Sage.

Barney, J. B. (1986). Organizational culture: Can it be a source of sustained competitive advantage? *Academy of Management Review, 11*, 656–665.

Buono, A. F., Bowditch, J. L., & Lewis, J. W. (1985). When cultures collide: The anatomy of a merger. *Human Relations, 38*, 477–500.

Cameron, K. S., & Quinn, R. E. (1999). *Diagnosing and changing organizational culture*. Reading, MA: Addison-Wesley.

Cartwright, S., & Cooper, C. L. (1993). The role of culture compatibility in successful organizational marriage. *Academy of Management Executive, 7*(2), 57–70.

Child, J., Faulkner, D., & Tallman, S. B. (2005). *Cooperative strategy.* New York, NY: Oxford University Press.

Cui, C. C., Ball, D. F., & Coyne, J. (2002). Working effectively in strategic alliances through managerial fit between partners: Some evidence from Sino-British joint ventures and the implications for R&D professionals. *R&D Management, 32,* 343–357.

Das, T. K., & Teng, B. (1997). Sustaining strategic alliances: Options and guidelines. *Journal of General Management, 22*(4), 49–64.

Datta, D. K. (1991). Organizational fit and acquisition performance: Effects of post-acquisition integration. *Strategic Management Journal, 12,* 281–297.

de Man, A-P, & Duysters, G. (2002). *The state of alliance management: Special ASAP report of research into alliance capability* (pp. 1–15). Association of Strategic Alliance Professionals.

Dyer, J. H., & Singh, H. (1998). The relational view: Cooperative strategies and sources of interorganizational competitive advantage. *Academy of Management Review, 23,* 660–679.

Granovetter, M. (1985). Economic action and social structure: The problem of embeddedness. *American Journal of Sociology, 91,* 481–510.

Kale, P., Dyer, J. H., & Singh, H. (2002). Alliance capability, stock market response, and long-term alliance success: The role of the alliance function. *Strategic Management Journal, 23,* 747–767.

Kale, P., Singh, H., & Perlmutter, H. (2000). Learning and protection of proprietary assets in strategic alliances: Building relational capital. *Strategic Management Journal, 21,* 217–237.

Khanna, T., Gulati, R., & Nohria, N. (1998). The dynamics of learning alliances: Competition, cooperation, and relative scope. *Strategic Management Journal, 19,* 193–210.

Kohli, A. K., & Jaworski, B. J. (1990). Market orientation: The construct, research propositions, and managerial implications. *Journal of Marketing, 54*(2), 1–18.

Lavie, D., Haunschild, P. R., & Khanna, P. (2012). Organizational differences, relational mechanisms and alliance performance. *Strategic Management Journal, 33*(12), 1453–1479.

Lui, S. S., & Ngo, H. Y. (2005). The influence of structural and process factors on partnership satisfaction in interfirm cooperation. *Group and Organization Management, 30,* 378–397.

Madhok, A. (1995). Revisiting multinational firms' tolerance for joint ventures: A trust-based approach. *Journal of International Business Studies, 26,* 117–137.

Madhok, A., & Tallman, S. B. (1998). Resources, transactions and rents: Managing value through interfirm collaborative relationships. *Organization Science, 9,* 326–339.

Nelson, R., & Winter, S. (1982). *An evolutionary theory of economic change.* Cambridge, MA: Belknap Press of Harvard University Press.

O'Reilly, C. A., Chatman, J., & Caldwell, D. F. (1991). People and organizational culture: A profile comparison approach to assessing person-organization fit. *Academy of Management Journal, 34,* 487–516.

Parkhe, A. (1993). Strategic alliance structuring: A game theoretic and transaction cost examination of interfirm cooperation. *Academy of Management Journal, 36,* 794–829.

Ring, P. S., & Van De Ven, A. H. (1992). Structuring cooperative relationships between organizations. *Strategic Management Journal, 13,* 483–498.

Rodriguez, C. M. (2005). Emergence of a third culture: Shared leadership in international strategic alliances. *International Marketing Review, 22*(1), 67–95.

Rosenkopf, L., & Padula, G. (2008). Investigating the microstructure of network evolution: Alliance formation in the mobile communications industry. *Organization Science, 19,* 669–687.

Sarkar, M. B., Echambadi, R., Cavusgil, S. T., & Aulakh, P. S. (2001). The influence of complementarity, compatibility, and relationship capital on alliance performance. *Journal of the Academy of Marketing Science, 29,* 358–373.

Saxton, T. (1997). The effects of partner and relationship characteristics on alliance outcomes. *Academy of Management Journal, 40*(2), 443–461.

Spekman, R. E., Forbes, T. M., Isabella, L. A., & MacAvoy, T. C. (1998). Alliance Management: A view from the past and a look to the future. *Journal of Management Studies, 35,* 747–772.

Stahl, G. K., & Voigt, A. (2008). Do cultural differences matter in mergers and acquisitions? A tentative model and examination. *Organization Science, 19,* 160–176.

Uzzi, B. (1996). The sources and consequences of embeddedness for the economic performance of organizations: The network effect. *American Sociological Review, 61,* 674–698.

Weber, Y. (2000). Measuring cultural fit in mergers and acquisitions. In N. M. Ashkanasy, C. P. M. Wilderon, & M. F. Peterson (Eds.), *Handbook of culture & climate* (pp. 309–320). Thousand Oaks, CA: Sage.

Zaheer, A., McEvily, B., & Perrone, V. (1998). Does trust matter? Exploring the effects of interorganizational and interpersonal trust on performance. *Organization Science, 9,* 141–159.

CHAPTER 3

# THE ROLES OF THIRD PARTIES IN STRATEGIC ALLIANCE GOVERNANCE

**Rosalinde Klein Woolthuis, Bart Nooteboom, Gjalt de Jong, and Dries Faems**

## ABSTRACT

The role of third parties in effective alliance management, especially with regards to innovation, has been identified recently but is still underexplored in the alliance literature. Whereas existing alliance governance literature mainly focuses on the role of third parties in stimulating trust building, this chapter develops a comprehensive framework, illuminating how third parties can influence the initiation and application of structural and relational governance mechanisms. In so doing, it provides a basis for further research on the role of third parties roles in alliance governance and the effects thereof on relationship quality and outcome.

## INTRODUCTION

Strategic alliances are increasingly common (Becerra, Lunnan, & Huemer, 2008) and considered essential for innovation and business success

*Interpartner Dynamics in Strategic Alliances*, pages 55–72
Copyright © 2013 by Information Age Publishing
All rights of reproduction in any form reserved.

(de Man & Duysters, 2005), but they do have high failure rates (Bleeke & Ernst, 1991; Das & Teng, 2001). Although alliance management has been studied extensively (Nooteboom, 1999c, 2002), studies on the role of third parties in governing alliances are virtually nonexistent. Although several studies point to the importance of third-party interventions for trust repair (Mesquita, 2007; Tomlinson & Mayer, 2009), innovation (Obstfeld, 2005), and enforcing cooperative behavior (Charness, Cobo-Reyes, & Jimenez, 2008; Fehr & Fischbacher, 2004; Stephens, Fulk, & Monge, 2009) in alliances, third party perspectives are still an under-theorized and poorly understood phenomenon.

In this chapter we therefore develop a comprehensive framework of third party roles in strategic alliance management. In particular, we present a comprehensive framework illuminating how third-party interventions might influence both the initiation and application of structural and relational governance mechanisms. The framework is built upon recent studies that have shed first light on certain aspects of third parties but have not yet provided an integrated overview of all potential roles of third parties in relationship governance. The reminder of this chapter is structured as follows. First, we define the concept of third parties. Subsequently, we discuss our framework on the role of third parties in alliance governance. In the concluding section of this chapter, we discuss the implications of our framework for future alliance governance research.

## THIRD PARTIES AND ALLIANCE GOVERNANCE

Alliances are governed by a particular combination of structural and relational governance mechanisms. Structural governance involves the use of contracts, monitoring, and contract enforcement to control and coordinate the relationship. Relational governance consists of using trust, norms of fair dealing (social obligation), values, and loyalty to govern the relationship. Below, we discuss the role of third parties regarding these different governance mechanisms. In particular, we show how third-party interventions might influence both the initiation and application of structural and relational governance mechanisms (see Table 3.1 for an overview).

Before doing so, it is worthwhile to make four comments about the peculiarities of third parties. First, we focus on the role of third parties that do not belong to the organizations of the collaborating actors and that do not have a relationship with these actors in the sense of a friendship or other connection that could corrupt their impartiality. These third parties can be specialist consultants, lawyers, researchers, and so on. Second, the third party should not have a permanent relationship with the other actors, for example, as an employee of the same organization or a family

## TABLE 3.1 The Roles of Third Parties in Alliance Governance

| Structural governance | Relational governance |
|---|---|
| **Initiating governance mechanisms** | |
| 1. Facilitate and speed up the implementation of an appropriate legal form/contracts | 1. Help with establishing shared social norms (Fehr & Fischbacher, 2004; Möllering, 2001, 2006) |
| 2. Provide trilateral governance if transaction is not worth drawing an extensive contract for (Williamson, 1985) | 2. Trust transfer to parties that lack history of prior relationship (Ferrin et al., 2006) |
| | 3. Prevent emergence of distrust during negotiations (Klein Woolthuis, Hillebarnd, & Nooteboom, 2005) |
| **Applying governance mechanisms** | |
| 1. Provide coordination (Obstfeld, 2005) | 1. Bridge cultural distance (Nooteboom 1999a,b; Bijlsma-Frankema, Sitkin, & Weibel, 2008) |
| 2. Provide impartial, objective information for effective monitoring and control | 2. Solve the idea problem (myopia and group-think) (Li, 1997; Obstfeld, 2005) by means of a gatekeeper (Katz & Tushman, 1981) |
| 3. Bridge cognitive distance (Baker, 2000; Nooteboom, Van Haverbeke, Duysters, Gilsing, & van den Oord, 2007), enabling understanding and reaching of an agreement | 3. Preventing blind trust (Nooteboom, 2004; Tomlinson & Mayer, 2009) |
| 4. Informal arbitration: judging contract deviation and punish the abuse of power (Fehr & Fischbacher, 2004), thereby reducing behavior that deviates from the social norm/contract (Charness, Cobo-Reyes, & Jimenez, 2008) and preventing the case going to court | 4. Trust repair (Tomlinson & Mayer 2009): obtain objective and accurate information, thereby judging and ascribing the causes of deviance (attribution) |
| 5. Prevent reputation damage by solving problems according to the "spirit of the contract" or industry norms (Klein-Woolthuis et al., 2005) | 5. Reputation management and blocking exit for deviant parties (Nooteboom, 2004) |
| 6. Help the parties to "get through" the legal system in situation where a dispute is taken to court | 6. Timely and minimally destructive relationship termination (Nooteboom, 2004) |

member. Third, the third party should not be servicing the interests of one actor more than those of the other: he or she should be chosen and paid by all the parties involved and not benefit from the gains of one of the parties. The latter two conditions assure the independence of the third party and distinguish the role of the third party from other roles such as a team leader. Finally, a third party should be trusted in his or her competences and intentions, and he or she should be known to be impartial and incorruptible to be suitable as an effective third. He or she should have an interest in acting scrupulously, with a view to his or her reputation as a third party. Note also that a third party does not have to play all roles—quite to the contrary. There is a range of actors who can play these roles, and the desired intervention should be leading in the choice for a certain third party. For legal issues, lawyers, for instance, are logical candidates, whereas consultants or project managers will more likely solve organizational issues.

## The Impact of Third Parties on Structural Governance

Structural governance entails the governance of relationships through the use of contracts, formal control, and monitoring mechanisms (Poppo & Zenger, 2002; Reuer, Arino, & Mellewigt, 2006). In a context of innovation, legal ordering can be expected to be problematic (Williamson, 1975, 1985). Contracts will be hard to specify *ex ante* because of uncertain development trajectories, and this may lead to undesirable rigidity in project execution (Nooteboom, 1999b). There is also a more technical obstacle to the full enforcement of contracts (Rosenkopf & Tushman, 1994; Rowley, Behrens, & Krackhardt, 2000). The agreements that characterize "relational contracting" will often include elements that are not legally enforceable. These might be agreements in the form of poorly specified intentions and/or promises. Deakin and Wilkinson (2000, p. 150) note that "such arrangements may easily be misinterpreted by the courts, which do not have access to the specialized knowledge or assumptions shared by the parties." Such an incomplete contract goes beyond what is verifiable—for example, with agreements on a quality level that cannot be verified (Chen, 2000). Moreover, monitoring can be difficult if contracts are incomplete, when monitoring requires specialist knowledge in the partner's technological field, or when it requires close interaction.

Too much attention to legal structural governance might have a negative effect on trust, can be time-consuming, and can distract from value creation (Klein-Woolthuis, Hillebrand, & Nooteboom, 2005). For this reason trust is often considered a substitute for contract, as trust reduces the need for formal control (Gulati, 1995; Zaheer, McEvily, & Perrone, 1998). Fehr and Fischbacher (2004, p. 185) furthermore emphasize that legal enforcement mechanisms cannot function without a broad consensus about the normative legitimacy of the rules—that is, the social norms.

## Phase 1: Initiating Structural Governance Mechanisms

### 1. Help with Establishing the Appropriate Legal Form/Contracts

The third party might help partners to construct the right legal governance—that is, helping parties to find the appropriate form of cooperation and draw up a sufficiently but not overly detailed contract to govern and safeguard the relationship successfully. Especially in the case of smaller firms, companies will often not have the staff and experience to design a suitable contract (Nooteboom, 2004). Specialist consultants or public agents, for example, can play an important role by guiding contract negotiations as an impartial, independent chair and by providing the specialist knowledge on how the contract should be designed. Such a guiding role of an independent third party can not only increase the quality of the contractual design but might also reduce the time needed for drawing up the contract.

*2. Provide Trilateral Governance*

A third party can provide trilateral governance (Williamson, 1985) when transactions are small or infrequent and it is not worth the cost and effort of setting up an extensive scheme for governance. In this case, it is more efficient to engage a third party to serve as an arbitrator or mediator to complement a simple, limited contract (Nooteboom, 2004).

## Phase 2: Applying Structural Governance Mechanisms

*1. Provide Coordination*

Simmel (1950) already wrote that the *tertius* could have two roles: mediating between parties with conflicting interests and becoming involved in a relationship where parties share the same goals. It is in this latter case that third parties merely serve the function of aiding coordination (Obstfeld, 2005)—for instance, by helping previously unacquainted parties to get to know each other. Third parties suitable for such roles are likely to be project managers or consultants. Parties in the collaboration could decide to resort to this function rather than drawing up an extensive contract. A precondition for such a choice, however, is that interests are well aligned and there is a basis for trust.

*2. Provide Impartial, Objective Information for Effective Monitoring and Control*

As discussed previously, it may be hard to draw up or enforce contracts. Third parties may play a role in informally monitoring and enforcing agreements. This might circumvent the ultimate appeal to court that might permanently harm the relationship and endanger the firm's reputation and future potential relations (Nooteboom, 1999a, 1999b). Burt (1992) already underlines the role of the *tertius* in complementing a contract and argues "that control is uncertain, that no one can act as if they have absolute authority.... There is no long-term contract that keeps a relationship strong, no legal binding that can secure the trust necessary to a productive relationship" (1992, p. 78). Therefore, a third party may help monitor the execution of the contract and monitor spillover risks. If parties perform these roles themselves, this may lead to defensive behavior or a breakdown of trust, and it may eventually put both the project and relationship at risk. A third party may fulfill the monitoring role as an independent mediator without causing the negative effects described. Moreover, since the third party has no direct commercial interest in the information, he or she may find it easier to gain access to companies and information, rendering monitoring more possible (Nooteboom, 1999a, 1999b).

*3. Bridge Cognitive Distance*

Whereas complementary knowledge and knowhow are often the key rationales for engaging in interfirm relationships, they also entail cognitive distance (Nooteboom, 2000). The gap that exists between companies with regard to their cognitive frameworks and specialist knowledge might form an important obstacle to mutual understanding, learning, innovation, and effective monitoring (Nooteboom, Van Haverbeke, Duysters, Gilsing, & van den Oord, 2007) and thus an important obstacle for establishing trust, reaching an agreement, and drawing up and monitoring a contract. The third party can help to bridge the gap between cognitive frameworks, that is, help to cross cognitive distance. Third parties can "translate" behavior to optimize "absorptive capacity" (Cohen & Levinthal, 1990). This has been defined as the role of knowledge broker (Hargadon, 1998; Wolpert, 2002). Translation activities might be necessary if highly specialized researchers have trouble understanding each other's work and thus appreciating each other's competences and expertise. Third-party intervention might also be valuable to bridge the cultural gap between technology-oriented people and market-oriented people, who often experience great difficulty understanding each other's language, competences, and even attitudes, which provides a fertile ground for misunderstanding and distrust. To be able to fulfill this role, the third party must be an expert or specialist in his or her field and be recognized as such by the collaborating parties. Potential third parties for this role are thus (top) researchers or other specialists who have a reputation in their field, but who, at the same time, are able to oversee, and connect to, other fields.

*4. Informal Arbitration and Preventing a Case Going to Court*

Recent insights from game theory find that conditional cooperation is the norm for human cooperation—that is, actors cooperate if the other group members also cooperate, whereas the defection of others is a legitimate excuse for individual defection (Fehr & Fischbacher, 2004).They see the third party as a type of arbitrator that can punish and reward, thereby maintaining the social norm. Experiments in this field show how third-party intervention can prevent opportunistic behavior in investment games. For instance, Charness et al. (2008) explore the effect of third-party punishment and reward in the "Investment Game" introduced by Berg, Dickhaut, and McCabe (1995), in which a first mover can pass all of his or her endowment to a responder, who receives three times the amount sent by the first mover. The responder then selects an amount to pass back to the first mover. The behavior shown by the players is seen as a proxy for trusting and trustworthy behavior. Charness et al. (2008) introduced the role of a third party to this game. They found that the presence of a person who can observe and punish the violation of the distribution norm, which is the social norm on how gains should be distributed (Fehr & Fischbacher, 2004), significantly and substantially increases the amount of money sent by the first mover. In addition, the responder's return is significantly higher. A third party can thus have an important role in deterring opportunism or arbitrating uncooperative behavior. This does not just aid the relationship by "enforcing" trustworthy behavior; it can also prevent the cost, effort, and damage of taking a case to court. Important preconditions for this are that both parties accept third-party interference and potential punishment and trust the fairness of the third party's judgment.

## 5. *Prevent Reputation Damage*

Coercive contract enforcement might be detrimental to the efficiency and effectiveness of the relationship because it can yield unwanted side effects, such as breakdown of trust, evoking conflict (Gaski, 1986; Gaski & Nevin, 1985; Ghoshal & Moran, 1996; Hunt & Nevin, 1974), opportunism, and defensive behavior (Hirschman, 1970; Zand, 1972). A well-known saying in business is that things are definitely wrong if the contract is pulled out of the drawer; that is, contracts are primarily intended to indicate how the project and relationship should proceed and they are considered an indication of nonresolvable conflict if they are actually called upon. In other words, if a third party can prevent the parties from quarrelling about the exact execution of the contract (the letter of the contract), this will not just potentially prevent trust from breaking down, but also the parties' reputations in terms of how they view each other and how external parties view them will be preserved. This can be attempted by solving problems according to the "spirit of the contract" or industry norm (Klein Woolthuis et al., 2005), and falling back upon social ordering mechanisms such as trust, loyalty, and social obligation.

## 6. *Help Parties "Get Through" the Legal System*

If neither of the parties in the collaboration nor the third party can solve the conflict that has arisen in a relationship or the case goes to court, third parties can play a role in helping the parties get through the process as best as possible. Contract enforcement through the courts is very expensive in terms of money, time, and delay. This is especially the case for small firms that lack a legal department (Nooteboom, 1993). A third party, most likely in the form of a legal advisor or experienced manager who has gone through the process before, can guide parties through the process without too much cost and delay.

In sum, a third party can not only improve the quality and effectiveness of structural governance mechanisms in place to govern the relationship, but he or she may also prevent conflicts from arising and the breakdown of trust as a result of misunderstandings, haggling, or threats to take a case to court. As such, a third party can play an important role in preventing the negative effects of formal aspects of the relationship on trust development and maintenance.

## THE IMPACT OF THIRD PARTIES ON RELATIONAL GOVERNANCE

Relational governance consists of using trust, norms of fair dealing (social obligation), values, and loyalty to control and coordinate the relationship. Although relational governance appears at first to be a very personal matter in which third parties have no role to play, a closer examination of the downside of trust gives considerable hints as to how the third party could play a role here. This explains the recent attention to the role of third parties' intervention in trust building and trust repair (Mesquita, 2007; Tomlinson & Mayer, 2009). Potential actors that can transfer and mediate trust are representatives of industry associations, development agencies, or technology transfer offices. These are parties that are independent and have a good knowledge of companies in a field or area, and are thus able to bring actors together.

### Phase 1: Initiating Relational Governance Mechanisms

*1. Help with Establishing Social Ordering and Speeding Up the Trust-Building Process*

The importance of relational governance, especially in the form of trust, has been acknowledged many times (Bachmann, 1998; Gambetta, 1988; Möllering, 2006; Nooteboom, 2002). Fehr and Fischbacher (2004) refer to this phenomenon as the shared social norm (see also Fehr & Gachter, 2002, or Gintis, Bowles, Boyd, & Fehr, 2003). They see it as the shared belief in how individual group members ought to behave in a given situation. Trustworthiness consequently refers to the adherence to these norms. In bilateral relationship development, there is a risk that many of these norms will be implicit: the actors assume that people will have similar ideas over what is fair and what is the appropriate behavior in certain circumstances. These ideas may vary greatly, however, from person to person and also within firms or industries. A third party can help to clarify ideas and make the social norm explicit. Furthermore, the third party can help in the process of developing a shared language and understanding, and can help to establish shared visions and goals regarding the collaborative venture (Larson, 1992; Ring & Van de Ven, 1994). The third party can thus help to build trust and speed up the process by providing guidance and advice.

### 2. Trust Transfer to Parties that Lack History of Prior Relationship

As trust is important and takes time to develop, the existence of prior ties has been stressed as important to relationship success (Blumberg, 2001). As we have already argued, it is often hard to establish trust between unfamiliar parties. However, new developments and the prevention of myopia and lock-in require the parties to collaborate with new, unknown partners as well. Furthermore, innovation often requires highly specialized but different skills and knowledge, contributing to the cognitive gap between the parties involved. In these circumstances, third parties can provide at least a partial solution to this problem. They can refer parties to each other and help in the first stages of relationship development. The trust that parties have in the actor who refers them to each other will mean that they are more likely and ready to trust each other (Baker, 2000; Ferrin, Dirks, & Shah, 2006). This is because they trust the third party to recommend only a partner that is both competent and benevolent (Nooteboom, 2004).

### 3. Prevent Emergence of Distrust During Negotiations

Alliance negotiation can be a very sensitive process in which different functions (i.e., lawyers, operational managers, top managers) have to communicate with each other. As such, negotiations might easily trigger feelings of misunderstanding and even distrust. The intervention of the third party can reduce the likelihood of such negative relational dynamics by providing a more impartial perspective on the demands and wishes of both parties. Moreover, experienced third party mediators can frame and translate the concerns of both partners in such a way that misunderstanding is less likely to occur. This can prevent a negative spiral of distrust and haggling, which might take a long time to resolve before an agreement can be reached.

## Phase 2: Application of Relational Governance Mechanisms

### 1. Bridge Cultural Distance

As trust is a social phenomenon, it is the product of communication and understanding. Misunderstandings, as well as differences in perception, make the trust-building process more difficult. Cultural distance can therefore be an important hindrance to trust development (Bijlsma-Frankema, Sitkin, & Weibel, 2008; Nooteboom, 1999c). Cultures may differ between companies (more entrepreneurial versus large bureaucratic firms, for instance) or between professions, knowledge fields, regions, or countries. Actors with different dominant logics have difficulty understanding each other and as a result knowledge transfer and learning will be hampered (Lane & Lubatkin, 1998). Third parties can, as in the case of bridging cognitive distance, fulfill the role of a translator in aiding this process. The third party can explain behavior and translate the underlying logic and intentions to the partner that is not (yet) capable of understanding this.

## 2. Solving the Idea Problem (Myopia and Group-Think)

Whereas trust is mostly associated with positive aspects, the "danger" of a very strong trust basis is an "unhealthy" closeness between partners that might lead to myopia, inertia, and hence lack of openness to new opportunities (Li, 1997, 1998). This will be detrimental for innovation because there will be a redundancy of information between parties (they tend to know and think the same; Granovetter, 1973; Obstfeld, 2005) and a lack of variation in knowledge and perspectives (Nooteboom, 2004). In such situations, a third party can be important for ensuring there is sufficient new input from outside the relatively closed collaboration. A third party might help to establish a cooperative structure that does not entail "barriers to entry" for potential new entrants; he or she might regularly introduce new potential parties, keep track of new developments and opportunities, and/or make the parties aware of the negative aspects too-close relationships might have. Another function is that of the gatekeeper, who keeps track of relevant developments, potential partners, and new opportunities (Tushman & Katz, 1980).

## 3. Preventing Blind Trust

A closed attitude as described with reference to the idea problem may not only refer to the object of collaboration (knowledge exchange, innovation), but also to the relationship itself. Tomlinson and Mayer (2009) refer to the latter situation as a stable attribution. They argue that partners may have such strong beliefs about each other and the other's behavior that a trustor can be blind to evidence that the partner is, in fact, behaving opportunistically (Tomlinson & Mayer, 2009). In this respect, Lewicki and Bunker (1996) mention the role of the objective third party as he or she who can observe and signal such behavior, without being swayed by stable or blind beliefs. As such, a third party can mirror the parties' behavior and beliefs and bring certain aspects to the discussion.

## 4. Trust Repair

Trust and the possibility of trust repair have only recently received more specific attention (Bijlsma-Frankema et al., 2008; Lewicki & Bunker, 1996). Tomlinson and Mayer (2009) examine the possibilities of trust repair using the causal attribution dimensions of Weiner (1986), arguing that actors who believe in the goodwill of others can interpret behavior positively when factually it is not (which is attribution). In other words, the authors argue that trust can be repaired if the breaking of trust (e.g., not performing according to agreement) can be ascribed to (1) external factors beyond the control of the partner; (2) a lack of ability, benevolence, or integrity beyond the partner's control; and (3) a lack of stability in the perception of the given trait (e.g., partners in long-established relationships will interpret individual actions in the light of previous cooperation and hence have more stable perceptions of the other's trustworthiness in the various aspects) (Tomlinson & Mayer, 2009). Alongside the reference to ability, benevolence, and integrity in trust repair, they also mention the role of denial and excuse in repairing trust. In this case, taking responsibility for what went wrong, issuing apologies or justifications that reduce the perceived negativity, and/or promising that things will not happen again are ways of repairing trust. A number of studies have shown this to be effective (Kim, Ferrin, Cooper, & Dirks, 2004; Tomlinson, Dineen, & Lewicki, 2004). Note that both Tomlinson and Mayer (2009) and Nooteboom (2004) stress the importance of obtaining objective and accurate information in this process of finding the true cause of norm deviance. A correct judgment can be made of the causes of deviance based on objective information. A third party can be very valuable in this process, not only because she will be impartial but also because her external role is likely to give her better access to information on all sides, which will help her reach a correct judgment.

## 5. Reputation Management and Blocking Exit for Deviant Actors

Apart from trust, reputation has been considered as an important relational governance mechanism in alliances. A third party can play a crucial role with regard to the reputation mechanism. Nooteboom describes how a third party can "spread the news" through his network: he can transmit a party's reputation without giving in to gossip and slander. His independent judgment of the parties' benevolence or opportunism will have more credibility than the word of parties that have a direct interest, which may be seen as malicious, strategic gossip. The third party can thus aid the reputation mechanism in several ways. First, as already discussed, the third party will have easier access to information, thereby enabling the third party to have more accurate and objective information that can signal deviance from the agreement and judge the grounds for such deviance (lack of loyalty, lack of competence). Second, the third party can use her network of weak ties to "spread the word" more easily and credibly to potential future partners. Because the third party cannot afford to be part of a "gossip campaign," she can be trusted to function as a sieve and amplifier by checking accusations of opportunistic or incompetent behavior and transmitting them only if correct. Third, although the third party is perhaps not able to prevent an opportunistic or incompetent party exiting by taking on another identity or "escaping" to new markets, he will certainly have more means to broadcast defection than the parties to the agreement (Nooteboom, 1999a, 1999b). When third parties are part of, for example, development agencies, innovation centers, research communities, or other government and semi-government organizations in particular, the parties often have ample contacts and opportunities to transmit a reputation.

### 6. Timely and Minimally Destructive Relationship Termination

Nooteboom (2004) describes how third parties can also play a role in terminating a relationship. If relationships end in a fight, the damage will often prevent parties from engaging in future collaboration (despite the fact that there may be a business rationale for doing so). In addition, future relationships with other parties may be at stake as a result of reputation damage. A third party can play an important role in reducing the negative effects of conflict and relationship breakdown. It is important here that the relationship is terminated before it turns sour and damage is irreparable. Mediators will be suitable third parties who can mediate in this process.

## CONCLUSIONS

A growing body of literature points to the added value third parties can have in relationship management (Nooteboom, 2004), interfirm coordination (Obstfeld, 2005), and the management of network ties (Burt, 2000). Yet no structural connection has been made to the mix of legal, private, and social ordering mechanisms of relationship governance, or to the role of third parties along the stages of relationship development. This chapter contributes to the alliance literature by providing a comprehensive framework on third-party roles, integrating existing third-party perspectives with alliance management insights from the organization, network, innovation, and trust literature (Howells, 2006). Third parties have an important role to play in relationship governance as their independence and impartiality makes them more suitable than the parties involved, for instance, to mediate and arbitrate. As a result of their "outside" position, they can contribute to establishing and maintaining strategic alliances, as they can provide help to make an assessment of risks, provide advice on suitable governance structures, and provide help when problems occur. In other words, by aiding the governance of a strategic alliance, they support the establishment and maintenance of high interfirm performance.

Existing studies of third-party intervention generally focus on *one* particular element out of the mix of governance mechanisms. Transaction cost economics, for instance, describes how third parties can complement legal governance or incomplete contracts (Williamson, 1985). In the same realm, attention has been given to how third parties can help in private ordering—for example, by aligning interests and providing coordination (Obstfeld, 2005; Simmel, 1950)—and in third-party mediation and arbitration in social ordering, for instance in trust building and repair (Möllering, 2006; Tomlinson & Mayer, 2009). This study contributes to this literature by presenting a coherent framework in which third party roles are structured along the various governance mechanisms and the stages of relationship development. In this way, first of all, the various third-party roles are explicitly coupled to the specific governance forms, providing insight into how roles differ per ordering mechanism, and hence which type of third party may be needed to assist. For instance, the type of intervention for supporting the drawing of a contract is very different from the process of transferring trust. Yet, these processes are highly interdependent.

The underlying logic of the framework is that it is not the *facts* such as asymmetric dependence or absence of prior trust that determine the quality of the relationship, but the ways that parties deal with their differences and governance problems. Third parties can fulfill many different roles in aiding this process. The framework elaborates on how third parties can not only help to set up an appropriate governance structure, but also how they can help to prevent the negative consequences of misuse or misinterpretation of governance mechanisms. In this way, governance mechanisms can be used in a constructive way, without provoking negative side effects. Hence, in our framework we theorize *how* third parties can prevent such negative consequences to occur, and *how* governance structures can be established that are supportive for the alliance.

We find that third party roles vary widely according to the stage of relationships development and the governance mechanism used. In the build-up and management stage of a relationship's development, third parties' help will mainly focus on establishing an appropriate governance structure. For example, the third party helps to balance the interests in the relationship and complements an incomplete contract with trilateral governance in such a way that the level of trust, flexibility, and openness essential for innovation can be maintained. When problems and conflicts occur in a relationship's development, different roles of third parties come to light. More attention will have to be focused on solving problems, realigning interests, adjusting the mix of governance, repairing trust, or simply limiting the damage of conflict and relationship termination. In this phase, governance is less concerned with creating value and more with limiting damage.

In a similar fashion, roles vary according to the governance mechanism in which third parties provide aid or guidance. In structural governance, roles such as specialized legal advice on contractual forms and formal and informal arbitration may play an important role. Also, mediation may be more important to align or realign interest between parties. Industry or technology specialists will be actors who have sufficient knowledge to value inputs and can hence provide help in balancing interests. In relational governance, again, other capabilities will be needed and hence other actors may become important. Trust, impartiality, and independence are crucial aspects to transfer, mediate, and potentially repair trust, and hence trusted mediators or consultants may prove valuable in this process. This in itself is a challenge for alliance governance, as several actors may be needed for the various aspects of relationship governance in the different phases of relationship development.

Our framework provides a basis for further research and theory building on the important and delicate role that third parties fill in relationship governance, taking into account the many aspects and subtleties of these interventions. Limited attention had been paid to the interrelatedness between the various ordering mechanisms and to the question of how third parties can help to establish an appropriate governance structure. This chapter can form a basis for future research as it makes the various potential roles of third parties explicit and explores the interrelatedness between the governance mechanisms. Although attention has been paid, for example, to the relationship between trust and contracts (Lane, 2000), and to how trust, contracts, and dependence interrelate (Klein-Woolthuis, 1999), no empirical or theoretical studies have structurally examined the roles of third parties in helping to establish an appropriate governance mix by, for example, substituting or complementing these governance mechanisms. Such insights are essential as the use and potential misuse of certain governance mechanisms are important ingredients for successful high-tech alliances.

An important next step is the empirical testing of the different roles that we hypothesize third parties to have. Questions arise, such as: Can third parties counterbalance asymmetric dependence in alliances by providing independent project management or installing administrative procedures that counteract potential opportunism by a more powerful party? And if this is possible, can trust exist despite the relationship's imbalance? Another important question would be whether third parties could complement incomplete contracts. Trust is often considered a complement or even substitute for contracts, but it is also fragile in its use. Could third-party intervention provide a reliable alternative? Empirical studies into these questions, as well as the question of who these third parties are, and how they fulfill their role, are all topics that call for additional theoretical and empirical studies on the role of third parties in relationship governance and trust.

## REFERENCES

Bachmann, R. (1998). Conclusion: Trust—conceptual aspects of a complex phenomenon. In C. Lane & R. Bachmann (Eds.), *Trust within and between organizations* (pp. 298–322). Oxford, UK: Oxford University Press.

Baker, W. E. (2000). *Achieving success through social capital: Tapping hidden resources in your personal and business networks*. San Francisco, CA: Jossey-Bass.

Becerra, M., Lunnan, R., & Huemer, L. (2008). Trustworthiness, risk, and the transfer of tacit and explicit knowledge between alliance partners. *Journal of Management Studies, 45*, 1024–1024.

Berg, J., Dickhaut, J., & McCabe, K. (1995). Trust, reciprocity and social history. *Games and Economic Behavior, 10*, 122–142.

Bijlsma-Frankema, K., Sitkin, S., & Weibel, A. (2008, July). *Breaking out of distrust: Judges and administrators in a court of law*. Paper presented at the EGOS Conference, Bergen, Norway.

Bleeke, J., & Ernst, D. (1991). The way to win in cross-border alliances. *Harvard Business Review, 69*(6), 127–135.

Blumberg, B. F. (2001). Cooperation contracts between embedded firms. *Organization Studies 22*, 825–852.

Burt, R. S. (1992). *Structural holes*. Cambridge, MA: Harvard University Press.

Burt, R. S. (2000). The network structure of social capital. *Research in Organizational Behavior, 22*, 345–376.

Charness, G., Cobo-Reyes, R., & Jimenez, N. (2008). An investment game with third-party intervention. *Journal of Economic Behavior & Organization, 68*, 18–28.

Chen, Y. M. (2000). Promises, trust, and contracts. *Journal of Law, Economics & Organization, 16*(1), 209–232.

Cohen, W. M., & Levinthal, D. (1990). Absorptive capacity: A new perspective on learning and innovation. *Administrative Science Quarterly, 35*, 128–152.

Das, T. K., & Teng, B. (2001). Trust, control, and risk in strategic alliances: An integrated framework. *Organization Studies, 22*(2), 251–283.

Deakin, S, & Wilkinson, F. (2000). Capabilities, spontaneous order and social rights. ESRC Centre for Business Research Working Paper No. 174. Cambridge, UK: University of Cambridge.

de Man, A. P., & Duysters, G. (2005). Collaboration and innovation: A review of the effects of mergers, acquisitions and alliances on innovation. *Technovation, 25*, 1377–1387.

Fehr, E., & Fischbacher, U. (2004). Social norms and human cooperation. *Trends in Cognitive Sciences, 8*(4), 185–190.

Fehr, E., & Gachter, S. (2002). Human behaviour: Egalitarian motive and altruistic punishment. *Nature, 415*, 137–140.

Ferrin, D. L., Dirks, K. T., & Shah, P. P. (2006). Direct and indirect effects of third-party relationships on interpersonal trust. *Journal of Applied Psychology, 91*, 870–883.

Gambetta, D. (1988). *Trust: Making and breaking cooperative relations*. Oxford, UK: Basil Blackwell.

Gaski, J. F. (1986). Interrelations among a channel entity power sources: Impact of the exercise of reward and coercion on expert, referent, and legitimate power sources. *Journal of Marketing Research, 23*(1), 62–77.

Gaski, J. F., & Nevin, J. R. (1985). The differential-effects of exercised and unexercized power sources in a marketing channel. *Journal of Marketing Research, 22*(2), 130–142.

Ghoshal, S., & Moran, P. (1996). Bad for practice: A critique of the transaction cost theory. *Academy of Management Review, 21*, 13–47.

Gintis, H., Bowles, S., Boyd, R., & Fehr, S. (2003). Explaining altruistic behavior in humans. *Evolution and Human Behavior, 24*, 153–172.

Granovetter, M. S. (1973). The strength of weak ties. *American Journal of Sociology, 78*, 1360–1381.

Gulati, R. (1995). Does familiarity breed trust: The implications of repeated ties for contractual choice in alliances. *Academy of Management Journal, 38*(1), 85–112.

Hargadon, A. B. (1998). Firms as knowledge brokers: Lessons in pursuing continuous innovation. *California Management Review, 40*, 209–227.

Hirschman, A. O. (1970). *Exit, voice and loyalty: Responses to decline in firms, organizations and states*. Cambridge, MA: Harvard University Press.

Howells, J. (2006). Intermediation and the role of intermediaries in innovation. *Research Policy, 35*, 715–728.

Hunt, S. D., & Nevin, J. R. (1974). Power in a channel of distribution: Sources and consequences. *Journal of Marketing Research, 11*, 186–193.

Katz, R., & Tushman, M. (1981). An investigation into the managerial roles and career paths of gatekeepers and project supervisors in a major R&D facility. *R&D Management, 11*(3), 103–110.

Kim, P. H., Ferrin, D. L., Cooper, C. D., & Dirks, K. T. (2004). Removing the shadow of suspicion: The effects of apology versus denial for repairing competence- versus integrity-based trust violations. *Journal of Applied Psychology, 89*, 104–118.

Klein Woolthuis, R. J. A. (1999). *Sleeping with the enemy: Trust, dependence, and contracts in interorganizational relationships*. Unpublished paper, University of Twente Entrepreneurship Centre, Enschede, Netherlands.

Klein Woolthuis, R. J. A., Hillebrand, B., & Nooteboom, B. (2005). Trust, contract and relationship development. *Organization Studies, 26*, 813–840.

Lane, C. (2000). Introduction: Theories and issues in the study of trust. In C. Lane & R. Bachmann (Eds.), *Trust within and between organizations* (pp. 1–30). Oxford, UK: Oxford University Press.

Lane, P. J., & Lubatkin, M. (1998). Relative absorptive capacity and interorganizational learning. *Strategic Management Journal, 19*, 461–477.

Larson, A. (1992). Network dyads in entrepreneurial settings: A study of the governance of exchange relationships. *Administrative Science Quarterly, 37*, 76–104.

Lewicki, R. J., & Bunker, B. B. (1996). Developing and maintaining trust in work relationships. In R. J. Lewicki, B. B. Bunker, R. M. Kramer, & T. R. Tyler (Eds.), *Trust in organizations: Frontiers of theory and research* (pp. 114–139). Thousand Oaks, CA: Sage.

Li, P. P. (1997). Towards an interdisciplinary concept of trust. A typological approach. *Management and Organization Review, 3*, 421–445.

Li, P. P. (1998). Towards a geocentric framework of trust. An application to organizational trust. *Management and Organization Review, 4*, 413–439.

Mesquita, L. F. (2007). Starting over when the bickering never ends: Rebuilding aggregate trust among clustered firms through trust facilitators. *Academy of Management Review, 32*(1), 72–91.

Möllering, G. (2001). The nature of trust. From George Simmel to a theory of expectation, interpretation and suspension. *Sociology, 35*, 403–420.

Möllering, G. (Ed.). (2006). *Trust: Reason, routine, reflexivity.* Oxford, UK: Elsevier.

Nooteboom, B. (1993). Firm size effects on transaction costs. *Small Business Economics, 5*, 283–295.

Nooteboom, B. (1999a). Innovation and inter-firm linkages: New implications for policy. *Research Policy, 28*, 793–805.

Nooteboom, B. (1999b). Innovation, learning and industrial organisation. *Cambridge Journal of Economics, 23*(2), 127–150.

Nooteboom, B. (1999c). *Inter-firm alliances: Analysis and design.* London, UK: Routledge.

Nooteboom, B. (2000). Institutions and forms of co-ordination in innovation systems. *Organization Studies, 21*, 915–939.

Nooteboom, B. (2002). *Trust: Forms, foundations, functions, failures and figures.* Cheltenham, UK: Edward Elgar.

Nooteboom, B. (2004). *Inter-firm collaboration, learning and networks: An integrated approach.* London, UK: Routledge.

Nooteboom, B., Van Haverbeke, W., Duysters, G., Gilsing, V., & van den Oord, A. (2007). Optimal cognitive distance and absorptive capacity. *Research Policy, 36*, 1016–1034.

Obstfeld, D. (2005). Social networks, the tertius iungens and orientation involvement in innovation. *Administrative Science Quarterly, 50*, 100–130.

Poppo, L. & Zenger, T. (2002). Do formal contracts and relational governance function as substitutes or complements? *Strategic Management Journal, 23*, 707–725.

Reuer, J. J., Arino, A., & Mellewigt, T. (2006). Entrepreneurial alliances as contractual forms. *Journal of Business Venturing, 26*, 306–325.

Ring, P. S., & Van de Ven, A. H. (1994). Developmental processes of cooperative interorganizational relationships. *Academy of Management Review, 19*, 90–118.

Rosenkopf, L., & Tushman, M. (1994). The coevolution of technology and organization. In J. A. C. Baum & J. V. Singh (Eds.), *Evolutionary dynamics of organizations* (pp. 403–424). Oxford: Oxford University Press.

Rowley, T., Behrens, D., & Krackhardt, D. (2000). Redundant governance structures: An analysis of structural and relational embeddedness in the steel and semiconductor industries. *Strategic Management Journal, 26*, 369–386.

Simmel, G. (1950). *The sociology of Georg Simmel.* Trans., ed., and intro. by K. H. Wolff. [German original, 1908]. New York, NY: Free Press.

Stephens, K. J., Fulk, J., & Monge, P. R. (2009). Constrained choices in alliance formations: Cupids and organizational marriages. *Human Relations, 62*, 501–536.

Tomlinson, E. C., Dineen, B. R., & Lewicki, R. J. (2004). The road to reconciliation: Antecedents of victim willingness to reconcile following a broken promise. *Journal of Management, 30*, 165–187.

Tomlinson, E. C., & Mayer, R. C. (2009). The role of causal attribution dimensions in trust repair. *Academy of Management Review, 34*, 85–104.

Tushman, M. L., & Katz, R. (1980). External communication and project performance–an investigation into the role of gatekeepers. *Management Science, 26*, 1071–1085.

Weiner, B. (1986). *An attributional theory of motivation and emotion.* New York, NY: Springer-Verlag.

Williamson, O. E. (1975). *Markets and hierarchies: Analysis and antitrust implications.* New York, NY: Free Press.

Williamson, O. E. (1985). *The economic institutions of capitalism.* New York, NY: Free Press.

Wolpert, J. D. (2002). Breaking out of the innovation box. *Harvard Business Review, 80*(8), 76–83.

Zaheer, A., McEvily, B., & Perrone, V. (1998). Does trust matter? Exploring the effects of interorganizational and interpersonal trust on performance. *Organization Science, 9*, 141–159.

Zand, D. E. (1972). Trust and managerial problem solving. *Administrative Science Quarterly, 17*, 229–239.

CHAPTER 4

# A NATURAL-RESOURCE-BASED EXAMINATION OF STRATEGIC ALLIANCE FORMATION

**Anne Norheim-Hansen**

## ABSTRACT

Firms frequently form strategic alliances with the aim of competing more effectively and efficiently by means of access to other firms' resources. Hence, when selecting a partner, the initiating (focal) firm in an alliance project tends to assess the relative attractiveness of prospective partner firms primarily based on their resource profiles. This chapter is the first study to argue that, considering the increased focus on environmental sustainability, natural resources resulting from proactive environmental strategies can have implications for alliance formation. Specifically, I examine strategic alliance formation under the natural-resource-based view (NRBV) of the firm and find that a strong environmental reputation (i.e., environmental credibility) makes a prospective partner firm more attractive to the focal firm—this through signaling resource-richness and opportunity for favorable reputational spillovers. To paraphrase, resources allowing for the protection of the natural environment can facilitate alliance formation. Whereas the pivotal role of resources in determining strategic alliance partner attractiveness is well documented in the literature, this chapter contributes to answering a call in recent research for more evidence on the influence of specific organizational resources in alliance formation. It is furthermore, to the best of my knowledge, the first study to apply the NRBV to the strategic alliance context.

## INTRODUCTION

With the rise of the knowledge-based economy and rapidly changing globalized markets, forming strategic alliances has become a common tactic used by companies in their quest to attain or maintain competitive advantages. Strategic alliances—that is, interfirm cooperative agreements aimed at generating competitive advantage through exchanging, sharing, or jointly developing resources (Das & Teng, 1999; Hoetker & Mellewigt, 2009; Mohr & Spekman, 1994)—allow companies to access resources they lack to compete effectively or efficiently (Lambe, Spekman, & Hunt, 2002; Teng & Das, 2008) and resources that are unavailable in factor markets (Bae & Gargiulo, 2004; Das & Teng, 2000; Oliver, 1997). As noted by Parmigiani and Rivera-Santos (2011), these interorganizational relationships "typically provide quicker access to resources than internal development does, allow to access tacit and imperfectly tradable resources, and are less costly than acquiring an entire firm" (p. 1114). Das and Teng (2000), proposing a resource-based theory of strategic alliances, underline that the resource characteristics of imperfect mobility, imitability, and substitutability "promise accentuated value-creation, and thus facilitate alliance formation" (p. 31).

While alliance formation has been extensively researched from a resource-based perspective (Das & Teng, 2000; Eisenhardt & Schoonhoven, 1996; Lavie, 2006; Lin, Yang, & Arya, 2009), a comprehensive search of the extant literature indicates that it has yet to be examined under the *natural-resource-based view* (NRBV) of the firm (e.g., Aragón-Correa & Sharma, 2003; Berchicci & King, 2007; Chan, 2005; Hart, 1995; Hart & Ahuja, 1996; Hart & Dowell, 2011; Sharma & Vredenburg, 1998) asserting that companies' resources and capabilities allowing for the protection of the natural environment are sources of competitive advantage. That such an undertaking has theoretical and practical value is evident when considering simultaneously (1) the growing pressure on and incentives for firms to become "greener" (Ambec & Lanoie, 2008; Chan, 2005; Hart & Dowell, 2011; Moon, 2007); (2) firms having, according to the NRBV, underinvested in environmental capabilities (Berchicci & King, 2007; Hart & Dowell, 2011); and (3) environmental capabilities being resource-intensive, complex, and time-consuming to build (Aragón-Correa & Sharma, 2003; Sharma & Vredenburg, 1998), suggesting that firms lacking or having few of these capabilities may well see forming strategic alliances with firms having attained "green credence" (Aragón-Correa & Sharma, 2003) as constructive (Parmigiani & Rivera-Santos, 2011).

These arguments are detailed in the next sections. The main objective of this chapter is to theoretically investigate whether and to what extent an initiating (focal) firm in an alliance project can be expected to assess prospective partner firms with strong environmental reputations as attractive. Strong environmental reputations are defined as environmental credibility (Brady, 2005) resulting from long-term (Barney, 1991; Dierickx & Cool, 1989; Hall, 1993), proactive environmental strategies (Aragón-Correa & Sharma, 2003; Hart & Dowell, 2011; Sharma & Vredenburg, 1998). Furthermore, for the purposes of this study, I employ the definition of partner attractiveness provided by Shah and Swaminathan (2008): "the degree to which the initiating [focal] firm in a particular alliance project sees a partner as desirable, favorable, appealing and valuable" (p. 473). I also incorporate Shah and Swaminathan's (2008) claim that the higher the attractiveness of a given partner, the higher the likelihood that the focal firm will select that particular partner. Nevertheless, it should be noted that higher attractiveness does not automatically *cause* selection. Partner selection is a contingent and complex decision based on additional criteria (see Dacin, Reid, & Ring, 2008, and Shah & Swaminathan, 2008, for relevant reviews).

The rest of this chapter is structured as follows. I first describe the resource-based view (RBV) and NRBV. Next, I justify the aforementioned arguments through a broad literature review. In my theoretical analysis leading up to the propositions of this chapter, the particular role of reputation in alliance formation is discussed—further justifying employing the proxy of strong environmental reputation for firms' long-term proactive environmental strategies. A concluding section discusses the findings and contributions to theory and practice, as well as the limitations pointing out possible areas for future research.

First and foremost, the study answers Mitsuhashi and Greve's (2009) call for evidence "on how specific organizational resources affect alliance formation" (p. 976). By examining strategic alliance formation under the NRBV of the firm, it contributes to both the strategic alliance and NRBV literatures, but it also provides useful insights for other streams such as corporate reputation and corporate social responsibility (CSR) research—on which this research draws upon recurrently.

## THE NATURAL-RESOURCE-BASED VIEW (NRBV) OF THE FIRM: AN EXTENDED RESOURCE-BASED VIEW

Penrose (1959) is generally considered the seminal work of what later became known as the resource-based view of the firm (Barney, 1991;

Wernerfelt, 1984), commonly abbreviated RBV. This strategic management research stream introduced novel, complementary lenses for determining a firm's competitive position by focusing inwards on its resources portfolio (Barney, 1995) rather than on the external competitive environment or industry structure (Porter, 1985)—acknowledging, though, that attention outwards is still vital as "firm resources are not valuable in a vacuum, but rather are valuable only when they exploit opportunities and/or neutralize threats" (Barney, 1995, p. 52). The main assumption of the RBV is that firms are heterogeneous over time (Grant, 1991; Mahoney & Pandian, 1992) with idiosyncratic and immobile resources (Peteraf, 1993) that can, if valuable, rare, and non-substitutable, be sources of competitive advantage and, if also costly to imitate or inimitable, be sources of sustained competitive advantage (Barney, 1991). The resource-based view, now and then referred to as the resource-based *theory* (Barney, 2001a; Hart & Dowell, 2011), has not developed without fierce criticism (Priem & Butler, 2001a, 2001b)—sometimes followed by an equally powerful counter-attack (Barney, 2001b)—but the great number of published articles under this framework speaks for itself with respect to its utility for strategic management researchers. Despite its original static and rather firm-specific approach, the RBV has evolved and has been successfully applied to both dynamic capabilities of the firm (Teece, Pisano, & Shuen, 1997) and strategic alliances (Das & Teng, 2000; Dyer & Singh, 1998; Eisenhardt & Schoonhoven, 1996; Lavie, 2006). Das and Teng (2000) argue that a resource-based view is "particularly appropriate for examining strategic alliances because firms essentially use alliances to gain access to other firms' valuable resources" (p. 33).

The *natural*-resource-based view (NRBV) was born with Hart's (1995) seminal paper—recently revisited by Hart and Dowell (2011)—where he extended the RBV to include the constraints imposed by the natural environment. Hart's motivation is depicted in the following quotation: "Given the growing magnitude of ecological problems...this omission has rendered existing theory inadequate as a basis for identifying important emerging sources of competitive advantage" (p. 987). As stated above, the essence of this view, or theory (Berchicci & King, 2007), is that companies' resources and capabilities allowing for the protection of the natural environment are sources of competitive advantage. These resources and capabilities are built and leveraged through proactive environmental strategies (Aragón-Correa & Sharma, 2003; Michalisin & Stinchfield, 2010; Sharma & Vredenburg, 1998) fostering, for instance, complex and path-dependent environmental capabilities of higher-order learning and productive problem solving with stakeholders (Aragón-Correa & Sharma, 2003; Sharma & Vredenburg, 1998), again leading to, for example, lower costs and/or reputation-based benefits (Hart & Dowell, 2011). Hart's (1995) framework is a typology of four stages of corporate environmental strategies: one reactive (i.e., pollution control), and three increasingly advanced proactive strategies (i.e., pollution prevention, product stewardship, and sustainable development). The concept of proactive environmental strategy is "a pattern of environmental practices that [go] beyond compliance with environmental regulations" (Aragón-Correa & Sharma, 2003, p. 71). To be considered proactive, a firm "should have exhibited a consistent pattern of such voluntary actions over time" (Sharma & Vredenburg, 1998, p. 733). Hart and Dowell (2011) argue that there are different competitive advantage outcomes of the three different levels of proactive environmental strategy (Hart, 1995). Due to the lack of research on the implications of sustainable development strategies for firm performance (Hart & Dowell, 2011), this study solely takes into account the lower level strategies of pollution prevention and product stewardship—linked to a number of firm effectiveness and efficiency improvements, which have been validated in empirical studies (Hart & Ahuja, 1996; Sharma & Vredenburg, 1998). According to Hart and Dowell (2011), reputation is the key competitive advantage driver of the proactive environmental strategy of product stewardship, which goes beyond simple pollution prevention—where the key driver is allegedly lower costs.

Apart from focusing on a certain resource category, the extended RBV differs from the classic RBV (Barney, 1991; Wernerfelt, 1984) in two of its assertions. The NRBV assumes that "managers make systematic errors" (Berchicci & King, 2007, p. 516), that is, that they systematically invest too little in developing environmental capabilities; this is mainly through the reasoning that there are particularly strong valuation difficulties related to environmental performance (Russo & Fouts, 1997; Stanwick & Stanwick, 1998) and that a number of cognitive heuristics and biases linked to these difficulties cause underinvestment (see Berchicci & King, 2007, and Hart & Dowell, 2011, for a detailed account of these mechanisms). The NRBV further differentiates itself from the classic RBV in arguing that external stakeholder involvement can "foster better decision making, and thereby cause managers to uncover hidden value" (Berchicci & King, 2007, p. 520). Examples include the access to beneficial information and assistance from liaising with environmental groups (Stafford, Polonsky, & Hartman, 2000) and waste prevention through customer-initiated collaborative actions (Klassen & Vachon, 2003). Fowler and Hope (2007), testing Hart's (1995) framework through a case study of the company Patagonia, found broad evidence of positive outcomes from interactions with external stakeholders. Both Berchicci and King (2007) and Hart and Dowell (2011) provide extensive reviews of empirical evidence supporting the arguments of the NRBV.

In accordance with the classic RBV, the NRBV holds that firms having made inferior investments in resources can encounter subsequent adjustment problems and competitive barriers (Berchicci & King, 2007). It also follows the classic RBV in emphasizing that market conditions affect the value of resources (Aragón-Correa & Sharma, 2003; Barney, 1995, 2001a, 2001b); thus, "the efficacy of organizational capabilities varies with market dynamism" (Aragón-Correa & Sharma, 2003, p. 72).

## NEW MARKET PRESSURES AND INCENTIVES ESCALATING FIRMS' ENVIRONMENTAL CAPABILITY AMBITIONS

As confirmed by Hart and Dowell (2011), there is a strengthened focus on the natural environment since Hart's (1995) relatively early paper. They state the following: "Climate change, for example, was known to be a significant issue in 1995..., but the full implications of climate change and the degree to which it is considered an issue for top management to consider is only now being understood" (pp. 1475–1476). In the midst of the enhanced societal awareness and concern about environmental issues (Ambec & Lanoie, 2008; Cacioppe, Forster, & Fox, 2008) such as climate change (Hart & Dowell, 2011; Michalisin & Stinchfield, 2010), companies are increasingly being scrutinized with regards to their environmental conduct. Moreover, there is a continual stream of emergent regulations and standards (Dowell, Hart, & Yeung, 2000; Gallarotti, 1995; Rugman & Verbeke, 1998) as well as ever-increasing stakeholder pressure on companies to improve (Waddock, Bodwell, & Graves, 2002). Even operations in emerging economies are being included (Chan, 2005; Dowell et al., 2000). In this business setting, where it has become progressively crucial to attend to the natural environment (Shrivastava, 1995), more firms than before integrate corporate environmentalism in their strategic plans (Banerjee, Iyer, & Kashyap, 2003; Berry & Rondinelli, 1998; Judge & Douglas, 1998).

Whereas scores of firms continue to follow a reactive strategy (Sharma & Vredenburg, 1998; Simpson, Taylor, & Barker, 2004), and many CEOs still adhere to the traditional paradigm associating "green" mainly with costs and disadvantages (Nidumolu, Prahalad, & Rangaswami, 2009), more evidence on the advantages has made companies increasingly more proactive in their efforts (Berry & Rondinelli, 1998; Chan, 2005). As noted by Chan (2005): "In the face of diminishing opportunities to develop value-generating capabilities in today's highly dynamic and competitive marketplace (Hart, 1995), proactive strategies to address problems inherent at the interface between the enterprise and ecological issues may represent one of the few alternatives available to sustain organizational growth" (p. 658). Both Aragón-Correa and Sharma (2003) and Hart and Dowell (2011) add further support to this argument by maintaining that proactive environmental strategies are in themselves dynamic capabilities, particularly valuable in rapidly changing markets (Hart & Dowell, 2011; Teece et al., 1997).

At the very minimum, it is safe to claim that there is growing adherence among firms to what Berchicci and King (2007) refer to as the "pays-to-be-green" (PTBG) literature (Ambec & Lanoie, 2008; Gallarotti, 1995; Porter & van der Linde, 1995a, 1995b) and therefore the NRBV (Hart, 1995)—both linking environmental capabilities to competitive advantages (Hart & Dowell, 2011; Sharma & Vredenburg, 1998; Simpson et al., 2004) through waste and cost reductions, improved processes and operations, improved product quality, product innovations and differentiations, higher employee morale, and, not least, better relations with stakeholders and an enhanced corporate reputation. With the strengthened societal attention to environmental issues, researchers have uncovered that perceived corporate environmental performance has become an integral part of the reputation construct (Barnett, Jermier, & Lafferty, 2006; Bertels & Peloza, 2008; Hillenbrand & Money, 2007; Quevedo-Puente, Fuente-Sabaté, & Delgado-García, 2007). Environmental performance is defined as the "firms' effectiveness in meeting and exceeding societal expectations with respect to concerns about the natural environment" (Chan, 2005, p. 632, referring to Judge & Douglas, 1998); "[i]t is about the firm's proactive stance concerning future environmental considerations, and extends beyond mere compliance with existing regulations" (p. 632). Such performance has become an important element of stakeholders' perceptual representation of companies (Brady, 2005) on which, for example, they base their purchasing or investment decisions (Lange, Lee, & Dai, 2011; Walker, 2010). High environmental performance has furthermore been found to enhance organizational attractiveness to prospective employees (Aiman-Smith, Bauer, & Cable, 2001). Lastly, although the relationship between environmental performance and financial performance (Russo & Fouts, 1997; Stanwick & Stanwick, 1998) is complex, and various contingency factors matter (Allouche & Laroche, 2005; Ambec & Lanoie, 2008; Aragón-Correa & Sharma, 2003; Chan, 2005; Hart & Dowell, 2011), recent meta-analyses have found that the two are positively correlated (Allouche & Laroche, 2005; Margolis & Walsh, 2003; Orlitzky, Schmidt, & Rynes, 2003).

In the next section, I investigate the probable implications these new market pressures and incentives escalating firms' environmental capability ambitions have for strategic alliance formation. More specifically, I examine the effects strong environmental reputations of prospective partner firms have on the extent to which the initiating (focal) firm in an alliance project considers them as attractive partners. However, beforehand, a discussion of the notion of partner attractiveness is warranted.

## STRATEGIC ALLIANCE FORMATION AND THE PREREQUISITE OF PARTNER ATTRACTIVENESS

Although prior studies on alliance formation rightly stress that it takes two to tango or two willing parties for alliance formation to occur (Mitsuhashi & Greve, 2009), "the decision to partner is typically initiated by one firm" (Shah & Swaminathan, 2008, p. 473). Moreover, in the formation phase of strategic alliances, "[the focal] firm deciding to initiate an alliance selects an appropriate partner" (Kale & Singh, 2009, p. 46), normally after an "assessment of the relative attractiveness of various partners" (Shah & Swaminathan, 2008, p. 473). Firms select strategic alliance partners based on different organizational characteristics of the prospective partner firms (Mitsuhashi & Greve, 2009), and partner selection tends to be a contingent (Shah & Swaminathan, 2008) and complex decision (Sarkar, Echambadi, Cavusgil, & Aulakh, 2001). It is also a highly important decision, as it is widely accepted that partner selection affects strategic alliance performance (e.g., Dacin, Hitt, & Levitas, 1997; Geringer, 1991; Holmberg & Cummings, 2009; Sarkar et al., 2001; Saxton, 1997; Shah & Swaminathan, 2008).

While individual criteria or organizational characteristics do not on their own *cause* partner selection, they can contribute to the attractiveness of prospective partners as perceived by the focal firm—and thereby increase the likelihood of selection (Shah & Swaminathan, 2008). As previously discussed, this study adopts the conceptualization of the construct of partner attractiveness provided by Shah and Swaminathan (2008): "the degree to which the initiating firm in a particular alliance project sees a partner as desirable, favorable, appealing and valuable" (p. 473).

There is a vast literature addressing determinants of partner attractiveness and selection (e.g., Ahuja, 2000; Bae & Gargiulo, 2004; Beckman, Haunschild, & Phillips, 2004; Chung, Singh, & Lee, 2000; Dollinger, Golden, & Saxton, 1997; Geringer, 1988; Mitsuhashi & Greve, 2009). However, considering that a full discussion seems unnecessary for the purposes of this chapter, I merely refer to a review performed by Shah and Swaminathan (2008) of more than 40 studies, where the factors of trust, commitment, financial payoff, and especially complementary resources (and skills) were "consistently identified as being important to partner attractiveness and selection." (p. 472). As this study takes a natural-resource-based perspective, I focus on the latter. Through this lens, the definition of partner attractiveness provided above can be understood as the degree to which the focal firm sees a prospective partner's *resource profile* as "desirable, favorable, appealing and valuable" (Shah & Swaminathan, 2008, p. 473).

## LINKING ENVIRONMENTAL REPUTATION TO STRATEGIC ALLIANCE PARTNER ATTRACTIVENESS

Earlier, I explained that firms presently operate in a business setting where the issue of environmental sustainability has become pressing to attend to—due to both constraints and opportunities. Accordingly, I argued that there has been an escalation in firms' environmental capability ambitions. Yet, whereas firms increasingly implement environmental strategies, improving environmental performance to the extent of acquiring a strong environmental reputation (i.e., environmental credibility) among stakeholders—where a large part of the potential harvest from environmental capabilities is situated (Allouche & Laroche, 2005; Hart & Dowell, 2011; Orlitzky et al., 2003; Surroca, Tribó, & Waddock, 2010)—is a long-term process. Developing credibility on this matter, as developing any reputational dimension (Dollinger et al., 1997), takes considerable time (Barney, 1991; Dierickx & Cool, 1989; Hall, 1993; Mayer, 2006; Roberts & Dowling, 2002) and consistent performance (Ang & Wight, 2009; Carter & Ruefli, 2006; Hastings, 1999; Roberts & Dowling, 2002). The sophisticated and time-consuming process of building up the comprehensive resource base (Chan, 2005; Hart, 1995) and highly complex and path-dependent environmental capabilities (Aragón-Correa & Sharma, 2003; Sharma & Vredenburg, 1998), associated with environmental credibility, is another aspect preventing companies from acquiring a strong environmental reputation "overnight."

In view of the fact that strategic alliances "typically provide quicker access to resources than internal development does, allow to access tacit and imperfectly tradable resources, and are less costly than acquiring an entire firm" (Parmigiani & Rivera-Santos, 2011, p. 1114), it is reasonable to argue that allying with partner firms in possession of resources and capabilities allowing for high environmental performance represents an adjustment solution for the focal firm's inferior investments (Berchicci & King, 2007), thus allowing the focal firm to adapt more effectively and efficiently to market requirements for environmental performance. Besides, as noted by Child, Faulkner, and Tallman (2005), "firms are more likely to ally if they see their potential partner as being able to strengthen their position in relation to the [market]" (p. 120)—for instance through providing resources of which they deem there are few or an absence of alternative providers (Bae & Gargiulo, 2004).

Naturally, to make informed decisions related to alliance formation, the initiating (focal) firm in an alliance project needs accurate information on the prospective partners. There is always a risk that partner firms knowingly or unknowingly misrepresent their resources and capabilities (Hoetker & Mellewigt, 2009); many companies have been accused of "greenwash" (Brady, 2005), meaning environmental communication and public relations (PR) "spin" with a lack of real substance. Where there are no prior ties (Gulati, 1995a, 1995b), and therefore restricted familiarity with prospective partners' resource profiles, reputations serve as informational signals on the underlying resources that have allowed for the construction of the reputation (Eisenhardt & Schoonhoven, 1996; Fombrun & Shanley, 1990; Gatewood, Gowan, & Lautenschlager, 1993). As such, a strong environmental reputation signals to the focal firm the real existence of valuable environmentally protective resources and capabilities to tap into. All of the above lead to the following proposition:

**Proposition 1:** *Initiating (focal) firms in alliance projects are more likely to see prospective partner firms with strong environmental reputations as attractive, and are consequently more likely to establish alliances with such firms.*

## ROLE OF CORPORATE REPUTATION IN FACILITATING STRATEGIC ALLIANCE FORMATION

While scarcely researched (Lui, Ngo, & Hon, 2006; Royer, Simons, & Waldersee, 2003), there are a handful of previous studies examining the role of corporate reputation in facilitating strategic alliance formation (Arend, 2009; Dollinger et al., 1997; Hirsch & Meyer, 2010; Royer & Simons, 2009; Royer et al., 2003). Dollinger et al. (1997), who authored the most cited paper on reputation effects in the strategic alliance context, argue from several theoretical perspectives—and find empirical evidence—that positive corporate reputations enhance partner attractiveness and thereby the likelihood of selection (Shah & Swaminathan, 2008). They furthermore demonstrate that corporation reputation is a multidimensional construct (Brady, 2005; Carter & Ruefli, 2006; Fombrun, Gardberg, & Sever, 2000; Rhee & Valdez, 2009; Walker, 2010) with disparate outcomes of the different dimensions or reputational issues—making apparent the need for separate analyses (Deephouse, 2000; Dollinger et al., 1997). Not isolated in the analysis of Dollinger et al. (1997) nor, to the best of my knowledge, in any other study in the strategic alliance context, the environmental dimension has today become an issue central to the corporate reputation construct (Barnett et al., 2006; Bertels & Peloza, 2008) that deserves attention. Corporate reputation is a dynamic construct evolving with society (Lange et al., 2011; Quevedo-Puente et al., 2007).

Apart from Dollinger et al. (1997)—including the RBV and several reputational dimensions in their analysis—previous studies mostly take game theoretic and/or transaction cost perspectives and are focused on reputation for cooperation. Given that this chapter analyzes alliance formation under the NRBV, only resource-based mechanisms pertaining to environmental reputation are attended to. With the intention, however, to complete a deeper scrutiny of the proposed relationship spelled out in Proposition 1, the resource-based mediators of the relationship are discussed in the subsequent sections. The rationale for this undertaking is that the extant literature (including the literature already reviewed in this chapter) reveals two distinct mediators: (1) the degree to which the initiating (focal) firm in a particular alliance project sees a partner as resource-rich (Bae & Gargiulo, 2004) and (2) the degree to which the initiating (focal) firm in a particular alliance project sees a partner as granting opportunity for favorable reputational spillovers (Yu & Lester, 2008). These arguments are detailed next.

## The Impact of Strong Environmental Reputation on Perceived Resource-Richness

There are various rationales or strategic objectives (Eisenhardt & Schoonhoven, 1996; Glaister & Buckley, 1996; Gulati & Singh, 1998) for entering into strategic alliances (those formed specifically to develop green technologies, etc. are outside the scope of this study), such as sharing costs and/or risks, sharing complementary technology, and reducing the time span of innovation (Gulati & Singh, 1998). However, "firms essentially use alliances to gain access to other firms' valuable resources" (Das & Teng, 2000, p. 33). The centrality of resource considerations in strategic alliance formation is highlighted in prior studies (Chung et al., 2000; Kale & Singh, 2009), as aforementioned, including in the extensive literature review performed by Shah and Swaminathan (2008). Bae and Gargiulo (2004) note that "the benefit a [focal] firm receives from an alliance increases with the resource endowment of the alliance partners" (p. 844), and "actors' resource endowments can determine...their attractiveness as partners" (p. 857). Similarly, Ahuja (2000) argues that "the greater a firm's stock of resources, the greater the firm's attractiveness [as] partners, and the greater the firm's collaboration opportunities" (p. 319). Das and Teng (2000), proposing a resource-based theory of strategic alliances, underline the influence of certain resource characteristics. Imperfect mobility, imitability, and substitutability, accredited to reputation among other resources (Barney, 1991; Dierickx & Cool, 1989; Hastings, 1999), "promise accentuated value-creation, and thus facilitate alliance formation" (Das & Teng, 2000, p. 31). In sum, these arguments suggest that partner attractiveness is dependent on the degree to which the focal firm perceives the partner as resource-rich, where resource-richness is conceptualized as including the quantity as well as quality of resources (Bae & Gargiulo, 2004); quality refers here to the extent to which the resources are sources of competitive advantage (Barney, 1991; Das & Teng, 2000).

As detailed in the previous sections, the underlying resources and capabilities of strong environmental reputations are according to the NRBV literature extensive, and embody to a large degree the decisive factors of competitive advantage (Barney, 1991; Dierickx & Cool, 1989; Hart, 1995). Aragón-Correa and Sharma (2003) note that such resources and capabilities include technology, managerial skills, attitudes and interpretations, complex environmental capabilities for pollution prevention, continuous innovation, and stakeholder integration. In other words, a strong environmental reputation is a signal of a range of underlying sophisticated resources that have permitted the organization to acquire such a positive reputation (Fombrun & Shanley, 1990; Gatewood et al., 1993) and that are found to enhance organizational efficiency and effectiveness in a number of ways (Sharma & Vredenburg, 1998). It can therefore indicate that a prospective strategic alliance partner's resources are of high quantity as well as high quality. These arguments are conducive to the following prediction:

**Proposition 2:** *Initiating (focal) firms in alliance projects are more likely to see prospective partner firms with strong environmental reputations as resource-rich, and are consequently more likely to see such firms as attractive.*

## The Impact of Strong Environmental Reputation on Perceived Opportunity for Favorable Reputational Spillovers

A firm's reputation, assuming it is positive, is in addition to being a signal in itself a resource and a source of competitive advantage (Barney, 1991; Das & Teng, 2000; Dierickx & Cool, 1989; Hall, 1993; Yu & Lester, 2008). Reputations' idiosyncratic nature makes them non-tradable (Dierickx & Cool, 1989), and the prospect of imitation is low since "a positive reputation usually depends upon specific difficult-to-duplicate historical settings" (Barney, 1991, p. 115) and socially complex informal relations with stakeholders. While guarantees and long-term contracts have been suggested as possible substitutes for reputation, Barney (1991) puts forward the counterargument that some firms invest in both a strong reputation and guarantees. A strong reputation can also be rare (e.g., environmental credibility) and is by classification valuable since "firm attributes must be valuable in order to be considered resources" (Barney, 1991, p. 106). It is commonly associated with business success (Hall, 1992), and the ability to attract other firms in the context of alliance formation (Dollinger et al., 1997) is only one of many ways positive reputations have been found to enhance companies' efficiency and effectiveness (Dowling, 2006; Lange et al., 2011; Walker, 2010).

The potential outcomes (Rindova, Williamson, Petkova, & Sever, 2005) of a strong corporate reputation have been extensively studied (see Rhee and Valdez, 2009, for a summary of prior reputation studies across disciplines and Lange et al., 2011, for another recent review of organizational reputation research). Among the advantages and organizational performance enhancers attributed to reputation in the extant literature (Deephouse, 2000; Fombrun & Shanley, 1990; Fuente-Sabaté & Quevedo-Puente, 2003; Hall, 1992; Roberts & Dowling, 2002) are the ability to charge higher prices (Bandyopadhyay & Kao, 2001; Klein & Leffler, 1981; Milgrom & Roberts, 1986), improve profits (Chu & Chu, 1994), attract customers (Chu, Choi, & Song, 2005), attract prospective employees (Gatewood et al., 1993; Turban & Greening, 1996), attract funding (Shane & Cable, 2002), and attract initiating firms in alliance projects (Dollinger et al., 1997; Goldberg, Cohen, & Fiegenbaum, 2003). Moreover, as previously discussed, the environmental dimension of the multidimensional reputation construct has, when isolated, been found to positively influence several stakeholder categories' decisions to contract with a company—for example, customers and investors (Lange et al., 2011; Walker, 2010) and prospective employees (Aiman-Smith et al., 2001). This is, to the best of my knowledge, the first study to analyze the influence on alliance formation—that is, the influence on the focal firm's decision to establish an alliance.

It was argued above that the focal firm in an alliance might be attracted by the opportunity to access a favorable reputation indirectly from accessing underlying resources (Roberts & Dowling, 2002). Another possible motivator could be accessing the reputations of strategic alliance partner firms directly (Dyer & Singh, 1998; Houston, 2003; Oliver, 1997); this is possible through reputational spillovers (Ferguson, Deephouse, & Ferguson, 2000; Houston, 2003; Lavie, 2006; Mayer, 2006; Simonin & Ruth, 1998) due to the proximity between the two firms (Yu & Lester, 2008). The underlying logic of this mechanism is, according to Yu and Lester (2008), that more frequent communications and interactions between organizations will make them resemble one another in strategies as well as orientations and values. Besides, such affiliations indicate transfers of skills and resources (Lange et al., 2011). These factors are anticipated by external stakeholders such as consumers (Simonin & Ruth, 1998). Referring to Ferguson et al. (2000)'s study of reputational spillover effects in strategic groups, Yu and Lester (2008) note that "by establishing strategic alliances, reputational information may spread through the inter-organizational ties and over time coalesce into a reputation for both partners as a whole" (p. 99). Alliancing with high-reputation partners can also enhance initiating firms' own reputation through endorsement effects (Houston, 2003; Lange et al.,

2011; Lavie, 2006; Rhee & Valdez, 2009; Stuart, Hoang, & Hybels, 1999); this since alliancing is a signal to other stakeholders that the two (or more) firms approve of each other's behavior—for instance with respect to the natural environment. Goldberg et al. (2003) suggest strategic alliances as a reputation-building strategy. Moen, Bakås, Bolstad, and Pedersen (2010) found evidence that companies are taking reputational spillovers into consideration in international strategic alliance partner selection. Interestingly, Costa and Vasconcelos (2010) show that allying with a high-reputation partner is not always preferable as contrasting, and blame effects can come into play when things go wrong. This is equally noted by Houston (2003), who adds high costs as a disincentive for partnering with high-reputation firms. I, however, find no theoretical or empirical evidence in prior studies indicating that initiating (focal) firms in alliance projects actively make these considerations (the same holds for high costs related to partnering with resource-rich firms; Bae & Gargiulo, 2004)—where a strong reputation could lower partner attractiveness! To avoid speculative arguments, I note, but leave out of this study, a further analysis of such possible dynamics. Thus, I formulate the following proposition:

**Proposition 3:** *Initiating (focal) firms in alliance projects are more likely to see prospective partner firms with strong environmental reputations as providing opportunity for favorable reputational spillovers, and are consequently more likely to see such firms as attractive.*

A conceptual model based on the propositions of this chapter, on the relationship between a strong environmental reputation—that is, environmental credibility—and strategic alliance partner attractiveness, is illustrated in Figure 4.1.

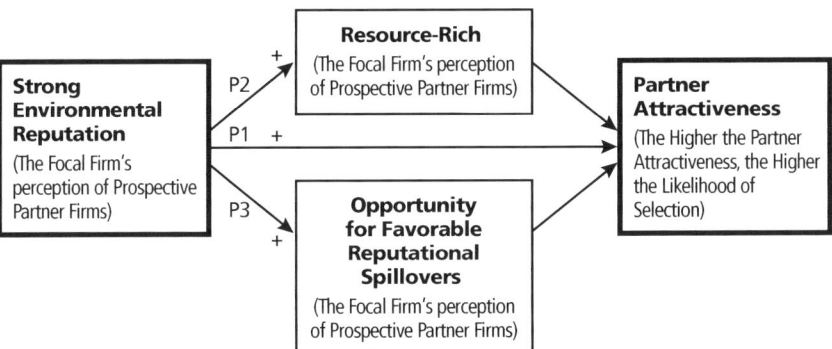

**Figure 4.1** Conceptual model.

## CONCLUDING REMARKS

This chapter is the first study to examine strategic alliance formation under the natural-resource-based view (NRBV) of the firm. I initially presented a threefold argument indicating that such an undertaking has theoretical and practical value: (1) the growing pressure on and incentives for firms to become "greener"; (2) firms having, according to the NRBV, underinvested in environmental capabilities; and (3) environmental capabilities being resource-intensive, complex, and time-consuming to build. I argued that these factors, combined, suggest that firms lacking or having few of these capabilities may well see forming strategic alliances with firms having attained "green credence" as constructive. Through exploring these arguments theoretically, I found that initiating firms in alliance projects are more likely to establish alliances with prospective partners that hold strong environmental reputation—resulting from long-term, proactive environmental strategies. Specifically, I found that the initiating (focal) firm sees such partners as more resource-rich, as well as providing opportunity for favorable reputational spillovers.

First and foremost, this chapter contributes to answering Mitsuhashi and Greve's (2009) recent call for more evidence for how specific organizational resources affect strategic alliance formation. Additionally, it provides new theoretical evidence in support of the NRBV and the related "pays-to-be-green" (PTBG) literature. Moreover, the findings grant insights of use to the corporate social responsibility (CSR) and reputation literatures, on which this chapter draws upon recurrently.

Several interesting research paths will hopefully surface from this pioneering study in the application of the NRBV to the strategic alliance context, the most imminent being empirical testing of my propositions. Scenario-based surveys should be one appropriate method, ensuring the avoidance of retrospective bias (Shah & Swaminathan, 2008). Furthermore, firm characteristics such as resource profiles are commonly avowed to have consequences for the subsequent alliance phases of alliance design and management, as well as alliance performance (e.g., Dacin et al., 1997; Das & Teng, 2003; Holmberg & Cummings, 2009; Oxley & Sampson, 2004; Sarkar et al., 2001; Saxton, 1997; Shah & Swaminathan, 2008). What are the implications of strong environmental reputation? Taking into consideration the extant literature on reputation effects in alliance formation (Dollinger et al., 1997), researchers may also be encouraged to draw on other theoretical frameworks to explore additional outcomes of environmental reputation in the strategic alliance context.

An obvious limitation of this study, pointing to avenues for future research, is not accounting for the probable moderating effects of alliance type and scope, allowing for different levels of access to resources—including reputation. In addition, other potential moderators could be explored, such as industry, size, origin and temporal orientation of the focal firm (Das, 2006), its level of absorptive capacity (Cohen & Levinthal, 1990), factors of the alliance formation environment (Das, 2006), as well as the match quality between the focal firm and partner firm's resources (Mitsuhashi & Greve, 2009), just to name a few. According to Shah and Swaminathan (2008), there is inadequate research on contingency factors in the partner attractiveness and selection literature.

Another important remark, also a limitation and call for further research, is the fact that this chapter does not study the likelihood that the focal firm is *accepted* by the partner firm it has selected. As briefly mentioned, it takes two (or more) willing parties for alliance formation to occur. Accordingly, several authors have drawn attention to the reality that firms' success as alliance partner suitors are reliant on firms' own resources (Ahuja, 2000; Bae & Gargiulo, 2004; Dacin et al., 1997; Das & Teng, 2000; Eisenhardt & Schoonhoven, 1996; Mitsuhashi & Greve, 2009). Strong environmental reputation can, according to the argumentation of this chapter, serve to provide partner firms with a competitive advantage in the strategic alliance market—and consequently allow *partner firms* to be highly selective. From this angle, the firm with a strong environmental reputation becomes the focal firm (Das, 2006). As noted by Das (2006), "we need of course to remember that the logic of the focal firm applies to the partner also, because the latter then becomes the focal firm for analytical purposes" (p. 7). In other words, further studies should explore what criteria or organizational characteristics firms with strong environmental reputations emphasize when selecting partners for alliance projects—and thereby offer recommendations for focal firms (as conceptualized throughout this chapter) that wish to establish alliances with "green" partners. For instance, returning to the logic of reputational spillovers, it seems unlikely that "green" partners would accept to ally with initiating firms in an alliance project having *negative* (as opposed to more neutral or slightly positive) environmental reputation, as it would represent a risk to their own reputation.

In conclusion, for strategic alliance practitioners, the arguments of this chapter indicate that there are additional incentives for firms to implement long-term proactive environmental strategies, adjoining those presented in the extant literature. If my propositions hold true, in empirical testing, it is clear that "going green" can make firms both more successful as alliance partner suitors *and* enhance their alliance opportunities. In today's highly competitive markets, where access to other firms' valuable resources has become strategically important, these findings are undeniably useful for managers.

## ACKNOWLEDGMENTS

I would like to thank Pierre-Xavier Meschi for insightful and detailed comments on each draft version of this chapter. I am also grateful to Gautam Ahuja, Ludovic DiBiaggio, Lars Frederiksen, and Lionel Nesta for their valuable suggestions. Lastly, I would like to acknowledge that this chapter benefited greatly from the extremely helpful and thoughtful comments of Editor T. K. Das.

## REFERENCES

Ahuja, G. (2000). The duality of collaboration: Inducements and opportunities in the formation of interfirm linkages. *Strategic Management Journal, 21,* 317–343.

Aiman-Smith, L., Bauer, T. N., & Cable, D. M. (2001). Are you attracted? Do you intend to pursue? A recruiting policy-capturing study. *Journal of Business and Psychology, 16,* 219–237.

Allouche, J., & Laroche, P. (2005). A meta-analytical investigation of the relationship between corporate social and financial performance. *Revue de Gestion des Ressources Humaines, 57*(3), 18–41.

Ambec, S., & Lanoie, P. (2008). Does it pay to be green? A systematic overview. *Academy of Management Perspectives, 22*(4), 45–62.

Ang, S. H., & Wight, A. (2009). Building intangible resources: The stickiness of reputation. *Corporate Reputation Review, 12*(1), 21–32.

Aragón-Correa, J. A., & Sharma, S. (2003). A contingent resource-based view of proactive corporate environmental strategy. *Academy of Management Review, 28,* 71–88.

Arend, R. J. (2009). Reputation for cooperation: Contingent benefits in alliance activity. *Strategic Management Journal, 30,* 371–385.

Bae, J., & Gargiulo, M. (2004). Partner substitutability, alliance network structure, and firm profitability in the telecommunications industry. *Academy of Management Journal, 47,* 843–859.

Bandyopadhyay, S. P., & Kao, J. L. (2001). Competition and Big 6 brand name reputation: Evidence from the Ontario municipal audit market. *Contemporary Accounting Research, 18,* 27–64.

Banerjee, S. B., Iyer, E. S., & Kashyap, R. K. (2003). Corporate environmentalism: Antecedents and influence of industry type. *Journal of Marketing, 67*(2), 106–122.

Barnett, M. L., Jermier, J. M., & Lafferty, B. A. (2006). Corporate reputation: The definitional landscape. *Corporate Reputation Review, 9*(1), 26–38.

Barney, J. B. (1991). Firm resources and sustained competitive advantage. *Journal of Management, 17,* 99–120.

Barney, J. B. (1995). Look inside for competitive advantage. *Academy of Management Executive, 9*(4), 49–61.

Barney, J. B. (2001a). Resource-based *theories* of competitive advantage: A ten-year retrospective on the resource-based view. *Journal of Management, 27,* 43–50.

Barney, J. B. (2001b). Is the resource-based "view" a useful perspective for strategic management research? Yes. *Academy of Management Review, 26,* 41–56.

Beckman, C. M., Haunschild, P. R., & Phillips, D. J. (2004). Friends or strangers? Firm-specific uncertainty, market uncertainty, and network partner selection. *Organization Science, 15,* 259–275.

Berchicci, L., & King, A. (2007). Postcards from the edge: A review of the business and environment literature. *Academy of Management Annals, 1,* 513–547.

Berry, M. A., & Rondinelli, D. A. (1998). Proactive corporate environmental management: A new industrial revolution. *Academy of Management Executive, 12*(2), 38–50.

Bertels, S., & Peloza, J. (2008). Running just to stand still? Managing CSR reputation in an era of ratcheting expectations. *Corporate Reputation Review, 11*(1), 56–72.

Brady, A. (2005). *The sustainability effect.* New York, NY: Palgrave MacMillan.

Cacioppe, R., Forster, N., & Fox, M. (2008). A survey of managers' perceptions of corporate ethics and social responsibility and actions that may affect companies' success. *Journal of Business Ethics, 82,* 681–700.

Carter, S. M., & Ruefli, T. W. (2006). Intra-industry reputation dynamics under a resource-based framework: Assessing the durability factor. *Corporate Reputation Review, 9*(1), 3–25.

Chan, Y. K. (2005). Does the natural-resource-based view of the firm apply in an emerging economy? A survey of foreign invested enterprises in China. *Journal of Management Studies, 42,* 625–672.

Child, J., Faulkner, D., & Tallman, S. (2005). *Cooperative strategy.* New York, NY: Oxford University Press.

Chu, W., Choi, B., & Song, M. R. (2005). The role of on-line retailer brand and infomediary reputation in increasing consumer purchase intention. *International Journal of Electronic Commerce, 9*(3), 115–127.

Chu, W., & Chu, W. (1994). Signaling quality by selling through a reputable retailer: An example of renting the reputation of another agent. *Marketing Science, 13,* 177–189.

Chung, S., Singh, H., & Lee, K. (2000). Complementarity, status similarity and social capital as drivers of alliance formation. *Strategic Management Journal, 21,* 1–22.

Cohen, W. M., & Levinthal, D. A. (1990). Absorptive capacity: A new perspective on learning and innovation. *Administrative Science Quarterly, 35,* 128–152.

Costa, L. A., & Vasconcelos, L. (2010). Share the fame or share the blame? The reputational implications of partnerships. *Journal of Economics & Management Strategy, 19,* 259–301.

Dacin, M. T., Hitt, M. A., & Levitas, E. (1997). Selecting partners for successful international alliances: Examination of U.S. and Korean firms. *Journal of World Business, 32*(1), 3–16.

Dacin, T., Reid, D., & Ring, P. S. (2008). Alliances and joint ventures: The role of partner selection from an embeddedness perspective. In S. Cropper, M. Ebers, C. Huxham, & P. S. Ring (Eds.), *The Oxford handbook of inter-organizational relations* (pp. 90–117). New York, NY: Oxford University Press.

Das, T. K. (2006). Strategic alliance temporalities and partner opportunism. *British Journal of Management, 13,* 1–21.

Das, T. K., & Teng, B. (1999). Managing risks in strategic alliances. *Academy of Management Executive, 13*(4), 50–62.

Das, T. K., & Teng, B. (2000). A resource-based theory of strategic alliances. *Journal of Management, 26,* 31–61.

Das, T. K., & Teng, B. (2003). Partner analysis and alliance performance. *Scandinavian Journal of Management, 19,* 279–308.

Deephouse, D. L. (2000). Media reputation as a strategic resource: An integration of mass-communication and resource-based theories. *Journal of Management, 26,* 1091–1112.

Dierickx, I., & Cool, K. (1989). Asset stock accumulation and sustainability of competitive advantage. *Management Science, 35*(12), 1504–1511.

Dollinger, M. J., Golden, P. A., & Saxton, T. (1997). The effect of reputation on the decision to joint venture. *Strategic Management Journal, 18,* 127–140.

Dowell, G., Hart, S., & Yeung, B. (2000). Do corporate global environmental standards create or destroy market value? *Management Science, 46,* 1059-1074.

Dowling, G. (2006). How good corporate reputations create corporate value. *Corporate Reputation Review, 9*(2), 134–143.

Dyer, J. H., & Singh, H. (1998). The relational view: Cooperative strategy and sources of interorganizational competitive advantage. *Academy of Management Review, 23,* 660–679.

Eisenhardt, K. M., & Schoonhoven, C. B. (1996). Resource-based view of strategic alliance formation: Strategic and social effects in entrepreneurial firms. *Organization Science, 7,* 136–150.

Ferguson, T. D., Deephouse, D. L., & Ferguson, W. L. (2000). Do strategic groups differ in reputation? *Strategic Management Journal, 21,* 1195–1214.

Fombrun, C. J., Gardberg, N. A., & Sever, J. M. (2000). The reputation quotient: A multi-stakeholder measure of corporate reputation. *Journal of Brand Management, 7,* 241–255.

Fombrun, C. J., & Shanley, M. (1990). What's in a name? Reputation building and corporate strategy. *Academy of Management Journal, 33,* 233–258.

Fowler, S. J., & Hope, C. (2007). Incorporating sustainable business practices into company strategy. *Business Strategy and the Environment, 16,* 26–38.

Fuente-Sabaté, J. M., & Quevedo-Puente, E. (2003). Empirical analysis of the relationship between corporate reputation and financial performance: A survey of the literature. *Corporate Reputation Review, 6*(2), 161–177.

Gallarotti, G. M. (1995). It pays to be green: The managerial incentive structure and environmentally sound strategies. *Columbia Journal of World Business, 30*(4), 38–57.

Gatewood, R. D., Gowan, M. A., & Lautenschlager, G. J. (1993). Corporate image, recruitment image, and initial job choice decisions. *Academy of Management Journal, 36,* 414–427.

Geringer, J. M. (1988). Partner selection criteria for developed country joint ventures. *Business Quarterly, 53*(1), 55–62.

Geringer, J. M. (1991). Strategic determinants of partner selection criteria in international joint ventures. *Journal of International Business Studies, 22,* 41–62.

Glaister, K. W., & Buckley, P. J. (1996). Strategic motives for international alliance formation. *Journal of Management Studies, 33,* 301–332.

Goldberg, A. I., Cohen, G., & Fiegenbaum, A. (2003). Reputation building: Small business strategies for successful venture development. *Journal of Small Business Management, 41*, 168–186.

Grant, R. M. (1991). The resource-based theory of competitive advantage: Implications for strategy formulation. *California Management Review, 33*(3), 114–135.

Gulati, R. (1995a). Does familiarity breed trust? The implications of repeated ties for contractual choice in alliances. *Academy of Management Journal, 38*, 85–112.

Gulati, R. (1995b). Social structure and alliance formation patterns: A longitudinal analysis. *Administrative Science Quarterly, 40*, 619–652.

Gulati, R., & Singh, H. (1998). The architecture of cooperation: Managing coordination costs and appropriation concerns in strategic alliances. *Administrative Science Quarterly, 43*, 781–814.

Hall, R. (1992). The strategic analysis of intangible resources. *Strategic Management Journal, 13*, 135–144.

Hall, R. (1993). A framework linking intangible resources and capabilities to sustainable competitive advantage. *Strategic Management Journal, 14*, 607–618.

Hart, S. L. (1995). A natural-resource-based view of the firm. *Academy of Management Review, 20*, 986–1014.

Hart, S. L., & Ahuja, G. (1996). Does it pay to be green? An empirical examination of the relationship between emission reduction and firm performance. *Business Strategy and the Environment, 5*, 30–37.

Hart, S. L., & Dowell, G. (2011). A natural-resource-based view of the firm: Fifteen years after. *Journal of Management, 37*, 1464–1479.

Hastings, M. (1999). A new operational paradigm for oil operations in sensitive environments: An analysis of social pressure, corporate capabilities and competitive advantage. *Business Strategy and the Environment, 8*, 267–280.

Hillenbrand, C., & Money, K. (2007). Corporate responsibility and corporate reputation: Two separate concepts or two sides of the same coin? *Corporate Reputation Review, 10*(4), 261–277.

Hirsch, B., & Meyer, M. (2010). Integrating soft factors into the assessment of cooperative relationships between firms: Accounting for reputation and ethical values. *Business Ethics: A European Review, 19*(1), 81–94.

Hoetker, G., & Mellewigt, T. (2009). Choice and performance of governance mechanisms: Matching alliance governance to asset type. *Strategic Management Journal, 30*, 1025–1044.

Holmberg, S. R., & Cummings, J. L. (2009). Building successful strategic alliances: Strategic process and analytical tool for selecting partner industries and firms. *Long Range Planning, 42*, 164–193.

Houston, M. B. (2003). Alliance partner reputation as a signal to the market: Evidence from bank loan alliances. *Corporate Reputation Review, 5*(4), 330–342.

Judge, W. Q., & Douglas, T. J. (1998). Performance implications of incorporating natural environmental issues into the strategic planning process: An empirical assessment. *Journal of Management Studies, 35*, 241–262.

Kale, P., & Singh, H. (2009). Managing strategic alliances: What do we know now, and where do we go from here? *Academy of Management Perspectives, 23*(3), 45–62.

Klassen, R. D., & Vachon, S. (2003). Collaboration and evaluation in the supply chain: The impact on plant-level environmental investment. *Production and Operations Management, 12*, 336–352.

Klein, B., & Leffler, K. B. (1981). The role of market forces in assuring contractual performance. *Journal of Political Economy, 89*, 615–641.

Lambe, C. J., Spekman, R. E., & Hunt, S. D. (2002). Alliance competence, resources, and alliance success: Conceptualization, measurement, and initial test. *Journal of the Academy of Marketing Science, 30*, 141–158.

Lange, D., Lee, P. M., & Dai, Y. (2011). Organizational reputation: A review. *Journal of Management, 37*, 153–184.

Lavie, D. (2006). The competitive advantage of interconnected firms: An extension of the resource-based view. *Academy of Management Review, 31*, 638–658.

Lin, Z., Yang, H., & Arya, B. (2009). Alliance partners and firm performance: Resource complementarity and status association. *Strategic Management Journal, 30*, 921–940.

Lui, S. S., Ngo, H., & Hon, A. H. Y. (2006). Coercive strategy in interfirm cooperation: Mediating roles of interpersonal and interorganizational trust. *Journal of Business Research, 59*, 466–474.

Mahoney, J. T., & Pandian, J. R. (1992). The resource-based view within the conversation of strategic management. *Strategic Management Journal, 13*, 363–380.

Margolis, J. D., & Walsh, J. P. (2003). Misery loves companies: Rethinking social initiatives by business. *Administrative Science Quarterly, 48*, 268–305.

Mayer, K. J. (2006). Spillovers and governance: An analysis of knowledge and reputational spillovers in information technology. *Academy of Management Journal, 49*, 69–84.

Michalisin, M. D., & Stinchfield, B. T. (2010). Climate change strategies and firm performance: An empirical investigation of the natural resource-based view of the firm. *Journal of Business Strategies, 27*(2), 123–149.

Milgrom, P., & Roberts, J. (1986). Price and advertising signals of product quality. *Journal of Political Economy, 94*, 796–821.

Mitsuhashi, H., & Greve, H. R. (2009). A matching theory of alliance formation and organizational success: Complementarity and compatibility. *Academy of Management Journal, 52*, 975–995.

Moen, Ø., Bakås, O., Bolstad, A., & Pedersen, V. (2010). International market expansion strategies for high-tech firms: Partnership selection criteria for forming strategic alliances. *International Journal of Business and Management, 5*(1), 20–30.

Mohr, J., & Spekman, R. (1994). Characteristics of partnership success: Partnership attributes, communication behavior, and conflict resolution techniques. *Strategic Management Journal, 15*, 135–152.

Moon, J. (2007). The contribution of corporate social responsibility to sustainable development. *Sustainable Development, 15*, 296–306.

Nidumolu, R., Prahalad, C. K., & Rangaswami, M. R. (2009). Why sustainability is now the key driver of innovation. *Harvard Business Review, 87*(9), 56–64.

Oliver, C. (1997). Sustainable competitive advantage: Combining institutional and resource-based views. *Strategic Management Journal, 18*, 697–713.

Orlitzky, M., Schmidt, F. L., & Rynes, S. L. (2003). Corporate social and financial performance: A meta-analysis. *Organization Studies, 24*, 403–441.

Oxley, J. E., & Sampson, R. C. (2004). The scope and governance of international R&D alliances. *Strategic Management Journal, 25*, 723–749.

Parmigiani, A., & Rivera-Santos, M. (2011). Clearing a path through the forest: A meta-review of interorganizational relationships. *Journal of Management, 37*, 1108–1136.

Penrose, E. T. (1959). *The theory of the growth of the firm.* New York, NY: John Wiley.

Peteraf, M. A. (1993). The cornerstones of competitive advantage: A resource-based view. *Strategic Management Journal, 14*, 179–191.

Porter, M. E. (1985). *Competitive advantage.* New York, NY: Free Press.

Porter, M. E., & van der Linde, C. (1995a). Green and competitive: Ending the stalemate. *Harvard Business Review, 73*(5), 120–134.

Porter, M. E., & van der Linde, C. (1995b). Toward a new conception of the environment-competitiveness relationship. *Journal of Economic Perspectives, 9*(4), 97–118.

Priem, R. L., & Butler, J. E. (2001a). Is the resource-based "view" a useful perspective for strategic management research? *Academy of Management Review, 26*, 22–40.

Priem, R. L., & Butler, J. E. (2001b). Tautology in the resource-based view and the implications of externally determined resource value: Further comments. *Academy of Management Review, 26*, 57–66.

Quevedo-Puente, E., Fuente-Sabaté, J. M., & Delgado-García, J. B. (2007). Corporate social performance and corporate reputation: Two interwoven perspectives. *Corporate Reputation Review, 10*(1), 60–72.

Rhee, M., & Valdez, M. E. (2009). Contextual factors surrounding reputation damage with potential implications for reputation repair. *Academy of Management Review, 34*, 146–168.

Rindova, V. P., Williamson, I. O., Petkova, A. P., & Sever, J. M. (2005). Being good or being known: An empirical examination of the dimensions, antecedents, and consequences of organizational reputation. *Academy of Management Journal, 48*, 1033–1049.

Roberts, P. W., & Dowling, G. R. (2002). Corporate reputation and sustained superior financial performance. *Strategic Management Journal, 23*, 1077–1093.

Royer, S., & Simons, R. H. (2009). Evolution of cooperation and dynamics of expectations— implications for strategic alliances. *International Journal of Strategic Business Alliances, 1*, 73–88.

Royer, S., Simons, R. H., & Waldersee, R. W. (2003). Perceived reputation and alliance building in the public and private sectors. *International Public Management Journal, 6*(2), 199–218.

Rugman, A. M., & Verbeke, A. (1998). Corporate strategies and environmental regulations: An organizing framework. *Strategic Management Journal, 19*, 363–375.

Russo, M. V., & Fouts, P. A. (1997). A resource-based perspective on corporate environmental performance and profitability. *Academy of Management Journal, 40*, 534–559.

Sarkar, M. B., Echambadi, R., Cavusgil, S. T., & Aulakh, P. S. (2001). The influence of complementarity, compatibility, and relationship capital on alliance performance. *Journal of the Academy of Marketing Science, 29,* 358–373.

Saxton, T. (1997). The effects of partner and relationship characteristics on alliance outcomes. *Academy of Management Journal, 40,* 443–461.

Shah, R. H., & Swaminathan, V. (2008). Factors influencing partner selection in strategic alliances: The moderating role of alliance context. *Strategic Management Journal, 29,* 471–494.

Shane, S., & Cable, D. (2002). Network ties, reputation, and the financing of new ventures. *Management Science, 48,* 364–381.

Sharma, S., & Vredenburg, H. (1998). Proactive corporate environmental strategy and the development of competitively valuable organizational capabilities. *Strategic Management Journal, 19,* 729–753.

Shrivastava, P. (1995). Environmental technologies and competitive advantage. *Strategic Management Journal, 16,* 183–200.

Simonin, B. L., & Ruth, J. A. (1998). Is a company known by the company it keeps? Assessing the spillover effects of brand alliances on consumer brand attitudes. *Journal of Marketing Research, 35,* 30–42.

Simpson, M., Taylor, N., & Barker, K. (2004). Environmental responsibility in SMEs: Does it deliver competitive advantage? *Business Strategy and the Environment, 13,* 156–171.

Stafford, E. R., Polonsky, M. J., & Hartman, C. L. (2000). Environmental NGO-business collaboration and strategic bridging: A case analysis of the Greenpeace–Foron alliance. *Business Strategy and the Environment, 9*(2), 122–135.

Stanwick, P. A., & Stanwick, S. D. (1998). The relationship between corporate social performance, and organizational size, financial performance, and environmental performance: An empirical examination. *Journal of Business Ethics, 17,* 195–204.

Stuart, T. E., Hoang, H., & Hybels, R. C. (1999). Interorganizational endorsements and the performance of entrepreneurial ventures. *Administrative Science Quarterly, 44,* 315–349.

Surroca, J., Tribó, J. A., & Waddock, S. (2010). Corporate responsibility and financial performance: The role of intangible resources. *Strategic Management Journal, 31,* 463–490.

Teece, D. J., Pisano, G., & Shuen, A. (1997). Dynamic capabilities and strategic management. *Strategic Management Journal, 18,* 509–533.

Teng, B., & Das, T. K. (2008). Governance structure choice in strategic alliances: The roles of alliance objectives, alliance management expertise, and international partners. *Management Decision, 46,* 725–742.

Turban, D. B., & Greening, D. W. (1996). Corporate social performance and organizational attractiveness to prospective employees. *Academy of Management Journal, 40,* 658–672.

Waddock, S. A., Bodwell, C., & Graves, S. B. (2002). Responsibility: The new business imperative. *Academy of Management Executive, 16*(2), 132–148.

Walker, K. (2010). A systematic review of the corporate reputation literature: Definition, measurement, and theory. *Corporate Reputation Review, 12*(4), 357–387.

Wernerfelt, B. (1984). A resource-based view of the firm. *Strategic Management Journal, 5*, 171–180.
Yu, T., & Lester, R. H. (2008). Moving beyond firm boundaries: A social network perspective on reputation spillover. *Corporate Reputation Review, 11*(1), 94–108.

CHAPTER 5

# A CIRCUMPLEX APPROACH TO INTERPARTNER DYNAMICS IN STRATEGIC ALLIANCES

Olivier Furrer, Brian Tjemkes, Pepijn Vos, Carmen Boymans, and Marit Ubachs

### ABSTRACT

This chapter reports data from a longitudinal exploratory case study of two strategic alliances with the aim of achieving a better understanding of interpartner dynamics. Combining insights from the response strategy perspective and interpersonal theory, we propose that response strategies are organized along the circumference of a circle in a two-dimensional space. In such a circumplex structure, the complementarity principle, explaining how partners respond to each other, is composed of two rules: the rule of reciprocity and the rule of correspondence. The objective of this chapter is to explain when and why alliance partners follow or deviate from these rules. Evidence from the two strategic alliances indicates that the response behaviors derived from interpersonal theory can be identified at the interorganizational level in a strategic alliance. Moreover, partners often use a complementary behavior. The findings, however, also provide insights into three mechanisms that trigger partners to use noncomplementary behavior. This study provides a fine-grained explanation for alliance partner interaction and offers a tentative first step in building an integrative model of interpartner dynamics in strategic alliances.

## INTRODUCTION

A strategic alliance is a long-term contractual agreement between two or more firms to share resources and realize individual and common objectives (Das & Teng, 2000a). Although alliances nowadays constitute the cornerstone of many firms' strategies, they also tend to exhibit a mix of promise and peril, resulting in a high failure rate of up to 50% (Das & Teng, 2000b). Such a high failure rate highlights the need for alliance managers to overcome adverse situations by responding to their partners' self-serving behaviors (Luo, Shenkar, & Gurnani, 2008) as well as unforeseen circumstances (Tjemkes & Furrer, 2010). While there is a large amount of scholarly work on alliance formation and governance structure, little is known about interpartner dynamics in strategic alliances once the partners reached an initial agreement (De Rond & Bouchikhi, 2004). Therefore, opening the black box of interpartner dynamic behavior is salient, as it would enable managers to better steer their alliance relationships toward success (Das & Teng, 2000b).

To understand alliance dynamics, a few studies have examined how strategic alliances evolve over time (see De Rond & Bouchikhi, 2004, for a review). However, these studies mostly investigated the effects of structural conditions on alliance processes, and relational norms and quality (e.g., Ariño & De la Torre, 1998; Doz, 1996). They neglected partners' behavioral dynamic interactions. While these studies thus contribute to the understanding of alliance evolution and processes, they do not completely account for the richness of interpartner dynamics. In order to examine these dynamics, this study draws on two theoretical perspectives to investigate partner interactions in strategic alliances: response strategy perspective (Tjemkes & Furrer, 2011) and interpersonal theory (Horowitz ,Wilson, Turan, Zolotsev, Constantin, & Henderson, 2006).

Originating from strategic management literature at the interorganizational level, the response strategy perspective focuses on alliance partners' responses and factors influencing this behavior (Tjemkes & Furrer, 2010, 2011). However, this perspective neglects an important aspect of alliance dynamics, which is how one partner's behavior influences the response of the other partner. This is the focus of interpersonal theory (Horowitz et al., 2006). Developed in individual personality and social psychology literature, interpersonal theory describes how actors respond to each other based on the complementarity principle. It stipulates that the main purpose of interpersonal behavior is to invite a complementary response from counterparts (Kiesler, 1983).

In this chapter we proffer that these two perspectives can be combined to develop unique insights into interpartner dynamics. However, before combining these two perspectives, it is critical to assess whether the processes described by interpersonal theory also apply in interorganizational relationships. In doing so, we empirically assess the relevance of interpersonal theory's complementarity principle to describe partners' behavior in strategic alliances. Then, by combining the insights from the response strategy perspective and interpersonal theory, we explore when and why alliance partners might deviate from the complementarity principle. To accomplish this twofold objective, in-depth case studies of two strategic alliances have been conducted that investigate the interactive behavior of the partners.

This methodological approach differs from previous studies on alliance behavior in three fundamental ways. First, an in-depth content analysis of partners' behavior in two strategic alliances was conducted. This differs from that of previous alliance process studies (e.g., Ariño & Ring, 2010; Faems, Janssens, Madhok, & Van Looy, 2008), which only assessed the consequences of this behavior at the alliance level. Second, previous researchers have mostly taken a static view on response strategies, measuring them at a single point in time (e.g., Furrer, Tjemkes, Ulgen Aydinlik, & Adolfs, 2012; Tjemkes & Furrer, 2010). This study instead applies a longitudinal view to examine how one partner's behavior invites or triggers response from the other partner over time. Third, this study deviates from previous interpersonal research by examining interpartner behaviors in their natural setting. Interpersonal studies have mainly relied on experimental design and manipulating partners' behavior (e.g., Locke & Sadler, 2007; Markey, Funder, & Ozer, 2003). Using a natural setting increases the external validity of the results. These three points of difference allow for extended and deeper interpartner dynamics research and enable us to take a tentative first step in building up an integrative model of interpartner dynamics in strategic alliances.

## INTERPARTNER DYNAMICS: CONCEPTUAL FOUNDATIONS

### Response Strategy Perspective

The response strategy perspective (Furrer et al., 2012; Tjemkes & Furrer, 2010, 2011, Tjemkes, Furrer, Adolfs, & Ulgen Aydinlik, 2012) defines response strategies as alliance managers' reactions to dissatisfaction resulting from adverse situations. Seven response strategies have been distinguished. These can be classified according to their degree of activeness–passiveness and constructiveness–destructiveness (Furrer et al., 2012).

- *Exit* refers to the termination of the current alliance. It is the most destructive response to an adverse situation.
- *Opportunism* is an active–destructive response used by alliance partners to increase their benefits from the alliance in ways that are explicitly or implicitly prohibited in the contract.
- *Considerate voice* is a constructive and slightly active response strategy used to change an adverse situation by communicating in a relationship-preserving manner and discussing problems cooperatively with the partner.
- *Aggressive voice* is more destructive and active than *considerate voice*. It refers to the forceful imposition of views on partners without making any attempt to avoid conflicts.
- *Creative voice* refers to the creation of innovative and potentially useful solutions to address the adverse situation. This makes it both active and constructive.
- *Patience* refers to the silent acceptance of the issues in the belief that the situation will improve. Patience is both constructive and passive because it involves voluntarily ignoring the issue in the hope that the situation will resolve itself.
- *Neglect* is passive but destructive because the alliance partner allows the relationship to deteriorate. A neglectful manager believes that the alliance does not deserve to be salvaged and expends little effort keeping it afloat.

Building on the active–passive and constructive–destructive dimensions, Furrer et al. (2012) demonstrated that, instead of viewing responses as independent and discrete, response strategies are organized within a two-dimensional space along the circumference of a circle according to their degree of compatibility and incompatibility (Fabrigar, Visser, & Browne, 1997). This structure is referred to as a circumplex structure. Compatible response strategies are located close to each other on the response strategy circle, and incompatible responses are located opposite to each other (see Figure 5.1). One salient implication of the circumplex structure of response strategies is that when managers are confronted with an unchanged situation, they tend to use the same or a compatible (i.e., adjacent) response rather than an incompatible (i.e., opposed on the circle) response (Furrer et al., 2012).

The response strategy perspective also proposes that the use of, or preferences for, active–passive and constructive–destructive response strategies depends on relationship-level exchange variables, such as partners' satisfaction and exit barriers. Tjemkes and Furrer (2010) found that economic dissatisfaction invoked by the relationship and the lack of attractive alternatives influence preferences for active response strategies. Furthermore, social satisfaction with the relationship and investments in alliance-specific

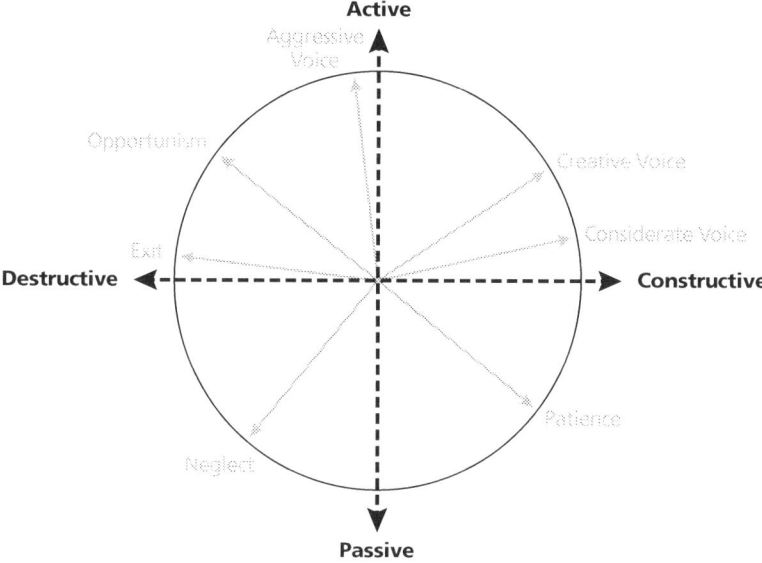

**Figure 5.1** Circumplex structure of response strategies.

assets influence constructive preferences for active response strategies. These results were later corroborated by Tjemkes et al. (2012) in a five-country study. However, the use of response strategies is also influenced by the behaviors of the alliance partners (Tjemkes & Furrer, 2011). Alliance partners are likely to develop dynamic interaction patterns of actions/reactions to respond to their partner's behavior, which to date have been unaccounted for by prior response strategy research.

## Interpersonal Theory

Interpersonal theory (Carson, 1969; Kiesler, 1983; Leary, 1957; Wiggins, 1979) has emerged in personality and social psychology as a dominant model to study phenomena related to social interaction (Horowitz et al., 2006). The theory is based on the interpersonal circumplex, which is defined by two orthogonal axes: a vertical axis (of dominance, agency, status, power, or control) and a horizontal axis (of friendliness, communion, solidarity, warmth, or love). These two dimensions are equivalent to the active–passive and constructive–destructive dimensions of the response strategy circumplex (Tjemkes & Furrer, 2011), making these perspectives compatible.

Interpersonal theory based on the interpersonal circumplex proposes that patterns of actions/reactions are governed by the principle of complementarity (Kiesler, 1983; Leary, 1957; Sullivan, 1953). As formulated by Kiesler (1983), the theory proposes that the main purpose of interpersonal behavior is to invite a complementary response from counterparts (Horowitz et al., 2006). The theory defines complementarity in terms of the two-dimensional interpersonal circumplex. Complementary responses tend to be similar with respect to the horizontal dimension but opposite or reciprocal with respect to the vertical dimension (Carson, 1969; Kiesler, 1983; Leary, 1957). An active–constructive behavior invites a passive–constructive response and vice-versa. An active–destructive behavior invites a passive–destructive response and vice-versa (see Figure 5.2a). Thus, the complementarity principle consists of two rules: the rule of reciprocity on the vertical active–passive dimension and the rule of correspondence on the constructive–destructive horizontal dimension.

Interpersonal theory further states that complementary interactions tend to be more mutually rewarding and satisfying, as they enhance partners' feelings of security (Carson, 1969; Kiesler, 1983). When a person's motivated interpersonal behavior provokes a complementary response from another person, this reinforces the first person's original action (Kiesler, 1983) and creates a dynamic pattern of complementary behavior. This is what Leary (1957) calls "the reinforcing quality of social interaction" (p. 123), which implies that complementary behavior is the most "natural" behavior in a satisfying relationship.

If complementary behavior is not forthcoming from partners, the relationship will either not endure or it will be altered in such a manner that complementarity is established (Kiesler, 1983). However, people do not always accept their partner's invitation to complementarily respond because they do not accept the motives behind the behavior or misinterpret these motives. This results in noncomplementary behavior (Horowitz et al., 2006).

Carson (1969) distinguishes between two forms of noncomplementary behavior: anticomplementary and acomplementary. Anticomplementary behavior refers to the response of a person who rejects the other person's motive on both dimensions of the circumplex. For example, an individual may respond to an active–destructive behavior with an active–constructive response, or to a passive–constructive behavior with a passive–destructive response (see Figure 5.2d). Acomplementary behavior refers to the response behavior of a person who only accepts the other person's motive on one dimension of the circumplex. Building on Carson's conceptualization, Kiesler (1983) further distinguishes between two types of acomplementary behavior. Semi-morphic acomplementary behavior breaks the rule of correspondence by responding to an active–destructive behavior with a passive–constructive response or an active–constructive behavior with a passive–destructive response (see Figure 5.2b). Isomorphic acomplementary

# A Circumplex Approach to Interpartner Dynamics in Strategic Alliances ■ 103

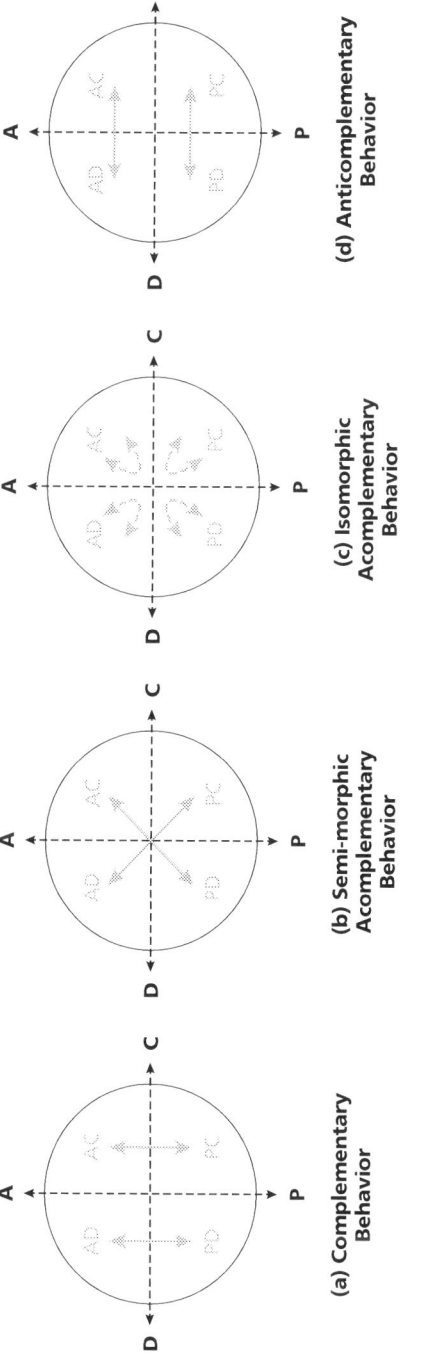

**Figure 5.2** Partner interactions and response strategies.

A = Active; P = Passive; C = Constructive; D = Destructive

behavior breaks the rule of reciprocity by responding to an active–destructive behavior with an active–destructive response, or a passive–constructive behavior with a passive–constructive response (see Figure 5.2c).

Building on interpersonal theory's insights, we seek to explore interpartner behaviors in strategic alliances by examining if alliance partners follow the principles of complementarity:

**Research Question 1:** *How does a strategic alliance partner respond to its counterpart's interactive behavior?*

Extant studies have tested the principle of complementarity in interpersonal relationships, but the results have not been consistent (see Horowitz et al., 2006, for a review). In general, the principle of complementarity has been reasonably well supported for behaviors on the constructive side of the interpersonal circumplex (e.g., Locke & Sadler, 2007; Markey et al., 2003; Tiedens & Fragale, 2003). However, results are more ambiguous on the destructive side of the interpersonal circumplex (e.g., Orford, 1986; Tracey, 1994). Moreover, interpersonal theory conceptualizes partners' behavior during an interaction not only as a function of the influence of each partner's behavior on the other, but also as a function of interpersonal dispositions and situational variables (Locke & Sadler, 2007; Orford, 1986; Strong et al., 1988). Noncomplementary behavior in alliances might be influenced by situational factors such as exchange variables (Tjemkes & Furrer, 2010). Thus, the second objective of this study is to explore the factors that might push strategic alliance partners to deviate from the complementarity principle by breaking the reciprocity and/or correspondence rules:

**Research Question 2:** *What are the factors that influence alliance partners' noncomplementary response behavior?*

## METHOD

Exploration of interpartner dynamics is facilitated by qualitative methods (Markey et al., 2003) such as an approach using longitudinal case studies (Ariño & Ring, 2010; Faems et al., 2008). Following the procedure used by Ariño and Ring (2010), Appendix 5.1 outlines the steps we took to ensure the validity of the research design. These steps are further documented, when appropriate, in the remainder of this section. However, as in many alliance studies (e.g., Ariño & Ring, 2010), the firms' real names cannot be revealed, even though it would have enhanced reliability.

## Research Setting

We conducted an in-depth exploratory case study of the same focal firm with two different alliance partners. The first case is used to answer the first research question and to assess the application of the complementarity principle to describe interpartner behavior in strategic alliances. The second case is used to replicate the findings of the first case study and to explore the factors influencing alliance partners to select noncomplementary response behaviors.

Interdy, the focal firm, is a semi-governmental Dutch knowledge-transfer company that connects science to business. Interdy's mission is to apply scientific knowledge to strengthen the innovative power of industry and government in the Netherlands. It assists firms through the different stages of product and process innovation, from idea generation to implementation. The firm is divided into seven divisions, each related to a different scientific domain. The first strategic alliance is related to Interdy's information and communication technology division (Interdy–ICT). The second strategic alliance is related to the information society division (Interdy–IS), which focuses on astronautics and telecommunication. Interdy's partner in the first strategic alliance case is Hortic, a Dutch supplier of innovative computers and IT systems for the horticultural industry. The firm's products control climatic conditions in greenhouses, and it is globally active through a dedicated distribution network. Interdy's partner in the second strategic alliance case is Hitec Communications (hereafter Hitec), a Canadian firm that provides tools for service management and field testing. Hitec is a global leader in measurement and test equipment for development labs, communication networks, and IT firms.

## Data Collection and Analysis

Data on the two strategic alliances were retrospectively collected (per Faems et al., 2008). Retrospective data collection allowed for a more focused process because it reduced the danger of data overload and collecting unusable data (Leonard-Barton, 1990; Poole, Van de Ven, Dooley, & Holmes, 2000). However, retrospectively documenting cases also has disadvantages. For instance, respondents have the tendency to filter out events that do not fit or that render their story less coherent (Poole et al., 2000). To improve the validity of these retrospective reports and prevent accepting respondent bias, a number of strategies were applied. First, data were triangulated by using two data sources: interviews and archival documents (Eisenhardt, 1989; Yin, 2003). Second, informants were asked to reflect on concrete events rather than abstract concepts to reduce the risk of cognitive biases and impression management (Miller, Cardinal, & Glick, 1997). Finally, individual reports were verified by asking similar questions to informants from both sides of the alliances (Cardinal, Sitkin, & Long, 2004).

Two of the authors independently collected data about the two alliances. For each of the alliances, archival data included management reports and minutes of key meetings covering the alliance's duration. For Case Study 2, a database was provided with more than 700 e-mails from February 2008 until September 2010. Five semi-structured interviews with managers from both partners of the first alliance and three interviews from the second alliance provided additional insights into key interactions between the partners. These also served to triangulate the other two data sources (Eisenhardt, 1989). Relying on Miles and Huberman (1994), data reduction techniques were used. A chronology was prepared of the various events that occurred during the evolutions of the alliances (per Ariño & Ring, 2010, and as recommended by Tracey, 1994). The study used Ring and Van de Ven's (1994, p. 112) definition of *events* as "critical incidents when parties engage in actions related to the development of their relationship." These events are briefly described in Tables 5.2 and 5.3.

A series of information displays was initially used to systematically handle the data (per Ariño & Ring, 2010). The contents of each document were classified in categories reflecting the theoretical concepts. Transcripts from the interviews and archival documents were explored for evidence that might support the premise that complementarity might be an important principle in explaining interpartner dynamics in strategic alliances. The operational indicators of the different response strategies and exchange variables are set forth in Table 5.1. They were primarily derived from Tjemkes and Furrer (2010). For each case, one of the authors classified the data and reviewed their categorizations with one of the alliance managers at the focal firm. It is worth noting that each firm's group of boundary spanners—that is, the alliance managers representing each partner (Luo, 2007)—is generally referred to by the company name. Thus, when referencing the use of response strategies by Interdy or one of its partners, this means the use of the response strategy by the firms' boundary spanners.

## CASE STUDY 1: INTERDY–HORTIC

This section presents a case study of the alliance between Interdy and Hortic between 2007 and 2009. Interdy and Hortic developed and marketed Wiregreen, a system based on wireless technology that measures the soil humidity of potted plants. Wiregreen provides the grower with continuous objective information that gives plants the right amount of water when

**TABLE 5.1   Indicators of Response Strategies and Exchange Variables**

**Response strategies**

| | |
|---|---|
| Exit propensity | The disinclination to continue the current relationship |
| Opportunism | Self-interested behavior that is explicitly or implicitly prohibited |
| Aggressive voice | A form of voice that consists of efforts to win without consideration for the concerns of the exchange partner |
| Creative voice | A form of voice that consists of the generation of novel and potentially useful ideas |
| Considerate voice | A form of voice that consists of attempts to solve the situation by considering one's own concerns as well as those of the partner |
| Patience | Accepting relationship issues in silence with the confidence that things will get better |
| Neglect | Passively allowing the relationship to deteriorate |

**Exchange variables**

| | |
|---|---|
| Economic satisfaction | Managers' evaluation of the financial outcomes of the strategic alliance |
| Social satisfaction | Managers' evaluations of the psycho-social aspects of a strategic alliance, which implies that interactions with their counterparts are fulfilling, gratifying, and facile |
| Alliance-specific investments | Represent sunk costs that cannot be easily redeployed to another alliance without some sacrifice in the productivity of the assets or cost to adapt them to the new relationship |
| Attractive alternatives | The extent to which the firm possesses attractive alternatives outside the alliance that could enable it to attain its objectives |

*Source:* Adapted from Tjemkes & Furrer (2010).

needed. After initial explorations to develop and commercialize wireless sensor technology in greenhouse horticulture, Interdy and Hortic signed a letter of intent in 2005. The parties formally expressed their intention to proceed with the product development roadmap to the point that an agreement was set for further commercializing Wiregreen. Interdy primarily contributed the necessary software, whereas Hortic was responsible for hardware development, sales, and distribution. Preceding the signing of the definitive license agreement, Interdy and Hortic made a business case together. After settling issues about the license fee, the partners reached agreement, and the alliance effectively became operational on July 1, 2007. During the development of the alliance, a number of critical events instigated different behavioral response patterns between the partners (see Table 5.2).

**TABLE 5.2 Case 1: Overview of the Critical Events and Response Behaviors**

| Event | Partners' interactive pattern | Response behavior | Interpretation |
|---|---|---|---|
| 1 Hardware redesign by third party (Fall 2007) | Hortic used creative voice by contracting a third party to solve hardware problems, which resulted in patience by Interdy | Complementary | Hortic actively and constructively considered Interdy's interests, which invited a passive and constructive response |
| 2 Wiregreen 1.1 is withdrawn from the market (January 2008) | Hortic behaved opportunistically by discontinuing sales without informing Interdy. Interdy responded with patience | Semi-morphic acomplementary | Hortic actively and destructively withheld information. Interdy's constructive and passive accommodating response broke the rule of correspondence |
| 3 Market launch of Wiregreen 1.2 (April 2008) | Interdy used creative voice to deal with design issues. Hortic responded with patience | Complementary | Interdy actively and constructively seek solutions, which invited a passive–constructive response from Hortic |
| 4 Hortic discontinues sales of Wiregreen (Fall 2008) | Hortic acted opportunistically by withholding critical complaints and sales information. Interdy responded with neglect | Complementary | Hortic actively and destructively withheld information, which invited a passive–destructive response from Interdy |
| 5 Two managers from Hortic leave the company (January 2009) | Hortic used considerate voice by appointing new managers, which was responded to with considerate voice by Interdy | Isomorphic acomplementary | Hortic actively and constructively considered the alliance's interest. Interdy's active and constructive accommodating response broke the rule of reciprocity |

*(continued)*

# A Circumplex Approach to Interpartner Dynamics in Strategic Alliances ■ 109

**TABLE 5.2 Case 1: Overview of the Critical Events and Response Behaviors (continued)**

| Event | Partners' interactive pattern | Response behavior | Interpretation |
|---|---|---|---|
| 6 Investing or discontinuing Wiregreen (January 2009) | Hortic used considerate voice as it composed a crisis team, to which Interdy responded with patience | Complementary | Hortic actively and constructively considered Interdy's interests, which invited a passive–constructive response from Interdy |
| 7 The user acceptance agreement is signed by Hortic (January 2009) | Interdy used aggressive voice to force Hortic to sign the agreement, which resulted in a considerate voice response by Hortic | Anticomplementary | Interdy actively and destructively imposed its solution. Hortic's constructive and active accommodating response broke the both reciprocity and correspondence rules |
| 8 Wiregreen 1.3 is launched on the market (February 2009) | Hortic used considerate voice by pro-actively resolving technical problems, which was responded to with patience by Interdy | Complementary | Hortic actively and constructively considered the alliance's interests, which invited a passive–constructive response from Interdy |
| 9 Budget and objectives' readjustment (March 2009) | Hortic used considerate voice by asking for payment postponement, and Interdy responded with considerate voice | Isomorphic acomplementary | Hortic actively and constructively considered Interdy's interest. Interdy's constructive and active accommodating response broke the rule of reciprocity |

## Overview of Critical Events: Interdy–Hortic Alliance

### Event 1: Hardware Redesign by Third Party (Fall 2007)

A number of problems occurred during development, resulting in Wiregreen's (version 1.0) market introduction not being as successful as expected. Based on customer feedback, several design issues were identified that caused the product to malfunction. To solve the problems, Interdy developed new software but discovered that the problems resulted from incompatibilities between software and hardware. In addition, hardware was still not performing up to expectations. Hortic recognized the need for specific knowledge and brought in a third party (creative voice), Wico, to troubleshoot the actual hardware. Interdy, confident in the quality of their software solution, refrained from further action and let Hortic solve the situation (patience). Wico discovered some bugs in the software, in addition to hardware problems, and blamed Interdy. Interdy kept its distance, although it felt that the other two firms were pairing up against it. To investigate Wiregreen's malfunctioning, Wico reassessed the development trajectory and concluded that the main cause of failure was hardware-related. Although Wico fixed the hardware issues, the launch of Wiregreen 1.1 had to be postponed.

The behavioral pattern emerging from this event is complementary. The initial active–constructive response by Hortic invited a passive–constructive response from Interdy. This interactive behavioral pattern is consistent with the rules of reciprocity and correspondence.

### Event 2: Wiregreen 1.1 is Launched in the Market (January 2008)

The upgraded version of Wiregreen functioned satisfactorily during Hortic's testing. The alliance partners decided to launch Wiregreen 1.1 in the market. The presales started in January 2008, and the official launch was scheduled for April. However, after receiving negative feedback from customers, Hortic decided, without informing Interdy, to immediately stop all sales activities to limit its financial and reputational losses (opportunism). Hortic informed Interdy about this decision only at the next scheduled quarterly meeting and justified its decision by arguing that hardware was again malfunctioning. It also stated it was working on a solution. Interdy was surprised and upset by Hortic's unilateral decision. In its view, the premature launch of version 1.1 resulted from Hortic's desire to secure cash flow. However, Interdy decided to not get actively involved, saying that Hortic possessed industry knowhow, and thus was responsible for marketing and distribution. Moreover, it was Hortic's choice to launch the product. Interdy trusted Hortic to choose the best launch strategy. Despite this setback, Interdy remained optimistic about the chance of Wiregreen's success and assisted Hortic in resolving hardware issues.

A semi-morphic acomplementary behavior describes Interdy's response during this event. Consistent with the complementarity principle, Hortic's initial active–destructive action invited Interdy to respond with a passive–destructive response (that is, neglect). However, Interdy accommodatingly responded with a passive–constructive response, thus breaking the rule of correspondence in order to preserve the relationship.

*Event 3: Market Launch of Wiregreen 1.2 (April 2008)*
Feedback reports from customers conveyed both positive and negative critiques. For example, prelaunch tests indicated that 20-meter cables would be sufficient to support Wiregreen, but customers mentioned they required 50-meter cables. In addition, it became apparent that Wiregreen only worked for specific types of soils. Hortic anticipated this problem, but did not thoroughly test for it. During development, Interdy trusted Hortic to fully commit its technological competences and knowledge of the greenhouse industry. However, Interdy realized that Hortic did not allocate sufficient engineering staff to the project. To solve the issue, and being aware of Hortic's tight financial situation, Interdy decided to help with hardware problems. It also actively assisted Hortic in obtaining the international certificates required to globally commercialize Wiregreen. Overall, Interdy reacted actively and constructively to rectify the situation and deal with customer feedback (considerate voice). During this period, Hortic accepted Interdy's assistance and became passive (patience). For instance, Hortic awaited Interdy's suggestions and did not fully commit its competences to improve the technological features of Wiregreen. Despite these minor setbacks, Wiregreen 1.2 was released in April 2008.

The behavioral pattern described above is complementary, as an initial active–constructive behavior by Interdy invited a passive–constructive response from Hortic.

*Event 4: Hortic Discontinues Sales of Wiregreen 1.2 (Fall 2008)*
Based on Wiregreen 1.0 sales and promising forecasts, the sales goal for 2008 was set as up to 40 Wiregreens 1.2 in the Netherlands and 10 Wiregreens internationally. Interdy was not informed about any customer complaints, so it believed sales were progressing according to expectations. However, prior to a quarterly meeting, they received an e-mail from Hortic with the actual sales figures for Wiregreen, which were disappointing. Moreover, because a substantial number of customers complained about the instability of the system, Hortic decided to discontinue sales without informing Interdy (opportunism). Hortic believed that the product was not functioning according to specifications, and the system had to be redesigned. These criticisms came as a complete surprise to Interdy. Hortic justified its decisions by claiming it only realized 20% of the sales target.

Although Interdy received a compensating minimum fee, which covered part of the investments made during the development phase, it was dissatisfied and decided to temporarily disregard the relationship (neglect) by reconsidering the initial partnership with Hortic.

The behavioral pattern emerging from this event can be described as complementary. Hortic's initial active–destructive behavior invited a passive–destructive response from Interdy. This interactive behavioral pattern is consistent with the rules of reciprocity and correspondence.

*Event 5: Two Managers from Hortic Leave the Firm (January 2009)*

In January 2009, a technical product manager and a sales manager left Hortic. They were involved in the alliance from its beginning. Hortic immediately appointed new managers to the alliance. Contrary to the previous managers, who were involved in several projects, the new managers were specifically allocated to the alliance with the main responsibility to make Wiregreen succeed (considerate voice). This initiative was welcomed, as Interdy resented Hortic's earlier lack of commitment. This was a critical barrier impeding alliance development. Interdy started to communicate actively and regularly with the new managers to inform them about the situation and reestablish the relationship (considerate voice).

The emerging behavioral pattern is isomorphic acomplementary. Hortic's initial active–constructive behavior invited a passive–constructive response (that is, patience). However, to accelerate the alliance's progress, Interdy broke the rule of reciprocity and responded by mimicking Hortic's active–constructive behavior.

*Event 6: Further Investing in or Discontinuing Wiregreen (January 2009)*

In January 2009, Hortic and Interdy considered the future of the Wiregreen project in light of design problems, negative customer feedback, and disappointing sales. Hortic was in favor of terminating the project, whereas Interdy still believed in the technology and saw market potential. After several meetings, the partners decided to continue with the project and to redesign and upgrade Wiregreen. Hortic first created a crisis project team (creative voice) to search for solutions. Its R&D department started to develop innovative technological features for the hardware. Meanwhile, Interdy waited on the sidelines (patience), as hardware design was beyond their responsibilities.

This behavioral pattern is complementary. The initial active–constructive behavior by Hortic invited a passive–constructive response from Interdy.

*Event 7: Hortic Signs the User-Acceptance Agreement (January 2009)*

It was critical to Interdy that Hortic signed the software user-acceptance agreement. This was necessary for Interdy to receive license payments.

However, Hortic procrastinated in formalizing the agreement. It argued that as long as Wiregreen was not functioning according to specifications, it did not want to pay even the agreed minimum fee. According to Interdy, the software had complied with specifications since the summer of 2008. Interdy managers felt they had been very accommodating to Hortic, but were now frustrated with the situation; customers had stated the problems originated in hardware design. Although Interdy recognized the importance of being lenient, it imposed substantial pressure on Hortic to promptly sign the user-acceptance agreement. If Hortic did not do so, Interdy threatened to discontinue software development (aggressive voice). Hortic finally signed the agreement during the quarterly meeting of January 2009 (considerate voice).

The behavioral pattern depicted is anticomplementary. The initial active–destructive behavior from Interdy would invite passive–destructive behavior (that is, neglect). However, Hortic recognized the pressing need to signal long-term commitment and behaved actively and constructively. This broke the rules of reciprocity and correspondence.

### *Event 8: Launch of Wiregreen 1.3 (February 2009)*

Building on a plan developed by Hortic, both partners agreed to upgrade Wiregreen. Hortic allocated time and resources to develop Wiregreen 1.3 within six weeks. The partners had learned from previous experiences and used this knowhow to accelerate the development process. However, the Wiregreen 1.3 market launch was delayed because the hardware manufacturer that Hortic subcontracted had filed for bankruptcy. Despite this setback, Hortic continued to make significant efforts to improve Wiregreen (considerate voice). Although it took some time to relaunch the product, Interdy trusted that Hortic would be able to successfully market the new product and was anticipating the Wiregreen 1.3 arrival (patience). It was released to the market in February 2009.

The behavioral pattern emerging during this event is complementary. Hortic's active–constructive behavior invited a passive–constructive response from Interdy.

### *Event 9: Budget and Objectives Readjustment (March 2009)*

The economic crisis and the delay in launching Wiregreen 1.3 generated financial problems for Hortic. Although Hortic was aware that Interdy was keen to recover initial investments, it was forced to ask for postponement of the license fee's payment (considerate voice). Board members from both Interdy and Hortic met to discuss their concerns and mutual interests. These meetings resulted in an adjusted payment scheme. Interdy considered negotiations about financial payments and contracts as inherently tied to alliance management. Moreover, acknowledging Hortic's situation, it primarily attributed Wiregreen's underperformance to the economic crisis rather than a delayed market launch. Therefore, Interdy remained active during negotiations in providing substantial support, stimulating communication and development activities without charging a fee (considerate voice).

The pattern emerging from this event depicts isomorphic acomplementary behavior. Initial active–constructive behavior from Hortic invited a passive–constructive response (that is, patience) from Interdy. However, Interdy responded actively and constructively to accommodate Hortic's interests, thereby breaking the rule of reciprocity.

### Interpretation: Complementarity in Response Behavior

Analysis of the events that shaped the evolution of the Interdy–Hortic alliance provides an answer to the first research question: *How does a strategic alliance partner respond to its counterpart's interactive behavior?* There was evidence of the four types of response behavior derived from interpersonal theory. Event 1 provides evidence of a complementary response, consistent with the rules of reciprocity and correspondence, in which Interdy responded in a passive–constructive way (patience) to Hortic's active–constructive behavior (creative voice). Event 2 provides an example of acomplementary semi-morphic behavior, in which a partner responds to its counterpart's invitation by breaking the rule of correspondence. In this event, Interdy responded to Hortic active–destructive behavior (opportunism) with passive–constructive behavior (patience). Event 5 shows a isomorphic acomplementary behavior. Interdy broke the rule of reciprocity with an active–constructive response (considerate voice) to Hortic's active–constructive behavior (considerate voice). Event 7 showed an anticomplementary response when Hortic actively and constructively (considerate) responded to Interdy's active–destructive behavior (aggressive voice). This broke the rules of reciprocity and correspondence. Based on these empirical findings, we developed the following proposition.

> **Proposition 1:** *Interpartner interactions in strategic alliances occur through four types of behavioral patterns: (1) complementary, (2) acomplementary isomorphic, (3) acomplementary semi-morphic, and (4) anticomplementary.*

The evidence also indicates that complementary is the most frequent way of interacting with a partner. More specifically, among the nine critical events, complementary behavior occurred five times, and acomplementary isomorphic behavior occurred twice. Acomplementary, semi-morphic and anticomplementary behavior each occurred one time. These findings are consistent with interpersonal theory stating that complementary behavior is the most rewarding interactive behavior (Kiesler, 1983). The involved parties recognize each other's motives behind the behavior and accept this when responding (Horowitz et al., 2006). A partner interaction becomes rewarding as it is guided by the rules of reciprocity and correspondence.

**Proposition 2:** *Within strategic alliances, complementary behavior on the basis of (a) reciprocity along the active–passive dimension (activeness invites passiveness, passiveness invites activeness) and (b) correspondence along the constructive–destructive dimension (constructiveness invites constructiveness, destructiveness invites destructiveness) is the expected response to interpartner behavior.*

Although the results suggest that complementary behavior is the expected way of interacting in strategic alliances, they also indicate that partners may respond with noncomplementary behavior under certain conditions (that is, deviating from reciprocity and/or correspondence rules). For example, during Event 5, Interdy's active and constructive response to Hortic's active and constructive behavior was isomorphic acomplementary. Interdy broke the rule of reciprocity to accommodate Hortic's interests. A second alliance was studied to more systematically explore the underlying mechanisms that inform noncomplementary behavior.

## CASE STUDY 2: INTERDY–HITEC COMMUNICATIONS

The strategic alliance between Interdy and Hitec was forged in 2008 to develop and commercialize IT solutions for xDSL noise impairment to extend the lifetime of copper lines in the advent of optical fiber cables. Noises (electromagnetic interferences) are problematic for xDSL transmissions because they reduce the quality of the signals. Prior to this alliance, Interdy and Hitec successfully collaborated in a distribution alliance in which they combined software and hardware. At the time of the start of the alliance, the partners decided to develop and market two new products: Biks and Boks. Both are software developed by Interdy, based on Hitec's hardware technology. Biks is a flexible tool that allows easy creation and customization of impulse noises to help to produce unlimited impulse scenarios to identify the impact of noise on xDSL transmissions. Boks predicts the performance of an xDSL system for a determined impulse scenario, including the types of xDSL system, cable, and disturbances. As the alliance progressed, five critical events arose to exemplify why partners respond with noncomplementary behavior (see Table 5.3).

116 ■ O. FURRER et al.

**TABLE 5.3  Case 2: Overview of Critical Events and Behavioral Patterns**

| Event | Partners' responses | Behavioral pattern | Interpretation |
|---|---|---|---|
| 1  Critical e-mail to Hitec (February 2008) | Hitec let the relationship deteriorate by redirecting its efforts (neglect), which invited Interdy to send a pressing email (aggressive voice). In turn, Hitec recommitted itself to the alliance project by responding constructively (considerate voice). | Complementary, Anticomplementary | Hitec's recognition that the window of opportunity was closing, putting time pressure on the alliance, made it break the rules of reciprocity and correspondence |
| 2  Negotiation of the Biks's license (May 2009) | Interdy proposed a minimum fee payment (considerate voice) to which Hitec responded by imposing pressure on Interdy to accept its conditions (aggressive voice). In turn, Interdy proposed an alternative payment scheme (creative voice), which was refused by Hitech (aggressive voice). Interdy finally agreed to lower prices (considerate voice) to which Hitec responded by signing the agreement (considerate voice). | Anticomplementary, Anticomplementary, Anticomplementary, Anticomplementary, Acomplementary isomorphic | The break of the rules of reciprocity and correspondence by Hitec was induced by internal pressures and the advent of the economic crisis. Interdy's long-term commitment triggered it to break the rules of reciprocity and correspondence to accommodate its partner. |
| 3  Expiration of the Boks contract (Dec. 2009–Jan. 2010) | Hitec let the relationship deteriorate (neglect) by not responding to Interdy's request to renew the Boks contract (considerate voice). Recognizing the salience of contract renewal Hitec explained the delay and promised to respond (considerate voice) which invited Interdy to wait (patience). Then, Hitec asked Interdy to come up with suggestions for contractual renewal (considerate voice). | Semi-morphic acomplementary, isomorphic acomplementary, Complementary, Complementary | The break of the rule of reciprocity by Interdy was triggered by its long-term commitment and intention to recommit Hitec to the alliance. Hitec responded positively by breaking the rule of correspondence to indicate its acceptance of Interdy' intentions. This behavior put the alliance back on track and both partners then responded with complementary behavior. |

*(continued)*

**TABLE 5.3  Case 2: Overview of Critical Events and Behavioral Patterns (continued)**

| Event | Partners' responses | Behavioral pattern | Interpretation |
|---|---|---|---|
| 4 Pricing issue Boks (Feb. 2009–Apr. 2010) | Interdy and Hitec both constructively discussed price levels (considerate voice), then Interdy awaited Hitec proposal (patience). Then, Hitec imposed demands on Interdy (aggressive voice), which were accepted by Interdy (considerate voice) | Acomplementary isomorphic, Complementary, Acomplementary semi-morphic, Anticomplementary | The partners broke the rules of reciprocity and correspondence. Driven by high social satisfaction, they were eager to resolve the pricing issue. Hitec broke the rule of correspondence to pursue self-interest. Interdy broke the rules of reciprocity and correspondence to preserve the relationship |
| 5 New Vice-President at Hitec (May 2010) | Hitec did not respond to Interdy's request to finalize contractual negotiations (neglect). Once Interdy imposed pressure (aggressive voice), Hitec responded by demanding additional contractual changes (aggressive voice). Interdy complied with the new demands (considerate voice), but Hitec unexpectedly demanded new negotiations (aggressive voice). | Complementary, Acomplementary isomorphic, Anticomplementary, Anticomplementary | Hitec breaks the rule of reciprocity triggered by internal pressure. Hitec breaks the rules of reciprocity and correspondence as the new VP shifts Hitec's disposition towards the alliance Interdy breaks the rules of reciprocity and correspondence to preserve the relationship. |

## Overview of Critical Events: Interdy–Hitec

### Event 1: Critical E-mail to Hitec (February 2008)

After a series of enthusiastic exploration and troubleshooting meetings to improve the performance of both hardware and software, Hitec's motivation started to slow down. Facing new technological advancements in its industry and some problems with a supplier that had to be replaced, Hitec somewhat neglected the Biks alliance (neglect). It did not dedicate enough time and resources to manage the alliance and primarily focused efforts on other hardware development. Interdy realized the window of opportunity for impulse noise testing would soon end, due to the maturity of copper cables and the rise of optical fiber. Interdy sent a pressing e-mail asking whether Hitec shared its view on the industry's technological development and if Hitec was still committed to the project (aggressive voice). Interdy also explicitly asked Hitec to become more actively involved. Hitec responded positively and said it was very interested in leveraging its existing portfolio of hardware devices with Interdy software, rather than developing new products. Hitec also requested more information about Biks' characteristics and hardware requirements (considerate voice). They recognized Biks' market potential and wanted to see if it could work on their existing hardware.

The partners' initial behavioral pattern is complementary, as initial passive–destructive behavior from Hitec invited an active–destructive response from Interdy. The recognition of the limited window of opportunity caused Hitec to shift from a long-term perspective for the alliance (new hardware development) to a short-term perspective (market for existing products). The shift in Hitec's disposition influenced it to break the rules of reciprocity and correspondence and give an (anticomplementary) active–constructive response.

### Event 2: Negotiation of Biks's License (May 2009)

Although the partners discussed royalties during initial contract negotiations, Interdy did not require royalty payments in the proposed final alliance contract. Building on prior experiences with Hitec and previous royalty payment agreements, Interdy proposed a minimum payment clause corresponding to sales of a specific number of units over two years (considerate voice). If sales met this target, this clause became invalid. From Interdy's point of view, this proposal was satisfactory, as it assured them minimum revenues and Hitec's commitment. At first, Hitec did not respond on the content of proposal. Instead, it put pressure on Interdy to speed up negotiations. Hitec stated it did not want any minimum requirements clauses in the contract (aggressive voice) because of the changing competitive conditions in the industry and the advent of the economic crisis. At the same time, it sought to convince Interdy of its commitment, noting their good relationship over the years. However, Interdy perceived that the relationship was based more on dependence than commitment and refused Hitec's demand, which they saw as a negotiation tactic. As Interdy felt that the partners were not likely to come to a satisfactory solution anytime soon, it came up with an alternative idea to solve the situation: a combination of license fees and minimal payment based on the number of products sold (creative voice). Hitec welcomed the proposition but suggested further lowering the price per product (aggressive voice). Interdy agreed to keep the project moving forward and ensure that Hitec stayed committed to push the Biks sales (considerate voice). The new agreement offered enough safety for both parties, as Hitec had no obligations if sales would be lower than expected and Interdy had some guaranteed revenues. Hitec positively responded to Interdy's proposition and signed the new contract (considerate voice).

The partners' initial behavior pattern is anticomplementary. Interdy's initial active–constructive behavior was countered with in an active–destructive response from Hitec, though it was invited to respond passively and constructively (that is, patience). Interdy did not accept Hitec motives and then used an active–constructive anticomplementary response (creative voice) to signal its long-term orientation towards the alliance. However, fueled by financial uncertainty, Hitec refused Interdy's invitation and responded with an anticomplementary behavior maintaining its active–destructive behavior (aggressive voice). In response, to accommodate Hitec and restating its long-term commitment to the alliance, Interdy also broke the rules of correspondence and reciprocity to use an anticomplementary behavior (considerate voice). Finally satisfied with Interdy's response, Hitec broke the rules of reciprocity and correspondence by signing the contract. That is, it gave an active–constructive response to signal commitment to the alliance.

### Event 3: Expiration of the Boks Contract (December 2009–January 2010)

The Boks project was also progressing. Interdy and Hitec had constructive discussions about how to proceed with the Boks upgrade in terms of software and pricing strategy. Interdy then reminded Hitec that the Boks license agreement had expired, and the extension of the exclusive license needed to be renewed (considerate voice). Hitec apologized for not responding sooner to Interdy's e-mails about the license agreement, explaining that e-mails were buried in the alliance manager's inbox (neglect). Hitec's alliance manager agreed to come back to Interdy in January 2010 (considerate voice). Interdy wondered why the alliance manager should be involved in such a standard renewal issue (patience). Hitec responded that if it was strictly about agreement renewal, there was no reason to delay signing the agreement and asked Interdy to highlight any changes in the document (considerate voice).

The initial behavioral pattern is semi-morphic acomplementary. Interdy responded with active–constructive behavior to Hitec's passive–destructive behavior to signal its long-term commitment to the alliance. In turn, Hitec responded with isomorphic acomplementary behavior (active–constructive) to signal that it understood and accepted Interdy's intentions. Interdy then gave a passive–constructive response, which reinforced Hitec's motives and produced an active–constructive behavior in a complementary interaction.

*Event 4: Boks Pricing Issues (February–April 2010)*

Hitec pointed out during a conference call that the 6X60 product was now at a good commercial price. Interdy also reconsidered the price for the PC-based Boks and wondered if Hitec thought it would help sales to bring down the price for 6X10. Hitec responded that high prices scare away customers. It had already addressed this issue several years ago. Hitec also mentioned that profit margins were tight. Interdy repeated it was open for discussion on lowering the minimum fee to help Hitec boost sales. Hitec felt that would be in the best interest to both of them. Lowering the list price would increase sales and decrease Hitec's cost of sales. It therefore asked for a lower minimum fee, which would provide more flexibility. Interdy felt it had opened Pandora's box by lowering the minimum fee and argued that if Hitec wanted to lower percentages, it should come up with a plan. Interdy became passive in telling Hitec to openly articulate all the issues (patience). A conference call took place in which it was decided to lower royalties on the 6X10, 6X11 and 6X12 products. Hitec also wanted to lower royalties on Boks to something that reflected the maturity of the DSL market place (aggressive voice). Interdy had an internal discussion and decided to go along to send a positive signal (considerate voice). Changes were made to the Boks license agreement.

The initial behavioral pattern is acomplementary isomorphic. Both Interdy and Hitec acted actively and constructively. Both partners broke the rule of correspondence because they were eager to solve issues. This was instigated by high levels of social satisfaction. Interdy then became patient, consistent with a complementary pattern, which triggered Hitec's acomplementary, semi-morphic, active–destructive response. This was then followed by anticomplementary behavior from Interdy, as it constructively complied with Hitec demands to maintain the alliance.

*Event 5: New Vice-President at Hitec (May 2010)*

Hitec did not initially respond to Interdy's multiple requests to finalize the license agreement (neglect). It only responded after Interdy imposed pressure (aggressive voice). Hitec's response entailed an amendment to the agreement by dropping the royalty percentages on the 6X10, 6X11 and 6X12. This would provide latitude to offer customers interesting discounts to boost sales. As the partners were coming to an agreement, Hitec requested an additional clause to reduce the minimum royalty fee (aggressive voice). Such a reduction would reflect the maturity of the DSL marketplace. Interdy hesitantly approved Hitec's proposition and drafted a readjusted contract (considerate voice). However, Hitec unexpectedly brought additional demands to the negotiation (aggressive voice). It argued that it had overpaid royalties on several Boks products and proposed a correction based on a revised agreement, rather than on the 2009 contract. It also became evident during these meetings that Hitec's newly appointed vice-president was opposed to any minimum volume commitments with any of their partners, not just Interdy. The alliance managers discussed the overall wire line business with him, but he was very aware that the business was declining. Hitec continued to promote 6X60 and sent out updated news flashes, dropping the 6X10 list price. However, at the current minimum royalty level, it felt it was too difficult to reach the minimum volume and requested new negotiations.

The initial behavior pattern is complementary. An initial passive–destructive behavior by Hitec (neglect) invited an active–destructive response from Interdy (aggressive voice). Hitec then gave an active–destructive response, depicting a complementary isomorphic behavior. Hitec broke the rule of reciprocity due to its short-term focus on financial interests. Interdy responded actively and constructively (considerate voice), reinforcing its long-term orientation towards the alliance, consistent with anticomplementary behavior. Due to unforeseen internal circumstances (new VP), Hitec broke the complimentarity principle and engaged in active–destructive, anticomplementary behavior (aggressive voice) by asking for new contractual adaptations.

## Interpretation: Breaking the Rules of Reciprocity and Correspondence

Although evidence seems to indicate that complementary behavior is the most frequent and natural response in strategic alliances, partners are sometimes required to break the reciprocity and/or correspondence rules. The alliance between Interdy and Hitec provides the empirical context to answer the second research question: *What are the factors that influence alliance partners' noncomplementary response behavior?* Empirical evidence from the case suggests that three sets of factors concur to explain why alliance partners deviate from the complementarity principle: partners' disposition, alliance exchange conditions, and partners' attempt to change their counterpart's behavior.

### Partners' Disposition

In strategic alliances, partners have diverging preferences or dispositions toward the alliance relationship. When partners have different dispositions, tensions arise that inform their response behavior. De Rond and Bouchiki (2004) argue that dialectical forces undermine alliance stability and thus account for response behavior among partners. These internal tensions should be taken into account to gain a better understanding of alliance partner interaction (Das & Teng, 2000b). More specifically, the empirical evidence from the Interdy–Hitec strategic alliance suggests that differences in partners' dispositions (that is, internal tension) trigger them to break the rules of reciprocity and correspondence. The critical events identified in the case indicate that two pairs of internal tensions were particularly salient in explaining response behavior: cooperation versus competition, and short-term versus long-term orientation.

Whereas cooperation pertains to the pursuit of mutual interests, competition entails pursuing one's own interests at the expense of the other partners (Das & Teng, 2000b). A partner's competitive disposition may influence it to refuse to respond complementarily to the cooperative behavior of its counterpart, and vice versa. For example, Event 5 provides evidence of how partners' different dispositions towards cooperation and competition resulted in acomplementary semi-morphic behavior. Whereas Interdy was holding a cooperative disposition and behaved passively and constructively, Hitec's competitive disposition influenced its active–destructive response. Such self-interested behavior reduced its financial risks and extracted additional revenues from the alliance. This is consistent with Luo et al.'s (2008) hypothesis that stipulates that when an alliance partner is behaving opportunistically, the other partner should respond by dominating the alliance, challenging the partner, or exiting the alliance. In a cooperative situation, Luo et al. (2008) argue that partners should accommodate, adapt, or comply with each other's requirements. The results of De Rond and Bouchikhi's (2004) study provide empirical support for the influence of the tension between cooperation and competition on partners' response behaviors.

The second salient internal tension present in the Interdy–Hitec alliance is related to differences in terms of short-term versus long-term orientations. A short-term orientation entails that a partner views an alliance as transitional, with a demand for quick and tangible results. A long-term orientation suggests a partner considers an alliance as (at least) a semi-permanent entity. More patience and commitment are exercised (Das & Teng, 2000b). Evidence from the case indicates that partners' temporal disposition towards the alliance may cause them to break the rules of reciprocity and correspondence. For example, in Event 1, Hitec's short-term orientation influenced Interdy's response when it engaged in anticomplementary active–constructive behavior in response to Interdy's active–destructive behavior.

This is consistent with previous empirical studies (e.g., Bello, Katsikeas, & Robson, 2010; Pajunen & Fang, in press). Bello et al. (2010) found that accommodation, defined as responding constructively to a destructive behavior (that is, semi-morphic acomplementary or anticomplementary behavior), is frequent in a strategic alliance for which one of the partners holds a long-term orientation. On the other hand, Pajunen and Fang (in press) also found that a short-term orientation might lead to retaliatory behavior (that is, isomorphic acomplementary behavior), likely to result in termination of the alliance. In sum, a short-term or a long-term orientation disposition may push a partner to either accommodate or retaliate against the counterpart's behavior by breaking the reciprocity and/or correspondence rules.

**Proposition 3:** *Within interpartner interactions in strategic alliances, a partner is likely to break the rules of reciprocity and correspondence when its disposition towards the alliance (e.g., cooperation versus competition or short-term versus long-term) conflicts with the intent of its counterpart's behavior.*

### *Exchange Conditions*

Consistent with the response strategy framework (Tjemkes & Furrer, 2011), which explains under what exchange conditions specific response strategies are more likely to occur, the case study indicates that a change in alliance conditions may influence a partner to break the rules of reciprocity and/or correspondence. Even though a partner's response invites its counterpart to act consistently with the complementarity principle, exchange conditions may trigger a departure from the expected response. For example, whereas economic dissatisfaction and the lack of attractive alternatives influence preferences for active response strategies (Tjemkes & Furrer, 2010), an active–constructive act by one partner invites a passive–constructive response. This presents an alliance partner with a dilemma: comply with complementarity principle or act in response to exchange conditions. Similarly, whereas social satisfaction and investments in alliance-specific assets influence constructive preferences for active response strategies (Tjemkes & Furrer, 2010), an active–destructive act invites a passive–destructive response.

Evidence from the Interdy–Hitec alliance provides support for such a dilemma between complementary behavior and that triggered by exchange conditions. In Event 2, Hitec's low economic satisfaction with the alliance influenced its active–destructive response to Interdy's active–constructive behavior. By doing so, Hitec responded in an anticomplementary way, breaking both correspondence and reciprocity rules. In contrast, Interdy's high social satisfaction in Event 4 influenced its isomorphic acomplementary response. Interdy mimicked Hitec's active–constructive behavior. Building on these insights, we propose:

**Proposition 4:** *Within interpartner interactions in strategic alliances, a partner is likely to break the rules of reciprocity and correspondence when exchange conditions conflict with the intent of its counterpart's behavior.*

### Partner's Attempt to Change Counterpart's Behavior

Interpersonal theory (Horowitz et al., 2006) suggests that an actor may deviate from an expected (that is, complementary) response to signal to their counterpart that a change in behavior is deemed necessary. How one person behaves profoundly influences how the other responds to that person (Kiesler, 1983). Partners may respond with specific behaviors to signal to their counterpart that they need to change their behavior. For example, a partner may mimic their counterpart's behavior (that is, isomorphic acomplementary behavior) to signal that they want to take the lead in the alliance, thereby inviting their counterpart to become more passive. Similarly, a partner may engage in anticomplementary behavior by an active–constructive response to an active–destructive action. This signals commitment to the relationship and invites in turn a passive–constructive response from the partner.

The results of Case Study 2 provide support for the prediction that one partner may respond with noncomplementary behavior to tell its counterpart to act more constructively. In Event 4, Hitec used an isomorphic acomplementary (that is, active–constructive) response to Interdy's active–constructive behavior to signal its commitment to the alliance, inviting the latter to respond in a passive–constructive way. In Event 3, Hitec acted neglectfully. Interdy responded in an acomplementary semi-morphic active–constructive manner (that is, considerate voice) to steer Hitec towards the constructive side of the circumplex. Hitec understood Interdy's intention and responded by breaking the principle of complementarity, using an active–constructive (considerate voice) to rebalance the internal tension in the alliance and inviting Interdy to respond with passive–constructive behavior (patience). Taken together:

**Proposition 5:** *Within interpartner interactions in strategic alliances, a partner is likely to break the rules of reciprocity and correspondence to trigger a change in its counterpart's behavior.*

## CONCLUSION

The objective of the study was to assess the relevance of interpersonal theory's complementarity principle to describe partners' behavior dynamic in strategic alliances. By combining the insights from interpersonal theory and response strategy perspective, this research sought to understand when and why alliance partners might deviate from the complementarity principle. The results of two exploratory case studies indicated that the four response behaviors theoretically derived from interpersonal psychology (complementary, isomorphic acomplementary, semi-morphic acomplementary, and anticomplementary) can be identified at the interorganizational level in a strategic alliance context. The findings also indicated that partners more often use a complementary behavior. In addition, the findings provided insights into three underlying mechanisms that trigger partners to act defiantly or accommodatingly, and respond with noncomplementary behavior: partners' disposition, exchange conditions, and a partner's attempt to change its counterpart's behavior.

The alliance literature is advanced by this new theoretical lens to study alliance interpartner behavior. This research validates that theoretical mechanisms operating at the individual level also apply at the interorganizational level. Moreover, these arguments can be effectively reconciled with existing alliance literature on internal tensions. The results indicated that partners' behaviors, in addition to exchange conditions and partner's past behaviors, are influenced by internal tensions inherently built into alliance relationships (Das & Teng, 2000b). Taken together, these findings account for behavioral patterns not sufficiently addressed by prior interpartner dynamics literature. By aligning the response strategy perspective, interpersonal theory, and the internal tensions perspectives, this study provides a first step toward an integrative perspective on interpartner dynamics in strategic alliances.

Integrating interpersonal theory with the response strategy perspective provides novel insight. For example, the core logic underpinning an integrative framework is that alliance interpartner behavior signals intentions to a partner's counterpart. More specifically, building on the circumplex structure of the response strategy perspective, partners are likely to continue to use similar or neighboring response strategies if the situation with the alliance is stable. From interpersonal theory, when partners are satisfied with the outcomes and process of the alliance, they are likely to follow the complementarity principle, a behavior that contributes to a rewarding and stable alliance relationship. However, following the complementarity principle on the destructive side of the circumplex structure is likely to create alliance instability. Then noncomplementary behavior is used to reestablish a balance in the internal tension. This pattern of motivated actions and reactions drives the development of a strategic alliance over time.

Although this research opened the black box of interpartner dynamics, it has several limitations. First, case studies are exploratory in nature, which did not allow for empirically testing the propositions. However, the propositions are testable. Future research could use a quantitative approach based on a representative sample of alliances to corroborate the propositions. Second, the case study approach retrospectively looked at a selection of critical events that might be subject to recollection bias and alliance managers' subjective memories, despite the data triangulation. Therefore, future research might use ethnographic techniques to study interpartner dynamics while following alliance development as partners' behaviors occur. Third, one of the aims of the study was to identify triggers of noncomplementary behavior. By doing so, some explanatory factors were singled out. However, multiple factors are likely to interact in explaining alliance partners' behavior and would need to be theoretically and empirically disentangled by future research.

Interpartner dynamics is understudied, but it is critical to alliance success. By validating the relevance of interpersonal theory for understanding interpartner dynamics at the alliance level, this study advances a more fine-grained explanation for alliance partner interaction. Taken together, the developed propositions provide a first tentative step in building an integrative model of interpartner dynamics in strategic alliances.

## APPENDIX: TACTICS USED FOR ENSURING VALIDITY OF RESEARCH DESIGN

| Validity tests[a] | Suggested case study tactics and rationale[b] | Implementation of case study tactics |
|---|---|---|
| *Construct validity:* Establishing correct operational measures for the concepts being studied. | *Use multiple sources of evidence.* This tactic allows triangulation and the development of converging lines of inquiry. | The following sources of evidence were used: (1) written documentation, such as management reports and minutes of key meetings; (2) data-based e-mail communication, and (3) semi-structured interviews with representatives of all partners. |
| | *Establish chain of evidence.* This allows an external observer to follow the derivation of any evidence from initial research questions to ultimate case study conclusions. | The following steps were taken to establish a chain of evidence: (1) the case reports cite the relevant portions of the case database; (2) the case database reveals the actual evidence and indicates the circumstances under which the evidence was collected. |
| | *Have informants review draft case study report.* This corroborates the essential facts and evidence presented in the case report, reducing the likelihood of false reporting. | The key informants reviewed the timeline of events and the case reports. |
| *Internal validity:* Establishing a causal relationship, whereby certain conditions, as distinguished from spurious relationships. | *Have a general analytical strategy:* (1) relying on a theoretical orientation to guide the analysis, or (2) developing a case description. This helps the researcher choose among different analytical techniques. | We relied on response strategy research and interpersonal theory to guide our organization and analysis of the case evidence. |
| | *Have a dominant analytical procedure:* (1) pattern matching, (2) explanation building, or (3) time series analysis. This ensures that inferences based on the case evidence are correct, ruling out alternative explanations. | The dominant analytical procedure was to use narrative to build an explanation that reflects theoretically significant propositions. |

*(continued)*

| Validity tests[a] | Suggested case study tactics and rationale[b] | Implementation of case study tactics |
|---|---|---|
| | *Use analytical techniques to manipulate the data.* This allows putting the evidence in some order prior to actual analysis. | Following Miles and Huberman's (1994) suggestions, the following techniques were used to organize the case evidence: (1) the information was placed in different displays such as comparative summaries and timelines of critical events; (2) tables were created to summarize the evidence in terms of response strategies and exchange variables by event and partner firm while keeping track of the chronological order. |
| *External validity:* Establishing the domain to which a study's findings can be generalized, keeping in mind that the aim is to generalize to theory, not to the population. | *Use replication logic in multiple case studies.* This allows researchers to establish the conditions under which a phenomenon is likely to be found and those where it is not likely to be found. | We used the second case as a replication study to corroborate the findings of the first study. |
| *Reliability:* Demonstrating that the operations of a study—such as the data collection procedures—can be repeated, with the same results. | *Develop case study database.* This allows other researchers to retrieve the evidence directly. | The case database includes case study notes, transcripts of interviews, and case study documents. |

[a] Source: Yin (2003, p. 34)
[b] Adapted from Ariño and Ring (2010) and Yin (2003).

## REFERENCES

Ariño, A., & De la Torre, J. (1998). Learning from failure: Towards an evolutionary model of collaborative ventures. *Organization Science, 9*, 306–325.

Ariño, A., & Ring, P. S. (2010). The role of fairness in alliance formation. *Strategic Management Journal, 31*, 1054–1087.

Bello, D. C., Katsikeas, C. S., & Robson, M. J. (2010). Does accommodating a self-serving partner in an international marketing alliance pay off? *Journal of Marketing, 74*(6), 77–93.

Cardinal, L. B., Sitkin, S. B., & Long, C. P. (2004). Balancing and rebalancing in the creation and evolution of organizational control. *Organization Science, 15*, 411–431.

Carson, R. C. (1969). *Interactional concepts of personality*. Chicago, IL: Aldine.

Das, T. K., & Teng, B. (2000a). A resource-based theory of strategic alliances. *Journal of Management, 26*, 31–61.

Das, T. K., & Teng, B. (2000b). Instabilities of strategic alliances: An internal tensions perspective. *Organization Science, 11*, 77–101.

De Rond, M., & Bouchikhi, H. (2004). On the dialectics of strategic alliances. *Organization Science, 15*, 56–69.

Doz, Y. L. (1996). The evolution of cooperation in strategic alliances: initial conditions or learning processes? *Strategic Management Journal, 17*, 55–83.

Eisenhardt, K. M. (1989). Building theories from case study research. *Academy of Management Review, 14*, 532–550.

Fabrigar, L. R., Visser, P. S., & Browne, M. W. (1997). Conceptual and methodological issues in testing the circumplex structure of data in personality and social psychology. *Personality and Social Psychology Review, 1*, 184–203.

Faems, D., Janssens, M., Madhok, A., & Van Looy, B. (2008). Toward an integrative perspective on alliance governance: Connecting contract design, trust dynamics, and contract application. *Academy of Management Journal, 51*, 1053–1078.

Furrer, O., Tjemkes, B. V., Ulgen Aydinlik, A., & Adolfs, K. (2012). Responding to adverse situations within exchange relationships: The cross-cultural validity of a circumplex model. *Journal of Cross-Cultural Psychology, 43*(6), 943–966.

Horowitz, L. M., Wilson, K. R., Turan, B., Zolotsev, P. Constantin, M. J., & Henderson, L. (2006). How interpersonal motives clarify the meaning of interpersonal behavior: A revised circumplex model. *Personality and Social Psychology Review, 10*(1), 67–86.

Kiesler, D. J. (1983). The 1982 interpersonal circle: A taxonomy for complementarity in human transactions. *Psychological Review, 90*, 185–214.

Leary, T. (1957). *Interpersonal diagnosis of personality*. New York, NY: Ronald.

Leonard-Barton, D. (1990). A dual methodology for case studies: Synergistic use of a longitudinal single site with replicated multiple studies. *Organization Science, 1*, 248–266.

Locke, K. D., & Sadler, P. (2007). Self-efficacy, values, and complementarity in dyadic interactions: integrating interpersonal and social cognitive theory. *Personality and Social Psychology Bulletin, 33*(1), 94–109.

Luo, Y. (2007). The independent and interactive roles of procedural, distributive, and interactional justice in strategic alliances. *Academy of Management Journal, 50*(3), 644–664.

Luo, Y., Shenkar, O., & Gurnani, H. (2008). Control-cooperation interfaces in global strategic alliances: A situational typology and strategic responses. *Journal of International Business Studies, 39*, 428–453.

Markey, P. M., Funder, D. C., & Ozer, D. J. (2003). Complementarity of interpersonal behaviors in dyadic interactions. *Personality and Social Psychology Bulletin, 29*, 1082–1090.

Miles, M. B., & Huberman, A. M. (1994). *Qualitative data analysis: An expanded sourcebook.* Newbury Park, CA: Sage.

Miller, C. C., Cardinal, L. B., & Glick, W. H. (1997). Retrospective reports in organizational research: A reexamination of recent evidence. *Academy of Management Journal, 40*, 189–204.

Orford, J. (1986). The rules of interpersonal complementarity: Does hostility beget hostility and dominance, submission? *Psychological Review, 93*, 365–377.

Pajunen, K., & Fang, L. (in press). Dialectical tensions and path dependence in international joint venture evolution and termination. *Asia Pacific Journal of Management.*

Poole, M. S., Van de Ven, A. H., Dooley, K., & Holmes, M. E. (2000). *Organizational change and innovation processes: Theory and methods for research.* Oxford, UK: Oxford University Press.

Ring, P. S., & Van de Ven, A. H. (1994). Developmental processes of cooperative interorganizational relationships. *Academy of Management Review, 19*, 90–118.

Strong, S. R., Hills, H. I., Kilmartin, C. T., De Vries, H. Lanier, K. Nelson, B. N., Strickland, D., & Meyer, C. W., III (1988). The dynamic relations among interpersonal behaviors: A test of complementary and anticomplementarity. *Journal of Personality and Social Psychology, 54*, 798–810.

Sullivan, H. S. (1953). *The interpersonal theory of psychiatry.* New York, NY: Academic Press.

Tiedens, L. Z., & Fragale, A. R. (2003). Power moves: Complementarity in dominant and submissive nonverbal behavior. *Journal of Personality and Social Psychology, 84*, 558–568.

Tjemkes, B. V., & Furrer, O. (2010). The antecedents of response strategies in strategic alliances. *Management Decision, 48*, 1103–1133.

Tjemkes, B. V., & Furrer, O. (2011). Behavioral responses to adverse situations in strategic alliances. In T. K. Das (Ed.), *Behavioral perspectives on strategic alliances: Emerging perspectives* (pp. 227–249). Charlotte, NC: Information Age Publishing.

Tjemkes, B. V., Furrer, O., Adolfs, K., & Ulgen Aydinlik, A. (2012). Response strategies in an international strategic alliance experimental context: Cross-country differences, *Journal of International Management, 18*(1), 66–84.

Tracey, T. J. (1994). An examination of the complementarity of interpersonal behavior. *Journal of Personality and Social Psychology, 67*, 864–878.

Wiggins, J. S. (1979). A psychological taxonomy of trait-descriptive terms: the interpersonal domain. *Journal of Personality and Social Psychology, 33*, 409–420.

Yin, R. K. (2003). *Case study research: Design and methods.* Newbury Park, CA: Sage.

CHAPTER 6

# MULTILEVEL EMBEDDEDNESS IN MULTILATERAL ALLIANCES

## A Conceptual Framework

Sveinn Vidar Gudmundsson, Christian Lechner,
and Hans van Kranenburg

### ABSTRACT

In this chapter we propose a conceptual framework for understanding interpartner dynamics in multilateral alliances involving common alliance processes, dyadic ties, and external transaction networks. The difference between alliance networks and multilateral alliances is the formalization of organization and common alliance processes in the latter. The firm-specific value in multilateral alliances is often buried in dyadic ties, which can be the prime motivator to join in the first place, but at the same time hindering common alliance processes. This multiplexity of relations, multilevel embeddedness, is a source of both strategic constraints and opportunities. Multilateral alliances set firms heading towards increased rigidity, cooperation and long-term orientation, requiring careful management of rising exit barriers to preserve strategic flexibility.

## INTRODUCTION

Alliance relations are institutional arrangements in which transactions take place (Lomi, 1995; Richardson, 1972). They constitute a transaction sphere that is an alternative governance mode to market transactions and vertical integration (Richardson, 1972). Alliances have commonly been formed among two firms, a dyad, but increasingly by a block of firms, an alliance network (Doz & Hamel, 1998; Gomes-Casseres, 1996; Lazzarini, 2007; Vanhaverbeke & Noorderhaven, 2001). The literature draws up a picture of alliance networks and constellations clustering around a focal firm or a focal project (Das & Teng, 2002; Doz & Hamel, 1998; Vanhaverbeke & Noorderhaven, 2001), while our definition of multilateral alliances (MLA) is formalized multipartner interfirm relations that involve not only a collection of dyads, but also central organization and common alliance processes.

Doz and Hamel (1998, p. 221) suggest that firms engaged in multilateral alliances are "entangled in a complex web of interdependent relationships that tax their strategic cleverness and managerial skills." One way to understand the "complex web" is by engaging embeddedness theory. We understand interfirm relations as a complex set of relations influencing and influenced by society they are embedded in. Embeddedness theory (Granovetter, 1985) helps to understand how networks of relations discourage mischief and influence choices through past interactions. Researchers have extended this work in various contexts such as cross-level embeddedness and overembeddedness (Hagedoorn, 2006; Hagedoorn & Frankort, 2008). Most of this research has focused on the influence of embeddedness on alliance formation but less on its influence on alliance dynamics.

In alliance networks, when there is an advantage in connecting resources through common processes and standards, a central organization needs to be formed due to the relational complexity. With formal organization, closure (Coleman, 1988) takes place, at the same time that dyadic relations continue to exist both internal and external to MLA. Instead of viewing MLA as replacing dyadic relations, it can be seen as icing on the cake, an additional set of strong ties on top of the existing relations, a mix of network closure (Coleman, 1988) and exploitation of structural holes (Burt, 2001). However, little research exists on the benefits of closure and structural holes in combination on one and the same alliance (Burt, 2001; Gudmundsson & Lechner, 2006).

Our objective in this chapter is to explore the important question of how multilevel embeddedness influences MLA tensions, the exploitation of opportunities, and how perceived barriers to exit influence the entry decision. We start by discussing definitions of different forms of multipartner alliances and particularly MLA; we then proceed to the theoretical perspectives that can be used to explain the multiplexity of MLA, we develop several propositions around our conceptual framework; and finally discuss the implications of our work.

## DEFINING MULTILATERAL ALLIANCES

A body of research has examined alliance networks, alliance constellations, and MLA (Das & Teng, 2002; Doz & Hamel, 1998; Gomes-Casseres, 1996; Gudmundsson & Lechner, 2006; Lazzarini, 2008; Vanhaverbeke & Noorderhaven, 2001). For the sake of clarity in the remainder of this chapter, we have listed definitions and the corresponding references in Table 6.1 to demonstrate how these three concepts have evolved.

**TABLE 6.1  Defining Multipartner Alliances**

| Concept | Definition | Reference |
|---|---|---|
| Multilateral alliance | "composed of overarching agreements applicable to all members of the group (Doz & Hamel, 1998)" | Lazzarini (2008, p. 20) |
| | "A multilateral alliance has at least three members who have cooperative relationships with each other involving elements of commonality across all partners" | Gudmundsson, De Boer, & Lechner (2002, p. 410) |
| | "formalized multipartner interfirm relations that involve not only a collection of dyads, but also central organization and common alliance processes." | Used in this chapter. |
| Constellation | "alliances formed by at least three partner firms—or multiple-partner alliances." | Das & Teng (2002, p. 446) |
| | "an explicit constellation is a broad multiple-firm alliance (Das & Teng, 2002)" | Lazzarini (2007, p. 346) |
| | "a set of firms linked together through alliances and that competes in a particular competitive domain." | Gomes-Casseres (2004, p. 44) |
| Alliance network | "a network consists of all interactions between organizations in a population" | Whetten (1981, p. 8) |
| | "A business network can be defined as a set of two or more connected business relationships, in which each exchange relation is between business firms that are conceptualized as collective actors (Emerson, 1981)." | Anderson, Hakansson, & Johanson (1994, p. 2) |
| | "A set of linkages between many relatively comparable firms . . . or an international network of independent local . . . firms" | Doz & Hamel (1998, p. 222) |
| | "consists of at least two alliances, each with two partners or with multiple partners." | Das & Teng (2002, p. 446) |

Lazzarini (2008) notes that the term alliance constellation has been used to denote both alliance networks (Gomes-Casseres, 1996) and multilateral alliances, and the two are not the same (Das & Teng, 2002). A perspective from technology and software industries is likely to see a focal firm at the center of alliance relations or a single project into which all the firms are linked, such as the RISC (project) processor alliance described by Vanhaverbeke and Noorderhaven (2001) or Fujitsu (focal firm) mainframe computer alliance described by Doz and Hamel (1998). Such alliances are inherently short-term as the project either fails or is completed. This brings up the question of whether constellations are more about projects and focal firms rather than a more permanent configuration of alliance relations. We could denote constellations as a ring of firms that constantly rearrange relations around projects and add or shed participants with redundant ties. These configurations are common in many industries, including software and aerospace. However, permanent alliance arrangements are rarer such as we find in the airline industry (oneworld, Skyteam and STAR) where the project is the alliance itself, a long-term vision of commonalities, but without any fixed completion time after which the partners rearrange within the alliance network. These arrangements are frequently found in network industries and services where interlinking of rights networks (legal operational boundaries) and the use of common standards are important.

We like to draw a line between constellations that describe project- or focal firm-focused alliance networks as having some formal arrangements between all partners, and MLAs, where formal arrangements are not project- or focal firm-focused and are not rearranged upon completion of projects. In other words, a constellation and MLA are not the same, but both constitute a group of firms that compete with other groups of firms. Our work focuses on multilateral alliances with central organization, so we favor the term multilateral alliance (MLA) rather than constellation to underline a difference.

## THEORETICAL PERSPECTIVES

To understand the multiplexity of MLAs it is necessary to engage several theoretical perspectives: tensions perspective (Das & Teng, 2000; De Rond & Bouchikhi, 2004), social network theory (Burt, 1992; Coleman, 1988, 1990), and embeddedness perspective (Granovetter, 1985). We cover each of these theoretical perspectives to unravel their significance in explaining MLA dynamics.

### Tensions Perspective

The dynamism of relations within MLAs can be understood using a tensions perspective (Das & Teng, 2000). The tensions perspective sees alliances being subject to competing forces across three spectrums: cooperation versus competition, rigidity versus flexibility, and short-term versus long-term.

Competition is defined (Das & Teng, 2000, p. 85) "as pursuing one's own interest at the expense of others," and cooperation "is the pursuit of mutual interests and common benefits." In MLAs, a stronger opportunistic focal firm may attempt to contribute fewer resources and control more of the alliance benefits. In MLAs where one firm is larger than the rest or is financially superior, opportunistic self-interest can develop and overtake cooperation. Since cooperation and competition are opposing forces, an imbalance must be resolved (Das & Teng, 2000; Gudmundsson, 2011). Too much competition will see one partner seeking to internalize the gains and unique resources of other partners (Khanna, Gulati, & Nohria, 1998; Yoshino & Rangan, 1995) or to control their actions. However, MLAs can be considered to move along a continuum from competition to cooperation and balance the tension between competition and cooperation. Too much competition due to high density in MLAs will cause the exit of partners with redundant ties, while too much cooperation in MLAs will lead to lock-in, strategic constraints, and eventually a merger of inseparable firms (Gudmundsson & Lechner, 2006).[1]

Rigidity (Das & Teng, 2000, p. 86) is defined "in terms of the degree of connectedness of members with each other in an ongoing relationship." While flexibility is an opposing force, freedom of action or loose coupling is usually considered integral to alliance formation. Firms start alliances as opposed to mergers to retain flexibility. Flexibility allows faster realignment of resources to take advantage of opportunities, but rigidity reduces coordination costs through stability and greater cohesion. From the perspective of the social network theory, firms should focus on opportunities generated by structural holes, but exercise a degree of closure to realize the value buried in the holes (Burt, 2001). This is best accomplished in a multilateral alliance by balancing flexibility and rigidity. MLAs increase rigidity as the connectedness among partners increases and cohesion through control escalates. The formalization of the MLA through a central organization increases rigidity and relational trust by regulating opportunistic behavior. The tension associated with too much rigidity, becoming tangled in one's own web or overembedded (Hagedoorn & Frankort, 2008), poses a real paradox for MLA partners, reinforcing their desire to balance rigidity and flexibility.

The third tension is between short-term and long-term orientation. The MLA, by nature of its central organization and required upfront investment, pushes firms to take the long view upon joining. The more relational features there are in the MLA the greater the relations-specific investment, the stronger the long-term orientation of the alliance. The directional arrows in Figure 6.1 show the movement along the three tensions when firms enter MLAs. Upon entry to the MLA, partners move in certain directions,

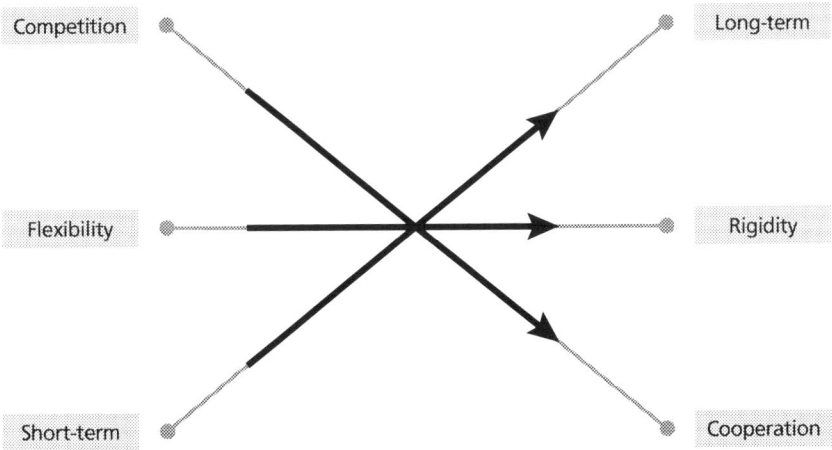

**Figure 6.1** Directional movement along the three tensions when entering MLA.

all of which increase the likely duration of attachment (Gudmundsson, 2011). However, this does not exclude the possibility of imbalance leading to instability. There is tension between common benefits and specific benefits, and MLAs are likely to move towards too much rigidity, too much cooperation, and lock-in unless managers maintain balance. MLAs are no different from any other type of alliance when it comes to exploiting opportunities, to leveraging unique resources to the maximum, and to maintaining enough strategic flexibility to exit if needed.

### Social Network Theory

We draw a parallel between social network theory (Barnes, 1954; Burt, 1992; Granovetter, 1973) and network opportunities and constraints to explain the link between MLA processes, the pursuit of opportunities, and structural holes and closure (Burt, 2001). Alliance processes can be described as the effective strengthening of alliance ties along a continuum between strong and weak ties (Granovetter, 1973). In the language of social network theory, a structural hole (Burt, 1992, 2001) represents an opportunity, an unserved sphere that can be exploited by brokering connections between actors. The theory has been applied to alliance networks that have weak ties and lack central organization. A central position in a network is not the same as central organization in an MLA that rather resembles network closure (Coleman, 1988). Little research exists that explains networks having traits of both closure and structural holes (Burt, 2001; Gudmundsson & Lechner, 2006). This poses a particularly interesting dynamic as firms can access opportunities embedded in structural holes across various levels and varying relational intensities within the boundaries of a single MLA. Such a group of firms is embedded in a closed network of common alliance processes with central organization, embedded in an alliance network of dyadic alliances (within the closed network), and the closed network in its entirety is embedded in the sum of all external transaction relations of the partner firms.

In an MLA, each partner occupies a central position characterized by weak to strong ties. The strong ties represent closure (Coleman, 1988) and the weak ties structural holes (Burt, 1992). Whereas strong ties represent high interaction, information flows, and mutual knowledge, they also imply greater redundancy as unique qualities are absorbed or suppressed by the group. Weak ties imply brokerage between unconnected positions in the network, and "the less one's contacts know and interact with each other, the more likely the information and knowledge available to these contacts will be non-redundant" (Moran, 2005, p. 1132). In other words, we can visualize each MLA partner as a doorkeeper between the inner and the outer world of interfirm relations. When managing the MLA, it is essential to keep the door open to both worlds and connect them to maintain constant stream of information about new opportunities.

## Embeddedness Theory

An embeddedness perspective (Baum & Dutton, 1996; Dacin, Ventresca & Beal, 1999; Granovetter, 1985; Polanyi, 1944) suggests that firms' actions are constrained on one hand by resource endowments and on the other hand by a network of relations. The concept of embeddedness in social networks comes from the simple observation that "most behavior is closely embedded in networks of inter-personal relations" (Granovetter, 1985, p. 504). The literature has examined the existence of embedded relations and how they create competitive advantage for firms and networks of firms (Granovetter, 1995; Gulati, 1995; Uzzi, 1997). Uzzi (1999, p. 482) defined embeddedness as "the degree to which commercial transactions take place through social relations and networks of relations that use exchange protocols associated with social, non-commercial attachments to govern business dealings." Alliance embeddedness, therefore, implies that actors are embedded in a network of enduring and repeated relations (Baum & Dutton, 1996; Burt, 1992; Dacin et al., 1999; Granovetter, 1992, 1985; Lomi, 1995).

The relational, positional, and structural constitute the usual embeddedness types considered to influence alliances (Gulati & Gargiulo, 1999). Relational embeddedness symbolizes cohesive ties between actors that channel information about capabilities and abilities of others (Gulati &

Gargiulo, 1999). Cohesive ties build trust and transparency and reduce uncertainty in existing and future partnerships (Burt & Knez 1995; Podolny, 1994). Positional embeddedness stands for the positional impact of the organization in the overall alliance network structure and decisions over new ties (Gulati & Gargiulo, 1999). This type of embeddedness encapsulates the system roles that actors occupy (Borgatti & Everett, 1994; Faust, 1988; Winship & Mandel, 1983). Structural embeddedness symbolizes the influence of relations around actors on their propensity to form relations with others (Granovetter, 1992; Gulati & Gargiulo, 1999). This type of embeddedness shifts the focus to groups of actors and to informal information channels (Gulati & Gargiulo, 1999).

Hagedoorn (2006) suggests that embeddedness traverses several levels depending on the social context surrounding partnerships: environmental, interorganizational, and dyadic. Overembeddedness takes place when actors are entrenched in their relational environment facing a reduced pool of potential new partners (Hagedoorn, 2006).

Based on the theoretical concepts we have covered so far in the chapter, we have the building blocks to conceptualize the structure and dynamics inherent in MLAs. In the section that follows we put forward a framework for MLAs and offer several derived propositions.

## A CONCEPTUAL FRAMEWORK OF MLAS

Firms engaged in MLA are embedded in interfirm relations on multiple levels, as shown in Figure 6.2. In the figure, solid lines denote relations links among firms $A$ through $X_i$, engaged in an MLA. The broken lines denote relations links outside the MLA, whereas the dotted rings show shared spheres, and solid rings denote proprietary (ego) spheres. $E$ denotes alliance relations within the MLA, and $E'_{ABCXi}$ ($i = 1 \ldots n$, partners, where $n > 2$) denotes a common sphere shared among all partners; $E_{AB} \ldots E_{CXi}$, denote dyadic shared spheres within the MLA. Dyadic links $E_{AC}$ and $E_{BXi}$ are omitted to symbolize the absence of structural holes between some partners; that is, all possible links will never be exploited. And $e$ denotes proprietary transaction partners; $e'_a \ldots e'_{xi}$ denote proprietary transaction partners shared in the alliance; $e_A \ldots e_{Xi}$, denote proprietary transaction partners not shared. Each relations layer is embedded ($\subseteq$ = subset of) in another until we reach the set of all possible relations in society ($E' \subseteq E \subseteq (e + e') \subseteq$ society). Interaction effects between MLA layers become more complex as the relations set becomes larger, but the intensity of relations becomes stronger as the relations set becomes smaller.

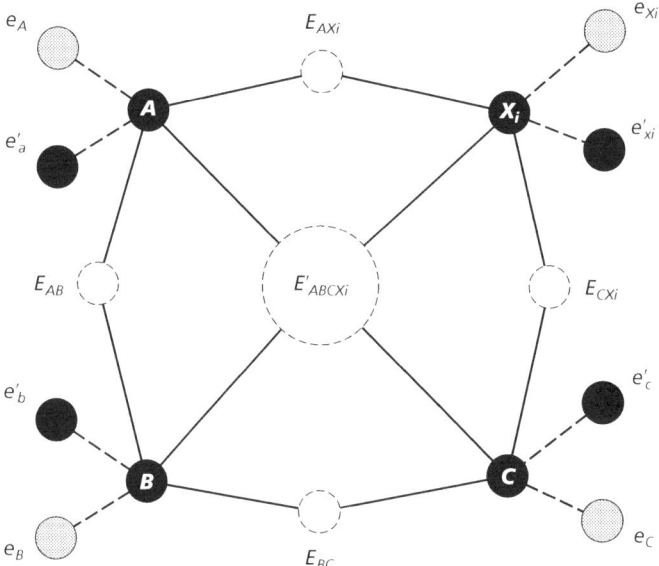

**Figure 6.2** A model of multilevel embeddedness in MLA. *Notes:* Solid lines denote relations links among firms $A \ldots X_i$, embedded in a multilateral alliance; broken lines denote relations links outside MLA; dotted rings show shared spheres; solid rings show proprietary (ego) spheres; $E$ ($E > 2$) = alliance relations within MLA; $i = 1 \ldots n$, partners; $e$ = proprietary (ego) transaction partners outside MLA; $e'_a \ldots e'_{xi}$ = proprietary (ego) transaction partners shared in MLA; $e_A \ldots e_{Xi}$, = proprietary (ego) transaction partners not shared in MLA; $E_{AB} \ldots E_{CXi}$ = dyadic relations within MLA (dyadic links $E_{AC}$, and $E_{BXi}$ are omitted to symbolize absence of structural holes); $E'_{ABCXi}$ = common relations within MLA. Multilevel embeddedness is denoted as ($E' \subseteq E \subseteq (e + e') \subseteq S$), where $\subseteq$ = subset of, and $S$ = society or set of all possible relations.

## Alliance Tensions and Proprietary Assets

The sharing of proprietary assets in MLAs can create an exit barrier if firms fear that ownership or uniqueness of the assets will become indistinct due to common alliance processes.[2] Thus, the propensity to enter an MLA increases if proprietary assets are either not shared at all or ring-fenced before sharing takes place. Ring-fencing means setting clear use and ownership rules: for example, who owns new or promiscuous customers?

Lazzarini (2008) argued that firms with extensive outside ties would have less commitment to the MLA, and sparseness would increase investment in formalization. We, however, argue that it is not the size of the external network that matters but the degree to which MLA partners can build and control proprietary assets embedded in the external network. Selective sharing may strengthen MLAs by balancing the tensions between flexibility and rigidity, cooperation and competition, increasing partner's commitment to low-intensity common alliance processes. In this regard, there must be a clear distinction between, on one hand, commitment to the MLA in its entirety and, on the other hand, commitment to common alliance processes. We can assume that the attraction of new partners to an MLA depends on potential exit costs. Since surprises are possible in any alliance, transaction networks and any unique resources need to be protected and tensions balanced.[3] Going to the extreme, being too cooperative straight-jackets the firm and leads to lock-in. A firm may want such an outcome, but that would be an exception rather than a rule.[4]

Multiple centers of gravity in MLA create opportunities for partners to mix or match resources, to exploit structural holes. Partners do not only exploit structural holes in the common sphere ($E_{ABCXi}$) but also in various dyadic spheres ($E_{AB} \ldots E_{CXi}$, $e_a \ldots e_{xi}$, $e_A \ldots e_{Xi}$). Shared spheres denote bridging of structural holes, exploitation of opportunities enabled by each partner's unique resources. The ability to exploit various relational spheres within an MLA balances alliance tensions (Das & Teng, 2000), containing potential instability. An MLA only focusing on the common sphere ($E_{ABCXi}$) would be considered too rigid and cooperative. Likewise, an MLA focusing only on the dyadic spheres and neglecting the common sphere would be considered too flexible and competitive.

Research has shown that the extensiveness of alliance features (number of different resources joined together between the various partners) increases duration (Gudmundsson, 2011; Gudmundsson & Rhoades, 2001).[5] In other words, an MLA containing many relational spheres embedded over several levels is a quintessence of balancing tensions. In MLAs the flexibility to enter and exit external and internal dyadic spheres in the pursuit of opportunities enhances partners' ability to develop and maintain competitive advantage.[6] Thus, MLA partners should enter and exit external and internal dyadic spheres more freely in the pursuit of opportunities than in a common sphere.

**Proposition 1a:** *Partners engaged in MLAs who are liberated to exploit multilevel embedded relational spheres perceive more balance between competition and cooperation and are less likely to defect (long-term orientation).*

**Proposition 1b:** *Partners engaged in MLAs sharing fewer assets in the common sphere and more assets in dyadic spheres perceive more balance between rigidity and flexibility and are less likely to defect (long-term orientation).*

**Proposition 1c:** *Partners engaged in an MLA who are liberated to exploit multilevel embedded relational spheres, entering and exiting external and internal dyadic spheres in the pursuit of opportunities, are more likely to enjoy competitive advantage and are less likely to defect (long-term orientation).*

## Structural Holes, Network Position and Partner Variety

McEvily and Zaheer (1999) pointed out that a network with a high ratio of structural holes can be a source of competitive advantage by providing ideas, knowledge and opportunities—we draw a parallel with this analogy. Thus, the higher the ratio of non-redundant ties within the MLA, the more value creating is the overall alliance for firms in central positions (Burt, 1992; Granovetter, 1974, 1985) and for partners having non-central but valuable positional assets attractive to bridge structural holes. The position of an actor within an alliance is an opportunity or a constraint. The more central an actor's position, the greater is his or her ability to exploit opportunities (Burt, 1992).

We draw parallel with recent organization- and management-related studies of networks, emphasizing that some network positions generate fewer constraints than others and have better access to information and resources (Burt, 1992; Salancik, 1995). Firms can aim to maximize non-redundant ties by entering partners with non-redundant ties and exit partners with redundant ties: the greater the number of partners with largely redundant ties, the more intensive the competition between partners—for example, for the same customers. The more non-occupied structural holes within a network, the greater will be the positional strength of partners possessing such opportunities. This leads us to conclude that from an ego perspective, firms should maximize positional strength in MLAs even if that means defection and occasional rearrangement between different MLAs. Therefore, partner variety rather than partner homogeneity matters. To put it differently, MLAs with high degree of partner variety has structural holes best exploited through flexible dyadic spheres. Likewise, partners lacking variety, having many redundant ties, may have positional strength in another MLA. These dynamics may facilitate MLA processes by generating superior firm-specific and customer value.

If benefits can be derived from complementary assets that are inaccessible outside the dyad, it strengthens ties. Strong ties are characterized by frequency and duration of interaction leading to sharing and exchanging of important resources (Lomi, 1997). However, partners commanding superior faculty will not share entire transaction networks with inferior partners as uniqueness is a strategic asset, a source of competitive advantage. Thus, in MLAs with large number of structural holes, dyadic ties will be formed on the basis of complementary assets to fill the holes. Thus, exclusive dyads in MLA may mean direct benefit for some partners and indirect benefits for other partners. For example, B and C (see Figure 6.2) have a direct interface to serve customers; A and B also have direct interface to serve customers; however, A and C have indirect interface through B to provide service to A's customers requiring to pass through B to C. Since this is rare for A's customers the cost of a direct interface between A and C is higher than sharing the indirect interface through B. In other words, B becomes a broker that saves A transaction costs with C.

There is a dark side to dyadic ties in MLAs, namely their potential to block common MLA processes. MLA partners engaged in an advantageous exclusive dyadic sphere may resist common alliance processes that attempt to internalize their unique position for the good of all, raising alliance exit costs. Exit costs rise because of the tradeoff between MLA uniqueness and individual firm uniqueness. Retaining strategic flexibility revolves around keeping alliance exit barriers down despite of harmonization processes. On the expectation of high exit costs, a partner might be in a better position outside the MLA or in another MLA. A partner in a central position may gain from high intensity (high sunk costs and reversal costs) commonalities acting as lock-in, by internalizing other's unique resources, and control partners in non-central positions. Therefore, the stronger role various dyadic ties play in a multilateral alliance, the greater will be the resistance to move towards high intensity common alliance processes.[7]

**Proposition 2:** *Partners' variety in an MLA facilitates the exploitation of structural holes but impedes high intensity common alliance processes (closure), reinforcing positional strength of individual partners.*

## Multilevel Embeddedness

Different levels of embeddedness can be identified within MLA. At the lowest level (above society, the total set of all possible relations) we find transaction networks (arms-length relations), then alliance networks, and at the highest level MLA relations, with the strength of ties increasing from level to level (see Table 6.2).

Whereas multilevel embeddedness opens up a larger network of structural holes, it also invites constraints as each member must reconcile consequences of own actions on others, more so at a high embeddedness level than at a low level. In other words, the stronger the ties, the more embedded and constrained the action potential is with regard to other partners. Participating in an MLA reduces the flexibility of partners to explore the full transaction network. A growing MLA with increased density (unless

**TABLE 6.2  Multilevel Embeddedness in Multilateral Alliances**

| Embeddedness | Denotation[a] | Relations Type | Tensions | Spheres |
|---|---|---|---|---|
| Level 3 ($E'$) $\subseteq$[b] | $E'_{ABCXi}$ | Multilateral (MLA) | Rigid/cooperative/long-term | Common sphere |
| Level 2 ($E$) $\subseteq$ | $E_{AB} \ldots E_{CXi}$ | Dyadic (MLA) | Rigid/cooperative/medium-term | Dyadic sphere |
| Level 1 ($e + e'$) $\subseteq$ | $e_a \ldots e_{Xi}$ | Transaction network external not-shared | Flexible/competitive/short-term | Dyadic sphere |
| $S$ | $e'_a \ldots e'_{Xi}$ | Transaction network external shared | Flexible/competitive/short-term | Dyadic sphere |

[a] See Figure 6.2 for explanations.
[b] $\subseteq$ = subset-of.

fixed number of partners) will involve more territorial overlaps and more compromises, eventually greatly reducing the action potential of partners.

Overembeddedness, being trapped in one's own net, leads to inflexibility—in other words, constraints (Gargiulo & Benassi, 2000; Uzzi, 1997). We draw a parallel with this notion in how MLA partners are embedded on several levels, and over time the higher levels, the more constraining ones, are likely to play a greater role through steadily increasing relational intensity. However, each level implies both opportunities and constraints, and the overall balance of the two determines the overall value of belonging to the MLA.

**Proposition 3:** *Partners' higher level embeddedness will become more constraining as alliance processes strengthen ties over time, and the ability to bridge structural holes at the lower levels diminishes due to increased alliance density, leading to reduced positional strength of individual partners.*

## CONCLUSION

In the chapter we have proposed a conceptual framework for understanding multilateral alliances (MLAs) that involve common alliance processes, dyadic ties, and external transaction networks. Such alliances involve great complexity due to the nature of their multilevel embeddedness. MLAs emphasize a degree of commonality among partners to provide integrated products and services across firm boundaries yet multilevel embeddedness inhibits partners from going beyond low-intensity commonalities to manage exit barriers.

MLA partners in a central position can use common alliance processes to raise exit barriers for weaker partners and exercise control over them. Thus MLA managers need to balance a complex set of tensions to derive benefits at the same time that strategic flexibility is maintained. In other words, MLA partners need to balance the benefits derived from the heterogeneity of resources and the homogeneity of MLA products and services, rather than one exclusive of another. Partner variety increases the propensity to exploit structural holes, which can be both a dyadic and MLA relational opportunity. However, the more important the external transaction networks as proprietary asset the higher the perceived risk of sharing the asset in the MLA. To put it differently, the more crucial the firms in the external transaction network to a partner's competitive advantage, the lower the action potential on common alliance processes.

From a management viewpoint, MLAs need to be understood as complex relationship networks spanning multiple levels: external, dyadic, and multilateral. This research suggests a conceptual framework that results in a better understanding of partner behavior vis-à-vis harmonization of alliance processes. It tells us how sharing of proprietary assets and the progression of common alliance processes can act as barrier to exit for firms, a concern for firms wanting to enter the MLA. However, in a situation where MLA is covering several distinctive areas of cooperation, separation of proprietary assets and partner management of specific cooperation features becomes a boundary choice question. If the benefit of the alliance relationship is superior to not entering the alliance, yet the risk associated with lock-in is high, then it is necessary to ring-fence proprietary assets. By the same token, if firms contemplating to join MLA are free to exploit opportunities generated by multilevel embeddedness and can broker between external and internal ties, sharing the external transaction network is less likely to pose a perceived exit barrier, but may still pose a threat to high-intensity common alliance processes.

Finally, in MLA there is an inherent paradox: namely, the level of perceived entry barriers are reflected in the level of perceived exit barriers. In other words, low exit barriers facilitate alliance formation but act as an inhibitor for progressively stronger common alliance processes. This is because progressive increase in common processes increases sunk costs, inherent in the sharing of proprietary assets, facilitating alliance lock-in. In other words, there is an important tradeoff between firm and MLA uniqueness, requiring difficult management choices as MLA relations progress over time.

## NOTES

1. One can also see the possibility of a domino effect if one partner declares bankruptcy and other closely tied partners face the same fate unless the bankrupt firm is overtaken or merged to salvage common assets.
2. This was demonstrated when Austrian Airlines left Qualiflyer for Star Alliance and had no FFP program on its own as Qualiflyer had merged all into one.

Although each airline may have ownership of customer data records, other MLA airlines could theoretically access those records after any one airline left the alliance.
3. Small alliance groupings with limited opportunities: EQA, Atlantic Excellence, Global Excellence, and Qualiflyer Group all collapsed because key members defected to competing groupings with larger membership and grander global vision. The first three had limited coverage and the last one was dense employing an equity investment strategy in partners to retain control and prevent defection.
4. This would probably have been the outcome if the Alcazar project had come about, a 1993 proposal to tie up and then merge Austrian Airlines, KLM, Scandinavian Airlines System (SAS) and Swissair. The first known merger from within an MLA (oneworld) was the merger between British Airways and Iberia.
5. Having experienced a collapse of previous alliances by defecting partners, Swissair wanted to prevent this happening in their Qualiflyer Group by taking equity investment in all the partners. This strategy ran the company to the ground and failed to build a globally attractive alliance, to which type the previous partners defected.
6. The largest most, disperse multilateral airline alliance, STAR, has had turnover of up to 55% higher per employee compared to the next MLA. Being concerned about network linkages and passenger flow potentials, STAR had also about 40% more passengers per employee compared to the next MLA. STAR alliance has also the highest market share on three key transcontinental corridors out of four: Europe–Asia Pacific; N. America–Asia; and Europe–N. America.
7. High intensity alliance processes would denote, for example, the creation of central platforms for information systems, without which the firm could not operate.

## REFERENCES

Anderson, J. C., Hakansson, H., & Johanson, J. (1994). Dyadic business relationships within a business network context. *Journal of Marketing, 58*(4), 1–15.

Barnes, J. (1954). Class and committees in a Norwegian island parish. *Human Relations, 7,* 39–58.

Baum, J. C., & Dutton, J. E. (1996). Introduction: The embeddedness of strategy. *Advances in Strategic Management, 13,* 1–15.

Borgatti, S. P., & Everett, M. G. (1994). Ecological and perfect colorings. *Social Networks, 16,* 43–55.

Burt, R. S. (1992). *Structural holes.* Cambridge, MA: Harvard University Press.

Burt, R. S. (2001). Structural holes versus network closure as social capital. In N. Lin, K. S. Cook, & R. S. Burt (Eds.), *Social capital: Theory and research* (pp. 31–56). New York, NY: Aldine de Gruyter.

Burt, R. S., & Knez, M. (1995). Kinds of third-party effects on trust. *Rationality and Society, 7,* 255–292.

Coleman, J. S. (1988). Social capital in the creation of human capital. *American Journal of Sociology, 94*, 95–120.
Coleman, J. S. (1990). *Foundations of social theory.* Cambridge, MA: Harvard University.
Dacin, M. T., Ventresca, M. J., & Beal, B. D. (1999). The embeddedness of organizations: Dialogue & directions. *Journal of Management, 25*, 317–356.
Das, T. K., & Teng, B. (2000). Instabilities of strategic alliances: An internal tensions perspective. *Organization Science, 11*, 77–101.
Das, T. K., & Teng, B. (2002). Alliance constellations: A social exchange perspective. *Academy of Management Review, 27*, 445–456.
De Rond, M., & Bouchikhi, H. (2004). On the dialectics of strategic alliances. *Organization Science, 15*, 56–69.
Doz, Y. L. & Hamel, G. (1998). *Alliance advantage.* Boston, MA: Harvard Business School Press.
Emerson, R. M. (1981). Social exchange theory. In M. Rosenberg & R. H. Turner (Eds.), *Social psychology: Sociological perspectives* (pp. 30–65). New York, NY: Basic Books.
Faust, K. (1988). Comparison of methods for positional analysis: Structural and general equivalences. *Social Networks, 10*, 313–341.
Gargiulo, M., & Benassi, M. (2000). Trapped in your own net? Network cohesion, structural holes, and the adaptations of social capital. *Organization Science, 11* 183–196.
Gomes-Casseres, B. (1996). *The alliance revolution: The new shape of business rivalry.* Cambridge, MA: Harvard University Press.
Gomes-Casseres, B. (2004). Competing in alliance constellations: A primer for managers. In M. A. Trick (Ed.), *Global corporate evolution: Looking inward or looking outward?* (pp. 43–52). Pittsburgh, PA: Carnegie Mellon Press.
Granovetter, M. (1973). The strength of weak ties. *American Journal of Sociology, 78*, 1360–1380.
Granovetter, M. (1974). *Getting a job: A study of contacts and careers.* Cambridge, MA: Harvard University Press.
Granovetter, M. (1985). Economic action and social structure: The problem of embeddedness. *American Journal of Sociology, 91*, 481–510.
Granovetter, M. (1992). Problems of explanation in economic sociology. In N. Nohria & R. Eccles (Eds.), *Networks and organizations: Structures, form and action* (pp. 25–56). Boston, MA: Harvard Business School Press.
Granovetter, M. (1995). The economic sociology of firms and entrepreneurs. In A. Portes (Ed.), *The economic sociology of immigration* (pp. 128–165). New York, NY: Russell Sage Foundation.
Gudmundsson, S. V. (2011). An empirical test of the internal tensions perspective of strategic alliances. In T. K. Das (Ed.), *Behavioral perspectives on strategic alliances* (pp. 157–174). Charlotte, NC: Information Age Publishing.
Gudmundsson, S. V., de Boer, E. R. & Lechner, C., (2002). Integrating frequent flyer programs in multilateral airline alliances. *Journal of Air Transport Management, 8*, 409–417.

Gudmundsson, S. V., & Lechner, C. (2006). Multilateral airline alliances: Balancing strategic constraints and opportunities. *Journal of Air Transport Management 12*, 153–158.

Gudmundsson, S. V., & Rhoades, D. (2001). Airline alliance survival analysis: Typology, strategy and duration. *Transport Policy, 8*, 209–218.

Gulati, R. (1995). Social structure and alliance formation patterns: A longitudinal analysis. *Administrative Science Quarterly, 40*, 619–652.

Gulati, R., & Gargiulo, M. (1999). Where do interorganizational networks come from? *American Journal of Sociology, 104*, 1439–1493.

Hagedoorn, J. (2006). Understanding the cross-level embeddedness of interfirm partnership formation. *Academy of Management Review, 31*, 670–680.

Hagedoorn, J., & Frankort, H. T. W. (2008). The gloomy side of embeddedness: The effects of overembeddedness on inter-firm partnership formation. *Advances in Strategic Management, 25*, 503–530.

Khanna, T., Gulati, R., & Nohria, N. (1998). The dynamics of learning alliances: Competition, cooperation and relative scope. *Strategic Management Journal, 19*, 193–210.

Lazzarini, S. G. (2007). The impact of membership in competing alliance constellations: Evidence on the operational performance of global airlines. *Strategic Management Journal, 28*, 345–367

Lazzarini, S. G. (2008). The transition from alliance networks to multilateral alliances in the global airline industry. *Brazilian Administrative Review, 5*(1), 19–36.

Lomi, A. (1995). The population ecology of organizational founding: Location dependence and unobserved heterogeneity. *Administrative Science Quarterly, 40*, 111–144.

Lomi, A. (1997). Markets with hierarchies and network structure of organizational communities. *Journal of Management and Governance 1*(1), 49–66.

McEvily, B., & Zaheer, A. (1999). Bridging ties: A source of firm heterogeneity in competitive capabilities. *Strategic Management Journal, 20*, 1133–1156.

Moran, P. (2005). Structural vs. relational embeddedness: Social capital and managerial performance. *Strategic Management Journal, 26*, 1129–1151.

Podolny, J. (1994). Market uncertainty and the social character of economic exchange. *Administrative Science Quarterly, 39*, 458–483.

Polanyi, K. (1944). *The great transformation.* New York, NY: Rinehart.

Richardson, G. (1972). The organization of industry. *Economic Journal, 82*, 883–896.

Salancik, G. R. (1995). Wanted: A good network theory of organization. *Administrative Science Quarterly, 40*, 345–349.

Uzzi, B. (1997). Social structure and competition in interfirm networks: The paradox of embeddedness. *Administrative Science Quarterly, 42*, 35–67.

Uzzi, B. (1999). Embeddedness in the making of financial capital: How social relations and networks benefit firms seeking financing. *American Sociological Review, 64*, 481–505.

Vanhaverbeke, W., & Noorderhaven, N. G. (2001). Competition between alliance blocks: The case of the RISC-microprocessor technology. *Organization Studies, 22*, 1–30.

Whetten, D. (1981). Interorganizational relations: A review of the field. *Journal of Higher Education, 52,* 1–28.

Winship, C., & Mandel, N. J. (1983). Roles and positions: A critique and extension of the blockmodeling approach. In S. Leinhardt (Ed.), *Sociological Methodology 1983–1984* (pp. 314–344). San Francisco, CA: Jossey-Bass.

Yoshino, M. Y., & Rangan, U. S. (1995). *Strategic alliances: An entrepreneurial approach to globalization.* Boston, MA: Harvard Business School Press.

CHAPTER 7

# INTERPARTNER DYNAMICS IN ASYMMETRIC STRATEGIC ALLIANCES

## The Role of Interpersonal Networks

Annabelle Jaouen, Olivier Meier,
and Audrey Missonier

### ABSTRACT

The purpose of this chapter is to examine how asymmetric firms can achieve a balanced interorganizational relationship. It identifies the interpersonal dynamics that influence the relationship by focusing on a key period in the process of building a strategic alliance: negotiation. The negotiation process is characterized by differences in interests and power, the importance of context, and the individual or collective external actors who intervene in the process. We use a case study in the web industry and analyze the negotiations between two partners from a chronological and longitudinal perspective. Pre-alliance negotiation concerns four types of control issues: relational (based on trust), contractual, equity, and managerial. Moreover, several factors influence this process: the respective resources of the partners, their relative sizes, and the possibility of alternative solutions. This chapter focuses on a longitudinal case study of two asymmetric firms, X Telecom (320 employees) and Web Interactive (12 employees), which are direct competitors but using different technologies. Their activity is the development of web-based tools for decision making. Several methods are combined: immersion in Web Interactive over the entire process (19 months), 202 days of observation (participative and nonparticipative), 52 semi-directive interviews with employees and the main negotiators, and the analysis of 53 official documents concerning the alliance process. The case shows several stages: the failure of the first negotiation, a negotiation between X Telecom and the main competitor of Web Interactive, and a second successful negotiation between the two firms. Although the competitor of Web Interactive had a better technology, we show that informal variables such as shared social networks, past working relationships, and cultural proximity provided Web Interactive with the means to negotiate effectively with X Telecom and establish a balanced strategic alliance.

## INTRODUCTION

Asymmetric alliances are usually characterized by the domination of one partner by the other, and recent research shows that asymmetric alliances tend to favor opportunistic behavior (Das & Rahman, 2010). In certain cases, however, asymmetric firms can achieve a balanced interorganizational relationship. In this chapter, we identify the interpersonal dynamics that influence the relationship by focusing on a key period in the process: negotiation. The negotiation process is characterized by differences in interests and power, the importance of context, and the individual and collective external actors who intervene in the process.

Through a chronological and longitudinal approach, this chapter analyzes the negotiations between two asymmetric firms in the web industry, X Telecom (320 employees) and Web Interactive (12 employees), which are direct competitors but using different technologies. The negotiation process comprised three stages, and for each one we focus on the role of interpersonal networks and dynamics: the failure of the first negotiation, a negotiation between X Telecom and the main competitor of Web Interactive, and a second successful negotiation between the two firms. Although the competitor of Web Interactive had a better technology, we show that informal variables such as shared social networks, past working relationships, and cultural proximity provided Web Interactive with the means to negotiate effectively with X Telecom and establish a balanced strategic alliance.

## BACKGROUND ON INTERORGANIZATIONAL NEGOTIATION

Negotiation is a process that requires discussions between parties in order to reduce their differences and arrive at a mutual agreement (Carnevale & Pruitt, 1992). In the case of a potential alliance, the pre-alliance negotiation serves to determine the control issues. Indeed, this particular form of negotiation is carried out by top management, as the outcome is likely to profoundly modify the future of the respective companies.

In order to optimally manage and reduce risk in the alliance process, the partners need to be sensitive to the interrelationships of trust, control, and risk (Das & Teng, 2001). Four types of control issues tend to arise in strategic alliance negotiations. First, contractual control is based on clauses that guarantee the possibility of legal action. Second, relational control is based on the trust that emerges through repetitive interactions between the partners. Trust is a key factor of success in building strategic alliances (Das & Teng, 1998, 2001; Gulati, 1995). In the context of cooperation between partners, Das and Teng (1998, p. 491) define it as "a firm's perceived level of certainty that its partner firm will pursue mutually compatible interests in the alliance, rather than act opportunistically." The authors explain that the feeling of confidence is based on trust and a sense of control. The negotiation process is thus a period during which future partners can build this necessary confidence (Mockler & Gartenfeld, 2001) and achieve a unique and shared identity, which will ultimately become the identity of the alliance. Third, equity control is exerted through majority interests. Last, managerial control can be implemented by placing one's own executives in the partner firm and/or by integrating the information systems.

Several factors influence the pre-alliance negotiation: the relative size of the partners, the resources each possesses, and the possibility of alternative solutions. First, big enterprises usually have greater negotiating power when constructing alliances with small companies, notably because they can more easily make use of experts to guide and advise them (Gulbro & Herbig, 1996). Second, the possession of more critical resources confers greater negotiating power (Harrigan, 1986). Third, having alternative solutions influences the negotiations because the negotiator with at least one alternative knows that he or she can always choose other arrangements or other partners to achieve company objectives (Inkpen & Beamish, 1997). Das and Kumar (2011) identify four types of interpartner negotiating strategies: problem solving, contending, yielding, and compromising, and three stages in the alliance development process: formation, operation, and outcome. Yet, although the negotiation phase is acknowledged to be critical to the success of the alliance, few researchers have focused on it. Among them, Marks and Mirvis (2001) show that the negotiation process can explain merger and acquisition failures. They particularly focus on the complexity of financially assessing the partner and conclude that this is the main factor of failure. Strauss (1992) demonstrates the importance of focusing attention on the evolution of the negotiation.

A major reason for the paucity of research on the negotiation phase is the lack of sufficient data, as collecting information on the chronology of pre-alliance negotiations has proven to be quite difficult. For legal and competitive reasons, pre-alliance negotiations are often confidential. Researchers thus face two problems: their status as researchers within the firms and gaining access to sensitive information (Schmidt & Rühli, 2002). Yet the transcripts of oral discussions between negotiators are much more relevant to the analysis than the review of documents and newspaper articles (Druckman, 2002). In this case study, we were able to collect salient data through participative observation (Hopman, 2002) (writing up the minutes of key meetings) and nonparticipative observation over 19 months of immersion in Web Interactive. We attended all formal meetings related to the negotiations and conducted semi-structured interviews with 52 stakeholders (shareholders, negotiators, employees, etc.).

## A CHRONOLOGICAL SURVEY OF A NEGOTIATION PROCESS BETWEEN ASYMMETRIC PARTNERS

### Description of the Strategic Alliance Case

The market for Web Interactive and X Telecom is web-based tools for decision making and website audience measurement. This market is dominated by four domestic companies (including X Telecom and Web Interactive). Three of them are small firms that have developed powerful tools and maintained their market share.

Two types of tools are developed by these firms. The two types are based on very different criteria and do not take into account the same decision parameters. One is an "onboard" audience measure (technology based on the website) and the other is an "offshore" measure (technology based on the user). X Telecom has been the French market leader in offshore technology for the last 20 years. The company has more than 320 employees and makes a profit of about 2 to 3% per year, most of which is reinvested to improve services. In order to maintain its brand image and reputation, X Telecom wants to become the key player in onboard technology in addition to its offshore technology. After three years of internal effort and a high level of investment, its onboard technology is still criticized by customers, who have complained of the delay in publishing the data. Thus, to become the market leader, X Telecom needs greater technological knowhow and must make a

**TABLE 7.1 Strategic and Organizational Characteristics of the Partners**

|  | X Telecom | Web Interactive |
|---|---|---|
| Aims | 1. Benefit from the knowhow and technology of Web Interactive; however, Protic is likely to meet this specific need.<br>2. Renew, regenerate: Benefit from the dynamism and responsiveness of the start-up business model. | 1. Survival: the aim is to achieve a critical size and financial balance.<br>2. Sustainability: the combination of the two technologies is a strategic project for Web Interactive. |
| Critical resources | Only firm to control and develop the "offshore" technology on the market | Total mastery of "onboard" technology, although certain direct competitors also master and sell this technology. |
| Size and financial power | • 320 employees<br>• The stakeholders are media companies<br>• High economic and financial weight<br>• Profitable company | • 12 employees<br>• The stakeholders are employees<br>• Low economic and financial weight<br>• Unprofitable company |

choice: either to continue its strategy of in-house development (its research and development [R&D] budget will cover this) or to acquire the technology of one of its competitors through a strategic alliance (X Telecom has a choice between its two main competitors: Web Interactive and Protic).

Founded in 1998, Web Interactive develops and markets the onboard technology for companies in the web industry. Its technology is widely recognized on the market for its high reliability (see Table 7.1). However, despite technological advances and the development of specific expertise in key technical areas, the company has not yet achieved financial balance. In addition to being unprofitable, it faces growing competition in this sector, which is a distinct threat to its survival. The only recourse for Web Interactive at this point is to form an alliance with one of its competitors, as it lacks the financial resources to continue internal development (difficulty finding investors on the Internet market, and refusal of shareholders to invest more money). This situation has prompted Web Interactive to consider an alliance with its biggest rival on the market: X Telecom.

## Method

First, we collected data in three phases: exploratory, in-depth, and control phases. During these three stages, several collection methods were employed:

- Nonparticipative observation: 202 days of observation over a period of 19 months (these observations were frequently the subject of informal discussions with key negotiators)
- Participative observation: writing up the minutes of 16 executive committee meetings and participation in five general meetings
- 52 interviews with major stakeholders in the organization and the chief negotiators: founders; shareowners; executive committee members; technical, commercial, and marketing staff; two lawyers; an auditor; and a public accountant
- Collection of 53 documents: official alliance documents (memorandum of understanding, shareholder agreement), internal documents (financial and commercial reports, notes, etc.), and external documents (newspaper articles)

Second, for data coding, Miles and Huberman (1994) recommend preprocessing the collected documents before the final analysis. We therefore summarized each of the collected documents and transcribed interviews using their protocol (Miles & Huberman, 1994), namely by (1) locating the document in context, (2) explaining its scope, and (3) providing a brief summary of its contents. We also constructed a monograph to reduce the collected data and retain only those data necessary for the historical understanding of the observed phenomenon. We used ATLAS/TI software, which was specifically developed for qualitative research. The first step consisted of defining categories ("test list," Miles & Huberman, 1994, p. 114). The test list was applied to the raw data and then carefully examined to improve the relevance (matching the field data) and power (for a return to the literature). We then constructed "first level" codes to describe the negotiation process between X Telecom and Web Interactive. The following are examples of the codes:

- size of the partner: Tai-Part
- market power: Pv-March
- technology: Techno
- position: Position
- interests and objectives of the merger: Int-Obj
- alternatives: Alter

Sixteen codes were defined on the basis of our conceptual framework. The initial results revealed the dynamics of the negotiation process and the influences of the two parties but did not provide explanations.

Thus, we performed a second round of coding by analyzing the data using a different approach. This step took into account the perceptions, feelings, and influences of the negotiators during the pre-alliance process.

We therefore proceeded from first-level coding to "thematic coding" or "meta-codes" (Miles & Huberman, 1994). As recommended by the authors, the thematic codes emerged from the data ("extension") and were then linked to the literature ("linking") on social networks. The definition of our codes for each category thus emerged from an interaction between data and theory (Miles & Huberman, 1994).

## Chronology of the Negotiation and Alliance Construction

From the first meetings in February 2005 to the official signing of the alliance in June, several stages of negotiations occurred, punctuated by unexpected situations and the intervention of many actors. The main events during the negotiation process are presented in chronological order in Table 7.2.

**TABLE 7.2   Chronology of Pre-Alliance Negotiation**

| Date | Events | Description |
|---|---|---|
| February 2005 | First meeting between Web Interactive and X Telecom | The two cofounders of Web Interactive decide to meet the Internet manager of X Telecom and agree to provide him with strategic and confidential information (economic and financial balance sheet of the company, customer portfolio, etc.). X Telecom wants to control onboard technology. The discussions focus on the possible modalities for a partnership. |
| March 2005 | Negotiations stop | The cofounders of Web Interactive and the Internet manager of X Telecom realize they have different visions of the market and strategic priorities. The meeting ends in failure. |
| November 2005 | X Telecom meets other alliance candidates (notably Protic) | Protic is highly regarded in the market for its technology and business strategy. It has the largest client portfolio of all the competitors. |
| January 16, 2006 | X Telecom recruits a new Internet manager | His mission is to make X Telecom's product reliable, using state of the art high-tech. He is a former colleague of the Web Interactive owners. |
| February 2006 | X Telecom reconnects with Web Interactive | Two main reasons:<br>• The Web Interactive owners know the new Internet manager.<br>• X Telecom is continuing negotiations with Protic. |
| February 2006 | X Telecom asks Protic to exchange information | X Telecom wishes to reduce the asymmetry of information and pursue the negotiations with Protic in a more formal and official way. |

*(continued)*

### TABLE 7.2  Chronology of Pre-Alliance Negotiation (continued)

| Date | Events | Description |
|---|---|---|
| March 2006 | Negotiations stop between X Telecom and Protic | Protic hesitates to communicate sensitive and confidential information. The companies do not share the same strategic priorities and market perceptions. |
| April 4, 2006 | Resumption of negotiations between Web Interactive and X Telecom | Web Interactive is chosen as a partner for several reasons:<br>• "Affectio societatis."<br>• Strategic assets: the convergence of onboard and offshore technologies and the potential synergies.<br>• Complementary businesses and target markets. |
| April 2006 | X Telecom audits Web Interactive | The aim is to reassure the X Telecom stakeholders on the continuation of the alliance process (use of audits). The actors of Web Interactive explain that they have nothing to hide. They wish to be transparent. |
| May 2006 | Failure of the negotiation | X Telecom wants a complete buyout of Web Interactive, which refuses the deal. |
|  | Willingness to continue the negotiations | The negotiators express their willingness to find a common agreement. |
| June 11, 2006 | Signing of a Memorandum of Understanding between Web Interactive et X Telecom | X Telecom acquires 50% of the equity of Web Interactive.<br>• Capital increase of Web Interactive.<br>• Concession on the use of the X Telecom brand name.<br>Establishment of a steering committee (two members from each company). |

The alliance is formalized by two reciprocal acts: (1) X Telecom acquires 50% of the equity of Web Interactive via a capital increase and (2) X Telecom brings its goodwill through its web activity.

The chronological analysis of the negotiation process of X Telecom and Web Interactive shows three main stages:

- In the beginning, asymmetry in favor of X Telecom, in terms of economic and financial power and size (turnover, staff, organizational structure)
- The decision of X Telecom to continue negotiations with Web Interactive and stop those initiated with Protic, although the latter seem more likely to meet the strategic and technological expectations of the company
- A balanced final agreement, whereas in the beginning of the negotiation process X Telecom had a strong influence on Web Interactive

## ANALYSIS OF THE PROCESS: THE ROLE OF INTERPERSONAL NETWORKS

In this type of asymmetric situation, the literature assumes that the imbalance between the parties is likely to be expressed by the conclusion of an "unbalanced" contract in terms of value or power, to the detriment of the smaller company (Lasbordes, 2000). However, the relationship presented here does not support the literature. Most of the research on interorganizational negotiation has focused either on the formal process of negotiation (analysis of economic, strategic and technological conditions) or the sources of power (possession of critical resources, firm size, economic weight, etc.). But the factors that explain the negotiation between Web Interactive and X Telecom were not found in the formal processes or in the sources of power. The role of social networks was thus examined.

A link can be established between the course of the negotiation process and the social relationships maintained by the main players. According to the concept of social networks, objectives may be more easily reached if an organization has built a network of contacts beyond the more traditional available resources (financial, physical skills).

### The Influence of Social Capital on the Beginning of the Negotiation Process

Bourdieu (1992) defines social capital as the aggregation of actual and potential resources associated with the possession of a durable network of more or less institutionalized relationships of mutual knowledge or recognition. The research of Granovetter (1973) on weak ties is at the origin of this concept, and it has been enriched by more recent network sociologists (Burt, 2000; Podolny & Baron, 1997). It is assumed that a firm with social capital—that is, the traditional resources plus a durable network of knowledgeable contacts—will achieve its objectives more easily than a firm without such a network. Thus, the pursuit of self-interest is often supplanted by a desire to enrich relationships through trust and reciprocity. Because trust between partners reduces the risk related to transactions and protects against opportunism, companies often seek partnerships with firms whose leaders have close social or personal ties with their leader (DiMaggio & Louch, 1998; Saorin-Iborra, 2006).

In the present case, the new Internet manager got back in touch with the founders of Web Interactive after the failure of the first negotiation. The negotiation was resumed at this point because the founders of Web Interactive had known the new Internet manager hired by X Telecom before the negotiations and belonged to his social network. An executive of X Telecom says: "It worked because ultimately these processes are very much based on relationships: the fact that people know each other beforehand is a huge enabler. In fact, that's why it didn't work with the other one [Protic]. It is only because of relationships: the *affectio societatis*." One of the owners of Web Interactive explains: "The new Internet manager changed the negotiation process. We started to believe in it again. He thought, just as I did, that the fact of knowing each was going to facilitate the negotiation and 'grease the wheels.' And it was true: we had the same vision of the future and bringing together our technical knowhow seemed obvious to us."

### The Role of Cultural Proximity in Re-Launching the Negotiation

In an empirical study, Hill and Hellriegel (1994) show that the quality of relationships between firms is conditioned by similar operating philosophies or similar management styles. Graham (1987) focuses on the individual characteristics of the negotiators to explain success. Fang, Fridh, and Schultzberg (2004) emphasize the influence of cultural proximity on the negotiation process. According to the authors, given that objectives and strategic priorities derive from corporate culture, cultural proximity is a key factor in successful alliances. Strong cultural proximity will positively influence the continuation of negotiations, since the players have the same strategic priorities and share a common vision of the future.

The choice of X Telecom to continue negotiations with Web Interactive and not with Protic was based in part on cultural proximity. The negotiators in the second round identified themselves as complementary and culturally close, and thus saw opportunities for joining forces. In this case, the owner of X Telecom explains: "Cooperation was particularly perceived as something technical and cultural. We looked for coherence from strategic and commercial points of view." An executive of Web Interactive adds: "We had the same vision of the future."

### The Influence of Relational Norms on the Willingness to Contractualize

Social or relational norms are considered as the part of a firm culture that affects the interorganizational exchange relationship (Fréchet, 2004). These are the rules that people must follow when they interrelate. The set of these norms provides a framework to guide the behavior of the concerned parties in order to ensure the future of a partnership. These standards represent an image shared by the partners of what their behavior should be as contractors. While formal negotiations have not yet been started and therefore no contract has been signed, the standards provide guidelines for further negotiations (Fréchet, 2004).

During the negotiation process between X Telecom and Web Interactive, the relational norms are expressed as follows: mutuality (the conviction that responsibility for the project must be shared, as well as its ultimate success), conflict resolution (pursuing mutual agreement after Web Interactive refuses the price offered by X Telecom), limited power (the more powerful firm shows restraint and limits the use of its power), and information exchange (the parties are willing to provide confidential information useful to the other party to further the negotiations). Regarding this last element, Protic is reluctant to disclose confidential information, while Web Interactive provides it twice to X Telecom. An executive of X Telecom says that because of its behavior, "Protic made it hard to build a trusting relationship." Another executive of X Telecom explains: "When we asked the Protic executive to suggest a price for his firm, the proposal was completely disproportionate. This was a strong signal to us. It would be difficult to collaborate with someone with such an outsized ego."

Gradually, social capital, cultural proximity, and relational norms combine to create strong dynamics between the parties. To the simple informal relationships at the beginning of the negotiations (social capital), new elements are added (cultural proximity and relational norms) and allow the two parties to consolidate and formalize the negotiations, leading to an early conclusion of the negotiations with a fair deal for both parties. Our analysis of the negotiation process of X Telecom and Web Interactive supports the work developed by the new economic sociology, which emphasizes the importance of the social relationships between negotiators and the idea that companies, as well as markets and other institutions, are created by social construction (Abolafia, 1996; Berger & Luckmann, 1986; MacKenzie & Millo, 2003). In our case, the social relationships gradually blurred the visible differences between the parties (size, economic and financial weight). Thus, through an increasing number of exchanges over a four-year period, two companies with socially close ties managed to negotiate a fair and balanced alliance. X Telecom gradually changed its perception of Web Interactive as a small business and came to see it as a full partner with which to collaborate, share, and innovate. At the end of the negotiation process, when X Telecom proposed a 50/50 deal, Web Interactive, now confident, was willing to concede 50% of its equity.

## CONCLUSION

In conclusion, our case study shows the three stages of a pre-alliance negotiation process: first, the prior relationship with X Telecom encourages Web Interactive to reconnect with it despite the failure of the initial negotiation. Second, cultural proximity and affinity lead X Telecom to choose Web Interactive as a partner. Third, the advanced technology of Web Interactive and the informal variables identified during the negotiation process (social networks, previous relationships, relational and cultural proximity affinities) gradually give this firm ways to negotiate a fair deal.

More generally, the results of this study show that social networks provide a crucial source of power for small and medium enterprises (SMEs) wanting to engage in partnerships with large companies. They show that a strictly rational and economic analysis of the relationship is insufficient to understand the negotiation process. The informal process in the negotiations is crucial. While the formal process of negotiations reveals the sources of power for both parties in terms of size, market power, or strategic position, the study of the informal negotiation process shows the rarely studied impact of social ties and cultural affinity on the management of the negotiations.

In the case presented here, analyzing the informal process yielded much more useful information about the real issues in play and provided a better basis for anticipating the future issue of the negotiations. Thus, a manager engaged in a negotiation process must include the informal part of the negotiation in the analysis of risks and opportunities, in addition to the official discourses and behaviors. This reduces uncertainty and provides a more solid basis for responding to unexpected situations. The case presented in this chapter is rich in lessons for managers. It highlights the influence of social networks on the processes and conclusion of pre-alliance negotiations.

## REFERENCES

Abolafia, M. (1996). *Making markets: Opportunism and restraints on Wall Street*. Cambridge, MA: Harvard University Press.

Berger, P., & Luckmann, T. (1986). *La construction sociale de la réalité* [Social Construction of reality]. Paris, France: Méridiens Klincksieck.

Bourdieu, P. (1992). *Réponses: Pour une anthropologie réflexive* [Answers: For a reflexive anthropology]. Paris, France: Editions du Seuil.

Burt, R. S. (2000). The network structure of social capital. *Research in Organizational Behaviour, 22*, 345–423.

Carnevale, P. J., & Pruitt, D. G. (1992). Negotiation and mediation. *Annual Review Psychology, 43*, 531–582.

Das, T. K., & Kumar, R. (2011). Interpartner negotiations in alliances: A strategic framework. *Management Decision, 49*, 1235–1256.

Das, T. K., & Rahman, N. (2010). Determinants of partner opportunism in strategic alliances: A conceptual framework. *Journal of Business and Psychology, 25*, 55–74.

Das, T. K., & Teng, B. (2001). Trust, control, and risk in strategic alliances: An integrated framework. *Organization Studies, 22*, 251–284.

Das, T. K., & Teng, B. (1998). Between trust and control: Developing confidence in partner cooperation in alliances. *Academy of Management Review, 23*, 491–512.

DiMaggio, P., & Louch, H. (1998). Socially embedded consumer transactions: For what kind of purchases do people most often use networks? *American Sociological Review, 63*, 619–637.

Druckman, D. (2002). Case-based research on international negotiation: Approaches and data sets. *International Negotiation, 7*, 17–37.

Fang, T., Fridh, C., & Schultzberg, S. (2004). Why did the Telia-Telenor merger fail? *International Business Review, 13*, 573–594.

Fréchet, M. (2004). *Prévenir les conflits dans les partenariats d'innovation* [Prevent the conflicts in innovative partnerships]. Paris, France: Edition Vuibert.

Graham, J. L. (1987). A theory of interorganizational negotiations. *Research in Marketing, 9*, 163–184.

Granovetter, M. S. (1973). The strength of weak ties. *American Journal of Sociology, 78*, 1360–1380.

Gulati, R. (1995). Does familarity breed trust? The implications of repeated ties for contractual choice in alliances. *Academy of Management Journal, 38*, 85–112.

Gulbro, R., & Herbig, P. (1996). Negotiating successfully in cross-cultural situations. *Industrial Marketing Management, 25*, 235–241.

Harrigan, K. R. (1986). *Managing for joint venture success*. Lexington, MA: Lexington Books.

Hill, R. C., & Hellriegel, D. (1994). Critical contingencies in joint venture management: Some lessons from managers. *Organisation Science, 5*, 594–607.

Hopmann, P. T. (2002). Negotiating data: Reflections on the qualitative and quantitative analysis of negotiation processes. *International Negotiation, 7*, 67–85.

Inkpen, A. C., & Beamish, P. W. (1997). Knowledge bargaining power and the instability of international joint ventures. *Academy of Management Journal, 22*, 177–202.

Lasbordes, V. (2000). *Les contrats déséquilibrés* [Unbalanced contracts]. Paris, France: Edition Lavoisier.

MacKenzie, D., & Millo, Y. (2003). Constructing a market, performing theory: The historical sociology of a financial derivatives exchange. *American Journal of Sociology, 109*, 107–145.

Marks, M. L., & Mirvis, P. H. (2001). Making mergers and acquisitions work: Strategic and psychological preparation. *Academy of Management Journal, 15*, 80–94.

Miles, A. M., & Huberman, A. M. (1994). *Qualitative data analysis: An expanded sourcebook*. Thousand Oaks, CA: Sage.

Mockler, R. J., & Gartenfeld, M. E. (2001). Using multinational strategic alliance negotiations to help ensure alliance success: An entrepreneurial orientation. *Strategic Change, 10*, 215–221.

Podolny, J., & Baron, J. (1997). Resources and relationships: Social networks and mobility in the workplace. *American Sociological Review, 62*, 673–693.

Saorín-Iborra, M. C. (2006). A review of negotiation outcome: A proposal on delimitation and subsequent assessment in joint venture negotiations. *Canadian Journal of Administrative Sciences, 23*, 237–252.

Schmidt, S., & Rühli, E. (2002). Prior strategy processes as a key to understanding mega-mergers: The Novartis case. *European Management Journal, 20*, 223–234.

Strauss, A. (1992). *La trame de la négociation. Sociologie qualitative et interactionniste* [The frame of negotiation. Qualitative and interactionist sociology]. Paris, France: L'Harmattan.

CHAPTER 8

# DYNAMIC EVOLUTION OF EQUITY JOINT VENTURE RELATIONSHIPS

## Role of the Parent Companies and Joint Venture Control

Pieter E. Kamminga and Jeltje van der Meer-Kooistra

### ABSTRACT

Equity joint venture (JV) relationships are susceptible to dynamic evolution because of the complexity of their organizational form and their joint control by the parent companies. The organizational form includes a hierarchical relationship between the (two or more) parent companies of the joint venture and the joint venture management, and a horizontal relationship between the parent companies. JV relationships could be influenced by changes in the joint venture and its environment, but also by changes within the parent companies and their environment. This chapter aims at exploring the dynamic evolution of JV relationships over their lifetime and, more specifically, the parent companies' use of JV control (i.e., control of the JV relationship by the parent companies) to accommodate a weakened JV relationship. We investigate the main factors mentioned in the literature that can cause changes in JV relationships. We distinguish three scenarios of the dynamic evolution of JV relationships: (1) a strengthened JV relationship, (2) a weakened JV relationship, and (3) the natural termination of a JV relationship. In addition, for each scenario we provide one example of the dynamic evolution of a JV relationship in practice. These examples illustrate how specific factors influence JV relationships, how the parent companies respond to these influences and thereby use JV control, and the intended and unintended effects of these responses, which may lead to additional responses and effects. More specifically, the examples illustrate the crucial role of the parent companies in coping with uncertainty. By responding to unexpected problems and opportunities over time, they may be able to accommodate weakening effects on the JV relationship. Trustworthy relationships between the parent companies will make it easier to find adequate responses to those problems and opportunities.

## INTRODUCTION

Equity joint venture (JV) relationships have a complicated organizational form. A JV relationship is a long-term transactional relationship between at least two independent companies that have established a new legal entity for jointly executing new activities. The independent companies are the owners or parent companies of the new legal entity or joint venture (JV). A JV relationship includes both hierarchical and horizontal (or lateral) relationships. The relationship between the parent companies and the JV itself can be described as a hierarchical relationship (Kogut, 1988). Through their ownership, the parent companies have an authority position vis-à-vis the JV. However, as the parent companies possess this authority position jointly, the horizontal relationship between the parent companies also plays a crucial role in the control of JV relationships. In this horizontal relationship, parent companies cannot just enforce their will on each other by means of an authority position. To exercise control in such a horizontal relationship, parent companies have to turn to other control mechanisms, which obviously adds complexity to the control of a JV relationship (which we from now on call JV control).

Yan and Zeng (1999) argue that a JV relationship is susceptible to changes because of the complexity of its organizational form and its joint control. A JV relationship could be influenced by changes in the JV and its environment, but also by changes within the parent companies and their environment (Kamminga & Van der Meer-Kooistra, 2007). These influences may need responses by the parent companies. If these influences weaken the JV relationship, the parent companies can use the JV control to accommodate the weakening effects. This chapter aims at exploring the dynamic evolution of a JV relationship over its lifetime and, more specifically, the parent companies' use of JV control to accommodate a weakened relationship. We investigate the main factors mentioned in the literature that cause changes in a JV relationship (e.g., Hamel, 1991; Harrigan & Newman, 1990; Inkpen & Currall, 1998; Kale, Singh, & Perlmutter, 2000; Kamminga & Van der Meer-Kooistra, 2007), the responses of the parent companies to these changes, and subsequently, the effects of these responses on the JV relationship.

In this chapter, we distinguish three scenarios of the dynamic evolution of a JV relationship. The first scenario describes the dynamic evolution of a JV relationship that strengthens the relationship. Such an outcome does not need any responses by the parent companies. In the second scenario, the dynamic evolution weakens the JV relationship and the parent companies have to use the JV control to accommodate these weakening effects, as otherwise the JV relationship will be at risk. This scenario also includes dynamic evolutions that have the potential to weaken the JV relationship, but because the parent companies adequately respond to the changes, the JV relationship will not be weakened. The third scenario concerns the dynamic evolution of a JV relationship that leads to its natural termination. Such a natural termination indicates that the collaboration has been successful and underlines the temporary nature of JV relationships. Distinguishing these three scenarios of JV dynamics allows investigating how various factors can influence a JV relationship, the responses of the parent companies to these influences, and the effects of these responses on the JV relationship. Such an investigation provides a deeper insight into the dynamic evolution of JV relationships over their lifetime and the role of the parent companies and JV control in the evolution processes. In addition, for each scenario we will provide one example of the dynamic evolution of a JV relationship in practice. These examples illustrate how specific factors influence JV relationships, how the parent companies respond to these influences and thereby use JV control, and the intended and unintended effects of these responses, which may lead to additional responses and effects.

The structure of the chapter is as follows. First, we will present the theoretical framework of our study and discuss its concepts and how they relate to each other. Next, drawing on the literature, we will introduce the main factors that may lead to the dynamic evolution of a JV relationship. We will elaborate on possible influences of these factors on the JV relationship and how the parent companies could use JV control to respond to these influences. In addition, we will indicate the possible effects of these responses on the JV relationship and thereby describe the scenarios of JV dynamics. Then, for each scenario of JV dynamics, we will present an example that illustrates the dynamic evolution of a JV relationship in practice in more detail. These illustrations are based on a number of in-depth case studies of JV relationships. We will end the chapter by drawing some conclusions about the theoretical implications of our study.

# THEORETICAL FRAMEWORK

## Concepts of the Theoretical Framework

In this section we will develop the theoretical framework that underpins our study of the dynamic evolution of JV relationships over their lifetime. This framework is depicted in Figure 8.1.

The literature argues that various factors that can be found within the JV and its environment and/or within the parent companies and their environment may influence the JV relationship over time. These factors include the strategic motives of the parent companies (Harrigan & Newman, 1990), different types of learning (Hamel, 1991; Inkpen & Currall, 2004), the match of the JV control with the character of the JV relationship (Kamminga & Van der Meer-Kooistra, 2007; Van der Meer-Kooistra & Kamminga, 2010), the key individuals of a JV relationship (Ariño & De la Torre, 1998; Inkpen & Currall, 1998), the financial situation of the JV (Hennart, Roehl, & Zietlow, 1999; Killing, 1983), and developments in the (institutional) environment (Yan & Zeng, 1999). These factors can cause changes in a JV relationship. If the changes strengthen the JV relationship, the parent companies will be happy with these changes. We refer to such an evolution of a JV relationship as a scenario of a strengthened JV relationship.

However, if the changes weaken the JV relationship, the parent companies will not accept these changes and try to accommodate them by means of the existing JV control or by putting in place additional JV control. As the

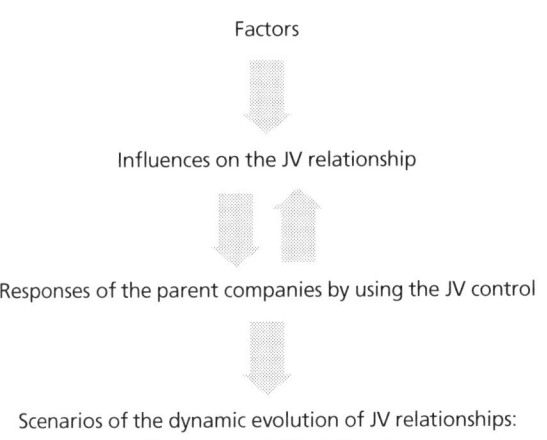

**Figure 8.1** Theoretical framework of the dynamic evolution of JV relationships.

parent companies share the ownership of the JV, they have to agree about the measures to be taken to accommodate the unwanted effects. If both parent companies want to continue the JV relationship, it will be easier to discuss the situation and to agree about the measures to be taken. If the parent companies are not able to fully accommodate the unwanted changes, the JV relationship may be weakened. Then, the parent companies have to take additional measures. The measures may also have unintended effects that weaken the JV relationship. In such a situation, the parent companies need to respond to accommodate these unintended effects. Such a need of successive responses by the parent companies is indicated by the two arrows between the boxes "Influences on the JV relationship" and "Responses by the parent companies" in Figure 8.1. It may be that the parent companies are not able to take adequate measures to reinforce a weakened JV relationship. Ultimately, this may lead to a premature termination of the JV relationship. Such a termination signals that the JV relationship has failed. Another possibility in the scenario of a weakened JV relationship is that the changes in the JV relationship have the potential to weaken the JV relationship, but that the parent companies are able to adequately respond to the changes such that no weakening effects occur.

The factors can also cause changes that lead to a natural termination of the JV relationship. If the changes imply that the parent companies have achieved their strategic motives to establish the JV relationship, the raison d'être of the relationship no longer exists.[1] As a consequence, the parent companies will terminate their relationship. Such a termination of a JV relationship is a self-explanatory outcome and does not mean that the relationship has failed. On the contrary, a natural termination of a JV relationship signals that the relationship was a success.

At the start of a JV relationship, the parent companies develop JV control to manage and control their relationship and usually lay it down in the JV contract. Geringer and Hebert (1989) define JV control as the process through which the parent companies influence the behavior of the personnel, the activities and the output of a JV, and the relationship between the parent companies "through the use of power, authority, and a wide range of bureaucratic, cultural and informal mechanisms" (pp. 236–237). They claim that JV control consists of the mechanisms that the parent companies use to exert control over the JV relationship, the extent or tightness with which the parent companies use these mechanisms, and the focus of (each of) the parent companies' control. The mechanisms, the extent or tightness, and the focus of the parent companies' control "are not incompatible, but rather complementary and interdependent" (Geringer & Hebert, 1989, p. 241).

Kamminga and Van der Meer-Kooistra (2007) argue that the JV control mechanisms parent companies put in place can consist of mechanisms that focus on the activities, processes, and output of the JV—which they call content-based control mechanisms—or on the relationship between the parent companies on the one hand and the relationship between the parent companies and the JV on the other—which they call context-based control mechanisms. In particular, when the activities, processes, and output of the JV cannot be measured well and/or in case of differences between the parent companies (e.g., different knowledge and experience, different strategic motives, or different norms and values), content-based mechanisms will not be very helpful and much more emphasis has to be placed on context-based control mechanisms. In such a situation, a trustworthy relationship helps to reduce uncertainty, as trust makes the parties' behavior more predictable. Hence, the parent companies have to develop context-based control mechanisms that stimulate the building of trust (see Kamminga & Van der Meer-Kooistra, 2007; Van der Meer-Kooistra & Kamminga, 2010; Van der Meer-Kooistra & Vosselman, 2010; Vosselman & Van der Meer-Kooistra, 2009).

To be able to effectively control a JV relationship, Kamminga and Van der Meer-Kooistra (2007) suggest that the package of JV control mechanisms, the focus of the control mechanisms, and the degree of tightness with which they are used have to match the character of the JV relationship. They distinguish three control patterns: a content-based, a consultation-based, and a context-based control pattern. Each control pattern consists of a specific package of control mechanisms and the focus and degree of tightness with which the control mechanisms are used. In the next section, we will explain the relationship between each control pattern and the character of the JV relationship. Kamminga and Van der Meer-Kooistra argue and found in practice that a mismatch between the control pattern being put in place and the character of the JV relationship weakens the relationship. Then the parent companies have to take measures to recover the match between the control pattern and the character of the JV relationship. In the next section, we will elaborate on the relations between the factors, their influences on the JV relationship, the responses by the parent companies, and their effects, which lead to one of the scenarios of JV dynamics: a strengthened relationship, a weakened relationship, or a natural termination of the relationship.

## Relations between Factors, Influences, Parent Companies Responses, and Scenarios of JV Dynamics

In this section, we will discuss in more detail what kinds of dynamic evolution the main factors mentioned in the literature may cause. First, we will discuss factors that relate to the JV relationship. Then we will discuss factors that relate to the environment of the JV relationship.

### Factors Related to the JV Relationship

**1. Strategic Motives.** An important condition for a viable JV relationship is for the parent companies to have compatible strategic motives (Contractor & Lorange, 1988; Lorange & Roos, 1992). The strategic motives are compatible if they are complementary (Ariño, 2003, speaks of private strategic motives) and/or similar (Ariño, 2003, speaks of common strategic motives). While it may be expected that the parent companies' strategic motives are compatible at the start of the JV relationship, over time, developments within and outside the JV relationship may harm this compatibility (Harrigan & Newman, 1990). These developments may lead to changes in the parent companies' interests in the JV relationship or to different opinions about how to continue the JV relationship. As a consequence, the JV relationship will weaken, which may eventually lead to an undesired and premature termination of the JV relationship. Such processes of JV dynamics are described in Scenario 2.

Over time the strategic motives of (one of) the parent companies, which motivated them to establish a JV relationship, could be achieved. If through this achievement the raison d'être of the JV relationship disappears, the JV relationship will also be terminated (Beamish & Delios, 1997; Parkhe, 1991). In this situation the termination is natural, as described in Scenario 3.

However, the achievement of the parent companies' strategic motives does not necessarily imply the end of the JV's raison d'être. If parent companies have established a JV relationship for such reasons as realizing economies of scale, overcoming governmental restrictions, or reducing risk, achieving these strategic motives implies that the JV relationship is successful and will be continued (see also Note 1).

If the strategic motives of one of the parent companies are achieved, the JV relationship may lose its raison d'être for that parent company but at the same time remain appropriate for the other parent company. In such a situation, the strategic motives for the former parent company have been achieved, as described in Scenario 3. However, if the JV relationship remains appropriate for the latter parent company, its termination will be undesired for this parent company. For this parent company, the dynamic evolution of the JV relationship (i.e., the termination of the JV relationship) occurs according to Scenario 2. It may be that this parent company is able to find another suitable partner and that the JV's activities can be continued in a new JV relationship.

**2. Learning.** Inkpen and Currall (2004) distinguish between learning how to cooperate with a partner (see also Das & Kumar, 2007; Kale et al., 2000) and learning about another partner's contributions to the JV (e.g., Das & Kumar, 2007; Hamel, 1991; Inkpen & Beamish, 1997; Inkpen & Currall, 2004; Kale et al., 2000; Yan, 1998). Learning how to cooperate could relate to both the *content* and the *context* of a JV relationship. With respect to the content, parties could, for instance, learn how to coordinate the different contributions of the parent companies more smoothly—for instance through more effective contracting (Mayer & Argyres, 2004). Learning about the context of a JV relationship may lead to a better understanding of each other's cultural backgrounds and norms and values. Through learning about the content and the context of a JV relationship, the parent companies will gain better insights into the JV's activities and acquire skills needed to cooperate, which will strengthen the JV relationship. Moreover, learning about the content and context of the JV relationship may lead to the development of trust (Sako, 1992; Zucker, 1986). This will further contribute to a strengthening of the JV relationship; a dynamic evolution that fits in with Scenario 1.

Parent companies may also learn about another partner's contributions to the JV (e.g., Das & Kumar, 2007; Hamel, 1991; Inkpen & Beamish, 1997; Inkpen & Currall, 2004; Kale et al., 2000; Yan, 1998). Hamel (1991) discusses how through such interpartner learning, the need for a partner's contributions may disappear over time. This may threaten the JV relationship, because for the parent company that acquired the partner's knowledge and expertise, the need to cooperate may disappear. Hence, learning about another partner's contributions may weaken the JV relationship and may even lead to its termination, especially if the strategic motive for establishing the JV was to gain access to the knowledge of the other partner. In such a case, the strategic motive for this parent company has been achieved, as described in Scenario 3. However, if the JV relationship remains appropriate for the other parent company, a termination of the JV relationship will be undesirable for this parent company, as described in Scenario 2.

**3. Mismatch of JV Control with the Character of the JV Relationship.** In Scenario 2, we describe how a weakening effect on the JV relationship may be accommodated by means of JV control. Then the JV control helps to reinforce the JV relationship. However, the JV control can also be the reason for a weakened JV relationship. Kamminga and Van der Meer-Kooistra (2007) argue that if the JV control does not match the character of the JV relationship, this could weaken the JV relationship.

According to Kamminga and Van der Meer-Kooistra (2007), how JV control is developed and exercised is influenced by three groups of characteristics: namely, (1) the transaction characteristics of a JV, (2) the relational characteristics of each of the JV parties, and (3) the characteristics of the institutional environment of the JV relationship.[2] First, a JV relationship with a *content-based control pattern* is characterized by little control complexity. It operates in a stable environment and there is little risk of opportunistic behavior. The transformation process of the JV is transparent, and the JV's activities and output are easily measurable. Therefore, parental control will be tightly focused on the JV's activities and/or output by means of content-based control mechanisms. Second, a JV relationship with a *consultation-based control pattern* is characterized by a medium level of control complexity as the parent companies contribute different but complementary resources to the JV, which creates information asymmetry between the parent companies. The coordination of the input and/or the exchange of these resources requires face-to-face consultations between the parent companies, especially when tacit knowledge is involved. Although in this control pattern parent companies can tightly control their own activities by means of content-based control mechanisms, their knowledge of the contributions of the other parent company is limited. Therefore, trust in each other's competences and goodwill is crucial for a successful relationship. In order to develop a trustworthy relationship control mechanisms that pay attention to the relationship between the JV parties and the atmosphere of the JV relationship—that is, context-based control mechanisms—will play a crucial role. They can stimulate the building of mutual trust and can iron out possible disturbances resulting from differences in the parent companies' backgrounds. Third, a JV relationship with a *context-based control pattern* is characterized by a high level of control complexity due to the characteristics of the JV's activities and output and/or the environment in which the JV operates. There will be a high level of information asymmetry between the parent companies and the JV management, and it will be difficult to prescribe the JV's activities in advance and to apply action and result controls. Mutual trust between the parent companies is indispensable to creating an atmosphere in which unexpected problems can be discussed and solutions can be found that pay attention to the interests of all the JV parties. Hence, context-based control mechanisms play the main role.

If there is a mismatch between the characteristics of the JV relationship and the JV control pattern, this will weaken the JV relationship. The parent companies can accommodate such a weakening effect by adjusting the JV control. These JV dynamics fit in with Scenario 2.

**4. Key Individuals.** A replacement of key individuals who are directly involved in the JV on behalf of a parent company may affect JV dynamics. Various researchers have argued that personal relationships between key individuals of cooperating organizations stabilize an interfirm relationship. For instance, according to Seabright, Levinthal, and Fichman (1992), a continuing exchange relationship leads to attachment between individuals involved in such a relationship. This attachment will counter pressure for changes in an interfirm relationship. Inkpen and Currall (1998) argue that personal relationships between key individuals of the cooperating organizations based upon trust "provide a buffer against the normal pressure of collaboration" (p. 9). Kamminga and Van der Meer-Kooistra (2007), however, argue that such a buffer of trust is not equally relevant in all types of JV relationships. Trust is especially important in JV relationships with substantial parental differences or high levels of uncertainty with respect to the environment and/or activities (described above as JV relationships with medium or high levels of control complexity). In JV relationships that have a transparent transformation process and operate in a stable environment (described above as JV relationships with little control complexity), trust is less relevant, as there is little uncertainty and risks can be covered by content-based control mechanisms.

If there are changes in the key individuals directly involved in a JV and the new individuals have little sense of and attention for the relational context of the JV relationship, the use of context-based control mechanisms will be limited and the control pattern will become more content-based. If the environment in which the JV operates is stable and the JV's transformation process is transparent, such a change in key individuals will not have a weakening effect on the JV relationship, because the control pattern that matches these transactional, relational, and environmental characteristics is a content-based control pattern.

However, if there are substantial parental differences or high levels of uncertainty with respect to the JV's environment and/or activities, those changes in key individuals will have a weakening effect on the JV relationship, because a content-based control pattern does not match these transactional, relational, and environmental characteristics. In such a situation the processes of dynamic evolution fit in with Scenario 2.

**5. Financial Situation of the JV.** Killing (1983) discusses how, in case of a well-performing JV, the parent companies may acquire trust in the competences of the JV management and increase the JV management's autonomy. As this autonomy, in turn, increases the JV management's possibilities of responding to new situations, the JV's performance may improve even more. This fits in with a strengthened JV relationship, as described in Scenario 1.

On the other hand, a JV experiencing substantial financial problems may lead to JV changes, which Killing describes as a "failure cycle." In case of a JV performing badly, the parent companies may lose their trust in the JV management, and as a consequence tighten their JV control. However, this tighter control is likely "to slow down and possibly even confuse decision-making processes," leading to yet worse performance and even tighter parental control; ultimately, this cycle can lead to "a major crisis" (Killing, 1983, pp. 82–83).

We argue, however, that Killing's failure cycle could be refined by taking into account the character of the JV relationship. In JV relationships with little control complexity, where the environment is stable and the transformation process is transparent, tight parental JV control can be expected (see Kamminga & Van der Meer-Kooistra, 2007). Therefore, in these kinds of JV relationships, we do not expect Killing's failure cycle to occur.

On the other hand, in JV relationships with more control complexity, where the level of information asymmetry between the parent companies and the JV management is high, tight parental control will be counterproductive. In these types of JV relationships, tighter parental JV control as a response to bad JV performance may indeed lead to Killing's failure cycle, which fits in with Scenario 2.

However, whether or not bad JV performance leads to a failure cycle, if a JV performs badly over an extended period of time, and no improvements are expected in the near future, it is very likely that the JV relationship will be terminated, as described in Scenario 2.

Changes in the financial situation of a parent company may also affect the JV relationship. If a parent company has financial problems and its JV has a bad performance as well, there is no longer a justification for that parent company to put much effort into the JV. Therefore, it is likely that the parent company will reconsider its strategy regarding the JV relationship and look for ways of withdrawing from the relationship (see also Hennart et al., 1999). Therefore, we expect that a situation in which a parent company faces financial problems and in which its JV performs badly as well will weaken the JV relationship, as described in Scenario 2. However, if a parent company has financial problems and its JV performs well, the JV's activities will become more important for that parent company, and it is likely that its interest in the JV relationship will increase. This will strengthen the JV relationship, as described in Scenario 1.

### *Factors Related to the Environment of the JV Relationship*

**1. Developments in the Institutional Environment.** While the institutional environment, including legal, governmental, and industry regulations, could reduce uncertainty, continuously changing regulations however could be a source of uncertainty (Kamminga & Van der Meer-Kooistra, 2007; Yan & Zeng, 1999). If developments in the institutional environment of a JV relationship create uncertainty, this may have JV control implications. Higher uncertainty will increase information asymmetry between the parent companies and the JV management. As a consequence, the JV management requires substantial autonomy in order to be able to respond (more) quickly to developments in the institutional environment (Kumar & Seth, 1998; Merchant & Van der Stede, 2003). In addition, given the behavioral risks in such a situation (Kamminga & Van der Meer-Kooistra, 2007), the parent companies have to create a trustworthy relational context by putting in place context-based control mechanisms. If the parent companies do not succeed in establishing these context-based control mechanisms, the JV relationship will weaken and will probably be terminated, as described in Scenario 2.

**2. Technological and Market Developments.** Environmental developments may lead to changes in the parent companies' strategic motives for establishing a JV relationship. For instance, if new opportunities arise in the market, a parent company may change its strategy. Such a strategic change could affect the strategic motives for setting up the JV relationship and thereby harm the similarity/complementarity of the strategic motives of the parent companies (Harrigan, 1986; Harrigan & Newman, 1990). This will weaken the JV relationship.

Technological developments may change the strategic importance of the JV's activities for one or more parent companies. For example, an important strategic motive for a JV relationship may be to gain access to the specific knowledge and experience of another partner. Over time, however, this knowledge may diffuse over the market and become less specific and more common knowledge (Kamminga & Van der Meer-Kooistra, 2007; Spender, 1989). As a result, the initial strategic motive will no longer be relevant, and this will weaken the JV relationship and may even lead to its termination.

Above we discussed how learning about how to cooperate with the JV parties can increase a parent company's understanding of the JV's activities and output and enable it to improve its measurement of and control over the JV's activities. A similar effect can be achieved by learning from external technological developments. Such technological developments may give all the JV parties better insights into the JV's transformation process (Johnson & Kaplan, 1987). If these developments also make the environment less uncertain, the control will shift to a more content-based pattern.

Developments in the market can affect a JV's financial position. A worsening market situation may change a successful JV into a loss maker, whereas an improving market situation may have an opposite effect. Such market changes, which affect a JV's financial position negatively (positively), may weaken (strengthen) the JV relationship (Hennart et al., 1999; Williamson, 1985).

## EXAMPLES OF THE SCENARIOS OF DYNAMIC EVOLUTION OF JV RELATIONSHIPS

In this section, we will describe one example for each of the three scenarios of JV dynamics. The information about these examples is derived from various in-depth case studies (Kamminga, 2003).

### Example of a Strengthened JV Relationship: Gas Sales

Gas Sales was a JV of American Corp (possessing 25% of the shares) and Electricity Corp (possessing 75% of the shares) that dealt with the marketing and sale of gas in the British gas market from 1992 to 1999. American Corp is an American utility company, while Electricity Corp is a British regional electricity company. Gas Sales was established in 1992, when the British gas market was being progressively deregulated and various business opportunities were beginning to emerge in the sale of gas initially to UK commercial customers and then to domestic customers.

The parental motives for establishing the JV relationship were broadly similar and complementary. On the one hand, American Corp, or more specifically, its British subsidiary Alpha Gas, wanted to exploit its knowhow in gas purchasing and the possibilities of gaining access to the emerging gas market. Moreover, it wanted to establish a reputation in the UK, but it did not have the customers. On the other hand, Electricity Corp wanted to apply to the gas market the experience that it had built up in marketing activities, billing customers, and collecting debts in the electricity market. Moreover, existing (electricity) customers provided a ready base for gas sales and new gas customers could also be sold electricity. However, it did not have access to gas and it had no expertise in the gas market. By collaborating in a JV relationship, both companies were able to share their different expertise, exploit their access to the gas and electricity markets, and to use and expand Electricity Corp's customer base.

During the first period of its operations, Gas Sales faced high levels of uncertainty. This uncertainty in particular concerned the institutional environment, which experienced substantial changes. In the early 1990s, the British government began to deregulate the British gas market. This had created opportunities for Electricity Corp and American Corp to enter this market. However, additional governmental regulations were expected, and their effects on the market were unknown. For instance, it was unclear whether the gas market would be deregulated for the most lucrative sector, namely households. Therefore, the parent companies were unsure of their ability to make Gas Sales a successful operation. The uncertainty concerning the institutional environment was also reflected in the uncertainty with respect to the building up and the operating of the JV's activities. Gas Sales had to build a completely new infrastructure in an evolving gas market. The JV needed Alpha Gas's knowledge in setting up information systems and the systems needed to coordinate the purchase and sale of gas. This required the sharing of knowledge and a lot of face-to-face discussions between the managers of Alpha Gas and the JV managers appointed by Electricity Corp, who did not have experience in cooperating with each other.

Due to the high levels of uncertainty about the institutional developments and about how to operate the JV's activities, the parent companies chose to remain at a distance and to organize the JV's activities as a standalone entity. As the uncertainty constrained the possibilities for the parent companies of gaining comprehensive insights into the JV's activities on a real-time basis, they decided to give extensive autonomy to a group of managers who directly dealt with the JV's activities, namely two managers appointed from within Electricity Corp and the managers of American Corp's British subsidiary Alpha Gas. This was a good way of dealing with the high level of information asymmetry between the parent companies and the managers directly involved, as in this way the managers directly involved could quickly respond to changes in the regulations and the new developments in the gas market (see Kumar & Seth, 1998; Merchant & Van der Stede, 2003). Another consideration for keeping the JV's activities at a distance from Electricity Corp, and not integrating them into Electricity Corp's existing activities, was the risk of failure that could harm Electricity Corp's reputation. As discussed above, due to institutional developments, it was still uncertain whether the parent companies were able to make the JV a success. By organizing the JV's activities separately from the parent companies' existing operations, the JV's activities could be terminated quite easily with little damage to the parent companies' reputations.

The control device of keeping the JV's activities separate from the parent companies also had dynamic implications. As discussed above, it was uncertain whether the managers of Alpha Gas and the managers appointed by Electricity Corp were able to successfully cooperate with each other. In fact, this cooperation worked out very well. There was a good personal fit between these managers, and this enabled them to build strong relationships based upon trust. Moreover, keeping the JV's activities separate from the parent companies further strengthened the personal relationships and built trust between the Electricity Corp appointed managers and the managers of Alpha Gas, as it created a Gas Sales team with its own culture and identity.

This, in turn, induced further dynamics by facilitating various types of learning: learning how to operate in the gas market, learning how to cooperate with the other partner, and learning from that partner. For instance, over time the managers appointed by Electricity Corp gained considerable knowledge about gas purchasing from Alpha Gas, and this enabled Electricity Corp to put in place the necessary infrastructure to manage gas-related activities. Both the building of trust and the various processes of learning greatly reduced the uncertainty within Gas Sales and gave it a flying start with very promising expectations for the future. These promising expectations further stimulated the building of trust and processes of learning between the managers appointed by Electricity Corp and the managers of Alpha Gas.

Over time, also, the uncertainty in the institutional environment substantially reduced. As the gas market changed from an "unexplored territory" into a known market, the uncertainty regarding the regulations significantly decreased, and it became much more clear which parties were involved in the gas market and how these parties operated in the chain of gas activities. One event that substantially decreased the uncertainty in the institutional environment was the British government's decision to open the entire gas market to competition, including households. Once this decision was made by the government, the gas market became much more attractive. This change into a "known market" also made it easier to measure the output of the JV. The accumulated knowledge regarding the selling of gas led to more sophisticated performance measures, and the market situation created new ways of assessing the JV's output.

The factors of learning, or more specifically the increasing knowledge about how to operate successfully in the market, together with the environmental developments, including the improvements in the measurability of the JV's activities and output and the opening up of the very profitable gas market, transformed Gas Sales into a very successful JV. Its customer base grew steadily, as did its financial results.

This brought into play the factor of financial success. In view of Gas Sales' success and because of the reduced uncertainty, Electricity Corp wanted to further exploit the potential of the gas market. As environmental uncertainty had decreased and Electricity Corp had learned how to operate in the gas market, it saw possibilities for strengthening the JV relationship by tightening its involvement in the JV's activities. Following the changes in the transactional, relational, and environmental characteristics of the JV relationship, Electricity Corp used more content-based control mechanisms and put in place a more content-based control pattern (see Kamminga & Van der Meer-Kooistra, 2007).

Therefore, the JV's information systems were integrated within Electricity Corp's systems, and Electricity Corp took a more direct role in directing the JV's strategy. This further strengthened the financial performance of the JV and the JV relationship. The JV thus became strategically important for Electricity Corp and it eventually came to consider it to be a core activity that required serious board-level attention. However, American Corp's position towards Gas Sales differed. It remained at a distance and left decision making largely to the managers of its British subsidiary, Alpha Gas. These managers were directly involved in the JV's activities, and they used their decision-making autonomy to realize their own goals by further expanding the JV's gas activities. As American Corp's strategic motives were more limited (i.e., establishing its name and reputation in the UK) and as it was not interested in the JV's gas retailing activities as such, it did not want direct involvement in the JV. It was the managers of Alpha Gas who were most involved, and they wanted to remain directly involved, especially as Gas Sales was becoming increasingly successful.

The above demonstrates how the factors of environmental developments, learning, and financial success led to a change in the JV control. Electricity Corp's involvement in the JV became more content-based. This change in the JV control, in turn, further strengthened the JV's financial performance and thereby the JV relationship.

## Example of a Weakened JV Relationship Where the Weakening Effect is Accommodated by JV Control Measures: JV Asia

JV Asia was a joint venture owned by a European company (EP) and an Asian company (AP). It was located in an Asian country and produced products that were sold to local customers. The idea for establishing JV Asia came from EP. EP is a company that produces and sells intermediate products all over the world. In the early 1980s, governmental restrictions on production volume led EP to investigate the possibilities of producing abroad. When at the beginning of the 1990s EP observed a substantial growth in the demand for its products in various Asian countries, it realized that setting up production activities in Asia would have two advantages. Firstly, a production site in Asia would give EP access to new sources of raw materials, which would also be much cheaper. Secondly, transportation costs would be reduced substantially and import duties avoided. These cost savings became even more of an issue because a large number of local Asian producers had entered the market, leading to downwards pressure on sales prices. Therefore, EP decided to set up a production site in an Asian country. As EP realized that the circumstances in the Asian country are quite different from those in Europe, EP came to the conclusion that it should set up the new production activities together with a local partner.

When starting up the production activities and designing the control structures, EP was strongly led by parsimoniousness. This parsimoniousness was caused by EP's difficult financial position. EP's weak position in the market and its high dependency on changing governmental regulations and subsidies meant EP constantly was facing financial problems. To reduce the costs, in EP's initial view, the JV would be managed without expatriates and controlled from a distant location by the Asia Pacific Region Sales Office. At the instigation of the (then) new corporate controller of EP, who had gained international experience in his former company, EP eventually decided to have an EP financial controller at the JV site. However, to save on expat salary costs, he was not immediately sent to the Asian country, but he first spent six months working within EP in Europe.

During the first few months, both parent companies worked separately on the issues that had been agreed: EP in Europe and AP in the Asian country. As a result, there was hardly any exchange of information between EP and AP, and face-to-face contacts were impossible. Therefore, while EP, having a technical and engineering orientation, carried out its preparations strictly according to the agreed time schedule, it did not really notice that the activities in the Asian country progressed less quickly. Although contractually agreed, AP did not come up with a JV managing director. It took five months for AP to be able to present a production manager who still needed to be trained. Also, AP generally took a waiting attitude. As AP saw that EP was taking the initiative, AP left it to them. A condition that determined AP's attitude was EP's dominant power position. As EP's financial controller said in retrospect: "AP was to some extent overwhelmed by the size and reputation of EP." The physical distance between both project organizations also made it difficult to build personal relationships based upon trust, whereas, according to EP's financial controller, "personal relationships and trust are highly crucial in this Asian country."

In fact, EP's parsimoniousness had caused a mismatch between the characteristics of the JV relationship and the applied control pattern (Kamminga & Van der Meer-Kooistra, 2007). While EP applied a content-based control pattern, the characteristics of the JV relationship required a consultation-based control pattern. Differences in both the parental cultural backgrounds and the parental contributions to the JV—EP contributed the production technology and the information and communication technology, and AP contributed their knowledge of the local market and the local norms and values and their relationships with governmental authorities—required regular face-to-face consultations and personnel and cultural controls. The effects of the mismatch became clear when EP's financial controller after six months eventually arrived at the JV site. He found that, in contrast to EP's expectations, there had been hardly any progress. All the paperwork still had to be done and, in particular, licences that had not been applied for caused considerable delay, as they were needed for the signing of contracts—for example, for the purchase of land and the import of machines. In other words, the mismatch had a weakening effect on the JV relationship.

However, once EP's financial controller finally arrived at the JV site, the situation changed. Through his arrival, communication between EP and AP became much easier. Furthermore, EP acquired an awareness of the importance of face-to-face contacts and building personal relationships with AP's representatives. There were regular face-to-face contacts between AP's managers and EP's Asia Pacific Region Sales Office. In quarterly sales meetings they discussed the JV's sales. Often, managers of the Asia Pacific Region Sales Office and AP jointly visited customers. Furthermore, EP put effort into getting AP actively involved in the JV's activities. EP tried to prevent AP from becoming too passive, for instance, by regularly inviting AP's managers to make product presentations. EP's financial controller regarded these personal interactions as a crucial instrument to strengthen the relationship and create a more open exchange of information and expertise.

The frequent face-to-face contacts and the direct involvement of AP in the decision making strongly strengthened the relationship between EP and AP. This smoothed the cooperation and resulted in high levels of trust between EP's and AP's representatives. It also changed the mismatch between the JV characteristics and the JV control into a match (the content-based control pattern was replaced by a consultation-based control pattern) and thereby accommodated the weakening effects and reinforced the JV relationship.

### Example of a Natural Termination of a JV Relationship: Gas Sales (Continuation of the First Example)

The different strategic motives of the parent companies, which were already present at the outset of the JV relationship, were a crucial factor in the termination of the Gas Sales JV. While Electricity Corp's strategic motive was to gain access to the gas market and establishing gas retailing activities, American Corp's strategic motive was more limited. American Corp was in the first place interested in establishing its name and reputation in the UK, and not in the JV's gas retailing activities as such. However, the different parent companies' strategic motives were a factor that only became important because of the effects of other factors. From the outset of Gas Sales, the relationship between American Corp and the managers of its British subsidiary, Alpha Gas, was quite strained. While the managers of Alpha Gas put considerable effort into developing Gas Sales, American Corp as a whole made hardly any contributions. American Corp was not particularly interested in the details of the JV's activities, as it was only interested in establishing its name and reputation in the UK. The differences in strategic motives between American Corp and Alpha Gas led to the Alpha Gas managers involved in the Gas Sales JV leaving Alpha Gas in 1996. They were replaced by other American Corp managers. This replacement can be considered as one of the factors that eventually led to the termination of the JV relationship. Because these managers were less skilled than their predecessors, and also because the JV managers appointed by Electricity Corp had no shared history with them, information sharing and trust between the JV parties declined substantially.

As a result, the relationship between the new managers and the Electricity Corp appointed managers became much more distant and more commercial. This strained the relationship between the parent companies. Furthermore, because of its success, Gas Sales wanted to further increase its activities in the gas market. This, however, created the need for additional working capital, but American Corp was unwilling to provide additional funds. The success of Gas Sales had enabled American Corp to establish its name and reputation in the UK, and this meant that it had achieved its strategic motive. Consequently, it decided to leave the JV relationship. Although Electricity Corp's strategic motives had not been achieved, due to what had been learned, it no longer needed the knowledge and experience of its partner, and so it decided to continue the JV's activities on its own. It thus integrated the JV's activities into its own business, merging the Gas Sales JV into the hierarchy of Electricity Corp. There was no longer any need for the protection by a JV relationship to exploit the gas market, and the JV relationship naturally terminated.

## DISCUSSION AND CONCLUSIONS

This chapter investigates the dynamic evolution of JV relationships over their lifetime. It takes a long-term perspective in order to study how specific factors cause changes within a JV relationship and how the parent companies respond to these changes and thereby use the JV control they have put in place. By taking a long-term perspective, the chapter demonstrates that the dynamic evolution of a JV relationship can have various outcomes. The chapter distinguishes three scenarios of evolution processes; the evolution processes may (1) strengthen a JV relationship, (2) weaken a JV relationship, or (3) lead to a natural termination of a JV relationship. It is indicated how specific factors could lead to one of these scenarios of JV dynamics. This analysis shows that the evolution processes and their outcome are determined by the factors that cause changes within the JV relationship and by the responses of the parent companies to these changes, but also by various characteristics of the JV relationship and its environment. As so many variables influence the evolution processes and their outcome, it is difficult to predict the effects of specific factors in general. Nevertheless, below we will try to develop some more general evolution patterns that help to explain evolution processes and their outcome in JV relationships in practice.

As JV relationships are intended for the longer term, the parent companies have to deal with uncertainty and, hence, cannot foresee all eventualities. It can be expected that the parent companies have to respond to unexpected problems and opportunities over time. The more the parent companies are committed to the JV relationship and trust each other, the easier it will be to find adequate responses to those problems and opportunities. Then the risk that the JV relationship will be terminated prematurely is low. Various scholars (Ariño & De la Torre, 1998; Luo, 2001; Ring & Van de Ven, 1994) have shown that personal relationships are crucial in long-term relationships, as they can reduce uncertainty. Trustworthy relationships between the individuals involved in a JV relationship help to share information, to discuss problems, to find solutions that are in the interest of all parties, to inform each other about developments in the near future, and to discuss possible effects. Therefore, changes in key individuals can hamper a JV relationship, which we saw in the last phase of Gas Sales.

A trustworthy JV relationship stimulates the use of JV control. Moreover, such a relationship makes it easier to make adaptations to the JV control when the character of the JV relationship changes. We saw in the first phase of Gas Sales that because of changes in the institutional environment and learning about how to operate in the gas market and how to cooperate, the JV control needed to be adapted to the changing characteristics of the JV relationship. As there was high trust between the JV parties, making these changes was only natural.

JV control is used by the parent companies to manage the JV's activities, but also to manage the relationship with each other. In other words, JV control helps the parent companies to cooperate successfully. On the other hand, JV control can also act as a factor that causes dynamic evolution of a JV relationship. When JV control is not geared to the character of the JV relationship, it may lead to tensions between the parent companies, as it does not adequately coordinate the JV's activities with those of the parent companies or is not able to prevent opportunistic behavior of one of the parties. Then the JV control needs to be adapted in such a way that it matches the character of the JV relationship. In JV Asia we saw such a mismatch of the JV control with the character of the JV relationship between EP and AP. As EP tried to manage the JV relationship from a distance, whereas the differences in the parental contributions and cultural backgrounds required regular face-to-face consultations, the parent companies were not able to set up the JV. Once EP's financial controller arrived at the JV site and had face-to-face contacts with AP, the parent companies were able to build the production site.

If the parent companies are not able to accommodate effects that weaken the JV relationship they are likely to decide to terminate the JV relationship. Then the weakening effects of one or more factors (e.g., the JV becomes a loss maker due to fierce competition in the market or one of the parent companies behaves opportunistically and causes mistrust) are outside the parent companies' control. In such a situation, the JV relationship ends prematurely and can be qualified as a failed relationship.

The examples show that the dynamic evolution of JV relationships is not a matter of the influence of one factor, but that more factors at the same time or successively affect a JV relationship. We saw that the termination of Gas Sales was not only the result of the replacement of key individuals by less committed individuals, who were primarily interested in their private goals, but that the realization of one of the parent companies' strategic motives quickened its decision to leave the JV relationship. JV Asia shows that the mismatch between the JV control and the character of the JV relationship was caused by the bad financial situation of EP.

JV relationships are usually established for a limited period of time. When the parent companies have achieved their strategic motives, the relationship will be terminated. Then the aim of the collaboration has been accomplished. It is likely that the parent companies will also terminate their relationship when they are able to perform the JV's activities themselves and when they have no other reasons to collaborate (for example, risk sharing). Then the JV's activities are brought under the umbrella of the hierarchy. Such a natural termination of JV relationships illustrates their strength. However, this study shows that the parent companies can only reap the benefits of a JV relationship if they are able to put in place adequate JV control at the outset and to adapt it when internal and external factors change the characteristics of the relationship over time.

## NOTES

1. If parent companies have established a JV relationship for such reasons as realizing economies of scale, overcoming governmental restrictions, or reducing risk, achieving these strategic motives implies that the JV relationship is successful and will be continued. In these cases, the JV relationship is appropriate for achieving these strategic motives. If the parent companies are not able to achieve these strategic motives, the JV relationship will be threatened, and this may lead to its termination.
2. We refer to Kamminga and Van der Meer-Kooistra (2007) for a comprehensive overview of the characteristics of the three control patterns (see Table 8, p. 151) and an in-depth discussion of the three matches between the characteristics of the JV relationship and the control pattern.

## REFERENCES

Ariño, A. (2003). Measures of strategic Alliance performance: An analysis of construct validity. *Journal of International Business Studies, 34*, 66–79.

Ariño, A., & De la Torre, J. (1998). Learning from failure: Towards an evolutionary model of collaborative ventures. *Organization Science, 9*, 306–325.

Beamish, P. W., & Delios, A. (1997). Improving joint venture performance through congruent measures of success. In P. W. Beamish & J. P. Killing (Eds.), *Cooperative strategies: European perspectives* (pp. 103–127). San Francisco, CA: New Lexington Press.

Contractor, F. J., & Lorange, P. (1988). Why should firms cooperate? The strategy and economics basis for cooperative ventures. In F. J. Contractor & P. Lorange (Eds.), *Cooperative strategies in international business* (pp. 3–30). Lexington, MA: Lexington Books.

Das, T. K., & Kumar, R. (2007). Learning dynamics in the alliance development process. *Management Decision, 45*, 684–707.

Geringer, J. M., & Hebert, L. (1989). Control and performance of international joint ventures. *Journal of International Business Studies, 20*, 235–254.

Hamel, G. (1991). Competition for competence and inter-partner learning within international strategic alliances. *Strategic Management Journal, 12* (Summer), 83–103.

Harrigan, K. R. (1986). *Managing for joint venture success.* Lexington, MA: Lexington Book Cooperation.

Harrigan, K. R., & Newman, W. H. (1990). Bases of interorganization cooperation: Propensity, power, persistence. *Journal of Management Studies, 27*(4), 417–434.

Hennart, J.-F., Roehl, T., & Zietlow, D.S. (1999). "Trojan horse" or "workhorse"? The evolution of U.S.-Japanese joint ventures in the United States. *Strategic Management Journal, 20*, 15–29.

Inkpen, A. C., & Beamish, P. W. (1997). Knowledge, bargaining power, and the instability of international joint ventures. *Academy of Management Review, 22*, 177–202.

Inkpen, A. C., & Currall, S. C. (1998). The nature, antecedents, and consequences of joint venture trust. *Journal of International Management, 4*, 1–20.

Inkpen, A. C., & Currall, S. C. (2004). The coevolution of trust, control, and learning in joint ventures. *Organization Science, 15*, 586–599.

Johnson, H. T., & Kaplan, R. S. (1987). *Relevance lost: The rise and fall of management accounting.* Boston, MA: Harvard Business School Press.

Kale, P., Singh, H., & Perlmutter, H. (2000). Learning and protection of proprietary assets in strategic alliances: Building relational capital. *Strategic Management Journal, 21*, 217–237.

Kamminga, P. E. (2003). *Management control of joint ventures.* Ridderkerk, Netherlands: Labyrint Publication.

Kamminga, P. E., & Van der Meer-Kooistra, J. (2007). Management control patterns in joint venture relationships: A model and an exploratory study, *Accounting, Organizations and Society, 32*, 135–158.

Killing, J. P. (1983). *Strategies for joint venture success.* Kent, UK: Croom Helm.

Kogut, B. (1988). Joint ventures: Theoretical and empirical perspectives. *Strategic Management Journal, 9*(4), 319–332.

Kumar, S., & Seth, A. A. (1998). The design of coordination and control mechanisms for managing joint venture-parent relationships. *Strategic Management Journal, 19*, 579–599.

Lorange, P., & Roos, J. (1992). *Strategic alliances: Formation, implementation and evolution.* Cambridge, UK: Blackwell Publishers.

Luo, Y. (2001). Antecedents and consequences of personal attachments in cross-cultural cooperative ventures. *Administrative Science Quarterly, 46*, 177–201.

Mayer, K. J., & Argyres, N.S. (2004). Learning to contract: Evidence from the personal computer industry. *Organizations Science, 15*, 394–410.

Merchant, K. A., & Van der Stede, W. A. (2003). *Management control systems, performance measurement, evaluations and incentives.* Upper Saddle River, NJ: Prentice Hall.

Parkhe, A. (1991). Interfirm diversity, organizational learning, and longevity in strategic global alliances. *Journal of International Business Studies, 22*, 579–601.

Ring, P. S., & Van de Ven, A. H. (1994). Developmental processes of cooperative interorganizational relationships. *Academy of Management Review, 19*, 90–118.

Sako, M. (1992). *Prices, quality and trust: Interfirm relationships in Britain and Japan.* Cambridge, UK: Cambridge University Press.

Seabright, M. A., Levinthal, D. A., & Fichman, M. (1992). Role of individual attachments in the dissolution of interorganizational relationships. *Academy of Management Journal, 35,* 122–160.

Spender, J.-C. (1989). *Industry recipes: An enquiry into the nature and sources of managerial judgement.* Oxford, UK: Basil Blackwell.

Van der Meer-Kooistra, J., & Kamminga, P. E. (2010). The role of management accounting in joint venture relationships: A dynamic perspective. In H. Håkansson, K. Kraus, & J. Lind (Eds.), *Accounting in networks* (pp. 80–112). New York, NY: Routledge.

Van der Meer-Kooistra, J., & Vosselman, E. G. J. (2010). Trust and control in strategic alliances: An instrumental perspective. In T. K. Das (Ed.), *Researching strategic alliances: Emerging perspectives* (pp. 77–103). Charlotte, NC: Information Age Publishing.

Vosselman, E. G. J., & Van der Meer-Kooistra, J. (2009). Accounting for control and trust building in interfirm transactional relationships. *Accounting, Organizations and Society, 34,* 267–283.

Williamson, O. E. (1985). *The economic institutions of capitalism: Firms, markets, relational contracting.* New York, NY: Free Press.

Yan, A. (1998). Structural stability and reconfiguration of international joint ventures. *Journal of International Business Studies, 29,* 773–798.

Yan, A., & Zeng, M. (1999). International joint venture instability: A critique of previous research, a reconceptualization, and directions for future research. *Journal of International Business Studies, 30,* 395–412.

Zucker, L. G. (1986). Production of trust: Institutional sources of economic structure, 1840–1920. *Research in Organizational Behavior, 8,* 53–111.

CHAPTER 9

# MANAGING CONFLICT IN INTERNATIONAL STRATEGIC ALLIANCES

Saleema Kauser

### ABSTRACT

International strategic alliances have become an important part of many firms' international business strategies. As such, it is important to understand what causes them to fail or succeed. One of the most common reasons for alliance failure in the literature is conflict between partners. The chapter will aim to investigate the dynamics of interpartner cooperation in strategic alliances by examining the linkages between conflict and communication, trust, commitment, coordination, and interdependence. Using a sample of UK, Japanese, European, and American alliances established during the period 1989 to 1985, the chapter will aim to show that partners who focus their attentions on managing interpersonal relationships will display lower levels of conflict in their relationships.

### INTRODUCTION

Collaborations across borders between firms are now so common that they are a growing subject of management research. Some firms perceive international alliances as strategic weapons (Doz & Hamel, 1998; Harrigan, 1988), while others consider them to be a superior method of investing corporate resources. In addition, competitive pressures are continuously forcing companies to partner with other firms, many of whom have different priorities, incentives, and ways of doing things. Several studies have shown that the number of alliances across borders being used by firms is increasing (Glaister & Buckley, 1994). The importance of managing successful international strategic alliances has been reflected extensively in the literature, and has primarily focused on the ex ante structuring of alliances (Parkhe, 1993). Researchers have examined the rationale for international alliances (Contractor & Lorange, 1988; Glaister & Buckley, 1994; Hagedoorn, 1993; Harrigan, 1988; Hennart, 1988; Kogut, 1988); partner selection and characteristics (Blodgett, 1991; Geringer, 1993); and the ownership, control, and performance relationship (Geringer & Hebert, 1989, 1991; Killing, 1983; Schaan, 1983; Tomlinson, 1970). The fundamental basis of these studies is that if the partners are not compatible, motivations of partners are not congruent, and ownership and control are not sorted out, the alliance is likely to experience difficulties and partners become dissatisfied with the outcomes.

Despite the initiatives to improve relationships between partners, international strategic alliances are plagued with problems because of potential problems associated with their management, poor perceived performance, and inflexibility (Geringer & Hebert, 1991; Parkhe, 1993). It has been estimated that between 30% and 70% of alliances fail (Bleeke & Ernst, 1991; Das & Kumar, 2009; Das & Teng, 2000; Park & Ungson, 2001). While several potential problems have been associated with their management, one main issue concerns the role of conflict in alliances and the ability of partners to deal with conflicting differences. Many researchers have emphasized the issue of managing conflict as a crucial organization process for alliance success (Ding, 1997; Geringer & Herbert, 1989, 1991; Gill & Butler, 2003; Yan & Gray, 1994). However, there is very little conceptual and empirical research available concerning the impact of partnership attributes on managing conflict (Das & Kumar, 2009; Das & Teng, 1998; Fey & Beamish, 2000).

Studies have investigated the operational aspects of international strategic alliances, including management and production control, human resources, marketing, and finance (Child & Faulkner, 1998). Researchers have found that conflict within international strategic alliances is inevitable due to the differing objectives, structures, and organizational cultures (Kauser & Shaw; 2004; Lane & Beamish, 1990). Much of this research emphasizes that while problems and disagreements are inevitable in every alliance relationship, partners can work together to develop mediating mechanisms to diffuse and settle their differences (Das & Kumar, 2009; Gulati & Singh, 1998; Kale, Singh, & Perlmutter, 2000; Kumar & Nti, 1998). One way to do this is to pay attention to relationship issues such as coordination, trust, commitment, and communication. These issues seem to be forgotten when it comes to launching alliance agreements (Das & Kumar, 2009) and have been shown to be critical in managing successful relationships (Fey & Beamish, 1999; Hambrick, Li, Xin, & Tsui, 2001; Hu & Chen, 1996; Mohr & Spekman, 1994; Yan & Gray, 1994). There is much in the literature that emphasizes the importance of managing the alliance relationship with regards to having clearly defined goals, contributing sufficient resources, having effective communication, managing commitment, and showing forbearance among others. (Das & Kumar, 2009; Geyskens, Steenkamp, Scheer, & Kumar, 1996; Holm, Eriksson, & Johanson, 1999; Kauser & Shaw, 2004; Mohr & Spekman, 1994). However, the impact of relationship dynamics on conflict within alliances has received little attention (Das & Teng, 1998).

To understand how partners address and deal with the issue of conflict in managing international alliances, we need to emphasize the complexity involved in managing relationship dynamics between companies from different national backgrounds and their impact on managing conflict in these relationships. This chapter proposes to address this gap in the existing literature by examining the impact of partnership attributes on managing conflict within international strategic alliances, (Dang, 1977; Geringer & Hebert, 1989, 1991; Kauser & Shaw, 2004). Specifically, the study aims to investigate the relationship between conflict and the development of commitment, trust, interdependence, coordination, and communication.

## CONFLICT RELATIONSHIP DYNAMICS

### Partnership Attributes

The conceptual framework for this study is based upon the premise that international strategic alliances are inherently characterized by conflict in their daily relationships. Based on a review of the relevant literature, the relationships between the factors are shown in Figure 9.1.

The importance of partnership attributes has been reflected extensively in the literature, which has focused on commitment, coordination, interdependence, trust, and communication (Anderson & Narus, 1991; Das & Kumar, 2009; Ding, 1997; Geyskens et al., 1996; Hu & Chen, 1996; Kauser & Shaw, 2004; Lee, 2001; Madhok, 1995; Mohr & Nevin, 1990; Mohr & Spekman, 1994; Monckza, Peterson, Handfield, & Ragatz, 1998; Morgan & Hunt, 1994). Theoretical contributions (Parkhe, 1993) as well as empirical and case study (Mohr & Spekman, 1994; Monckza et al., 1998) research have identified these attributes as the most important factors necessary for the development of successful alliance relationships. In such relationships

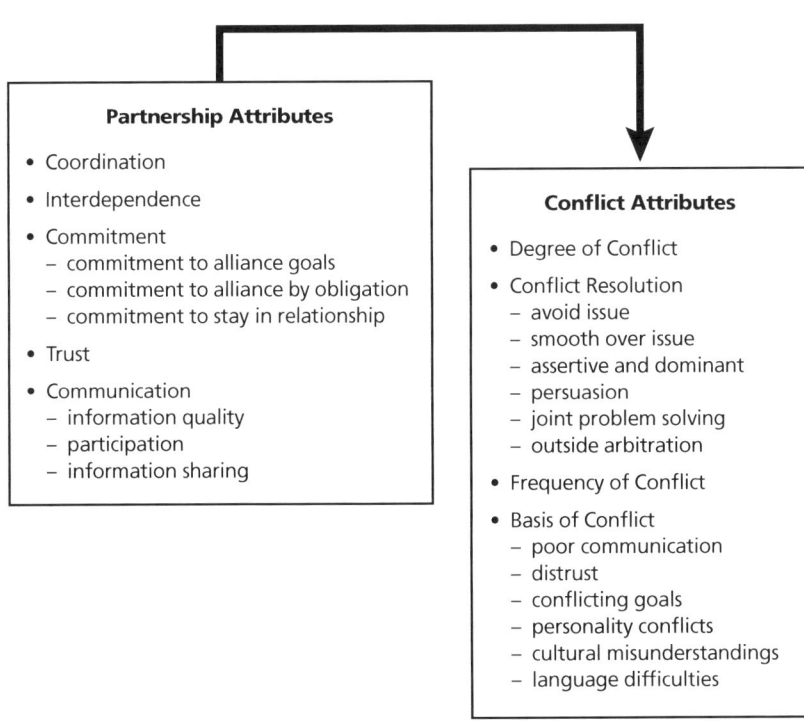

**Figure 9.1** Conflict and relationship dynamics.

there exist a set of commodities that help guide the flow of information between partners, manage the depth and breadth of interaction, and capture the complex and dynamic interchange between partners. Mohr and Spekman (1994) make the assumption that the existence of partnership attributes implies that both partners acknowledge their mutual dependence and their willingness to work for the survival of the relationship and thus reduce the potential for opportunistic behavior. Hu and Chen (1996) identified four characteristics that may impact the performance of partnerships: level of commitment, control, the number of partners, and the sociocultural distance. More recently, Das and Kumar (2009) have argued that because of the buoyant nature of partnerships, misunderstandings can be handled through managing both commitment and forbearance.

Many researchers also agree that conflict between partners is strongly related to the relationship dynamics of international alliances (Anderson & Narus, 1990; Child & Faulkner, 1998; Ding, 1997; Friedman & Beguin, 1971; Killing, 1983; Lane & Beamish, 1990; Lewis, 1990). One view is that international alliances try to maintain their autonomy in an interdependent relationship, which gives rise to conflicts (Van de Ven & Walker, 1984). The drive for both autonomy and cooperation can result in the coexistence of cooperative and conflictual motives within the partnership (Aldrich, 1979; Das & Teng, 2000; Khanna, Gulati, & Nohria, 1998). Conflicts between partners can result in misunderstandings and distrust, leading to reduced cooperation and thereby deteriorating the success of the alliance (Freidman & Beguin, 1971; Kauser, 2007; Killing, 1983; Lewis, 1990; Madhok, 1995; Wright, 1979).

Habib (1983, 1987) showed that the frequency and level of conflicts between partners led to problems of commitment to goals. Others have shown that frequent disagreements in a relationship tend to cause frustration and unpleasantness and impact the relationship dynamics within strategic alliances (Anderson & Narus, 1984, 1990; Kauser, 2007; Ding, 1997). In addition, conflict may harm accomplishment of the task of the relationships. Frequent disagreements may result in complex, time-consuming decision making or in obstructive behaviors that simply block any decision making (Killing, 1983). As a result, time and resources are devoted to conflict resolution rather than activities that are productive for the alliance. Such situations may limit an alliance's ability to cope with and to respond to changes in its environment and thus to be successful in its business. Conflicts may also result in firms from cooperating and from withholding resources that may be required by the other partner to achieve its objectives (Buckley & Casson, 1988; Lane & Beamish, 1990; Nti & Kumar, 2000). Transaction cost theory advocates that conflict breaks down trust and increases the potential for opportunistic behavior, thereby resulting in economically inefficient relationships (Beamish & Banks, 1987; Buckley & Casson, 1988).

**Proposition 1:** *International strategic alliances that exhibit coordination, interdependence, commitment, trust, and communication will display lower levels of conflict.*

There are many ways in which conflicts can arise between partners. Conflicts may arise from differences in cultural values, management styles, operational methods, and procedures, which may jeopardize the alliance (Jain, 1987). In international strategic alliances, the presence of two parent firms can lead to differences between them in terms of management style, culture, communication, and operational practices, which are conducive to conflict (Devlin & Bleackley, 1988; Ding, 1997; Glaister & Wu, 1994; Jain, 1987; Johnson, 1999; Killing, 1983; Lewis, 1990; Wright, 1979).

Wright (1979) examined 25 U.S. and Canadian joint ventures in Japan and found that conflicts between partners resulted from differences between the Japanese and the Western culture, which in turn reflected differences in management style. Glaister and Wu (1994), in their study of UK joint ventures in China, pointed out that differences in the economic systems and management systems impacted the management of the joint ventures. Cultural differences between the two countries made the actual management more difficult. These factors would appear to adversely affect the successful implementation of the joint ventures. Lewis (1990), from his investigation of 40 U.S. American and Asian alliances, observed that the potential for conflict resulted from cultural distance between alliance partners, which adversely affected the management of the alliance. Similarly, Simiar (1984) investigated the causes of failure in 29 international joint ventures in Iran and attributed the failure of ventures to conflicting goals between partners resulting from cultural misunderstandings. More recently, research has shown that the ways in which partnership relationships are managed affect conflict (Das & Kumar, 2009; Hoon-Halbauer, 1999; Hu & Chen, 1996; Johnson, Cullen, Sakano, & Bronson, 2001; Kauser, 2007; Kozan, 1997; Leung, Koch, & Lu, 2002). Essentially, the presence of conflict may monopolize the attention and the time of the management of the alliance relationship and thus is likely to block their communication, coordination, commitment, and trust. Ultimately, it may impede effective management of the alliances operations and implementation of strategy. Against this background, the following proposition was formulated:

**Proposition 2:** *International strategic alliances that exhibit coordination, interdependence, commitment, trust, and communication will impact the basis of conflict between partnerships.*

Given that a certain amount of conflict is expected, an understanding of how such conflicts can be resolved is also important (Borys & Jemison, 1989). Research has shown that the success of international strategic alliances is very much dependent upon how partners manage daily operations and the mechanism used to resolve conflicts (Das & Kumar, 2011; Lane & Beamish, 1990; Lin & Germain, 1998; Xie, Song, & Stringfellow, 1998). Researchers have identified a range of strategies in dealing with conflict in international partnerships. In their study of Sino–foreign partnerships, Lin and Germain (1998) identified four conflict resolution mechanisms: namely, joint problem solving, compromising through negotiation, unilateral control by the dominant party, and informal and formal contracts. They found that the use of joint problem solving was positively associated with more successful partnerships. Other research has also demonstrated that partnerships are more likely to use nonassertive strategies such as joint problem solving and compromise as the most preferred strategy for managing conflict (Mohr & Spekman, 1994; Xie et al., 1998). Joint problem solving allows a mutually satisfactory solution to be reached, thereby enhancing alliance success. Partners very often attempt to persuade each other to adopt particular solutions to the conflict situation, which appears to be more constructive than the use of coercion or domination (Deutsch, 1969;

Lin & Germain, 1998). Domination or coercion is seen as being the least preferred strategy, which is counterproductive and likely to strain the fabric of the strategic alliance relationship (Lin & Germain, 1998). In some strategic alliances, conflict resolution is institutionalized, and third party arbitration is recommended (Anderson & Narus, 1990). However, it has been suggested that internal resolution is more likely to lead to long-term success (Assael, 1969). Other conflict resolution techniques such as smoothing over or ignoring and avoiding the issue are somewhat at odds with the norms and values advocated in more successful strategic alliances. Such techniques do not fit in with alliances in which the problems of one party become the problems affecting both parties. Different conflict resolution strategies may also be used according to the circumstances, resulting in different outcomes (Das & Kumar, 2011; Lin & Germain, 1998). These findings suggest that managers in international partnerships are induced to use a particular conflict resolution strategy depending on the situation at hand.

Clearly, various conflict resolution strategies can be adopted in the management of international strategic alliances (Anderson & Narus, 1990; Das & Kumar, 2011; Ding, 1997; Friedman & Beguin, 1971; Killing, 1983; Lane & Beamish, 1990; Lewis, 1990; Lin & Germain, 1998).

**Proposition 3:** *International strategic alliances that exhibit coordination, interdependence, commitment, trust, and communication are more likely to resolve conflicts using joint problem solving.*

## METHODOLOGY

The propositions were tested on a sample of 600 international agreements that took place between 1988 and 1995. This sample included strategic alliances between British companies and their U.S., European, and Japanese partners. Information concerning these alliances was gathered from *The Economist* and *Financial Times* along the lines of similar databases constructed by other researchers (Glaister & Buckley, 1994; Hergert & Morris, 1988). All companies were contacted by telephone to request their participation in the study. Questionnaires were sent out to senior managers involved in the management of alliances. A total of 287 responses (63.7%) were received. In spite of having agreed to participate in the study when contacted by telephone, 173 respondents did not complete the questionnaire, giving the following reasons for non-response: the alliance had been terminated, contract confidentiality did not allow information to be divulged, and workload; some commented that the alliance was not strategic in nature. The length of the questionnaire may also have been an issue for some companies, but the usable response rate of 114 completed questionnaires (25.3%) compares well to other studies of a similar nature (Mohr & Spekman, 1994).

## Measurement of Variables

The domain of the measures used was specified and a sample of items was generated for each construct (Churchill, 1979). To ensure high content validity, all measurements developed were based on a comprehensive review of the literature and detailed evaluation by the researchers. The questionnaire developed was also pretested on a number of senior managers with extensive international strategic alliance management experience. All measures were evaluated for reliability and validity using Cronbach's alpha (see Tables 9.1 & 9.2). The majority of measures demonstrated a high degree of internal consistency, with alphas ranging from 0.58 to 0.93, falling within the range of acceptability recommended by Nunnally (1978).

**TABLE 9.1 Reliability Scales for Relationship Dynamic Variables**

| Relationship Dynamic Attributes | Original Number of Scale Items | Cronbach's Alpha |
|---|---|---|
| Co-ordination | 8 | .88 |
| Interdependence | 10 | .70 |
| Commitment/Goals and Values 1 | 10 | .93 |
| Commitment/Goals and Values 2 | 5 | .91 |
| Commitment/Obligations | 7 | .91 |
| Commitment/stay in relationship | 6 | .86 |
| Trust 1 | 5 | .90 |
| Trust 2 | 8 | .90 |
| Information Quality | 5 | .89 |
| Information Sharing | 4 | .72 |
| Participation | 5 | .79 |
| Total | 73 | |

**TABLE 9.2 Reliability Scales for Conflict**

| Conflict | Original Number of Scale Items | Cronbach's Alpha |
|---|---|---|
| Conflict Resolution | 6 | N/A |
| Conflict | 6 | .70 |
| Total | 12 | — |

## Dependent Measures

A fourteen-item scale was used to measure the conflict construct. The *conflict* measure concerns the level of conflict between the partner firms and was assessed in terms of the degree and frequency of conflict, the basis of conflict (Anderson & Narus, 1990; Kogut, 1988), and how conflicts may be resolved (Mohr & Spekman, 1994) between partners.

## Independent Measures

Much previous research into coordination has measured this construct using either a single or two items (Mohr & Spekman, 1994; Monckza et al., 1998; Olson & Singsuwan, 1997). By contrast, this study has used eight items derived from the literature. Interdependence was measured on two dimensions—replaceability and dependency on resources (Kumar, Scheer, & Steenkamp, 1995). Following reliability, all ten measures were used for further analysis. Commitment was operationalized using an organizational commitment questionnaire, which measured the extent to which each party identifies with the goals and objectives of the alliance, is willing to exert effort on behalf of the alliance, and intends to maintain the relationship (Porter, Steers, Mowday, & Boulian, 1974). These three dimensions were assessed using 28 items, all of which remained in the analysis after reliability tests. These items have been widely used in studies of organizational behavior (Mowday, Steers, & Porter, 1979; Randall, 1990). Although many studies have recognized the importance of trust for successful collaboration, the number of measures used has been low, with many authors acknowledging that the conceptualization and operationalization of trust often does not capture the many facets of the concept (Aulakh, Kotabe, & Sahay, 1996; Mohr & Spekman, 1994; Monckza et al., 1998). This study, therefore, has developed new measures of trust using 13 different dimensions that showed very high levels of reliability. Communication attributes were measured on three dimensions—information quality, information sharing, and participation in planning and goal setting (Daft & Lengel, 1986; Huber & Daft 1987; Mohr & Spekman, 1994). Information quality in this study refers to timeliness, accuracy, adequacy, and creditability of the information exchanged (Daft & Lengel, 1986; Huber & Daft, 1987). Information sharing measures the extent of information exchange between partners (Mohr & Spekman, 1994), and participation measures the extent to which partners engage jointly in planning and goal setting (Mohr & Spekman, 1994). A total of 14 items were used in subsequent analysis.

## FINDINGS

### Regression Model Testing

To investigate the effect of partnership characteristics on the level and basis of conflicts and how conflicts may be resolved in international alliances, regression analysis was undertaken with each of the dependent variables measuring conflict. All the identified factors from the factor analysis were used as the explanatory variables (see Tables 9.1 to 9.8). The predictors and independent measures are presented in Table 9.9. Partnership characteristic factors were regressed for each measure of the dependent variables in order to identify the influence of these that might be related to each of the different aspects of conflict measured. The justification for running the regression model for each single measure of the dependent variables was to realize how much explanatory power the independent variables have for each dependent measure. Therefore, fourteen separate regression models (one for each conflict measure) were examined and reported.

The regression analysis estimates the significance of the coefficients corresponding to the set of propositions and assesses the changes in the proportion of variance explained ($R^2$) and the statistical significance of each of the independent variables. The regression model was defined as:

$$Y = a + þ1\ X1 + þ2\ X2 + þ3\ X3 \ldots + þ11\ X16$$

**TABLE 9.3  Predictors and Dependent Variables**

| Independent Measures | Dependent Measures |
|---|---|
| **Relationship Atributes** | **Conflict Attributes** |
| **Coordination** | Degree of Conflict = Y1 |
| Factor 1 = Coordination between partner firms = þ1 | Frequency of Conflict = Y2 |
| **Interdependence** | **Conflict Resolution** |
| Factor 1 = Dependency on marketing capabilities = þ2 | Avoid issue = Y3 |
| Factor 2 = Dependency on administrative support = þ3 | Smooth over issue = Y4 |
| Factor 3 = Dependency on management skills = þ4 | Assertive and dominant = Y5 |
| **Commitment** | Persuasion = Y6 |
| Factor 1 = Commitment to alliance goals = þ5 | Joint problem solving = Y7 |
| Factor 2 = Commitment to alliance by obligation = þ6 | Outside arbitration = Y8 |
| Factor 3 = Commitment to stay in relationship = þ7 | **Basis of Conflict** |
| **Trust** | Poor communication = Y9 |
| Factor 1 = Trust in partner = þ8 | Distrust = Y10 |
| **Communication** | Conflicting goals = Y11 |
| Factor 1 = Information quality = þ9 | Personality conflicts = Y12 |
| Factor 12 = Participation = þ10 | Cultural misunderstanding = Y13 |
| Factor 13 = Information sharing = þ11 | Language difficulties = Y14 |

where $Y$ represents the measures of conflict (dependent measures) and a is the intercept. The intercept is the expected value of $Y$ when the value for each X variable is zero. The X1, X2, X3 are the partnership characteristics (independent variables), and þ1, þ2, þ3, are the regression coefficients for the eleven independent factors. The coefficients are the amount by which the expected value of y increases when X1 increases by a unit amount, when all the other X variables are held constant. The specific variables identified as significant predictors, the resulting standardized Beta weights, and the percentage of variance explained for each of the conflict items are presented in Table 9.9.

**TABLE 9.4 Coordination Factor Analyses Scores**

| Variables | Factor 1 |
|---|---|
| Teamwork with partner | .830 |
| Exchange of ideas with partner | .818 |
| UK firm integrated with part | .809 |
| High level of interaction between partners | .808 |
| Partner firm integrated with UK firm | .807 |
| Keep partner informed about important decisions | .727 |
| Partner activities an extension of UK firm | .570 |
| Eigen value | 4.169 |
| Percent of variance explained | 59.6 |
| KMO | .803 |
| Bartlett's Test of Sphericity | 472.402 |

**TABLE 9.5 Interdependence Factor Analysis Scores**

| Variables | Factor 1 | Factor 2 | Factor 3 |
|---|---|---|---|
| Dependency on marketing capability | .848 | | |
| Dependency on market information | .800 | | |
| Dependency on customer service | .759 | | |
| Dependency on sales/profits | .737 | | |
| Dependency on administration | | .834 | |
| Dependency on manpower resources | | .823 | |
| Dependency on financial resources | | | .836 |
| Dependency on management skills | | | .598 |
| Eigen value | 2.558 | | |
| Percent of variance explained | 31.9 | | |
| KMO | .654 | | |
| Bartlett's Test of Sphericity | 246.705 | | |

## TABLE 9.6 Commitment Factors Analysis Scores

| Variables | Factor 1 | Factor 2 | Factor 3 |
|---|---|---|---|
| Agreement over key decisions | .825 | | |
| Agreement over goals/objectives | .773 | | |
| Agreement over future plans | .740 | | |
| Agreement over strategic direction | .731 | | |
| Agreement over roles performed | .717 | | |
| Share understanding and vision | .705 | | |
| Agreement over contractual terms | .692 | | |
| Agreement over daily operations | .590 | | |
| Identify with goals/objectives | | .582 | |
| Obligated to compromise in achieving objectives | | .767 | |
| Obligated to be patient with partner over mistakes | | .759 | |
| Obligated to listen to problems of partner | | .741 | |
| Obligated to try to overcome problems | | .739 | |
| Obligated to encourage goal achievement | | .697 | |
| Obligated to satisfy partners needs | | .643 | |
| Obligated to help build the relationship | | .630 | |
| Relationship important to achieve strategic objectives | | | .849 |
| Long-term relationship will be profitable | | | .771 |
| Staying in relationship is a desire | | | .751 |
| Staying in relationship is a necessity | | | .741 |
| Partnership is valuable | | | .726 |
| Make sacrifices to achieve long-term objectives | | | .506 |
| Eigen value | 11.069 | | |
| Percent of variance explained | 50.3 | | |
| KMO | .992 | | |
| Bartlett's Test of Sphericity | 1912.365 | | |

To test the proposition that the amount of variation explained by the regression model is more than the variation explained by the average, the $F$ statistic was used. The $F$ statistic (Table 9.9) for the majority of the regression models exceeded the $F$ critical with 93 degrees of freedom at the 0.01 level and therefore offers significant explanatory power. This means collectively the predictors explain some variation in every case. The statistical significance of the individual regression coefficients are presented in Table 9.9. These coefficients indicate the relative importance of each predictor in the prediction of each of the dependent measures of conflict.

### TABLE 9.7 Trust Factor Analysis Scores

| Variables | Factor 1 |
|---|---|
| Partner trusted to show loyalty | .897 |
| We can always rely on each other | .888 |
| Partner makes effort to keep commitments | .881 |
| Relationship marked by a high degree of harmony | .834 |
| Partner trusted to be supportive | .806 |
| Partner trusted to keep promises | .802 |
| Partner trusted to be sincere | .786 |
| Relationship open and informal | .727 |
| We do not take advantage of each other | .727 |
| We share work related problems | .719 |
| Close personal ties between us | .623 |
| Eigen value | 6.937 |
| Percent of variance explained | 63.1 |
| KMO | .923 |
| Bartlett's Test of Sphericity | 952.158 |

### TABLE 9.8 Communication Factor Analysis Scores

| Variables | Factor 1 | Factor 2 | Factor 3 |
|---|---|---|---|
| Communication adequate/inadequate | .875 | | |
| Communication complete/incomplete | .868 | | |
| Communication credible/incredible | .779 | | |
| Communication accurate/inaccurate | .760 | | |
| Communication timely/untimely | .682 | | |
| Seek partners advice in decision making | | .804 | |
| Partner seeks advice before decision making | | .705 | |
| Both keep each informed about changes | | .690 | |
| Inform partner of changing needs | | .657 | |
| Participate in goal setting | | .574 | |
| Participate in planning activities | | | .773 |
| Share proprietary information | | | .690 |
| Participate in regular meetings | | | .538 |
| Eigen value | 5.541 | | |
| Percent of variance explained | 42.6 | | |
| KMO | .831 | | |
| Bartlett's Test of Sphericity | 781.429 | | |

## TABLE 9.9  Regression Analysis

| Dependent Measures | Y1 | Y2 | Y3 | Y4 | Y5 | Y6 | Y7 | Y8 | Y9 | Y10 | Y11 | Y12 | Y13 | Y14 |
|---|---|---|---|---|---|---|---|---|---|---|---|---|---|---|
| P1 | 0.041 | 0.298 | −0.010 | 0.186 | 0.370 | 0.144 | 0.051 | −0.236 | −0.436 | −0.382 | −0.042 | 0.011 | 0.104 | 0.014 |
| P2 | 0.139 | 0.030 | 0.015 | 0.052 | 0.100 | −0.043 | −0.046 | 0.018 | −0.033 | 0.037 | 0.070 | −0.057 | −0.037 | −0.205 |
| P3 | 0.115 | 0.087 | −0.084 | 0.072 | 0.064 | 0.023 | −0.095 | −0.081 | −0.080 | −0.131 | 0.160 | 0.228 | 0.055 | 0.042 |
| P4 | −0.130 | −0.034 | −0.063 | −0.095 | −0.066 | 0.041 | −0.103 | 0.057 | −0.136 | −0.013 | 0.035 | −0.006 | −0.004 | 0.130 |
| P5 | −0.275 | −0.363 | 0.022 | −0.269 | −0.334 | −0.094 | −0.063 | −0.190 | 0.295 | 0.203 | 0.389 | 0.257 | 0.016 | −0.026 |
| P6 | −0.096 | 0.063 | 0.118 | 0.004 | −0.122 | 0.001 | −0.193 | −0.247 | 0.240 | 0.163 | 0.066 | 0.272 | 0.279 | 0.235 |
| P7 | −0.125 | −0.052 | 0.070 | 0.048 | −0.387 | 0.004 | −0.032 | −0.029 | 0.176 | 0.171 | −0.014 | 0.172 | 0.87 | −0.042 |
| P8 | −0.553 | −0.430 | −0.062 | −0.511 | −0.375 | −0.183 | −0.261 | 0.440 | −0.055 | −0.112 | −0.280 | −0.159 | 0.429 | −0.082 |
| P9 | 0.057 | 0.019 | −0.192 | −0.184 | −0.023 | −0.218 | −0.063 | 0.095 | −0.237 | 0.010 | 0.083 | −0.131 | 0.062 | 0.068 |
| P10 | 0.134 | −0.057 | −0.042 | −0.003 | 0.044 | −0.120 | −0.235 | −0.092 | −0.098 | −0.125 | −0.175 | −0.088 | 0.022 | −0.020 |
| P11 | 0.140 | 0.021 | −010 | 0.222 | 0.169 | 0.010 | 0.249 | 0.140 | −0.089 | 0.170 | −0.043 | 0.018 | −0.180 | 0.045 |
| Adjusted $R^2$ | 0.386 | 0.280 | −0.040 | 0.665 | 0.265 | 0.035 | 0.502 | 0.065 | 0.111 | 0.082 | 0.033 | 0.053 | 0.356 | 0.029 |
| $F$ Statistic | 0.000 | 0.000 | 0.819 | 0.000 | 0.000 | 0.000 | 0.0019 | 0.081 | 0.015 | 0.046 | 0.209 | 0.119 | 0.000 | 0.233 |

## Effects of Partnership Characteristics on Managing Conflict within International Strategic Alliances

The results support Proposition 1, that conflict will be lower in international alliances that exhibit coordination, interdependence, commitment, trust, and communication, and it is consistent with previous findings that in order to reduce the number of disputes, partners need to work together (Fey & Beamish, 2000; Kauser & Shaw, 2004; Killing, 1983; Mohr & Spekman, 1994). In particular, the results suggest that trust and commitment in alliance relationships are a critical component in determining the level of hostility and mistrust.

The overall findings also show support for Proposition 2. Partnership attributes are shown to be strong predictors of distrust, conflicting goals, and cultural misunderstandings within international alliances. These findings support the view that conflicts can arise over just about anything from differences in management style, culture, and communication to misunderstandings in operational practices (Devlin & Bleackley, 1988; Jain, 1987; Killing 1983). The results also indicate that international alliances avoid or smooth over the issue of resolving conflicts. This may have been due to the cultural differences between the UK firms and their partners. Peterson and Shimada (1978) found cultural differences to be the most difficult problem in managing alliances. The regression analysis further indicated that alliances less likely to share information with their partner and keep each other informed about changing needs and activities have results in greater misunderstandings.

There is also ample support for Proposition 3. In alliances where conflicts are resolved through joint problem solving, the integration of activities, commitment, trust, and communication is expected to be higher. Similarly, the findings show negative coefficients for other conflict resolution mechanisms that may be utilized such as avoiding the issue, smoothing over things, the level of arbitration, and persuasion. These findings are consistent with previous research that reports that strategic alliances are encouraged to engage in joint problem solving so that they are able to manage the uncertain environment that they are faced with (Das & Kumar, 2011; Lane & Beamish, 1990; Lin & Germain, 1998; Xie et al., 1998). Similarly, previous research has also indicated that partners very often attempt to persuade each other to adopt particular solutions to the conflict situation, which appear to be more constructive than the use of coercion or domination (Deutsch, 1969). Domination or coercion is seen as being counterproductive and likely to strain the fabric of the strategic alliance. Other conflict resolution techniques such as smoothing over or ignoring and avoiding the issue are somewhat at odds with the norms and values advocated in more successful strategic alliances. Such techniques do not fit in with alliances in which the problems of one party become the problems affecting both. More recently, Weiss and Hughes (2005) proposed that to effectively resolve conflict, companies need to devise and implement strategies around a common method that integrates conflict resolution on day-to-day basis.

In light of the above findings, managers of international alliances need to be aware of the potential existence of conflict and the need to minimize cultural misunderstandings through building trust, commitment, and communication. It is also important for managers to keep in check the level of conflict within the alliance relationship by understanding the basis of where and why conflicting situations arise. Only then can managers decide on the optimum way of minimizing conflicting situations as they arise.

## DISCUSSION

The findings of this study have demonstrated that the presence of partnership attributes are associated with the level, degree, and type of conflict and that relationship dynamics play an important role in how these disputes are settled. This suggests that conflicting situations between international alliances are commonplace and not unique to any particular form of alliance relationship. They are a consequence of business relationships that extend across geographical and cultural boundaries.

The results of this study highlight three main points: first, conflict and cooperation coexist. Although relationships between different organizations require a great deal of cooperative effort, the relationship is also an arena for misunderstandings between partners, so conflicting situations are inherent characteristic in international partnerships (Child & Faulkner, 1998; Jain, 1987) because each party's relationship is characterized by competitive and joint efforts. Second, these disputes between partners can arise over just about anything, ranging from cultural misunderstandings to incompatibility in goals, capabilities, and reporting and communication processes. So conflicts can arise because members of each organization often fail to see what they have in common with their perspective partners. Partners within a strategic alliance relationship have a drive for both autonomy and cooperation, which results in the coexistence of cooperative and conflictual motives within the alliance (Aldrich, 1979). Third, the optimum way to resolve any conflicting situation is to utilize a method that will have a positive impact on developing the relationship. Given the inherent nature of conflicting situations in partnerships, attempting to resolve them through joint problem solving can help build trust, commitment, and communication.

The presence of conflict thus appears to give rise to distrust and a lack of communication and reduces the level of commitment and integration of activities in international alliances. This suggests that while conflicts are likely to result in misunderstandings and distrust, which leads to reduced cooperation and commitment, attempting to resolve them through joint problem solving helps build trust, commitment, and communication. Thus, these analyses indicate that commitment and trust play a strong part in the level of conflicts in partnerships. These strong, consistent findings for commitment and trust as a predictor of conflict for international alliances are similar to other findings (Anderson & Narus, 1990; Anderson & Weitz, 1989; Beamish, 1987; Das & Kumar, 2009; Kumar et al., 1995; Mohr & Spekman, 1994; Monckza et al., 1998; Morgan & Hunt, 1994; Noordewier, John, & Nevin, 1990).

There are a number of limitations to this study. First, given the lack of any documented official sources available on international alliances, the study relied on secondary data from press articles to identify the number of alliances for the later stage of the research. Thus there is likely to be a bias in the data as only well-known firms and alliance activities are likely to be reported in the press. However, the approach adopted is considered to be feasible, and there is a well-established precedent for researchers to compile their own database in this way (Ghemawat, Porter, & Rawlinson, 1986; Glaister & Buckley, 1994; Hergert & Morris, 1988). Second, data were collected from the perspective of the UK partners engaged in international alliances and therefore it does not capture the cooperative and conflicting nature of both partners. Thus, further research is encouraged to utilize dyadic responses from both partners in order to better understand the relationship between partnership attributes and conflict from the perspective of both firms. Third, despite the importance of these findings, knowledge concerning conflict with international alliances is at an early stage. While the concepts used in this study are highly reliable and show validity, it is not possible to capture all the complexities of the attributes studied when measuring these variables. Therefore, future research is encouraged to improve on the definitions of concepts and their operationalizations and to explore the many complexities inherent in managing international partnerships.

## CONCLUSIONS AND IMPLICATIONS

The chapter has highlighted the importance of a number of partnership attributes and the presence of conflict in the management of interorganizational relationships. This study represents the first systematic collection of data assessing the relationship between partnership attributes and the management of conflict within partnerships. The findings show that conflicts are commonplace within international alliances and that, to some degree, all types of relationships are characterized by a mixture of conflict and cooperation. To minimize conflicting situations, managers in both parties should aim to identify and agree on how to coordinate and adapt the activities that are particularly critical to the relationship. This requires both parties to become closely involved in their activities. Thus, partners should be in complete agreement about the purpose of the alliance and the process by which its goals can be achieved. This will require the different functional groups of both parties to work together toward achieving goals and objectives. This will also encourage a higher level of interaction between managers as well as heighten a regular exchange of ideas between partners and thus minimize the number of conflicts.

Owing to the mutual interdependencies of the companies, conflicts may also be minimized through relying on each other for mutual support and cooperation. This means that managers must realize that each firm needs the other to provide information and resources to complete their work and so must be aware of the connections between its own activities and those of its own. In addition to helping guide mutually dependent partners to coordinate their alliance activities, managers can also assist in the development of mutual trust and commitment to the relationship. The results of this study have suggested that building trust and commitment is essential in handling both cooperative and conflicting situations.

While this study has indicated that conflicts are characteristic of international alliances that exhibit lower levels of coordination, trust, commitment, and communication, it has been readily acknowledged that disagreements are inevitable in every alliance relationship. Each firm has its own agenda and goals for the alliance, which can result in conflicting goals. Further, differences between cultures of partners can lead to cultural misunderstandings. It is suggested that partners work jointly together to develop mediating mechanisms to defuse and settle their differences. Firms can train their personnel to be sensitive to each other's problems and deal with these problems through using joint problem solving techniques. In this way problems may be discussed to develop mutually acceptable solutions. Helping to blend in the different cultures of the partners will help to phase in the relationship between the partners.

## REFERENCES

Aldrich, H. E. (1979). *Organizations and environments*. Englewood Cliffs, NJ: Prentice Hall.

Anderson, J. C., & Narus, J. A. (1984). A model of the distributor's perspective of the distribution -manufacturer firm working relationships. *Journal of Marketing*. 48(4), 62–74.

Anderson, J. C., & Narus, J. A. (1990). A model of distributor firm and manufacturer firm working partnerships. *Journal of Marketing*, 54(1), 42–58.

Anderson, J. C., & Narus, J. A. (1991). Partnering as a focused marketing strategy. *California Management Review, 33*(3), 95–113.

Anderson, E., & Weitz, B. (1989). Determinants of continuity in conventional industrial channel dyads. *Marketing Science, 8*(4), 310–323.

Assael, H. (1969). Constructive role of organizational conflict. *Administrative Science Quarterly, 14*, 573–582.

Aulakh, P. S., Kotabe, M., & Sahay, A. (1996). Trust and performance in cross-border marketing partnerships: A behavioral approach. *Journal of International Business Studies, 27*, 1005–1032.

Beamish, P. W. (1987). Joint ventures in LDCs: Partner selection and performance. *Management International Review, 27*(1), 23–37.

Beamish, P. W., & Banks, J. C. (1987). Equity joint ventures and the theory of the multinational enterprise. *Journal of International Business Studies, 18*, 1–16.

Bleeke, J., & Ernst, D. (1991). The way to win in cross border alliances. *Harvard Business Review, 69*(6), 127–135.

Blodgett, L. L. (1991). Towards a resource-based theory of bargaining power in international joint ventures. *Journal of Global Marketing, 5*(1/2), 35–54.

Borys, B., & Jemison, D. B. (1989). Hybrid arrangements as strategic alliances: Theoretical issues in organizational combinations. *Academy of Management Review, 14*, 234–249.

Buckley, P. J., & Casson, M. C. (1988). A theory of cooperation in international business. In F. J. Contractor & P. Lorange (Eds.), *Cooperative strategies in international business* (pp. 31–53). Lexington, MA: Lexington Books.

Child, J., & Faulkner, D. (1998). *Strategies of cooperation: Managing alliances, networks and joint ventures.* Oxford, UK: Oxford University Press.

Contractor, F. J., & Lorange, P. (1988). Why should firms co-operate? The strategy and economics basis for cooperative ventures. In F. J. Contractor & P. Lorange (Eds.), *Cooperative strategies in international business* (pp. 3–20). Lexington, MA: Lexington Books.

Churchill, G. A. (1979). A paradigm for developing better measures of marketing constructs. *Journal of Marketing Research, 16*(2), 64–73.

Daft, R., & Lengel, R. (1986). Organizational information requirements, media richness and structural design. *Management Science, 32*(5), 554–571.

Dang, T. (1977). *Ownership, control and performance of the multinational corporation: A study of US wholly-owned subsidiaries and joint ventures in the Philippines and Taiwan.* Unpublished doctoral dissertation, University of California, Los Angeles, CA.

Das, T. K., & Kumar, R. (2009). Interpartner harmony in strategic alliances: Managing commitment and forbearance. *International Journal of Strategic Business Alliances, 1*, 24–52.

Das, T. K., & Kumar, R. (2011). Interpartner negotiations in alliances: A strategic framework. *Management Decision, 49*, 1235–1256.

Das, T. K., & Teng, B. (1998). Between trust and control: Developing confidence in partner cooperation in alliances. *Academy of Management Review, 23*, 491–512.

Das, T. K., & Teng, B. (2000). Instabilities of strategic alliances: An internal tensions perspective. *Organization Science, 11*, 77–101.

Deutsch, M. (1969). Conflicts: productive or destructive. *Journal of Social Issues, 25*(1), 7–41.

Devlin, G., & Bleackley, M. (1988). Strategic alliances-guidelines for success. *Long Range Planning, 21*(5), 18–23.

Ding, D. Z. (1997). Control, conflict, and performance: A study of U.S.–Chinese joint ventures. *Journal of International Marketing, 5*(3), 31–45.

Doz, Y. L., & Hamel, G. (1998). *The art of creating value through partnering*. Boston, MA: Harvard Business School Press.

Fey, C. F., & Beamish, P. W. (1999). Strategies for managing Russian international joint venture conflict. *European Management Journal, 17*(1), 99–105.

Fey, C. F., & Beamish, P. W. (2000). Joint venture conflict: The case of Russian joint ventures. *International Business Review, 9*, 139–162.

Friedman, W. G., & Beguin, J. P. (1971). *Joint international business ventures in developing countries*. New York, NY: Columbia University Press.

Geringer, J. M. (1993). Ownership and control in East-West joint ventures, In R. Culpan (Ed.), *Multinational strategic alliances* (pp. 203–218). New York, NY: International Business Press.

Geringer, J. M., & Hebert, L. (1989). Control and performance of international joint ventures. *Journal of International Business Studies, 20*, 235–254.

Geringer, J. M., & Hebert, L. (1991). Measuring performance of international joint ventures. *Journal of International Business Studies, 22*, 249–263.

Geyskens, J., Steenkamp, J. E. M., Scheer, L. K., & Kumar, N. (1996). The effects of trust and interdependence on relationship commitment: A transatlantic study. *International Journal of Research Marketing, 13*, 303–317.

Ghemawat, P., Porter, M., & Rawlinson R.A. (1986). Patterns in international coalition activity. In M. E. Porter (Ed.), *Competition in global industries* (pp. 345–366). Boston, MA: Harvard University Press.

Gill, J., & Butler, R. J. (2003). Managing instability in cross-cultural alliances. *Long Range Planning, 36*, 543–563.

Glaister, K. W., & Buckley, P. J. (1994). UK international joint ventures: An analysis of patterns of activity and distribution. *British Journal of Management, 5*, 35–51.

Glaister, K. W., & Wu, W. (1994). Management and performance of UK joint ventures in China. *Journal of Euromarketing, 4*(1), 23-43.

Gulati, R., & Singh, H. (1998). The architecture of cooperation: managing coordination costs and appropriation concerns in strategic alliances. *Administrative Science Quarterly, 43*, 781–814.

Habib, G. M. (1983). *Conflict measurement in the distribution channel of joint ventures: An empirical investigation*. Unpublished doctoral dissertation, Texas Tech University, Lubbock, TX.

Habib, G. M. (1987). Measures of manifest conflict in international joint ventures. *Academy of Management Journal, 30*, 808–816.

Hagedoorn, J. (1993). Understanding the rationale of strategic technology partnering: Inter organizational modes of cooperation and sectoral differences. *Strategic Management Journal, 14*, 371–385.

Hambrick, D., Li, J., Xin, K., & Tsui, A. (2001). Compositional gaps and downward spirals in international joint venture management groups. *Strategic Management Journal, 22*, 1033–1053.

Harrigan, K. R. (1988). Joint ventures and competitive strategy. *Strategic Management Journal, 9,* 141–158.

Hennart, J.-F. (1988). A transaction costs theory of equity joint ventures. *Strategic Management Journal, 9,* 361–374.

Hergert, M., & Morris, D. (1988). Trends in international collaborative agreements, In F. J. Contractor & P. Lorange (Eds.), *Cooperative strategies in international business* (pp. 99–109). Lexington, MA: Lexington Books.

Holm, D. B., Eriksson, K., & Johanson, J. (1999). Creating value through mutual commitment to business network relationships. *Strategic Management Journal, 20,* 467–486.

Hoon-Halbauer, S. K. (1999). Managing relationships within Sino-foreign joint ventures. *Journal of World Business, 34,* 344–371.

Hu, M., & Chen, H. (1996). An empirical analysis of factors explaining foreign joint performance in China. *Journal of Business Research, 35,* 165–173.

Huber, G., & Daft, R. (1987). The information environment of organizations. In F. M. Jablin, L. L. Putnam, K. H. Roberts, & L. W. Porter (Eds.), *Handbook of organizational communication* (pp. 130–164). Newbury Park, CA: Sage Publications.

Jain, C. S. (1987). Perspectives on international marketing strategic alliances. *Advances in International Marketing, 2,* 3–20.

Johnson, J. (1999). Multiple commitments and conflicting loyalties in international joint venture management teams. *International Journal of Organizational Analysis, 7,* 54–71.

Johnson, J., Cullen, J., Sakano, T., & Bronson, J. (2001). Drivers and outcomes of parent company intervention in IJV management: A cross-cultural comparison. *Journal of Business Research, 52,* 35–49.

Kale, P., Singh, H., & Perlmutter, H. (2000). Learning and protection of proprietary assets in strategic alliances: Building relational capital. *Strategic Management Journal, 21,* 217–237.

Kauser, S. (2007). Alliance relationship dynamics: Conflict, structure and control. *Journal of Euromarketing, 16*(3), 5–25.

Kauser, S., & Shaw, V. (2004). The influence of behavioral and organizational characteristics on the success of international strategic alliances. *International Marketing Review, 2*(1), 17–52.

Khanna, T., Gulati, R., & Nohria, N. (1998). The dynamics of learning alliances: Competition, cooperation and relative scope. *Strategic Management Journal, 19,* 193–210.

Killing, J. P. (1983). *Strategies for joint venture success,* New York, NY: Praeger.

Kogut, B. (1988). Joint ventures: Theoretical and empirical perspectives. *Strategic Management Journal, 9,* 319–332.

Kozan, M. K. (1997). Culture and conflict management: A theoretical framework. *International Journal of Conflict Management, 8,* 338–360.

Kumar, N., Scheer, L. K. & Steenkamp, J. E. M. (1995). The effects of perceived interdependence on dealer attitudes. *Journal of Marketing Research, 32*(3), 348–356.

Kumar, R., & Nti, K. O. (1998). Differential learning and interaction in alliance dynamics: A process and outcome discrepancy model. *Organization Science, 9*(3), 356–367.

Lane, H. W., & Beamish, P. W. (1990). Cross-cultural cooperative behavior in joint ventures in LDCs. *International Management Review, 30*(Special Issue), 87–102.

Lee, D. Y. (2001). Power, conflict and satisfaction in IJV supplier—Chinese distributor channels. *Journal of Business Research, 52*(2), 149–160.

Leung, K., Koch, P. T., & Lu, L. (2002). A dualistic model of harmony and its implications for conflict management in Asia. *Asia Pacific Journal of Management, 19*, 201–220.

Lewis. J. D. (1990). *Partnerships for profit: Structuring and managing strategic alliances.* New York, NY: Free Press.

Lin, X., & Germain, R. (1998). Sustaining satisfactory joint venture relationships: The role of conflict resolution strategy. *Journal of International Business Studies, 29*, 179–196.

Madhok, A. (1995). Opportunism and trust in joint venture relationships: An exploratory study and a model. *Scandinavian Journal of Management, 11*, 57–74.

Mohr, J., & Spekman, R. (1994). Characteristics of partnership success: Partnership attributes communication behavior and conflict resolution techniques. *Strategic Management Journal, 15*, 135–152.

Mohr, J., & Nevin, J. R. (1990). Communication strategies in marketing channels: A theoretical perspective. *Journal of Marketing, 54*(4), 36–51.

Monckza, R. M., Peterson, K. T., Handfield, R. B., & Ragatz, G. L. (1998). Success factors in strategic supplier alliances: The buying company perspective. *Decision Sciences, 29*, 553–576.

Morgan, R. M., & Hunt, S. D. (1994). The commitment trust theory of relationship marketing. *Journal of Marketing, 58*(3), 20–38.

Mowday, R. T., Steers, R. M., & Porter, L. W. (1979). The measurement of organizational commitment. *Journal of Vocational Behavior, 14*, 224–227.

Nti, K. O., & Kumar, R. (2000). Differential learning in alliances. In D. O. Faulkner & M. de Rond (Eds.), *Cooperative strategy: Economic, business and organizational issues* (pp. 119–150). Oxford, UK: Oxford University Press.

Nunnally, J. C. (1978). *Psychometric theory.* New York, NY: McGraw Hill.

Noordeweir, T. G., John, G., & Nevin, J. R. (1990). Performance outcomes of purchasing arrangements in industrial buyer-vendor relationships. *Journal of Marketing, 54*(4), 80–93.

Olson, L. B., & Singsuwan, K. (1997). The effect of partnership, communication, and conflict resolution behaviors on performance success of strategic alliances: American and Thai perspectives. In P. W. Beamish & J. P. Killing (Eds.), *Cooperative strategies: Asian Pacific perspectives* (pp. 245–267). San Francisco, CA: New Lexington Press.

Park, S. O., & Ungson, G. R. (2001). Interfirm rivalry and managerial complexity: A conceptual framework of alliance failure. *Organization Science, 12*, 37–53.

Parkhe, A. (1993). Messy research, methodological predispositions and theory development in international joint ventures. *Academy of Management Review, 18*, 227–268.

Peterson, R. B., & Shimada, J. Y. (1978). Sources of management problems in Japanese-American joint ventures. *Academy of Management Review, 3*, 796–804.

Porter, L. W., Steers, R. M., Mowday, R. T., & Boulian, P. V. (1974). Organizational commitment, job satisfaction and turnover among psychiatric technicians. *Journal of Applied Psychology, 59,* 603–609.

Randall, D. M. (1990). The consequences of organizational commitments: Methodological investigation. *Journal of Organizational Behavior, 11,* 361–378.

Schaan, J. C. (1983). *Parent control and joint venture success: The case of Mexico.* Unpublished doctoral dissertation, University of Western Ontario, London, Ontario, Canada.

Simiar, F. (1984). Major causes of joint venture failures in the Middle East: The case of Iran. *Management International Review, 23*(3), 58–68.

Tomlinson, J. W. C. (1970). *The joint venture process in international business: India and Pakistan.* Cambridge, MA: M.I.T. Press.

Van de Ven, A. H., & Walker, G. (1984). The dynamics of interorganizational coordination. *Administrative Science Quarterly, 29,* 598–621.

Weiss, J. & Hughes, J. (2005). Want collaboration? Accept—and actively manage—conflict. *Harvard Business Review, 83*(3), 93–101.

Wright, R. W. (1979). Joint venture problems in Japan. *Columbia Journal of World Business, 14*(1), 25–31.

Xie, J., Song, X. M., & Stringfellow, A. (1998). Interfunctional conflict, conflict resolution styles, and new product success: A four-culture comparison. *Management Science, 44*(12), S192–S206.

Yan, A., & Gray, B. (1994). Bargaining power, management control and performance in United States–China joint ventures: A comparative case study. *Academy of Management Journal, 37,* 1478–1517.

CHAPTER 10

# ACCOUNTING FOR PARTNERS THAT ARE WORTH TRUSTING

Morten Jakobsen

**ABSTRACT**

This chapter addresses the topic of interorganizational relationships and how the partner selection process affects the ability to influence the practices of suppliers in the later stages of the interorganizational relationship. The chapter shows how the partner selection process can function as a disciplinary procedure that lays the foundation for the future willingness of suppliers to accept interorganizational control defined by the buying company. This chapter is based on a qualitative case study of the practices of supplier selection within the purchasing department of an electronic manufacturing company. The chapter thereby provides insight into the practice of supplier selection processes. The theoretical basis of the chapter is the thoughts of Michel Foucault concerning governmentality. Governmentality is found to be a relevant framework for analyzing interpartner dynamics because it both contains an acceptance of an intention of intervention via governmental apparatuses and a recognition of the tensions between the partners; tensions that contain the potential for a successful outcome for both parties if the tensions are mobilized appropriately. The contribution of the chapter is to analyze the supplier selection process employed by the purchasers at an electronic manufacturing company. It will analyze how they use their initial bargaining power to construct a platform for further cooperation.

## INTRODUCTION

This chapter addresses the topic of interpartner dynamics during assessment and selection processes in relation to interorganizational relationships. The chapter shows how the use of accounts and standardized practices during the assessment process can function as forms of disciplinary power (Jackson & Carter, 2000) that lays the foundation for the future ability to conduct interorganizational control according to the objectives of the buying company. The chapter is based on a qualitative case study of the supplier assessment practices of an electronics manufacturing company. The case is interesting because the purchasers explicitly use power as the driving force to challenge and assess the potential suppliers during a formal partner assessment process. During this process, trust in the partners is implicitly developed. The chapter provides insight into the practice of supplier assessment and the interpartner dynamics illustrated by the specific case and their practices during their formal partner assessment processes.

The objective of the chapter is to analyze how certain practices of disciplinary power conducted during supplier assessment processes can form a foundation for intervention in the later stages of interorganizational relationships.

Similar to Oliver and Ebers (1998), this chapter defines an interorganizational relation as a close bilateral relationship between independent organizations, whereas a network is defined as cooperation among more than two organizations. The discussion of the theoretical positions within the field draws on both interorganizational and network-based contributions, whereas the empirical study focuses on the interpartner dynamics of interorganizational relationships.

One of the major motives for engaging in interorganizational relationships or networks is the ability to gain access to specific resources or competences faster than the internal capabilities of the company can be developed (e.g., Mouritsen & Thrane, 2006). However, before companies can benefit from the capabilities of their external relationships, they must create a contact to these external relations and construct an understanding of the possibilities represented by these external resources or competences. Gulati (1998) concludes that networks give companies access to information that puts them in a position to select and create a portfolio of potential partners to choose from. A number of formalized methods exist in order to assist supplier selection under such conditions. For instance, De Boer, Labro, and Morlacchi (2001) review a number of methods that can support the supplier selection process in situations where the buying company has a palette of possible suppliers to choose from. However, such condition may not always be present. The case to be presented later in this chapter is an example of such an instance. The company faces a situation where the number of potential suppliers is limited. In addition to this, the resources and competences that they seek from their suppliers are often not spelled out because the products where the resources and competences are going to be utilized have not yet been developed. Under such conditions, the supplier's ability to integrate and participate in the product development process becomes important (e.g., Humphreys, Huang, Cadden, & McIvor, 2007). Maneuvering in a field with a limited number of possible suppliers and undefined products requires a different approach to managing the supplier selection process than circulating and picking a partner within one's network. Supplier selection becomes an ongoing process where the assessment process influences both the buying and the supplying company, and therefore the assessment becomes a process of interpartner dynamics.

Another difficulty that companies seeking potential partners face is the ability to choose partners who actually possess the specific resources or competences that can form the basis for a synergetic relationship. Wilkinson, Young, and Freytag (2005) question the assumption that partner selection is based on rational choices concerning competences that can create synergetic effects. They base their study on findings from both biology and family partner selection practices. Within these contexts they find that partner selection is driven by an urge to find genes similar to one's own. They test this rationale within an interorganizational context and conclude that buyers and sellers tend to be similar concerning several attributes. Their results indicate that systematic partner selection practices are required in order to assure that partners are selected based on qualifications that can create synergies. Ittner, Larcker, Nagar, and Rajan (1999) find that advanced partner selection practices seem to increase the general outcome of interorganizational relationships. This indicates that interorganizational relationships can provide companies with competences that together with the competences of the buying company can enter a process of emergence that enhances the final product. However, the selection process needs direction, as otherwise emergence will not take place—only mergence.

Based on these initial considerations, this chapter addresses the research question: How can formal partner assessment technologies form both the foundation for disciplinary power and the basis of a controlled trusting relationship?

Three concepts are central in this chapter: power, control, and trust. The phenomenon of interest is the supplier assessment process, and it is the evolvement of the interplay between power, control, and trust during the supplier selection process and how they can form the foundation for future intervention that is of specific interest.

The focus of this chapter is to analyze the supplier assessment process employed by the purchasers at an electronic manufacturing company. It will be analyzed how they use their initial bargaining power to construct a foundation for intervention. They use the assessment process to determine areas of action where the supplier can be trusted and areas where control is needed. Finally, we analyze how trust, despite the outspoken focus on power, evolves during the relationship. In the terminology of Sako (1992), it is found that the confrontational use of a formalized supplier assessment method implicitly creates trust in the shape of competence trust and contractual trust. Accounts of the potential partners are thereby constructed during the assessment process that confirms that the potential partner is worth trusting.

## THEORETICAL ASPECTS OF DISCIPLINARY POWER

The theoretical framework for the analysis of the Case Company presented in the following section is the theory of governmentality (Foucault, 1991). In this section, the essential aspects of governmentality will be outlined. The theory is applied as a guide, a pair of glasses through which the dynamics of interpartner auditing within interorganizational relationships is going to be seen and understood. Choosing the theory of governmentality as the analytical framework is a consequence of the abduction method applied during the fieldwork. The abduction method will be discussed in the following section.

Initially, the fieldwork focused on the interplay between trust and control between the parties involved in interorganizational relationships. The initial fieldwork was inspired by authors such as Das and Teng (2001); Gulati (1995); Hedberg, Dahlgren, Hansson, and Olve (2000); and van der Meer-Kooistra and Vosselman (2000). Especially, the ideas of Dekker (2004), Langfield-Smith and Smith (2003), and Tomkins (2001) initially attracted attention since these specifically bring in the time horizon as an aspect that influences the relationship between trust and control. After a few interviews, however, the fieldwork revealed that the Case Company did not focus on trust. Instead, they used power as a means to gain control. This finding was in stark contrast to the initial literature, and since no explanation could be found in this literature to explain the findings made in the Case Company, a new framework was sought. It turned out that the theory of governmentality was able to form an applicable analytical framework for understanding and analyzing the Case Company.

### Basic Aspects of the Theory of Governmentality

The term *governmentality* stems from the neologism governmental rationality (Gordon, 1991). In the texts of Foucault, a single clear definition of the concept is not made. One definition he brings into play is that governmentality is a form of collective management rationality (found in institutions, procedures, analyses, and reflections) that is constituted in a number of methods and techniques (governmental apparatuses) outlining how government is organized and carried out (Foucault, 1991). In another text, he defines governmentality as the contact and interaction between technologies of domination of others and the technologies of the self (Foucault, 1988). Since the original source is not clear, other references have to be taken into account in order to clarify the concept of governmentality.

As research assistant to Foucault, Colin Gordon is perceived as a central reference for understanding the theory of governmentality. Gordon states:

> A rationality of government will thus mean a way or system of thinking about the nature of the practice of government (who can govern; what governing is; what or who is governed), capable of making some form of that activity thinkable and practicable both to its practitioners and to those upon whom it was practised. (Gordon, 1991, p. 3)

Another important contributor to the understanding of governmentality is Dean (1999). Dean suggests two broad meanings of the term governmentality. In the first sense, governmentality deals with the different mentalities of government, basically how people think about governing. This meaning is very much in line with the definition outlined by Gordon (1991). The second meaning suggested by Dean concerns governmentality as a new form of thinking about and exercising power, where power is directly related to the economy as a new conception of reality and the population as object for control. Also Raffnsøe, Gudmand-Høyer, and Thaning (2008) draw this conclusion. Raffnsøe et al. (2008) point out that government of today increasingly becomes government of self-government and that we—our self-government—increasingly take into account the government of us made by others and their government of themselves.

These definitions can thus be summarized: Governmentality is how control is carried out in a setting where independent free actors have a will to interrelate, which they do via certain governmental apparatuses. Within this constant attempt to interrelate is a certain rationality that defines how the interrelationship is to be interpreted and formed into a basis for action.

Foucault (1991) mentions *sovereignty–discipline–government* as a triangle that has the population as its main target. This triangle also points at three central and interdependent aspects of governmentality. The actors are sovereign; they have a free will. This free will holds the potential for conflicts and thereby a battle fought with disciplinary power is constantly going on. This fight is made with the purpose of governing and is made visible and conducted via governmental apparatuses. These three aspects of governmentality are found to be of particular importance in relation to this chapter and will be examined in the following subsections.

### Mobilizing the Free Will of the Governed

A central aspect of governmentality is the autonomous behavior of human beings as capable actors (Gordon, 1991). People, both the governor and the governed, are assumed to be free and they are expected to act accordingly. From this perspective, management takes more than mechanical programming of human behavior because those who are governed behave and think independently and often in unpredictable ways (Dean, 1999). Therefore, the governor seeks to define a certain truth and to construct models that outline possible actions. This represents the facilitation of restricted freedom, where the governed will carry out their activities (Burchell, 1991).

Governmentality takes place in an endless and open strategic game that the parties play in order to promote personal interests (Gordon, 1991). In an interorganizational setting, the strategic game manifests itself in the negotiation process between the parties that aims at reaching an agreement. The term "strategic" has three facets (Foucault, 1982). The first facet relates to the question of how to reach a given end. It is a matter of what rationalities are mobilized in order to achieve a certain objective. The second facet concerns reading the game. Reading has similarities to the game of chess, where the successful chess player is able to figure out the actions of the opponent several moves ahead. However, unlike chess, the strategic game does not consist of a fixed number of possible moves. In this facet, the rules are constantly revised due to the free will of the parties involved. As such, the ability to respond to the new rules becomes essential in order to succeed in this strategic game for power. The third facet is about signaling strength, in the sense of showing the other party that you intend to fight for your objectives and that you have the resources to do so. In terms of negotiation, it becomes a matter of having the convincing arguments at the right time.

The strategic game of power is rooted in the social (Foucault, 1982) and takes place in a "zone of (partially) interplay" (Gordon, 1991, p. 35). In this chapter, the term forum is applied to the situation of the strategic game. The term forum draws attention to the characteristic that governmentality takes place in a discursive frame of reference. With specific reference to the empirical setting of this chapter, the parties negotiate (as free subjects) in order to achieve their goals. They enter the forum in order to learn about their opponents and to figure out how to get the most out of them compared to their own ends without ever showing any sign of weakness in this battle of arguments.

### Focus on Disciplinary Power

As in most of Foucault's thinking, when it comes to governmentality, power is a central aspect in human relations. Though it may sound counterintuitive, power becomes central due to each individual's ability to act freely in one way or another (Gordon, 1991). Introducing power in relation to interorganizational relationships is unconventional, since within this field trust has been perceived as the dominant strategy for absorbing uncertainty and a facilitator for exchange of information among interorganizational participants (e.g., Das & Teng, 2001; Dekker, 2004; Gulati, 1995; Hedberg et al, 2000; Langfield-Smith & Smith, 2003; Tomkins, 2001; van der Meer-Kooistra & Vosselman, 2000). Power within interorganizational relationships has been discussed in prior studies (e.g., Bachmann, 2001; Kumar, 2005). However, applying governmentality in the context of interorganizational relationships is found to be novel.

Within the context of governmentality, power is defined as "actions on others' actions" (Gordon, 1991, p. 5). Power is not to be perceived as violence or as a ruler who has absolute domination over the subject (Foucault, 1982). Likewise power is not something you hold. Power is a practice that is exercised in the relationship between free people (Deleuze, 1999). In relation to governmentality, power is basically a mobilization of the free will, initiatives, and resources of the subjects, but still within the discursive frame of reference of what is true and what is not true (Dean, 1999). Freedom of the governed is a central element both because this state requires the handling of the many possible actions of the governed, and it also contains possibilities for the future (Foucault, 1982).

To sum up, power is about how you can influence the actions of fellow human beings when you relate to them, since power exists in the relation with others. Power relates to people's ability to act and react to the positive and negative actions and reactions of other people. Success in controlling other people's behavior is dependent on one's ability to foresee actions.

### *Conduct Exposed via Governmental Apparatuses*

Governmentality is always embedded in government in the shape of specific governmental apparatuses (Foucault, 1991). Governmental apparatuses have inherent rationalities. It is these rationalities that guide the involved people to act in certain ways. The combination of a specific understanding of the reality (the rationality) and a certain framework (the governmental apparatus) for making this reality explicit forms the foundation for managing.

Governmental apparatuses can be contracts, open-book accounts, self-assessment reports, and so on, just to mention a few specific examples relevant for managing interorganizational relationships. Through their construction, governmental apparatuses define the forum of government. For example, a contract that emphasizes certain aspects of the relationship will point attention towards these aspects and influence the actions of the people involved. By defining the area in which the suppliers are able to act, government at a distance becomes possible. The ability to set the agenda is central since the one who is able to set the agenda, and thereby to define governable forums, will inevitably have the power. (e.g., Jackson & Carter, 2000; Rose, 1999).

# A CASE STUDY OF THE INTERPARTNER DYNAMICS OF PURCHASING VITAL ELECTRONIC COMPONENTS

## Research Method and Design

The study was conducted as a qualitative case study based on the ideas of C. S. Peirce concerning abductive inference (e.g., Burks, 1946; Fann, 1970; Haig, 2005). Insight into the Case Company was gained through semistructured interviews. The interviews were carried out by using interview guides. The interview guide serves the purpose of keeping the interview on track. This should not be interpreted as an intention to rigidly stick to the prespecified topics. Instead it is important to follow up on new themes if such themes turn up during the interview. However, it is found that the conversation must have a starting point, and the interview guide serves this purpose. All interviews were recorded and subsequently transcribed by the author. This creates deep insight into the interviews, and thereby a solid foundation for the further analysis of the data.

The Case Company is the alias for a small electronics manufacturing company in which the fieldwork was conducted. The company prefers to be anonymous, and hence its details are veiled. Within the Case Company, the purchasing department is the center of supplier selection. In all, 13 people in this department were involved in the different aspects of purchasing, such as supplier selection, supplier management, project management, and supplier evaluation. Of the 13 people, the fieldwork involved interviews with six people who covered different positions in the purchasing department of the Case Company, and all had experience regarding managing supplier relations; two of these people were interviewed twice. In all, eight interviews were conducted, and the interviews lasted from one to two hours each. In addition to the interviews, access was given to relevant manuals and spreadsheets used in relation to managing supplier relationships.

The case study provides insight into the world of the purchasers from their perspective, and as such, the study is an example of how purchasing via an interorganizational relationship can be conducted.

## Description of the Case Company

The Case Company has been able to obtain a position at the high end of the product scale within their industry. This position gives the Case Company the possibility to obtain high prices that are justified by the unique design and longevity of their products. This position is recognized in the industry, and the brand of the Case Company has a good reputation. Concerning their products, the Case Company emphasizes the features design, functionality, quality, and longevity. Especially design is perceived by the Case Company as their core competence. This emphasis adds further dimensions to the sourcing task of the company. It is not enough to find the cheapest supplier of a given component; other qualitative dimensions also have to be incorporated into the buying process and the evaluation of suppliers.

The primary impression of the purchasing department in the Case Company is that they are very focused on their role in the organization. They are fully aware that purchasing in the Case Company is more than merely scanning the market in order to find the lowest price. In most situations it is a matter of finding the right partner and subsequently agreeing on the price. During the last 10 to 15 years, the Case Company has increased the number of outsourced components. At the time the fieldwork was carried out, 50% of the total costs of the company were related to products bought from sub-suppliers. Due to this rate, the purchasing function requires adequate managerial attention. Not only will their performance affect the cost level, but the performance of their suppliers will also have direct impact on customers' experience of the products bought from the Case Company.

The purchasing department has two major focus areas: inside components, which are mainly various kinds of electronic devices, and hardware components, frames, mechanical devices, and so on. In monetary terms, the inside components represent approximately 75% of product-related purchases, and hardware components represent approximately 25%.

In order to systemize and visualize the purchasing process, the Case Company has developed a matrix in which the different kinds of suppliers are grouped into four segments. The four segments are labeled: key suppliers, standard suppliers, system suppliers, and capacity suppliers. Two dimensions are used to distinguish between the segments. The first dimension refers to who defines the specifications of the product—that is, whether it is a standard commodity within the industry or it has been specified by the Case Company. The second dimension refers to the nature of the relationship with the supplier—that is, whether the sourcing strategy is founded on a relational-oriented basis or on competitive terms. During the case study, the focus was on the systems supplier segment. From this segment the Case Company sources components specified by the Case Company, and the sourcing strategy is founded on a relational-oriented basis. Sourcing from the system supplier segment involves high interaction, and relationships within this segment have significant consequences if they fail.

A system supplier has two major characteristics. First, he is able to deliver a complex product, which includes product development, subsequent production, and delivery. Second, he is able to manage and control the underlying supply chain, meaning that the Case Company does not have to get directly involved with second-tier suppliers. The typical system supplier is larger than the Case Company, which one might think would be a weak position for bargaining and setting demands. Though the strong brand of the Case Company is intended for its end customers, having the Case Company as a customer does have certain positive effects, even for large actors within the industry—a phenomenon that mostly prevails in relationships with companies located in Southeast Asia. In addition to this, the recognition of the quality standards of the Case Company means that the Case Company has knowledge to offer to the larger company. Cooperating with the Case Company gives the large company a possibility to learn from the Case Company, and in this way the Case Company becomes an attractive partner despite the relatively low volume of products involved. Being perceived as an attractive partner by the purchasers is found to be a main source of the initial bargaining power that the Case Company needs in order to roll out the formalized assessment procedure.

The Case Company has several objectives for engaging with system suppliers, two of which seem to be central. The Case Company wants to focus on their core competence, which is design. By involving system suppliers, the Case Company is able to release resources from activities peripheral to this core competence and at the same time to procure competences and knowledge superior to the ones given up by the Case Company. The second objective is flexibility. By outsourcing competences and knowledge, the Case Company can cut off these resources if they become obsolete.

The Case Company does not want to compromise quality and functionality. That is, the end customer still has to perceive the final product as a genuine Case Company product. This requires a lot of coordination and knowledge transfer with the system supplier. Coordination and knowledge transfer take place at all organizational levels in both the Case Company and at the system supplier. So although resources can be allocated to activities more closely related to the core competences of the Case Company, there is still an immense task of coordinating and securing that the outsourced activities comply with the Case Company's standards.

## The Formalized Audit Procedure for Selection of System Suppliers at Case Company

At the Case Company, the assessment of potential system suppliers goes through a formalized procedure. The people in the Case Company refer to this procedure as an "audit." The audit procedure for selecting new suppliers has three steps. The first step is a desk research, a screening of the potential supplier. If the results of the desk research seem interesting, the assessment process is taken into its second step, which is a formalized audit conducted by a sourcing team that consists of a purchaser assisted by relevant people from the development, quality, and logistics departments at the Case Company. The final step is a detailed investigation of the quality management system of the potential supplier. The information obtained through the audit procedure is used, first, in order to assess the potential supplier and, second, if the supplier gets through the eye of the needle, then the audit report is used as a basis for improving the cooperation, in order to enhance possible weak spots that could harm the relationship.

*First Step—The Desk Research*
A major aspect of the purchaser's job is to screen the market for potential suppliers. Initial contact between the Case Company and potential suppliers can happen in many ways. It can be based on contacts established through fairs, potential suppliers' own applications, advice from other non-competing suppliers, and so on. Sometimes the direction of the search is driven by a request from the development department, and in other cases a potential supplier offers a specific device that can be incorporated into a given project. So the focus on potential suppliers is not always the outcome of a deliberate strategy; sometimes potential suppliers just fall from the sky like manna and new possibilities emerge. In other cases, capacity suppliers develop their skills and competences and become system suppliers. They advance and offer more complicated tasks such as engaging in the development of products and carrying out larger parts of the managerial role of the underlying supply chain. However, this way of recruiting system suppliers is not the prevailing one.

No matter how a potential supplier gets the attention of the purchaser, the first step is to consider whether this potential supplier will ever be able to come into consideration as a supplier to the Case Company, considering its requirements for high quality standards. Often the purchaser is able to weed out inept suppliers just by a short glimpse. For instance, their financial situation may be obviously hopeless, their competences are insufficient in relation to the requirements of the Case Company, or their references are inferior. Such potential suppliers are not given any attention besides a polite rejection, though potential suppliers who look interesting, but with competences not required at the moment, are filed for future usage in case their competences will be required at some time in the future. If the potential supplier seems promising, then the auditing procedure moves into the second step.

*The Second Step—Systematic Assessment of the Potential Supplier*
In the second step, contact is made with the potential supplier. First of all, the contact is made in order to obtain a feeling of some basic aspects: for instance, ability to produce specific products, price level, and so on. If these conditions are found acceptable, a more formal supplier audit is made. This audit includes a visit at the premises of the potential supplier. During this visit, the sourcing team takes a closer look at the supplier in

order to get an impression of the capabilities of the potential supplier—is he really as good as he claims? The chief controller in the purchasing department describes these visits in these words: "You visit the supplier, get to talk with him, get access to his financial reports, and get an insight into his plans for development, where are they heading, etc."

The supplier audit is a formalized procedure, which is described and documented by the operations management system in the Case Company itself. The chief purchaser for electronic components explained: "We are ISO 9001 certified, and in relation to this certification we have our operations management system. In this system we have a description of how we do sourcing." The systemized supplier assessment procedure thereby has its origin in the quality management policies of the Case Company itself. The operations management system is the governmental apparatus that sets the frame for sourcing and to a large extent predetermines the foundation for doing business. In their work, the purchasers have to follow the operations management system, and they have to account for their work by reporting to the system. Thereby their work is dependent on their usage of the system.

During the formal supplier audit, an assessment report is made in order to account for the performance of the potential supplier. The assessment report has two parts, a basic part that is used for potential suppliers within the four supplier segments, and a part that is specific for system and capacity suppliers.

The basic part contains seven elements: master data concerning the potential supplier, details about the organization of the supplier, financial results and goals, an element concerning tariffs and other exogenous factors that could influence the price of the product, an element concerning quality, an element concerning logistics, and finally an element concerning the environmental policies of the potential supplier. In principle, it is the responsible purchaser who has to fill in the basic part. However, one of the interviewed purchasers uses another procedure: "Typically—or this is how I do it—I send the supplier assessment report to them in advance. Then they fill it in themselves, and then I can evaluate the answers afterwards." At the meeting the contents of the assessment report are discussed and possible misunderstandings are clarified. Sending the basic part of the assessment report in advance also enables the purchaser to set the agenda. He avoids details about topics that are irrelevant to him, and it enables him to stay in power even though the dialogue takes place on the home turf of the potential supplier.

The specific part intended for system and capacity suppliers contains six elements—an element concerning cooperation, one concerning logistics, one concerning the process technology of the potential supplier, one element concerning the productivity of the supplier, one that covers the treatment of tools specific to the production of items for the Case

Company—and then there is a final conclusion to the entire assessment including both the basic and the specific part. The element concerning cooperation reflects the expected ability of the potential supplier to cooperate with the Case Company, to live up to the requirements of open-books, joint development, ability to cooperate on many levels, etc. In short, this element is an investigation of the characteristics of a system supplier mentioned above. The logistics element seems to overlap with the logistics element in the basic part; however, in this specific part the logistics element only covers one item: lead time of the product category that the Case Company is interested in. The element concerning process technology reflects the present and future technologies of the potential supplier and thereby products that the supplier is able or will be able to deliver to the Case Company. The productivity element covers the factors that result in high costs during production of the products relevant to the Case Company. This goes for both the internal production of the potential supplier and their management of their suppliers—for instance, intervals between price negotiations with suppliers and number of alternative suppliers. The last element concerns the specific tools that have to be used in the production of the items for the Case Company. These tools are to be marked in order to signify the ownership of the Case Company; the tools must be stored in fire-proof rooms and the potential supplier should have routines for systematic maintenance of the tools. Finally, the entire assessment is evaluated and concluded upon. Within each element the sourcing team evaluates whether the items are at a satisfactory level. If too many elements are assessed as unsatisfactory, then the auditing procedure is terminated, and the potential supplier will not be part of the supplier portfolio of Case Company. If most elements get an adequate score, then the auditing process continues. However, for elements not found to be at an appropriate level, the potential supplier is requested to develop precise action plans for how he intends to live up to the required level, and these plans have to be carried out before the potential supplier can be a full member of the supplier portfolio of the Case Company. This practice shows how the operations management system defines the rationality of the cooperation. The system enables the Case Company not only to set the agenda for what is the expected performance level but also to mobilize the free will of the potential supplier by asking them to come up with solutions to the deficiencies accounted for during assessment. The potential suppliers are thereby enabled to conduct themselves based on the rationality inherent in the operations management system.

In addition to functioning as a kind of check-list in relation to the audit, the procedure also functions as a disciplining process that prepares the supplier for the role of being a supplier to the Case Company. The potential supplier commits itself to the procedures that the Case Company uses when it conducts projects in cooperation with their suppliers.

*The Third Step—In-Depth Evaluation of Compatibility*

If the potential supplier looks promising, and if the price level of the product in focus is interesting, the final step of the selection procedure is initiated. The third step includes a visit by an audit team to the potential supplier. The team goes through a meticulous procedure that involves the topics of quality management and process technologies. This audit is conducted with the specific purpose of ensuring that the quality management of the potential supplier really is compatible with the procedures at the Case Company. The same objective goes for process technologies. Here the audit team from the Case Company wants to make sure that the technologies of the potential supplier can live up to the standards of the Case Company. For both quality and technology, the audit team also brings back information to the Case Company—information needed for future coordination.

## Ways of Acting and Forming System Suppliers

So far the audit report as an account of the performance of suppliers has been introduced. The audit report is used to evaluate whether the potential supplier is able to live up to the standards required for suppliers cooperating with the Case Company. The report has the characteristic that the intended direction of intervention points towards the supplier. That is, it is the supplier who has to adjust to the requirements of the Case Company. This attitude is in line with the characteristics of system suppliers, namely that the Case Company wants to be in power. The chief purchaser for electronic components expressed it in this way: "They have to be aware that if they do not act on the hints we give them, then there will be consequences in the long run." This sentence contains several important aspects. The first is the sequence: "if they do not act," meaning that it is the suppliers who have to act. What they have to act upon is hints along with the accounts that the Case Company has defined and presented to the supplier. Also the part "there will be consequences" is relevant, as this indicates that if the supplier does not move in the right direction, then he will not be supplier to the Case Company. Though it is only a short sentence, it grasps some essential parts of the way in which the Case Company practices governmentality. First, it shows that the Case Company seeks to mobilize the free will of their potential suppliers. The Case Company gives them hints, but as these are unspecific, the potential suppliers have to find solutions by themselves. Also, the short sentence reveals the disciplinary power aspect. The description in the subsection above shows that the Case Company forces the potential suppliers to commit themselves to the standards set by the Case Company. The rationality that the Case Company mobilizes is that from the ISO standards and the related operations management system. Hence the truth and the proper behavior make the potential suppliers act upon hints stems from the ISO rationale of standards and quality.

The assessment process is a disciplining practice that prepares the suppliers for the future cooperation with the Case Company. When the supplier has entered the portfolio of suppliers at the Case Company, the cooperation concerning product development is similar to the assessment process. The similarity is found in the fact that the Case Company has a prespecified contract that is filled in and formulated during the product development process. The contract concerns technical aspects, open-book accounting, and terms of trade. The supplier is then expected to come up with proposals that can be negotiated. In that sense the assessment process for selecting the proper suppliers forms the foundation for controlling the suppliers.

During the interviews, it was quite surprising that none of the interviewed persons mentioned the word trust. However, when asked directly about the importance of trust, the interviewed people revealed that the audit as well as the subsequent plans for action also serve the purpose of building competence trust—not building trust in the persons involved, but in their ability to carry out a specific project. One of the purchasers described it like this: "If you cooperate with a supplier, you have to be able to trust that he conducts the processes agreed upon." Therefore, meeting the expectations of the Case Company sends a signal of trustworthiness from the potential suppliers to the Case Company. This signal makes the people at the Case Company confident in the ability of the supplier to enter a project that can reasonably be expected to have a successful outcome.

During the audits and the visits at the potential suppliers, the purchasers seek not to become personally involved with the people who represent the supplier. One purchaser said: "When I visit the supplier, we normally have dinner together. Here we of cause discuss personal topics, but I try not to become personally involved. It has to be kept as a professional relation." The chief purchaser is aware of situations where the purchaser and suppliers have become too close personally. He said: "I sometimes switch purchasers between suppliers if I feel that one of the purchasers becomes too familiar with the supplier." The chief purchaser is worried about the situation where a purchaser begins to trust the supplier at a personal level and to rely mainly on the good intentions of the supplier instead focusing on the information gathered through the audit process.

## DISCUSSION

The interesting part of this case is how a small electronics manufacturing company is able to conduct its potential suppliers despite the fact that many of them are much more significant players in the market compared to the

Case Company. The Case Company managed their supplier selection procedure by enforcing a huge battery of controls in the shape of a very systematized and thorough operations management system that strictly specified issues that had to be accounted for by the potential supplier if he should manage to become part of the portfolio of suppliers. The operations management system was part of the ISO 9001 certification that the Case Company used as a central part of its internal control system.

The Case Company explicitly stated that they want to be in power. In their self-perception, they expressed the belief that due to their position in the market and their reputation as a high-quality brand they were very attractive customers to potential suppliers. The people interviewed at the Case Company seemed to be able to force the potential suppliers to act according to the demands set by the Case Company. This indicates a kind of dominating power position. However, the governmentality analysis indicates that the ability to conduct the potential suppliers during the selection process has its roots in the governmental apparatuses applied—that is, the ISO 9001-driven operations management system. In that sense, the Case Company has power, not by dominating the potential suppliers, but via disciplinary power. Having the ISO 9001 governmental apparatus as the power base for conducting supplier relations raises a major problem because this source of power may be fragile in the hands of the Case Company.

In the theoretical section, it was discussed that disciplinary power relates to the ability to set the agenda in a relationship. It was also discussed that this ability is closely related to the design and the practice of the governmental apparatuses applied since these are the vehicles for conduct. In this specific case the governmental apparatus is the ISO 9001 operations management system. The whole idea of the apparatus is that it is an internationally recognized standardization system. This means that the potential suppliers who are assessed by the Case Company are familiar with the governmental apparatus that they face. The potential suppliers probably subscribe to the rationality inherent in this system. The potential suppliers thereby deliver the information that the Case Company requests, and the suppliers do so without consideration. The Case Company perceives this as being in power. What seems to be happening is that the Case Company reflects the potential suppliers in the image created by the ISO 9001 system. Consequently, the ability to set the agenda is not held by the Case Company—it is held by the International Organization for Standardization who defines the ISO 9001 system. Thus the Case Company becomes a governed part like the potential supplier because they are both acting based on the rationale inherent in the ISO 9001 standard. If the Case Company is unaware of the origin of their disciplinary power, they can easily squander their position, and this is what makes their source of power fragile.

The results indicate that the Case Company conducts the supplier selection process based on a different form of power than they believe. The potential suppliers do not deliver information and act upon the demands raised by the Case Company because the Case Company tells them to, but because it is part of the management system employed. Hence it is the ISO 9001 system that allows the parties to interact on a sophisticated level at very early stages in the relationship. This has also been discussed as a major advantage of ISO 9001 (e.g., Wilkinson & Dale, 2002). What the operations management system does is that it forms a forum where the conduct of the interorganizational relationship can be played out. This phenomenon has been discussed in relation to management accounting and interorganizational relationships. Håkansson and Lind (2004) found that interorganizational relationships are not a matter of two companies engaging very closely. Instead, a temporary unit is constructed between the two permanent companies, and it is within this temporary unit that management accounting is rolled out. The structures provided by management accounting provide a framework for a negotiation process that can lead to an agreement on solutions. In this process, management accounting facilitates the creation of the boundaries of the temporary unit. Other studies find that management accounting provides structures for cooperation through ongoing negotiations (e.g., Cuganesan & Lee, 2006; Mouritsen & Thrane, 2006; Seal, Cullen, Dunlop, Berry, & Ahmed, 1999). Arenas for the participants in the ongoing dispute of developing interorganizational relationships were thereby constructed, and intervention inside the interorganizational relationship was facilitated. Thrane and Hald (2006) contribute to this by showing how the interorganizational boundaries that separate the parties involved in the relationship develop through the interaction of rational deliberation, cultural symbols, and management accounting. Thrane (2007) explores this further by showing how management and change in interorganizational relations are acted out within a so-called space that is partly shaped by the controls applied in the process along with other factors. Jakobsen (2010) expands these findings and concludes that management accounting techniques are representations of the cooperation that functions as checkpoints where information is exchanged among the parties.

Though the people interviewed did not openly express the concept of trust, they admitted, when asked directly, that trust building during the selection process had an impact on the assessment of the potential suppliers. This finding reintroduces the concept of trust that ironically was abandoned to begin with due to the initial findings in the company. A possible explanation for the initial abandoning of trust is that in most of the relevant literature trust is either perceived as a substitute for control, or the concepts are thought of as complementary mechanisms for reducing uncertainty. The Case Company shows something else. The Case Company mobilizes a massive control system and thereby they create confidence and trust in the potential supplier. So what the case shows is a situation where the control part is constant and used to build up trust to a level that allows the potential suppliers to become possible suppliers for the Case Company. This finding calls for a revised understanding of the concept of trust than what has so far been outlined in this chapter.

The literature on trust seems to agree on one thing: namely, that trust is multifaceted (e.g., Baier, 1986; Khodyakov, 2007; Rousseau, Sitkin, Burt, & Camerer, 1998). Sako (1992) divided the trust concept into three different types of trust that are relevant in an interorganizational relationship. These types are contractual trust, competence trust, and goodwill trust. By dividing the trust concept, Sako succeeds in moving the concept beyond the general definition of trust that basically states that trust is an expectation that others have no intention of harming our well-being. This general definition only highlights a basic condition of life, assuming that life includes social interaction. Employing trust into the practice of management requires a more explicit understanding of where and when trust comes into play and how trust is likely to function in different settings. Within an interorganizational setting Sako is found to bring a contribution by the tripartition of trust, and as such, this framework has been used in other analyses of interorganizational relationships (e.g., Langfield-Smith & Smith, 2003).

Contractual trust concerns trust in the will of the partner to live up to the terms of cooperation agreed upon. For instance, a buyer will only enter an agreement if she expects that the supplier intends to deliver the right quantity at the agreed-upon time and place. From the viewpoint of the supplier, she will only enter the agreement if she expects that the buyer will pay for the goods actually delivered. The form of the contract is irrelevant in relation to contractual trust. A handshake on a market place can symbolize more trust than a twenty-page written contract (e.g., Macaulay, 1963). Hence, contractual trust concerns the willingness to keep promises, neither more than promised, nor less.

Competence trust refers to trust in the other party's ability to deliver the product agreed upon. This type of trust often has qualitative aspects—for instance, whether the supplier is able to live up to certain criteria of quality. It may also be relevant to consider aspects apart from the physical product, such as whether it is plausible that supplier will deliver the promised goods within the time frame agreed upon.

The final type of trust is goodwill trust. This type of trust is related to the degree of commitment that the parties invest in their mutual agreement. It concerns the willingness to do more than formally expected. Uzzi (1997) gives some examples of goodwill trust in his case study of small companies in the New York City apparel industry. He shows that through cooperativeness and caring for each other, these small companies are able to help each other and in the long run ensure efficiency and adaptability for each of the members of this close-knit network. Goodwill trust is quite similar to the kind of trust among close relatives and friends. Though such caring characteristics are pleasant in an interhuman context, they face some difficulties in interorganizational context. The creation of such close-knit bonds makes it difficult to break a relationship and options for renewal and flexibility are not utilized (e.g., Ahuja, 2000; Gulati & Gargiulo, 1999; Maravelias, 2001). Uzzi (1997) has labeled this phenomenon as the "paradox of embeddedness."

The supplier assessment process is used by the Case Company to build contractual and competence trust specifically. Building contractual trust is done when the potential supplier delivers answers to the questions raised during the assessment. At this stage the contract concerns assessment, and therefore an answer provided indicates that the potential supplier is willing to live up to the contract. Competence trust is built when the potential supplier provides answers that fit into the expectations of the Case Company. Does the potential supplier have adequate procedures for storing vital components in fire-safe rooms? Yes, we do it in this certified way. Such an answer would add to the competence trust level. Both contractual trust and competence trust add to the trustworthiness of the potential supplier, and thereby form the foundation for future cooperation. Goodwill trust is actively avoided. The reason is that the managers at the Case Company find that too much personal involvement will lead to decisions that are not beneficial for the company.

## CONCLUSIONS

This chapter has analyzed the supplier selection process at an electronics manufacturing company. The selection process has focused on a type of supplier that involves a high level of interaction during cooperation. The company explicitly states that they want to be in power in the relationship. They seek power through the employment of a massive and standardized supplier selection process, which has an operations management system as its pivotal point. Following this operations management system has two main managerial outcomes. First, it assists the purchasing department in selecting proper suppliers who are found qualified to live up to a number of different criteria within several dimensions. Second, the selection process constructs a foundation for cooperation with the suppliers in future projects. The foundation has two roots. One root prepares the suppliers for the form of cooperation that the Case Company wants to work by in future projects. In this sense, disciplinary power is achieved, and this will let the Case Company set the agenda in future projects. The other root is the contractual trust and the competence trust in the potential supplier, which are built during the supplier selection process. These findings indicate that the operations management enables accounting for partners who are worth trusting.

## REFERENCES

Ahuja, G. (2000). Collaboration networks, structural holes, and innovation: A longitudinal study. *Administrative Science Quarterly, 45*, 425–455.

Bachmann, R. (2001). Trust, power and control in trans-organizational relations. *Organization Studies, 22*, 337–365.

Baier, A. C. (1986). Trust and antitrust. *Ethics*, 96, 231–260.

Burchell, G. (1991). Peculiar interests: Civil society and governing "the system of natural liberty." In G. Burchell, C. Gordon, & P. Miller (Eds.), *The Foucault effect: Studies in governmentality* (pp. 119–150). Chicago, IL: University of Chicago Press.

Burks, A. W. (1946). Peirce's theory of abduction. *Philosophy of Science, 13*, 301–306.

Cuganesan, S., & Lee, R. (2006). Intra-organizational influences in procurement networks controls: The impact of information technology. *Management Accounting Research, 17*, 141–170.

Das, T. K., & Teng, B. (2001). Trust, control, and risk in strategic alliances: An integrated framework. *Organization Studies, 22*, 251–283.

Dean, M. (1999). *Governmentality: Power and rule in the modern society*, London, UK: Sage.

de Boer, L., Labro, E., & Morlacchi, P. (2001). A review of methods supporting supplier selection. *European Journal of Purchasing and Supply Management, 7*(2), 75–89.

Dekker, H. C. (2004). Control of inter-organizational relationships: Evidence on appropriation concerns and coordination requirements. *Accounting, Organizations and Society, 29*, 27–49.

Deleuze, G. (1999). *Foucault*. London, UK: Athlone Press.

Fann, K. T. (1970). *Peirce's theory of abduction*. Hague, Netherlands: Martinus Nijhoff.

Foucault, M. (1982). The subject and power. *Critical Inquiry, 8*, 777–795.

Foucault, M. (1988). Technologies of the self. In I. Martin, H. Gutman, & P. Hutton (Eds.), *Technologies of the self: A seminar with Michel Foucault* (pp. 16–49). Boston, MA: University of Massachusetts Press.

Foucault, M. (1991). Governmentality. In G. Burchell, C. Gordon, & P. Miller (Eds.), *The Foucault effect: Studies in governmentality* (pp. 87–104). Chicago, IL: University of Chicago Press.

Gordon, C. (1991). Governmental rationality: An introduction. In G. Burchell, C. Gordon, & P. Miller (Eds.), *The Foucault effect: Studies in governmentality* (pp. 1–52). Chicago, IL: University of Chicago Press.

Gulati, R. (1995). Does familiarity breed trust? The implications of repeated ties for contractual choice in alliances. *Academy of Management Journal, 38*, 85–112.

Gulati, R. (1998). Alliances and networks. *Strategic Management Journal, 19*, 293–317.

Gulati, R., & Gargiulo, M. (1999). Where do interorganizational networks come from? *American Journal of Sociology, 104*, 1439–1493.

Haig, B. D. (2005). An abductive theory of scientific method. *Psychological Methods, 10,* 371–388.

Håkansson, H., & Lind J. (2004). Accounting and network coordination. *Accounting, Organizations and Society, 29,* 51–72.

Hedberg, B., Dahlgren, G., Hansson, J., & Olve, N. (2000). *Virtual organizations and beyond: Discovering imaginary systems.* Chichester, UK: Wiley.

Humphreys, P., Huang, G., Caddena, T., & McIvor, R. (2007). Integrating design metrics within the early supplier selection process. *Journal of Purchasing and Supply Management, 13*(1), 42–52.

Ittner, C. D., Larcker, D. F., Nagar, V., & Rajan, M. V. (1999). Supplier selection, monitoring practices, and firm performance. *Journal of Accounting and Public Policy, 18,* 253–281.

Jackson, N., & Carter, P. (2000). *Rethinking organizational behavior.* London, UK: Prentice Hall.

Jakobsen, M. (2010). Management accounting as the inter-organizational boundary. *Journal of Accounting and Organizational Change, 6*(1), 96–122.

Khodyakov, D. (2007). Trust as a process: A three-dimensional approach. *Sociology, 41*(1), 115–132.

Kumar, N. (2005). The power of power in supplier–retailer relationships. *Industrial Marketing Management, 34,* 863–866.

Langfield-Smith, K., & Smith, D. (2003). Management control systems and trust in outsourcing relationships, *Management Accounting Research, 14,* 281–307.

Macaulay, S. (1963). Non-contractual relations in business: A preliminary study. *American Sociological Review, 28*(1), 55–67.

Maravelias, C. (2001). *Managing network organizations.* Unpublished doctoral dissertation, School of Business, Stockholm University, Sweden.

Mouritsen, J., & Thrane, S. (2006). Accounting, network complementarities and the development of inter-organizational relations. *Accounting, Organizations and Society, 31,* 241–275.

Oliver, A. L., & Ebers, M. (1998). Networking network studies: An analysis of conceptual configurations in the study of inter-organizational relationships. *Organization Studies 19,* 549–583.

Raffnsøe, S., Gudmand-Høyer, M., & Thaning, M. (2008). *Foucault.* Frederiksberg, Denmark. Samfundslitteratur.

Rose, N. (1999). *Powers of freedom: Reframing political thought.* Cambridge, UK: Cambridge University Press.

Rousseau, D., Sitkin, S. B., Burt, R. S., & Camerer, C. (1998). Not so different after all: A cross-discipline view of trust. *Academy of Management Review, 23,* 393–404.

Sako, M. (1992). *Prices, quality and trust: Inter-firm relations in Britain and Japan.* Cambridge, UK: Cambridge University Press.

Seal, W., Cullen, J., Dunlop, A., Berry, T., & Ahmed, M. (1999). Enacting a European supply chain: A case study on the role of management accounting. *Management Accounting Research, 10,* 303–322.

Thrane, S. (2007). The complexity of management accounting change: Bifurcation and oscillation in schizophrenic inter-organizational systems. *Management Accounting Research, 18,* 248–272.

Thrane, S., & Hald, K. S. (2006). The emergence of boundaries and accounting in supply fields: The dynamics of integration and fragmentation. *Management Accounting Research, 17,* 288–314.

Tomkins, C. (2001). Interdependencies, trust and information in relationships, alliances and networks. *Accounting, Organizations, and Society, 26,* 161–191.

Uzzi, B. (1997). Social structures and competition in interfirm networks: The paradox of embeddedness. *Administrative Science Quarterly, 42,* 35–67.

van der Meer-Kooistra, J., & Vosselman, E. G. J. (2000). Management control of interfirm transactional relationships: The case of industrial renovation and maintenance. *Accounting, Organizations, and Society, 25,* 51–77.

Wilkinson, G., & Dale, B. G. (2002). An examination of the ISO 9001:2000 standard and its influence on the integration of management systems. *Production Planning and Control, 13,* 284–297.

Wilkinson, I., Young, L., & Freytag, P. V. (2005). Business mating: Who chooses and who gets chosen? *Industrial Marketing Management, 34,* 669–680.

CHAPTER 11

# QUALITY OF PARTNER RELATIONS IN INTERNATIONAL CONSTRUCTION ALLIANCES

Beliz Ozorhon and David Arditi

## ABSTRACT

Construction companies consider strategic alliances as a vehicle to enter new markets and exploit business opportunities. Through such alliances, they take advantage of the distinctive competencies and the complementary resources of their partners. Such entities are very difficult to manage mainly due to their inherent complexity, involving a mixture of different cultures, managerial systems, philosophies, and attitudes. As a result, partners in strategic alliances in international construction have a hard time figuring how to achieve high levels of quality in interpartner relations. A better understanding is critical in selecting the right partners, in getting along well with partners, and in realizing anticipated synergies. In this chapter, the key factors that affect the quality of interpartner relations in strategic alliances in international construction are explored. In this respect, the issues related to interpartner relations—that is, (1) the strategic and organizational fit between partners, (2) the impact of cultural differences in national and organizational approaches, and (3) the structural characteristics of the strategic alliance—are operationalized and investigated.

A framework for analyzing the relationship between interpartner relations and these three issues is presented. The research makes use of data collected from a questionnaire survey administered to 28 Turkish contractors that entered into a total of 68 strategic alliances with non-Turkish partners. The data are analyzed by using structural equation modeling. It is expected that the information in the chapter will help professionals during the partner selection process and will result in a successful alliance that operates smoothly.

## INTRODUCTION

Alliances improve the strategic position of firms in competitive markets by providing resources from other firms that enable them to share costs and risks in product design, production, marketing, and distribution. Doing business within a strategic alliance (SA) provides the partnering firms the opportunity to share costs and risks, to acquire knowledge, to enter new markets, and to gain economies of scale or to rationalize operations (Contractor & Lorange, 1988). Despite their benefits, such entities are difficult to manage because of the presence of two or more partner organizations usually with different managerial systems, philosophies, values, and attitudes, which may be competitors as well as collaborators (Janger, 1980; Killing, 1983; Tatoglu & Glaister, 1998). Previous studies have shown that SAs have a high failure record, reporting on the dissolution rate but also on the ineffectiveness and the inefficiency of the SA management. The nature of the relationship between SA partners is likely to affect SA operations (Buckley & Casson, 1988; Parkhe, 1993). Many factors have been suggested in the literature as factors affecting the quality of partner relations in international construction alliances including the fit between the partner companies and the structural characteristics of the alliances.

The quality of partner relations in international construction alliances was modeled in Ozorhon's (2007) research based on the experiences of Turkish contractors and their foreign partners. The aim of this research was to explore the impact of various factors on the quality of partner relations. In this respect, the research investigated the impact of strategic and organizational fit between alliance partners, national and organizational cultural fit between alliance partners,; and the structural characteristics of the SA organization on the quality of partner relations. Based on the findings of this study, partner selection and alliance formation stages will be discussed for the SAs in international construction.

## PARTNER SELECTION AND PARTNER RELATIONS

With increasing levels of globalization in business, alliances between and among multinational firms have become popular. There are a number of overriding economic and political reasons for the rise in the popularity of SAs. These include the characteristics of foreign markets, such as access to suitable distribution channels; sharing heightened economic and political risks in new business ventures; government pressure; and technology transfer (Makino & Delios, 1996). Forging an alliance enables a firm to focus resources on its core skills and competencies while acquiring other components or capabilities it lacks from the marketplace (Zaman & Mavondo, 2002). Through the formation of SAs, companies are able to exploit business opportunities and enter new markets abroad. However, the benefits associated with SAs are counterbalanced by a wide range of problems. The failure rate of SAs, in general, is high (Makino & Beamish, 1998). Since SAs consist of at least two parent organizations, these entities may have different goals, management practices, and organizational cultures, and it becomes difficult to manage these organizations and achieve critical success criteria. The good intentions and rational motives behind these alliances are not always congruent with the strategic direction of either firm on its own, let alone the strategic direction of both in unison. Like in other industries, achieving high levels of performance is difficult in the construction industry as performance is extensively dependent on several internal and external factors.

In order to identify those factors contributing to the success of SAs, each stage of an alliance process should be investigated. The process of an SA is generally distinguished in three stages: namely, partner selection, formation, and operation. The selection of the appropriate partner constitutes one of the major success factors for an SA. Partner selection determines an SA's mix of skills, knowledge, and resources; its operating policies and procedures; and its vulnerability to indigenous conditions, structures, and institutional changes (Geringer, 1991). SAs are formed based on strategies of how to manage environmental uncertainties, how to overcome lack of resources and, in particular, how to manage the firm's range of interorganizational relations. During the formation stage, potential partners spend considerable time identifying their common compatible interests in the task-related areas. Kwok, Then, and Skitmore's (2000) study identified a number of these critical factors, including negotiation, profit and loss distribution, clarity of contribution among partners, control and decision making policy, clarity of sharing of risks and liabilities, composition of decision-making body, and dispute resolution procedures. During the operation of a project, it is important to enter into a fair engineering contract, employ qualified subcontractors and suppliers, maintain a good relationship with the host government and other parties, and adopt renegotiation as a dispute resolution and problem-solving technique (Bing & Tiong, 1999).

Geringer (1991) posits that the partner selection process is considered to be of crucial importance to the formation and operation of SAs. Partner consistency in terms of strategic goals and behaviors, cooperative culture, managerial philosophy, innovativeness, and long-term orientation influences mutual trust, commitment, and collaboration between parties (Parkhe, 1991). Killing (1983) states that it is impossible to identify an exhaustive list of criteria that an organization should meet when attempting to assess a potential complementary partner. Partner fit determines the extent to which partner firms can get along and realize anticipated synergies from the joint venture (Buckley & Casson, 1988; Hill & Hellriegel, 1994; Morris & Cadogan, 2001; Yan & Duan, 2003). The issue of partner fit has been widely discussed in the partner selection literature. For example, Geringer (1988) argues that selection of an SA partner needs to consider a fit in both task-related characteristics (e.g., resources and skills) and partner-related characteristics (e.g., size, objectives, and operating policies).

Most researchers suggest that a mismatch in terms of alliance fit is the most important reason for alliance failure. According to previous studies, the factors that affect interpartner fit commonly include strategic fit, resource fit, operational fit, organizational fit, and cultural fit (Luo, 1998; Morris & Cadogan, 2001; Ulijn, Duijsters, Schaetzlein, & Remer, 2005; Yan & Duan, 2003). According to Luo (1998), strategic, organizational, and financial attributes are all crucial to SA performance. A partner with superior strategic traits, but lacking strong organizational and financial characteristics, results in an unstable SA. The possession of desirable organizational attributes without corresponding strategic and financial competence leaves the SA unprofitable. A partner with superior financial strengths without strategic and organizational competencies can lead to an unsustainable venture.

The partner selection and venture formation processes set the basis of the relationship between the partners during the operation of the SA. The smooth operation of the SA is dependent mainly upon the interaction between the partners in making strategic and operational decisions (Sridharan, 1997). For SAs to survive, their parents must find a way to work together—that is, they must be able to agree on goals and policies and to renegotiate them in response to changes in the environment (Doz, 1996).

## MODELING INTERPARTNER RELATIONS IN INTERNATIONAL CONSTRUCTION ALLIANCES

This study is built upon the findings of a research by Ozorhon (2007), who proposed and tested a set of indicators and drivers for stronger partner relations in international construction alliances. The following sections present the research methodology, the data collection process, and the components of the framework developed by Ozorhon (2007).

The following five hypotheses were tested: the strategic fit between SA partners (H1), the organizational fit between SA partners (H2), the national culture fit between SA partners (H3), the organizational culture fit between SA partners (H4), and the effectiveness of structural characteristics of the SA organization (H5) have positive effects on the quality of partner relations.

## Operationalization of the "Quality of Partner Relations" in SAs

Extant literature has focused on commitment, cooperation, collaboration, communication, trust, and conflict resolution as the important components of alliance relationships (Luo, 2002). In this study, "quality of partner relations" is defined by the six indicators discussed below (Ozorhon, 2007).

### *Commitment*

Commitment can be described as the willingness of SA partners to exert effort on behalf of the SA (Mohr & Spekman, 1994). Committed partners are likely to consider long-term gains rather than short-term advantages. Committed partners are interested in creating and maintaining a good relationship with the other partners and thus are less likely to let differences in functional approaches result in conflicts and negatively affect SA performance. Committed partners are likely to be more cooperative, communicative, and flexible in accommodating conflict issues. When parties are committed to the relationship, cooperation evolves from "commitment to cooperation in its own right" (Buckley & Casson, 1988).

### *Effective Communication*

Effective communication between the SA partners is important for good partner relations since partners do not usually start an SA with a full understanding of each other's goals, capabilities, and behaviors; in many instances, these are revealed when the SA starts operating (Doz, 1996). Communication allows the partners to understand the goals of the alliance, and the roles and responsibilities of all the actors. Failure by parents to quickly learn about each other may lead to misunderstandings and suspicion, and eventually to lower commitment, poor economic results, and dissolution (Doz, 1996; Shenkar & Zeira, 1992). Communication helps with the sharing and dissemination of individual experiences (Inkpen, 1996).

### *Cooperation*

Cooperation is the key dimension of the SA relationship. Understanding the nature and scope of cooperation is essential in analyzing the operation and success of an alliance. Cooperation is a proxy for commitment, trust, and synergy. It is required to overcome the potential misunderstandings and coordination difficulties that can arise from differences in managerial or organizational practices (Das & Teng, 1998). Cooperation is critical to avoid possible conflicts (Ozorhon, Arditi, Dikmen, & Birgonul, 2010).

*Previous Cooperation*

Previous cooperation and experience earned from prior engagements between the partners allows the partners to justify subsequent risky steps (Das & Teng, 1998). In addition, prior relationships indicate a history of repeated interaction, which may lead to relational advantages and stability. Previous contact between partners also leads to the development of specialized skills and routines adapted to the exchange. These include specific knowledge about the structure and operation of the partner organization as well as familiarity with its executives and managers (Shenkar & Zeira, 1992). Previous cooperation also fosters a climate of openness that is essential for discussing behavioral problems that may be a barrier to learning (Doz, 1996).

*Conflict Resolution*

Conflict resolution refers to methods of resolving amicably the conflicts between partners. Fey and Beamish (1999) define SA conflict as the interaction between SA partners where the actions of one partner prevent or compel some outcome against the resistance of another partner. Conflict between the partners can indicate disagreement over goals and operational and managerial expectations, send confusing signals to the parent managers and employees, and thereby hamper performance levels (Yan & Gray, 2001). Such circumstances may also limit an SA's ability to respond to environmental changes (Hebert, 1994). Conflict may also result in the unwillingness of parent firms to contribute resources that the IJV needs to achieve its goals (Killing, 1983). Since extensive conflict negatively affects SA performance, the amicable resolution of disputes is essential for the continuity of an SA in harmony.

*Degree of Trust*

The degree of trust between the partners is one of the most critical indicators affecting the quality of partner relations since trust provides for greater adaptability in an SA, and enhances the exchange of knowledge, a key component of organizational learning and SA success (Bing, Tiong, Fan, & Chew, 1999; Das & Teng, 1998; Parkhe, 1993; Park & Ungson, 1997).

## Operationalization of the Variables Affecting the Quality of Partner Relations

The factors influencing the quality of partner relations were defined in terms of (1) strategic and organizational fit between SA partners, (2) national and organizational culture fit between SA partners, and (3) structural SA characteristics (Ozorhon, 2007).

### *Contextual Fit in SAs*

In forming SAs in construction, the SA partners expose themselves to several internal and external risks. These include but are not limited to inheriting a partner's financial problems, having disagreements about accounting standards, distrust between partner employees, policy changes in parent companies affecting the project, lack of management competence, disagreements about staff allocation and positions in the project team hierarchy, disagreement on allocation of work to be done, and technology-transfer disputes (Bing et al., 1999). In this study, factors related to contextual fit are grouped as strategic and organizational fit.

**Strategic fit:** The strategic orientation of a partner firm is important for a successful alliance operation. In this study, "strategic fit" consists of goal congruency between SA partners, previous experience in the host country, previous experience with similar projects, adequacy of management skills, technical skills and human resources, and quality of relationship with the client.

- Goal congruency between partners is one of the primary factors in SA success (Inkpen & Currall, 1998; Tomlinson & Thompson, 1977). Conflict between partners that may result from goal incongruity can negatively affect partner relations (Fey & Beamish, 1999).
- Complementarity of partners in terms of previous experience in host country is an important strategic asset since in this experiential process, foreign firms develop a general knowledge about the political, social, economic, and cultural aspects of the SA location and specific knowledge about local business practices and local networks (Johanson & Vahlne, 1977). This acquired knowledge stimulates the trust and collaboration between partners (Beamish, 1987; Luo, 1997; Shenkar, 1990).
- Complementarity of partners in terms of previous project experience may be critical for achieving stronger partner relations. The partners' ability to acquire, learn, process, assimilate, integrate, deploy, and exploit an inflow of new knowledge and skills may depend on how these relate to the skills already established (Luo, 1997). As Gunhan and Arditi (2005) state, having a special expertise can be a major strength for a company operating in international markets.
- Compatibility of partners' managerial skills, technical skills, and human resources is important in that it allows a firm to complete a project successfully. Compatible management skills not only enable partners to operate the SA effectively but also help them maintain good relations with other project participants. Compatible technical

skills are required to smoothly mitigate possible project risks that may lead to cost, time, and quality problems. Finally, human resources reflect the blending of partners' cultures and management styles, and as such affect the SA's joint human resources strategies.
- The quality of partners' relationship with the client is also a good indicator of strategic fit. Since client satisfaction is an important indicator of performance, strong relations with the client are useful in dealing with client-related issues.

**Organizational fit:** "Organizational fit" consists of complementarity/compatibility of partners' financial capabilities, company size, management systems, and national/international workload.

- Financial capability of partner firms is critical since a partner's profitability directly influences its ability to make a capital contribution, fulfill financial commitments, and dispense financial resources in the operation of the SA.
- Partner size may be a significant determinant of quality of partner relations and thereby SA performance (Hennart, Kim, & Zeng, 1998; Merchant, 2000; Pan & Chi, 1999; Pan & Li, 2000; Smith, Guthrie, & Chen, 1989). The literature suggests that asymmetry in partners' firm size has negative effects on the stability of an SA (Geringer, 1988; Gomes-Casseres, 1990; Harrigan, 1988; Killing, 1983).
- Similarity between partners' management systems is another important determinant of performance (Beamish, 1984; Killing, 1983). Differences in partners' management styles can result in conflict; nonresolution of such conflicts can eventually affect the success of SAs (Sridharan, 1997).
- Partners' national/international workload may influence the effort and time they allocate to the SA. A partner with extensive international spread tends to reduce its commitment to the SA (Beamish, 1984), which in turn may affect SA performance.

### *Cultural Fit in SAs*

Cultural distance has received a great deal of attention in the international business literature (Barkema, Shenkar, Vermeulen, & Bell, 1997; Evans & Mavondo, 2002; Kogut & Singh, 1988; Morosini, Shane, & Singh, 1998; O'Grady & Lane, 1996; Park & Ungson, 1997). Culture has been referred to as a set of shared experiences, understandings, and meanings among members of a group, an organization, a community, or a nation (Hofstede, 1991; Mead, 1998). Culture is also that complex whole that includes knowledge, beliefs, arts, morals, customs, and any other capabilities and habits acquired by men and women as members of a society (Low &

Leong, 2000). Culture is an ingrained behavioral influence that affects the way collective groups approach, evaluate, and negotiate opportunities for international business. The topics relating to the impact of culture on SAs span a number of areas such as national and organizational cultures.

It is hypothesized that cultural similarity increases harmony and reduces friction (Shenkar, 2001) in cross-cultural strategic partnerships. Arguments to support this proposition build on three primary insights. First, culturally similar managers are more likely to share the same attitudes, values, beliefs, knowledge, management systems (Lasserre, 1999), leadership styles, and scripts of behavior, as well as business, organizational, and administrative practices (Kogut & Singh, 1988). Second, such cultural similarities facilitate and enhance the ability to communicate, cooperate, integrate knowledge, and develop trust (Killing, 1983). Third, cultural dissimilarities increase the frequency and severity of communication difficulties (Brown, Rugman, & Verbeke, 1989), miscommunications (Park & Ungson, 1997), conflict (Sim & Ali, 2000), and misinterpretation of a foreigner's intentions, whether honest or opportunistic. In brief, past theoretical arguments can be captured in a single statement: Cultural similarity increases harmony and decreases friction in cross-cultural interactions and vice versa.

**National culture fit:** Several researchers reported that differences in national cultures are a source of poor communication, inadequate cooperation, lack of commitment, and ineffective conflict resolution between SA partners (Mohr & Spekman, 1994; Parkhe, 1991). These problems occur because of the dissimilarities of partners' interpretation of and responses to strategic and managerial issues.

Hofstede (1991) developed a pioneering and widely accepted classification scheme that breaks national culture into the following five indicators: *Power distance* focuses on the degree of equality or inequality between people in a country's society. *Individualism–collectivism* focuses on the degree the society reinforces individual or collective achievement and interpersonal relationship. *Masculinity–femininity* focuses on the degree the society reinforces the traditional masculine work role model of male achievement, control, and power. *Uncertainty avoidance* focuses on the level of tolerance for uncertainty and ambiguity within the society and the extent to which rules are obeyed and risks are avoided. *Long-term orientation* focuses on the degree to which the society embraces long-term devotion to traditional, forward-thinking values.

**Organizational culture fit:** Partners with dissimilar organizational cultures may expend time and energy to establish mutually agreeable managerial practices and routines to facilitate interaction (Park & Ungson, 1997), which can in turn lead to a significant negative influence on SA performance (Pothukuchi, Damanpour, Choi, Chen, & Park, 2002). Hofstede, Neuijen, Ohayv, and Sanders (1990) asserted that organizational culture is best measured by organizational practices instead of more abstract assumptions and values. Hofstede et al. (1990) empirically found six independent indicators that describe the numerous organizational practices. *Process-oriented vs. results-oriented culture* is related to the risk attitude of organizations; *employee-oriented vs. job-oriented culture* is about how the employees are valued; *professional vs. parochial approach* is related to how employees are identified; *open vs. closed system* refers to the perceived communication climate within the organization; *loose vs. tight control* dimension refers to the degree of internal structuring in the organization; and *normative vs. pragmatic* dimension considers the popular notion of customer orientation.

### *Structural Characteristics of the SA*

The structural characteristics related to the SA organization include the extent of management control imposed on the SA, ownership distribution, and the completeness of the contract (Ozorhon, 2007).

*The extent of management control* is one of the most tested drivers of performance in the research on SAs. Control is defined as the influence exercised by the SA partners over the management of the SA (Geringer & Hebert, 1989; Killing, 1983). The exercise of managerial control has been one of the most important subjects in the SA literature (Parkhe, 1993; Yan & Gray, 1994). In this study, adopting the approach of Choi and Beamish (2004), management control is divided into three categories, including (1) shared management for all activities, (2) dominant management for all activities by one of the partners, and (3) split management of activities for which each partner has competence. To improve performance, Mjoen and Tallman (1997) proposed that the activities controlled by each partner should be matched with their respective firm-specific strengths.

*Distribution of ownership* involves an SA's equal or unequal division of ownership and has been found to affect its performance (Blodgett, 1992; Geringer & Hebert, 1989; Killing, 1983). The ownership of an SA may be dominated by the respondent company, by a foreign partner, or equally shared by the partners. According to Killing (1983), the dominance of one partner will increase stability, avoiding the managerial costs inherent in an SA and potential conflicts between partners. However, Blodgett (1992) argued that roughly equal equity shares will result in greater stability because the partners are equally committed to the SA. It is proposed by Ozorhon (2007) that it is most advantageous when the partner from the host country has dominant ownership, and that the ownership structure has no effect on performance if the host is a third country.

*The completeness of the SA contract* is an essential success factor that can avoid a great deal of trouble and conflict in future SA operations (Bing & Tiong, 1999). An SA contract provides a legally bound, institutional framework in which each party's rights, duties, and responsibilities are codified and the goals, policies, and strategies underlying the anticipated SA are specified. Since there are many potential problems in construction projects, the contract between the SA partners should define the rights and responsibilities of each party clearly to ensure success (Luo, 2002). Basically, an SA should be established based on mutual trust and understanding, but the agreement must be more concrete and precise regarding liability (Bing & Tiong, 1999).

## DATA ANALYSIS

A questionnaire survey was administered to the Turkish partners of SAs. Almost half of the projects were undertaken in 18 foreign countries including Afghanistan, Bulgaria, Jordan, Russia, Iraq, India, the U.S., and others, whereas the remaining projects were undertaken in Turkey. Considering the fact that medium-to-large companies are likely to undertake SAs with more frequency compared to smaller firms, the target population was set as the members of the Turkish Contractors Association (TCA). All of the respondents were upper-level managers of large contractors with an average age of 39 years, operating both in domestic and international markets, and having expertise mainly in general contracting and infrastructure construction. The number of SA projects completed by Turkish construction companies with foreign partners in the last ten years is around 110 (TCA, 2005). A total of 68 completed questionnaires were returned for data analysis, 48 of which were administered through face-to-face interviews and 20 via e-mail. Around 60% of the target population was covered in this study. Data were collected from 28 Turkish partners that undertook 68 international construction projects. The choice of only one partner in an SA as opposed to all partners was motivated by the difficulties in obtaining data from all partners due to logistical and cost barriers. Survey respondents were asked to evaluate the level of the above-mentioned determinants of partner relations as well as the quality of the partner relations in their SA on a 1–5 point Likert scale.

The data were analyzed using a software package called EQS 6.1, a structural equation modeling (SEM) tool. The general form of SEM consists of (1) a measurement model that specifies how the hypothetical constructs are measured in terms of the observed variables and establishes the validity and reliability of the observed variables, and (2) a structural model that explores the causal relationships between the validated constructs and that tests the hypothesized causal effects (Bollen, 1989). In the first step, construct validity is tested through qualitative and empirical validity tests. Content validity is a qualitative test and refers to the degree to which the construct is represented by indicators that cover the domain of meaning of the construct (Dunn, Seaker, & Waller, 1994), whereas reliability, convergent, and discriminant validity tests compose the empirical part of the construct validity.

## RESULTS

Table 11.1 shows the factor loadings corresponding to the six constructs of the model. The factor loadings are important because indicators that do not have statistically significant loadings are to be deleted from the model. In this respect, uncertainty avoidance and long-term orientation are deleted from the "national culture fit" construct. The analysis is performed using the statistically significant indicators. In the second step, SEM tests the hypotheses between the validated constructs.

Figure 11.1 shows the hypothesized relations between the constructs of the model. The numbers on the arrows represent the path coefficients that are equivalent to regression weights. The analysis suggests that "strategic fit between SA partners" is the main driver of "quality of partner relations" with a path coefficient of 0.365. "Organizational culture fit" has a moderate effect on partner relations (path coefficient: 0.268), which is followed by "structural characteristics of the SA" (0.212). On the other hand, no significant influence of "organizational fit" and "national culture fit" on the "quality of partner relations" was found. Links that are not statistically significant at $\alpha = 0.05$ were eliminated from the model (shown in dashed lines in Figure 11.1).

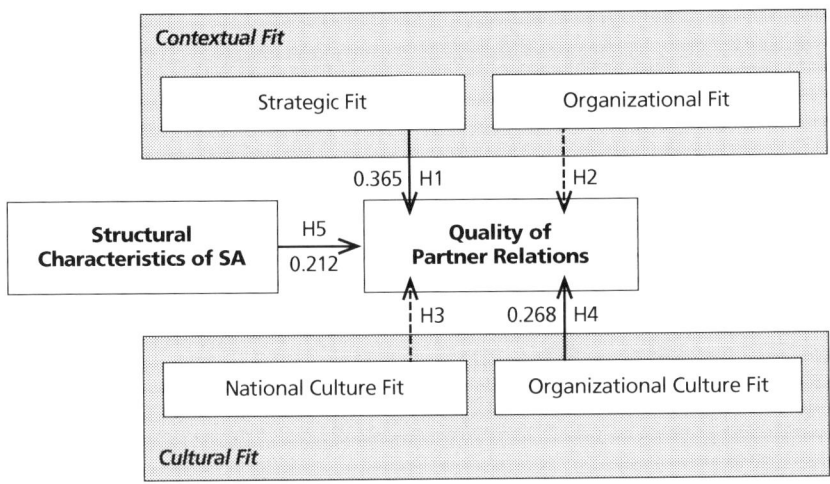

**Figure 11.1** The structural equation model for quality of partner relations (adapted from Ozorhon [2007]).

### TABLE 11.1 Variables of the Model

| Variables | Factor loading |
|---|---|
| **Quality of partner relations** | |
| Commitment | 0.901 |
| Communication | 0.751 |
| Cooperation | 0.796 |
| Previous cooperation | 0.939 |
| Conflict resolution | 0.651 |
| Trust | 0.730 |
| **Strategic fit** | |
| Goal congruency | 0.336 |
| Host country experience | 0.454 |
| Similar project experience | 0.734 |
| Managerial skills | 0.733 |
| Technical skills | 0.892 |
| Human resources | 0.674 |
| Client relations | 0.622 |
| **Organizational fit** | |
| Financial capability | 0.693 |
| Size of partners | 0.786 |
| Management systems | 0.622 |
| Workload of partners | 0.685 |
| **National culture fit** | |
| Power distance | 0.865 |
| Individualism | 0.541 |
| Masculinity | 0.688 |
| Uncertainty avoidance | * (0.054) |
| Long-term orientation | * (0.138) |
| **Organizational culture fit** | |
| Process vs. results-oriented culture | 0.668 |
| Employee vs. job-oriented culture | 0.545 |
| Parochial vs. professional practice | 0.712 |
| Open vs. closed system | 0.799 |
| Loose vs. tight system | 0.780 |
| Normative vs. pragmatic orientation | 0.674 |
| **Structural characteristics** | |
| Extent of management control | 0.665 |
| Distribution of ownership | 0.620 |
| Contract satisfaction | 0.533 |

## DISCUSSION

The model in Figure 11.1 indicates that previous cooperation between SA partners, commitment to the SA, cooperation of SA partners during strategic decision-making, and communication are the major indicators of "interpartner relations."

The first hypothesis that strategic fit between SA partners has a positive effect on the "quality of partner relations" is verified by the data. Strategic fit has the highest influence on partner relations compared to other factors. If one relies on the high factor loadings of the variables that constitute the "strategic fit" construct, one should recommend that for better partner relations, SA partners should have compatible technical (factor loading: 0.892) and managerial (0.733) skills and complementary experience in projects similar to the one being undertaken by the SA (0.734). It appears that SA partners that have complementary resources and skills enhance interpartner relations in terms of commitment, cooperation, communication, and trust in the operation of an SA. This finding also supports the earlier research by Luo (1998), Morris and Cadogan (2001), and Yan and Duan (2003), who stated that partner match in terms of strategic assets is critical for managing an SA since it increases the chance of achieving project objectives and leads to a high level of partner satisfaction. The strategic orientation of parent firms is important to venture success because how well it matches that of its partner influences interpartner consistency in terms of strategic goals and behaviors, cooperative culture, and investment commitment (Parkhe, 1991).

The second hypothesis that organizational fit between SA partners has a positive effect on the "quality of partner relations" is not verified by the data since the influence of the quality of partner relations fit was not significant at $\alpha = 0.05$. This finding is interesting since previous research indicated that organizational fit has a positive impact on partner relations. This difference might be due to the fact that in this research, strategic fit and organizational fit are investigated as two separate constructs and the impact of strategic fit on partner relations was found to be dominant. It could also be argued that similarities in parent firms' size, workload, management systems, and financial capability do not help achieve better partner relations.

The third hypothesis that national culture fit between SA partners has a positive effect on the "quality of partner relations" is not verified by the data either, since the influence of national culture fit was not significant at $\alpha = 0.05$. In this study, the differences in the national cultures of two firms were measured in terms of power distance, individualism, and masculinity. Similarity in the national cultures of SA partners was not found to affect the "quality of partner relations." This finding is in line with the findings of the studies conducted by Beamish and Kachra (2004); Luo, Shenkar, and Nyaw

(2001); Park and Ungson (1997); and Shenkar and Zeira (1992). However, it should also be stated that prior research has provided mixed empirical evidence regarding the specific influence of cultural distance on SA operation and performance (Brouthers & Brouthers, 2001). Although several researchers reported that differences in national culture are a source of poor communication, inadequate cooperation, lack of commitment, and ineffective conflict resolution between the SA partners (Harrigan, 1988; Mohr & Spekman, 1994; Parkhe, 1991) due to the dissimilarities of partners' interpretation of and responses to strategic and managerial issues, some argue that these differences may help SA partners learn how to operate with a foreign partner (Barkema & Vermeulen, 1997) and may enhance the firm's learning capabilities (Makhija & Ganesh, 1997). Other researchers like Beamish (1985) and Glaister and Buckley (1999) found no relation between the two variables.

The fourth hypothesis, that organizational culture fit between SA partners has a positive effect on the "quality of partner relations," is verified by the data. Differences in the organizational culture of two SA partners are manageable, since a firm's organizational culture can always be modified. The positive influence of SA partners' organizational culture fit is supported by other studies in the literature (e.g., Brown et al., 1989; Pothukuchi et al., 2002). When partners in an SA differ in their organizational culture, these differences may result in conflicting behaviors, leading to misunderstandings and interaction problems, which may lead to lower partner satisfaction and difficulties in achieving project targets. Based on the high factor loadings of the variables that constitute the "organizational culture fit" construct, one should recommend that for better partner relations SA partners should have compatible cultures in terms of communication climate; internal structuring; and employee identification that are measured in this study by open vs. closed system (factor loading: 0.799); loose vs. tight system (0.780); and parochial vs. professional practice (0.712), respectively.

The fifth hypothesis, that the effectiveness of the structural characteristics of an SA has a positive effect on the "quality of partner relations," is verified by the data. This finding also supports earlier research arguing that an appropriate structure allows the partner firms to integrate the SA's activities with their individual strategies and activities and protects against the loss of the venture's competitive advantage (Geringer & Hebert, 1989). This finding reveals the importance of the extent of management control (factor loading: 0.665), ownership distribution (0.620), and the completeness of the SA contract (0.533). Split management control is expected to increase the level of performance since the specific competencies of each partner could be utilized effectively. A home country partner that has majority ownership is likely to put into full use their being familiar with the conditions in the host country. For a successful SA organization, a complete contract should be prepared in which company and project objectives are reflected, roles and responsibilities of each party are defined, and ownership distribution together with control mechanisms are arranged based on the specific needs of the project and contribution of partners. A balanced control of the management, a balanced distribution of ownership, and a complete and thorough SA contract lead to smooth operation and enhances inter-partner relations as suggested by Ozorhon et al.'s (2010) findings.

## CONCLUSION

SAs are effective ways of combining distinctive resources and capabilities of parent organizations to become more competitive in business. Such entities have been active for many years in the construction industry. Due to globalization, construction firms are forced to establish SAs so as to enter and compete in international markets. The main principle behind forming construction alliances is to share financial and human resources as well as managerial and technical skills that are critical for accomplishing a successful project. Despite their popularity, SAs are very difficult to operate; failure rates of SAs are reported to be high. Success of partner relations is one of the main determinants of SA success. In this chapter, factors contributing to the quality of partner relations are explored.

Partner selection and alliance formation are critical stages of an SA where better partner relations may be achieved. If compatible and complementary partners come together under a well-working structure, it is likely that the SA will operate smoothly. This study builds upon the findings of a research by Ozorhon (2007) to examine the determinants of the quality of partner relations in international construction alliances. The research used SEM to test the hypotheses relative to the factors contributing to better partner relations. In this respect, strategic and organizational fit between SA partners, national and organizational culture fit between SA partners, and structural characteristics of SAs are investigated and their impacts on partner relations are analyzed.

Based on the findings of the study, it is suggested that the main indicators of partner relations in an international construction alliance are previous and current cooperation, communication between partners, and commitment to the alliance. The factors governing the smooth working relations are the strategic fit between the parent firms, the organizational culture fit between the parent firms, and the structural characteristics of the SA. Strategic fit is the most influential factor among the three. Partners having complementary technical, managerial, and human resources and similar project experience are expected to maintain better partner relations. Organizational culture fit between partners moderately affects the quality of partner relations. The most important dimensions relate to the similarity between partners in terms of the communication climate; internal structuring; and employee identification within the parent firms. Finally, the structural characteristics of the SA have less effect on partner relations. All the indicators of structure—namely extent of management control, ownership distribution, and a satisfactory contract—seem to somehow affect the quality of partner relations. It should also be noted that organizational fit and national culture fit between the partners have not been found to be related to partner relations.

The findings of the analysis indicate that for better working relations in an SA, construction companies should concentrate on selecting compatible partners that could best complement their capabilities in terms of strategic assets and organizational culture. In addition, they should establish an appropriate structure for the SA organization in which each partner controls the activities related to its core competency, and they should prepare a complete and thorough agreement that defines each partner's roles and responsibilities clearly. Ensuring good relations between partners will help companies achieve a higher business performance in the context of international construction alliances.

## REFERENCES

Barkema, H. G., Shenkar, O., Vermeulen, F., & Bell, J. H. J. (1997). Working abroad, working with others: How firms learn to operate international joint ventures. *Academy of Management Journal, 40*, 426–442.

Barkema, H. G., & Vermeulen, F. (1997). What differences in the cultural backgrounds of partners are detrimental for international joint ventures? *Journal of International Business Studies, 28*, 845–864.

Beamish, P. W. (1984). *Joint venture performance in developing countries.* Unpublished doctoral dissertation, University of Western Ontario, Canada.

Beamish, P. W. (1985). The characteristics of joint ventures in developed and developing countries. *Columbia Journal of World Business, 20*(3), 13–19.

Beamish, P. W. (1987). Joint ventures in LDCs: Partner selection and performance. *Management International Review, 27*(1), 23–37.

Beamish, P. W., & Kachra, A. (2004). Number of partners and JV performance. *Journal of World Business, 39*, 107–120.

Bing, L., & Tiong, R. L. K. (1999). Risk management model for international construction joint ventures. *Journal of Construction Engineering and Management, 125*, 377–384.

Bing, L., Tiong, R. L. K., Fan, W. W., & Chew, D. A. S. (1999). Risk management in international construction joint ventures. *Journal of Construction Engineering and Management, 125*, 277–284.

Blodgett, L. (1992). Factors in the instability of international joint ventures: an event history analysis. *Strategic Management Journal, 13*, 475–481.

Bollen, K. A. (1989). *Structural equations with latent variables.* New York, NY: Wiley.
Brouthers, K., & Brouthers, L. (2001). Explaining the national cultural distance paradox. *Journal of International Business Studies, 32,* 177–189.
Brown, L. T., Rugman, A. M., & Verbeke, A. (1989). Japanese joint ventures with Western multinationals: Synthesizing the economic and cultural explanations of failure. *Asia Pacific Journal of Management, 6,* 225–242.
Buckley, P. J., & Casson, M. (1988). A theory of co-operation in international business. In F. J. Contractor & P. Lorange (Eds.), *Cooperative strategies in international business* (pp. 31–53). Lexington, MA: Lexington Books.
Choi, C. B., & Beamish, P. W. (2004). Split management control and international joint venture performance. *Journal of International Business Studies, 35,* 201–215.
Contractor, F. J., & Lorange, P. (1988). Why should firms cooperate? The strategy and economics basis for cooperative ventures. In F. J. Contractor & P. Lorange (Eds.), *Cooperative strategies in international business* (pp. 3–30). Lexington, MA: Lexington Books.
Das, T. K., & Teng, B. (1998). Between trust and control: Developing confidence in partner cooperation in alliances. *Academy of Management Review, 23,* 491–512.
Doz, Y. L. (1996). The evolution of cooperation in strategic alliances: Initial conditions or learning processes? *Strategic Management Journal, 17,* 55–83.
Dunn, S. C., Seaker, R. F., & Waller, M. A. (1994). Latent variables in business logistics research: Scale development and validation. *Journal of Business Logistics, 15,* 145–172.
Evans, J., & Mavondo, F. T. (2002). Psychic distance and organizational performance: An empirical examination of international retailing operations. *Journal of International Business Studies, 33,* 515-532.
Fey, C. F., & Beamish, P. W. (1999). *Joint venture conflict: The case of Russian international joint ventures.* Working Paper #99-104, Stockholm School of Economics, St. Petersburg, Sweden.
Geringer, J. M. (1988). *Joint venture partner selection: Strategies for developing countries.* New York, NY: Quorum.
Geringer, J. M. (1991). Strategic determinants of partner selection criteria in international joint ventures. *Journal of International Business Studies, 22,* 41–62.
Geringer, J., & Hebert, L. (1989). Control and performance of international joint ventures. *Journal of International Business Studies, 20,* 235–254.
Glaister, K. W., & Buckley, P. J. (1999). Performance relationships in UK international alliances. *Management International Review, 39,* 123–147.
Gomes-Casseres, B. (2000) Mastering management. *Financial Times, 16*(10), 14–15.
Gunhan, S., & Arditi, A. (2005). Factors affecting international construction. *Journal of Construction Engineering and Management, 131,* 273–282.
Harrigan, K. (1988). Joint Ventures and competitive strategy. *Strategic Management Journal, 9,* 83–103.
Hebert, L. (1994). *Division of control, relationship dynamics and joint venture performance.* Unpublished doctoral dissertation, University of Western Ontario, Canada.
Hennart, J. F., Kim, D. J., & Zeng, M. (1998). The impact of joint venture status on the longevity of Japanese stakes in U.S. manufacturing affiliates. *Organization Science, 9,* 382–395.

Hill, R. C., & Hellriegel, D. (1994). Critical contingencies in joint venture management: Some lessons from managers. *Organization Science, 5*, 594–607.

Hofstede, G. (1991). *Cultures and organizations: Software of the mind, intercultural cooperation and its importance for survival.* New York, NY: McGraw-Hill.

Hofstede, G., Neuijen, B., Ohayv, D., & Sanders, G. (1990). Measuring organizational cultures: A qualitative and quantitative study across twenty cases. *Administrative Science Quarterly, 35*, 286–316.

Inkpen, A. C. (1996). Creating knowledge through collaboration. *California Management Review, 39*(1), 123–140.

Inkpen, A. C., & Currall, S. C. (1998). The nature, antecedents, and consequences of joint venture trust. *Journal of International Management, 4*, 1–20.

Janger, A. R. (1980). *Organization of international joint ventures.* New York, NY: Conference Board.

Johanson, J., & Vahlne, J. E. (1977). The internationalization process of the firm: A model of knowledge development and increasing foreign market commitments. *Journal of International Business Studies, 8*, 23–32.

Killing, J.P. (1983). *Strategies for joint venture success.* New York, NY: Routledge.

Kogut, B., & Singh, H. (1988). The effect of national culture on the choice of entry mode. *Journal of International Business Studies, 19*, 411–432.

Kwok, H. C. A., Then, D., & Skitmore, M. (2000). Risk management in Singapore construction joint ventures. *Journal of Construction Research, 1*, 139–149.

Lasserre, P. (1999). Joint venture satisfaction in Asia-Pacific. *Asia-Pacific Journal of Management, 16*, 1–28.

Low, P. S., & Leong, C. H. Y. (2000). Cross-cultural project management for international construction in China. *International Journal of Project Management, 18*, 307–316.

Luo, Y. (1997). Partner selection and venturing success: The case of joint ventures with firms in the People's Republic of China. *Organization Science, 8*(6), 648–662.

Luo, Y. (1998). Joint venture success in China: How should we select a good partner? *Journal of World Business, 33*, 145–166.

Luo, Y. (2002). Contract, cooperation, and performance in international joint ventures. *Strategic Management Journal, 23*, 903–919.

Luo, Y., Shenkar, O., & Nyaw, M. K. (2001). A dual parent perspective on control and performance in international joint ventures: Lessons from a developing economy. *Journal of International Business Studies, 32*, 41–58.

Makhija, M. V., & Ganesh, U. (1997). The relationship between control and partner learning in learning-related joint-ventures. *Organization Science, 8*, 508–527.

Makino, S., & Beamish, P. W. (1998). Performance and survival of international joint ventures with non-conventional ownership structures. *Journal of International Business Studies, 29*, 797–818.

Makino, S., & Delios, A. (1996) Local knowledge transfer and performance: Implications for alliance formation in Asia. *Journal of International Business Studies, 27*, 905–928.

Mead, R. (1998). *International management: cross-cultural dimensions.* Malden, MA: Blackwell Publishers.

Merchant, H. (2000). Configuration of international joint ventures. *Management International Review, 40*, 107–140.

Mjoen, H., & Tallman, H. (1997). Control and performance in international joint ventures. *Organization Science, 8*, 257–274.

Mohr, J., & Spekman, R. (1994). Characteristics of partnership success: Partnership attributes, communication behavior, and conflict resolution techniques. *Strategic Management Journal, 15*, 135–152.

Morosini, P., Shane, S., & Singh, H. (1998). Cultural distance and cross-border acquisition performance. *Journal of International Business Studies, 29*, 137–158.

Morris, B., & Cadogan, J.W. (2001). Partner symmetries, partner conflict and the quality of joint venture marketing strategy: an empirical investigation. *Journal of Marketing Management, 17*, 223–256.

O'Grady, S., & Lane, H. W. (1996). The psychic distance paradox. *Journal of International Business Studies, 27*, 309–333.

Ozorhon, B. (2007). *Modeling the performance of international construction joint ventures.* Unpublished doctoral dissertation, Middle East Technical University, Ankara, Turkey.

Ozorhon, B., Arditi, D., Dikmen, I., & Birgonul, M. T. (2010). The performance of international joint ventures in construction. *Journal of Management in Engineering, 26*, 209–222.

Pan, Y., & Chi, P. S. K. (1999). Financial performance and survival of multinational corporations in China. *Strategic Management Journal, 20*, 359–374.

Pan, Y., & Li, X. (2000). Joint venture formation of very large multinational firms. *Journal of International Business Studies, 31*, 179–189.

Park, S. H., & Ungson, G. R. (1997). The effect of national culture, organizational complementarity, and economic motivation on joint venture dissolution. *Academy of Management Journal, 40*, 279–307.

Parkhe, A. (1991). Interfirm diversity, organizational learning, and longevity in global strategic alliances. *Journal of International Business Studies, 22*, 579–601.

Parkhe, A. (1993). Messy research, methodological predispositions, and theory development in international joint ventures. *Academy of Management Review, 18*, 227–268.

Pothukuchi, V., Damanpour, F., Choi, J., Chen, C. C., & Park, S. H. (2002). National and organizational culture differences and international joint venture performance. *Journal of International Business Studies, 33*, 243–265.

Shenkar, O. (1990). International joint ventures' problems in China: Risks and remedies. *Long Range Planning, 23*, 80–90.

Shenkar, O. (2001). Cultural distance revisited: Towards more rigorous conceptualization and measurement of cultural differences. *Journal of International Business Studies, 32*, 519–535.

Shenkar, O., & Zeira, Y. (1992). Role conflict and role ambiguity of chief executive officers in international joint ventures. *Journal of International Business Studies, 23*, 55–75.

Sim, A. B., & Ali, M. Y. (2000). Determinants of stability in international joint ventures: Evidence from a developing country context. *Asia-Pacific Journal of Management, 17*, 373–397.

Smith, K. G., Guthrie, J. P., &Chen, M. (1989). Strategy, size and performance. *Organization Studies, 10*, 63–81.

Sridharan, G. (1997). *Factors affecting the performance of international joint ventures: A research model.* Proceedings of the First International Conference on Construction Industry Development, December 9–11, 1997, National University of Singapore, Singapore.

Tatoglu, E., & Glaister, K. W. (1998). Performance of international joint ventures in Turkey: Perspectives of Western firms and Turkish firms. *International Business Review, 7*, 635–656.

TCA. (2005). *Turkish Contractors Association* [in Turkish]. Retrieved from http://www.tmb.org.tr/genel.php?ID=2

Tomlinson, J. W. C., & Thompson, M. (1977). *A study of Canadian joint ventures in Mexico.* Ottawa, Canada: Office of Science and Technology, Department of Industry, Trade and Commerce.

Ulijn, J., Duijsters, G., Schaetzlein, R., & Remer, S. (2005). *Culture and its perception in strategic alliances, does it affect the performance? An exploratory study into Dutch–German ventures.* Working Paper 03.05, Eindhoven Centre for Innovation Studies, Netherlands.

Yan, A., & Duan, J. (2003). Interpartner fit and its performance implications: a four-case study of U.S.-China joint ventures. *Asia Pacific Journal of Management, 20*, 541–564.

Yan, A., & Gray, B. (1994). Bargaining power, management control, and performance in United States-China joint ventures: a comparative case study. *Academy of Management Journal, 37*, 1478–1517.

Yan, A., & Gray, B. (2001). Antecedents and effects of parent control in international joint ventures. *Journal of Management Studies, 38*, 393–416.

Zaman, M., & Mavondo, F. (2002) Measuring strategic alliance success: a conceptual framework. Retrieved April 7, 2007 from http://smib.vuw.ac.nz:8081/WWW/ANZMAC2001/anzmac/AUTHORS/pdfs/Zaman.pdf.

CHAPTER 12

# POWER AS A MANAGEMENT TOOL FOR STRATEGIC ALLIANCES

## A Study of Russian Agri-Food Business

Vera Belaya and Jon Henrich Hanf

### ABSTRACT

Recent research has shown that the role of power in the context of supply chains and strategic alliances is crucial in that, through its interactions with other elements of the relationship atmosphere, it can seriously impede cooperation, though others see power in strategic alliances not only as a negative force. It is agreed that power is central to understanding the nature of the collaboration, the power structures that exist within it, and implementing procurement and alliances strategies. Hence, power can be considered one of the strongest and most influential tools for the management of alliances. However, in order to discuss the effects of power, one needs to be specific on the nature of the power and its origins. Our research aims at investigating the role of power in supplier–buyer relationships in strategic alliances by using a classification of power into different types and sources with distinct attention to cooperation and coordination issues. Thus, our chapter aims to develop a theoretical framework for using power as managerial tool and to verify it in the context of Russian agri-food business. The framework was empirically tested in the context of Russian agri-food business, using expert interviews conducted with 97 representatives of companies with foreign direct investments in Russian agri-food business. The interviews were conducted on the basis of a designed survey tool. We analyze the results of these interviews using qualitative methods of research and discuss the results of the content analysis.

## INTRODUCTION

Recent research has shown that the role of power in the context of supply chains and strategic alliances is crucial in that through its interactions with other elements of the relationship atmosphere, it can seriously impede cooperation, though others see power in strategic alliances not merely as a negative force. It is agreed that power is central to understanding the nature of the collaboration, the power structures that exist within it, and implementing procurement and alliances strategies. Hence, power can be considered one of the strongest and influential tools for the management of alliances. However, in order to discuss the effects of power, one needs to be specific on the nature of the power and its origins.

There are six types of power, each based on its source or origin: coercive, reward, expert, legitimate, referent, and informational (French & Raven, 1959; Raven & Kruglanski, 1970). Coercive power enables an individual to punish others. In the strategic alliance context, it reflects the fear of an alliance member to be punished if it fails to comply with the requirements of the focal company. Reward power depends on the ability of the power holder to offer rewards to others. If a focal company has access to resources that are valuable for other network actors, it can make these network actors perform in a desired way. Expert power is derived from the skills or special knowledge of a particular subject. Expert power of a focal company can be achieved if the other actors believe that it possesses a special knowledge which is valuable to them. Legitimate power stems from a legitimate right to influence and an obligation to accept this influence. In this case, a focal actor is recognized in the eyes of the members as having a right to make specific decisions. Referent power depends on an ability to be attractive to others and depends on the charisma and interpersonal skills of the power holder. This power is observed when network actors want to join a network.

We use the described classification of the construct of power in order to shed new light on the management of relationships within strategic alliances. The main two management areas of interest are cooperation (aligning interests) and coordination (aligning actions), which should be addressed separately. Since solving the problems of cooperation does not automatically help to achieve coordination, there is a need to search for other mechanisms to reduce uncertainty and make knowledge about how others will behave available. Therefore, the challenge is to find out how different types of power based on different sources can be exercised through different means for managerial purposes with specific attention to cooperation and coordination issues. Our research aims to investigate the role of power in supplier–buyer relationships in strategic alliances by using a classification of power into different types and sources with distinct attention to cooperation and coordination issues. Thus, our chapter aims to develop a theoretical framework for using power as a managerial tool and to verify it in the context of Russian agri-food business.

The framework was empirically tested in the context of Russian agri-food business. This part is based on expert interviews conducted with 97 representatives of companies with foreign direct investments in Russian agri-food business. The interviews were conducted on the basis of a designed survey tool. We analyze the results of these interviews using qualitative methods of research and discuss the results of the contents analysis.

## THEORETICAL BACKGROUND, RESEARCH ASSUMPTIONS, AND STUDY DESIGN

### Power as a Management Tool

Most definitions of power within studies on supply chain marketing channels are based on the definition by El-Ansary and Stern (1972), who "define the *power* of a channel member as his *ability to control the decision variables in the marketing strategy of another member in a given channel at a different level of distribution*" (p. 47; emphasis in original). Power in supply chains is defined as "the ability of a firm (or an entrepreneur) to own and control critical assets in markets and supply chains that allow it to sustain its ability to appropriate and accumulate value for itself by constantly leveraging its customers, competitors and suppliers" (Cox, Ireland, Lonsdale, Sanderson, & Watson, 2002, p. 3). The concept of critical assets in supply chains is based on the idea that some resources are considered to be scarce or unique and that with the combination of high value, uniqueness, and scarcity, particular supply chain resources become critical assets. Hu and Sheu (2005) view power in terms of a strategy-influencing source that is oriented from one channel member to another. As a result, power is viewed as an effectively applied means to gain certain objectives by utilizing influence strategies once the power over another firm is attained (Hu & Sheu, 2003; Payan & McFarland, 2005). Other recent literature on power in supply chains and marketing channels uses more or less similar definitions of power and simply rephrases aspects of using power to influence other firms to act in a desired manner for economic gains (Ireland & Webb, 2007) or to get them do things that they would not normally do (Reid & Bojanic, 2009) and having a great deal of influence over the other members (Cant, Strydom, Jooste, & du Plessis, 2009).

French and Raven (1959) expressed a view that the actual effect of power will depend on its different types. We assume that the use of different types of power has different effects on supply chain management and specifically on coordination and cooperation. Even though both cooperation and coordination are equally important, most often they are researched separately. Problems of cooperation arise from conflicts of interest (Doz, 1996; Gottschalg & Zollo, 2007). For a strategic alliance to work more efficiently, all parties involved—from raw material suppliers to consumers and every touch-point in between—will need to work more collaboratively and invest in technology that enables them to more easily share accurate product information (Duysters, Heimeriks, & Jurriens, 2004). Collaboration proves to be important since, as Cooper, Lambert, and Pagh (1997) formulate, suboptimization occurs when each organization in the strategic alliance attempts to optimize its own results rather than integrate its goals and activities with the other organizations to optimize the results of the whole chain (Das & Teng, 2001). Successfully formulating the appropriate strategy in a particular supplier–buyer situation implies that all entities must work together, where financially independent entities try to get the dependent parts of the chain to "play" together (Dyer & Singh, 1998; Kampstra, Ashayeri & Gattorna, 2006).

Cooperation within the strategic alliance is based on individual motivation of its actors (Das & Teng, 2000). It is resolved by aligning interests through formal mechanisms such as contracting (where possible) (Williamson, 1975). Informal mechanisms such as identification and embeddedness may also serve to align interests (Granovetter, 1985; Gulati, 1995; Kogut & Zander, 1996). One can say that collaboration among the members of a strategic alliance is claimed to yield significant improvements in multiple performance areas (Kale, Dyer, & Singh 2002)—it is believed to reduce costs, increase quality, improve delivery, augment flexibility, cut procurement cost and lead time, and stimulate innovativeness.

Solving problems of cooperation, however, does not automatically help to achieve coordination (Gulati & Singh, 1998). Whereas cooperation problems are rooted in motivation, coordination problems arise due to the limitations of participating actors that hinder them from possessing comprehensive knowledge of how others will behave in situations of interdependence (Das & Teng, 2002). Problems of coordination emerge due to the lack of shared and accurate knowledge about the decision rules that others are likely to use and how one's own actions are interdependent with those of others (Geanakoplos, 1992; Milgrom & Roberts, 1992).

In order to be able to achieve successful performance of the strategic alliance, it is necessary to coordinate this whole system (Das & Teng, 1998) as well as facilitate intensive collaboration between enterprises for the improvement of all internal and external material, information, and finance flows. These two tasks can be fulfilled within successful supply chain management concepts using power as a tool for achieving compliance on the part of the power target.

In the following section, we present our argumentation on how the research assumptions A1–A5 about supplier–buyer relationships and their management and the existence, distribution, and use of power in the example of Russian agri-food business were developed.

## Supplier–Buyer Relationships in Russian Agri-Food Business and their Management

When entering Russia, many foreign companies encounter problems apart from high entry barriers in the form of complicated title registration procedures, unreliable quality of supplied products, a lack of production knowhow and financing for farmers, supply chains characterized by distrust, and absence of professionalism (Tretyak & Sheresheva, 2005) with the Russian management style, because it was so different from the Western management practices. In the Russian world and prior to the recent changes, the purpose of a company was to serve a centralized and planned economy by complying with some production standards (Yakovlev & Kokorev, 1995). Traditional Russian companies did not seem to be customer-oriented. If customers experienced a problem with a product just purchased, they must often solve the problem themselves (Fey, 1995). Therefore, since management concepts are different from those of the Western companies, one may assume that the foreign retailers and food manufacturers operating in Russia might experience problems in managing supply chain relationships with their local partners. Moreover, since chain management is not only about the alignment of actions (coordination), but also about the alignment of interests (cooperation), we present the following research assumptions about supply chains and networks and their management within the context of foreign and local companies.

**Assumption 1:** *Problems in relationships among Western and local partners exist.*

**Assumption 2:** *Problems of managing supplier–buyer relationships can be grouped into problems of cooperation (alignment of interests) and coordination (alignment of actions).*

## Existence, Distribution and Use of Power in Russian Agri-Food Business

In the background of evolving coordinated supply chains, the phenomenon of asymmetrical power distribution seems to exist. In fact, the natural state for supply chain relationships does not appear to be the one of symmetry and equilibrium (Ogbonna & Wilkinson, 1996). Hence, a number of authors (Medcof, 2001; Gulati & Sytch, 2007) address the issue of power in this context. One of the explanations is that such factors as the size differences in favor of the central buyer as well as size differences between suppliers themselves, buyer and suppliers' different areas of expertise, and different switching costs contribute to the power inequalities within a supply chain network (Helper, 1991). Thus, the asymmetrical power relationships are observable. In the majority of Western markets, retailers proved to be more dominant, since they positioned themselves as brand guarantors in the supply chain and made the shift in retail strategy from being a relatively passive assortment builder to the brand developer and manager of the whole chain. As a result, there has been a shift in power within food marketing channels towards the multiple retailer (Bourlakis, 2001; Fiddis, 1997) where the retailer is seen as the main gateway to consumers and gatekeeper between producer and consumer (Lang, 2003). Taking into account the described facts as well as the classification topology of French and Raven (1959) and Raven and Kruglanski (1970), we present the following research assumptions.

**Assumption 3:** *Power exists in supply chains and networks.*

**Assumption 4:** *Power is asymmetrically distributed among actors in supply chains and networks.*

**Assumption 5:** *Power can be classified according to the framework of French and Raven (1959) and Raven and Kruglanski (1970).*

## Study of Russian Agri-Food Business

To answer our research assumptions we conducted semi-structured in-depth interviews by telephone about relationships of international food retail and processing companies with their suppliers in Russia. We contacted the companies of foreign origin registered in Russia as companies operating in the area of food processing and food retailing in Russia with at least 10% of foreign direct investment capital. Ninety-seven complete telephone interviews were conducted, which represents a response rate of 9.7%. We made a thorough selection of the interviewees, who were chosen according to their leading positions in order to effectively gather relevant information (Blankertz, 1998; Merkens, 2000; Patton, 1990). Specifically, we employed an expert (concentration) sampling (Fritsch, 2007; Patton 1990). The persons chosen were in positions with a high level of concentration of appropriate information. The applied technique makes particular sense in view of the above-mentioned research questions.

Before contacting the companies from the database we made a thorough pretest study by contacting 15 experts from the field of agri-food business and conducting telephone conversations with them. This pretest allowed us to identify potential problems and to revise the proposed questionnaire before starting the actual fieldwork. After receiving their feedback and improving the questionnaire, we started the survey. The questionnaire was designed in three languages (Russian, English, and German) in order to allow experts speaking different languages to participate in the questionnaire. The translation of the questionnaire was done by the authors and cross-checked by two native speakers to help achieve reliability (Hingley, 2005; Patton, 2002). The interviewees were first informed about the interviews via email. After receiving their consent, the calls were made at the time indicated by the interviewees. Due to the fact that the majority of the respondents wanted to be treated anonymously and did not give their permission to tape-record the interviews, they were protocolled in written form.

One of the first questions asked was "Do you feel responsible to coordinate the supply chain of this product ('from the field to the fork')?" Two answer options were given: "yes" and "no." By means of this question, we selected the focal companies that were the target of our research.

Among the interviewed companies were two types of companies: processors (89) and retailers (8). Since the questionnaire was offered in three languages (Russian, English, and German), some interviewees made the use of this option and chose the language in which they were most sure. As the results show, most of the respondents chose Russian as the language of the interview (97%). Only 2% of them chose English and 1% German. Duration of interviews was between 10 and 45 minutes. The average duration per interview was about 16 minutes. The overall duration accounted for 1,534 minutes (or 25.5 hours).

The companies from our sample stem from a variety of different Western European and North American countries. Altogether, the number of countries of origin of the companies is 27. The biggest share among the interviewed countries belongs to Germany (21.65%). There are indeed a substantial number of German companies operating in Russia in different supply chains. Therefore, the number of those companies that replied to our invitation to participate in the expert interview was also high. The next largest group after Germany is the U.S. Again, the number of available companies from this country made it possible that so many of them replied positively to our invitation. Some other important big groups are from France, the Netherlands, and Italy; Asian countries (China and Singapore) were also included.

Among the companies that were called, the majority were from Moscow and the Moscow region (81%). The rest of the cities included St. Petersburg (8%) as well as some other Russian cities (Samara, Belgorod, Velikiy Novgorod, Novosibirsk, Kaluga, Kaliningrad, Pskov, Tula). In two cases when the respondents were not able to participate in the expert interview, they recommended us to contact their head offices in Warsaw (Poland) and St. Wendel (Germany). However, the respondents were all well informed about the situation of their company in Russia. Among the respondents were general directors, sales managers, category managers, logistics managers, quality managers, and supply chain managers. The interviewed respondents chose only one supply chain with respect to which they were reporting. In our sample we had 13 different supply chains. The most frequently chosen of them were dairy products (15.5%), vegetable products and plant oils (13.4%), sweets and confectionary products (11.3%), and bread and pastry products (11.3%).

## INTERPRETATION OF RESULTS

### Supplier–Buyer Relationships in Russia and Their Management

According to the conducted interviews (see Table 12.1), it was generally agreed that Western companies represented by famous retail and food processing enterprises have brought changes in the Russian supply chain landscape after their entrance to the market. In fact they were said to "have introduced new management approaches, new supply chain relationships," to have created new conditions and versions of cooperation between the supplier and retailer as well as to have put new requirements to the organization of commercial work. The relationships between suppliers and buyers in Russia were characterized by a high degree of interdependence. Since the prospects of survival and future prosperity of one party depend highly on the preparedness to cooperate of another party, building a partnership is very strategic, and "both sides understand that they will need to work not only today, but also tomorrow and the day after tomorrow." So there is a general understanding on both sides that just as the retailers cannot live without good suppliers, so suppliers cannot live well without buyers and retailers. Since the number of food manufacturers grows and the overabundance of supply offers and the available quantity of supermarket shelves do

### TABLE 12.1 Summary of Findings from Expert Interviews

| Research issue | Findings | Illustrative quotations |
|---|---|---|
| **Supplier–buyer relationships in Russian agri-food business** | | |
| General characteristics | Due to the different interests of both sides there is some tension in the supplier–buyer relationships. | "Both sides understand that they will need to work not only today, but also tomorrow and the day after tomorrow." "The problem of the supplier is to show and convince the representative of retail network that the offered version of cooperation will be favourable to both organizations." "If these are complex products having a low degree of standardization, then the creation of partner relationships with suppliers is very important." |
| Problems with suppliers | Problems with suppliers include: contractual conditions, lack of professionalism and reliability, absence of readiness to have long-term relationships, and logistics problems. | "One step to the left, you have earned some money; a step to the right and you are ruined." "One of the main problems is also catastrophically low level of trust. In Russia people have been cheated already so many times that they do not trust anyone at any conditions." "A supplier sends the offer to a network in such type, which you simply cannot imagine: text without a uniform blank and without paragraphs, half of text is emphasized with a computer since it is full of mistakes. Such suppliers will of course not be considered." "Supplier in the category which had the goods and a possibility to deliver in this network informed in 3 days after the price arrangement has been reached that its prices have grown by 30 %. This network accepted it. There was nothing to do but to accept the new price. But the main thing, that this supplier has raised the prices by additional 15 % in 2 days after the network has agreed on 30 % increase. The majority of suppliers act similarly." |
| Problems with retailers | Problems with retailers include: unfair policy of retailers, toughening of conditions and discrimination at the conclusion of delivery contracts. | Suppliers "suffer from retailers which take the delivered products and do not pay back for a long time." Retailers "reduce prices literally to the bottom threshold of profitability" of suppliers. Retailers "press on suppliers using a monopoly position in the market." "The giant manufacturers investing into promotion of brands billions of roubles may sometimes pay nothing to the retailers for accommodation of their goods." "Networks show rigid uniform style in work with suppliers." "No entrance bonuses are necessary to networks, since they have free money of suppliers on 90–120 days and besides, the additional discount." |

*(continued)*

**TABLE 12.1 Summary of Findings from Expert Interviews (continued)**

| Research issue | Findings | Illustrative quotations |
|---|---|---|
| **Existence and distribution of power in Russian agri-food business** | | |
| Existence of power | Existence of power was confirmed | "For the last years some networks have turned to be not only very powerful, but become the aggressive players which alter rules of work on the market under own discretion." |
| Distribution of power | The counterbalance of power is by all means on the side of buyers. | "This parity is frequently acting not in favor of suppliers."<br>"Since there are more suppliers than processors and retailers, suppliers have less power."<br>"When it is a preferred supplier, he has more power than a small and unknown supplier." |
| **Use of power in Russian agri-food business** | | |
| Coercive power | Coercive power was seen both in a negative and positive light, depending on the object and purpose of use. | "He fees paid by suppliers would be possible to recognize as the mechanism of competitive selection of the best manufacturers."<br>"It is economically inexpedient to use partner relationships with all suppliers."<br>"If we are speaking of the suppliers of simple products with a high degree of standardization, it could make sense to apply hard methods."<br>"Such mechanisms as threats and penalties are not very effective because they show that the company is aggressive."<br>"Such approach in short-term prospect can yield positive results, but in long-term is not always effective." |
| Reward power | Reward power was stated to be important. | "Certainly, it requires additional expenses of time and forces, but at the same time allows reducing expenses and to raise a degree of adaptation of the enterprise to changing market conditions not only in short-term, but also over the longer term."<br>"The company has simply terminated contracts with all networks this year and does not work with anybody except for Auchan because it pays without delays" |
| Expert power | Foreign retailers and manufacturers possessing more expertise use expert influence strategies. | "Western companies have brought not only new management approaches to Russia but also innovative products such as drinking yoghurts and curt (partly curt—partly yoghurt)."<br>Suppliers "have only minimal … [or] … zero information on work of commercial structures of the potential customer." |

*(continued)*

## TABLE 12.1 Summary of Findings from Expert Interviews (continued)

| Research issue | Findings | Illustrative quotations |
| --- | --- | --- |
| Informational power | Informational power and its positive sides were more praised and acknowledged than the expert ones. | "The fundamental importance has the creation of a database of the list of potential suppliers which allows obtaining information quickly about suppliers with desirable characteristics."<br>"By tradition manufacturers had the greatest market information concerning their products. Now it is not so. As retail commerce has cash department, and by means of a bar code of a product, can collect the information on the sold goods and on preferences of clients. The information is the powerful weapon in hands of trading chains."<br>"Supplier may be also interested in reception of trustworthy information how those or other types of the goods are getting sold." |
| Legitimate power | Use of legitimate power is the precondition of Harmonious relationships | "A contract with suppliers which defines the rights and duties of each side and also timeframes of payments. Both sides put the signatures, confirming, that conditions of the contract suit everyone. Therefore there is no room for conflicts."<br>"The system of justice in Russia works in such a way that the judges are not allowed to acquit more than 1% of all cases. Therefore, the chance that the legal proceedings will result in indictment is quite high." |
| Referent power | Use of referent power is observed. | "It is difficult to say who influences whom to what extent, because there are different sources of influence. For example, our company has a strong image and it gives us the basis for our influence."<br>"Among advantages of working with networks of the company mark the additional total profit received as a result of advancing growth of sales volumes in comparison with growth of costs." |

not correspond sometimes, the retailer faces the difficult task of choosing only those suppliers that can also offer marketable products. Retailers take care of effective filling of their trading areas and of their own profitability parameters; otherwise they will suffer essential financial and reputation losses. Therefore, "the problem of the supplier is to show and convince the representative of retail network that the offered version of cooperation will be favourable to both organizations." The aspiration to create partnerships with suppliers of strategically important materials or commodity groups was especially emphasized, since the supply of such products and materials may exert direct influence on the position of the enterprise. As one of the interviewees admitted, "If these are complex products having a low degree of standardization, then the creation of partner relationships with suppliers is very important." On the other side, relationships between suppliers and buyers in Russia underlie the same economic principles as in other countries: namely, the nature and the rules of business. In this regard it was stated that manufacturers and retail commerce have opposite interests. The retailers try to keep the cost of a sourced product as low as possible, and suppliers and manufacturers are interested in acquiring the highest margin at sale and the maximization of profit. Among advantages of work with retailers were mentioned the additional total profit received as a result of advancing growth of sales in comparison with growth of costs and favorable conditions from the point of view of volume and stability of sales. Therefore, due to the different interests of both sides, there is some tension in the supplier–buyer relationship from the very beginning. As stated by one of the interviewees, for suppliers "there is a question to cooperate or to not cooperate with retail networks."

The retailers undoubtedly also raise the same question with regard to suppliers, since some interviewees confessed that the work with some Russian suppliers was very insecure: "One step to the left, you have earned some money; a step to the right and you are ruined." Besides the problem of insecurity, absence of trust was mentioned by one of the interviewees, who stated: "One of the main problems is also catastrophically low levels of trust. In Russia people have been cheated already so many times that they do not trust anyone under any conditions." The main reason for conflicts among retailers and suppliers was said to be default of contractual conditions (terms of delivery, terms of payment). Others named some basic problems characteristic of relationships with suppliers in Russia such as the lack of professionalism and reliability, absence of readiness to have long-term relationships, and problems with logistics. The following example, explained by one of the interviewees, showed that the ability to send professionally written trade offers though being considered one of the basic requirements for a supplier still could be missing in Russia: "A supplier sends the offer to a network in such type, which you simply cannot imagine: text without a uniform blank and without paragraphs, half of the text is emphasized with a computer since it is full of mistakes. Such suppliers will of course not be considered." Another example was given to us by another interviewee as an illustration of some unreliable behavior of suppliers:

> Their unique supplier in the category which had the goods and a possibility to deliver in this network informed us three days after the price arrangement had been reached that its prices have increased by 30%. This network accepted it. There was nothing to do but to accept the new price. But the main thing is that this supplier raised the prices by an additional 15% two days after the network agreed on 30% increase. The majority of suppliers act similarly.

This example shows that some suppliers use their advantageous status in order to profit from raised price and do not care about the long-term relationships with their partners. The supplier felt that the situation was in its favor and took the chance and raised the prices. However, we were also told that there is also a new layer of suppliers in Russia that are ready to have long-term relationships and that such suppliers are willing to learn from their more competent Western partners and "ask the more knowledgeable partners about what to do exactly." More and more suppliers begin to perfectly understand that networks will continue grow and that working with networks is useful and strategically important for a long-term stability. As stated by one of the interviewees, "we are not on different sides of barricades, but on one side," or by another interviewee, "today there are also companies/suppliers that work with networks simply for the sake of maintenance of relationships."

Generally we get the impression that suppliers in Russia are rather more dissatisfied with their status than buyers or retailers. Our interviewees complained about unfair policy of retailers with respect to suppliers, toughening of conditions, and discrimination at the conclusion of delivery contracts, an indispensability to pay "entrance tickets," to render networks additional services without which the latter refuse to expose the goods on shelves. In fact, we were told that suppliers "work almost 'in a zero' despite good profitability of production and serious turnovers" and "suffer from retailers that take the delivered products and do not pay back for a long time." Also the fact was mentioned that retail networks "reduce prices literally to the bottom threshold of profitability" of suppliers, "press on suppliers using a monopoly position in the market," and assign to suppliers additional obligations and works related with additional expenses for suppliers such as entrance fees. Apparently retailers also seem to differentiate suppliers according to their status. It was mentioned that the size and the image of the supplier played an important role and made the retailers treat it differently than small suppliers, since "the giant manufacturers investing into promotion of brands billions of rubles may sometimes pay nothing to the retailers for accommodation of their goods." Generally it was noted that each retailer was using individual approaches or practices with suppliers: "some suppliers may count on discounts, others may not."

Our picture of retailers drawn by some interviewees in fact corresponded to the mentioned complaints of suppliers. The gradual strengthening position of retail operators in a chain of consumer goods tends to increase requirements for suppliers of manufactured goods. In connection with constant progress of these requirements and toughening of quality standards of production, retailers tend to exert more rigid control over the suppliers and the quality of the delivered goods. Some interviewees expressed the opinion that in observing the behavior of the trading networks of Petersburg in relation to Petersburg manufacturers, "you can say that... networks show rigid uniform style in work with suppliers." The observers of the Moscow market confessed that in their work with large traditional Russian suppliers of some basic foodstuffs like bread, dairy, and sausage products retailers put an amplifying pressure upon suppliers and that "the latter are compelled to agree for partially acceptable conditions." Others even described the relationships between suppliers and buyers using the word "dictatorship."

However, it was also stated that some retailers begin to be more aware of the fact that good suppliers are indeed a precious treasure and should be treated accordingly. Therefore, "retailers start to reconsider and reconstruct a pool of the suppliers; they look for the most reliable, loyal to a network, those suppliers on whom it is possible to rely." It is also necessary to mention that the state has already noticed that some retailers require too many conditions from their suppliers and has issued some laws in which they prohibit or limit the direct exploitation of suppliers. The reasonable treatment of suppliers by retailer networks is now tracked by the government and the state administration. As a result, retailers have been forced to soften their terms of trade. Most of them have cancelled entrance bonuses, but as compensation for that they have added new rigid conditions for suppliers concerning discounts and delays of payments. The following example told to us by one of the interviewees explains this situation:

> Many networks have started to cancel entrance bonuses. I consider that it is connected, first of all, with credits of the state and the trade laws concerning networks. The first has cancelled entrance bonuses X5 and, notice, this network has received among the first the big state credits. It is clear, what means "cancelled."

As stated by another interviewee, "no entrance bonuses are necessary to networks, since they have free money of suppliers on 90–120 days and besides, the additional discount."

## Existence, Distribution and Use of Power in Russian Agri-Food Business

According to the results of our interviews we were able to identify the main fact that the existence of power in supply chain relationships indeed was confirmed. For example, one of the interviewees stated that "for the last years some networks have turned to be not only very powerful, but have become the aggressive players who alter rules of work on the market under own discretion." We were even told that the counterbalance of power is by all means on the side of buyers. Qualitative statements also clearly indicated that the power disparity was in the favor of buyers. As stated by one of the interviewees "this parity frequently acts not in favor of suppliers." In fact, we could even determine several reasons for existence of such counterbalance. The reason which was mentioned most often is the number of trading partners: "Since there are more suppliers than processors and retailers, suppliers have less power." The position of the seller initially was stated to be stronger than a position of the supplier, since "there are many more candidates for one meter of a shelf than it can physically contain." Among other reasons that were said to be responsible for the larger portion of power among the supply chain participants were market share and size of area in the commodity market as well as the status of the trading partner. As for the market share, we learned that it was not the only factor necessary for the formation of power: "market share is not the sufficient condition of domination." Such factors as the company name and image turned out to be at least as important as other factors mentioned. As stated by one of the interviewees, "When it is a preferred supplier, he has more power than a small and unknown supplier."

As far as coercive power is concerned, we were able to receive quite a number of statements about both its existence and use within the context of Russian agri-food supply chains. For example, one of the methods of coercive power was said to be the entrance fee or "entrance ticket." We were told that the general "entrance sum" was influenced by some parameters such as "popularity of the manufacturer and volume of its advertising budget" or "commodity group represented (it is known that to place ketchup in a network is cheaper than beer)." Though the fact that suppliers are required to pay fees in order to be able to work with some big retailers is evidently negative for suppliers, retailers regard this method in a positive light and justify its use due to the fact that "the fees paid by suppliers would be possible to recognize as the mechanism of competitive selection of the best manufacturers." Besides, the positive view on the use of coercive means of management was further supported by the fact that "it is economically inexpedient to use partner relationships with all suppliers." This interviewee explained to us that as far as the principles of work on commodity groups of non-strategic character are concerned, it would be appropriate to use coercive methods: "In this case it is not necessary to be afraid that opportunistic attitudes with the supplier will negatively affect quality of a product." This fact was also confirmed by another interviewee, who stated, "If we are speaking of the suppliers of simple products with a high degree of standardization, it could make sense to apply hard methods." On the other side, some participants of our survey expressed the opinion that coercive methods should be used with caution, since, for example, "such mechanisms as threats and penalties are not very effective because they show that the company is aggressive." In general, we could see that coercive methods were seen both in a negative and positive light, depending on the object and purpose of use. One of the statements especially clearly explained this point: "Such approach in short-term prospect can yield positive results, but in long-term is not always effective."

The mechanisms of reward power were not left without remarks by our interviewees. For example, the assistance programs offered by dairies to their suppliers were stated to be important in fostering the high quality standards to guarantee long-shelf-life dairy products. Interviewee No. 6 especially highlighted the advantages of using assistance programs in the long term: "Certainly, it requires additional expenses of time and forces, but at the same time allows reducing expenses and to raise a degree of adaptation of the enterprise to changing market conditions not only in the short term, but also over the longer term." The attractiveness of reward mechanisms such as favorable payment conditions was explained on a specific case by one of the interviewees, stating that a supplier company even used it as choosing criterion for working with retailers: "The company has simply terminated contracts with all networks this year and does not work with anybody except for Auchan because it pays without delays." This interviewee also indicated that besides conditions of payment, other mechanisms of reward power such as "the granting of the greatest possible level of discounts" were also considered to be very attractive for suppliers.

The evidence on the existence of expert power which is undoubtedly based on the expertise and professionalism of supply chains partners was stated by many interviewees. In fact, it is quite obvious that some big foreign retailers and manufacturers indeed possess more expertise on supply chain management approaches and have quite some experience with using such approaches in other countries before. As one of the interviewees stated, "Western companies have brought not only new management approaches to Russia but also innovative products such as drinking yoghurts and curd (partly curd—partly yoghurt)." The fact that such Western companies do possess this specific expertise is readily recognized by some Russian suppliers, who confess their own lack of experience and try to learn from their partners by "asking the more knowledgeable partners about what to do exactly." We learned from our interviewees even further that suppliers evidently enter supply chain networks "having only minimal or zero information on work of commercial structures of the potential customer."

The use of informational power and its positive side was even more praised and acknowledged by our interviewees than the expert one. In fact, the importance of collecting information about partners and creating specific databases was mentioned: "Of fundamental importance is the creation of a database of the list of potential suppliers, which allows obtaining information quickly about suppliers with desirable characteristics." It was also stated that due to the favorable position of retailers in the chain and their closeness to the consumer, they end up possessing also more information and as a consequence more of an ability to use informational influence strategies. Another interviewee underlined this point: "By tradition manufacturers had the greatest market information concerning their products. Now it is not so. As retail commerce has cash department, and by means of a bar code of a product, can collect the information on the sold goods and on preferences of clients. The information is the powerful weapon in hands of trading chains." The fact that the possessed information could be very effectively used to gain the favor or interest of suppliers was quite obvious as well. One of the interviewees stated that "supplier may also be interested in reception of trustworthy information how those or other types of the goods are getting sold."

According to the statements of our interviewees the legitimate power was claimed to be the precondition harmonious relationships with suppliers. For example, Interviewee 27 reported: "There is a contract with suppliers that defines the rights and duties of each side and also timeframes of payments. Both sides put the signatures, confirming, that conditions of the contract suit everyone. Therefore there is no room for conflicts." The effective use of legitimate power was further confirmed by some other participants of our survey. We learned that it was connected with the organization of the system of justice in Russia and its perception by other partners. Interviewee 83 expressed the opinion that especially threats on the legal basis are very effective. "The system of justice in Russia works in such a way that the judges are not allowed to acquit more than 1% of all cases. Therefore, the chance that the legal proceedings will result in indictment is quite high."

It is interesting to remark that some interviewees confessed that they do observe the clear existence and use of referent influence strategies. For example, one of the interviewees clearly stated that "it is difficult to say who influences whom to what extent, because there are different sources of influence. For example, our company has a strong image and it gives us the basis for our influence." Others only saw it indirectly or even call this phenomenon "paradox": "Sometimes there is such a paradox that the company wishes to enter our network at any cost." In general, all the factors making the company so attractive to other partners though a solid reputation and established sales volumes do contribute to the company's ability to use referent influence strategies. Another interviewee stated that "among advantages of work with networks of the company mark the additional total profit received as a result of advancing growth of sales volumes in comparison with growth of costs." Still others admitted that they observed in the behavior of suppliers working with big retailers, because they seem to feel like they are "on the safe side."

## DISCUSSION AND CONCLUSIONS

The results of the qualitative analysis of the interviews show that the retailers and their suppliers still have some tensions and problems in their relationships. Since the number of available suppliers is large, the focal companies have the difficult task of choosing reliable suppliers who offer well marketable products. Suppliers, in turn, feel the "dictatorship" of retailers by having to pay high entrance fees and sell their goods at lower prices. Some suppliers of strategic materials of goods try to use any chance to increase the price whenever they feel that the retailer is more dependent on them and cannot change the partner right away. The behavior of some Russian suppliers was described as a "no-go." Moreover, we were told that suppliers have a low level of professionalism, do not trust anyone, and try to take advantage of any situation as soon as there is a chance for it. Some suppliers do not consider the importance of investing in long-term relationships and being a fair business partner. However, we were also told that nowadays there is a new layer of suppliers who show more understanding towards the strategic character of relationships. Therefore, suppliers and buyers have some problems that are very characteristic for a transition economy like Russia. Russian suppliers have inherited their management style and the mentality influenced by the Soviet-planned economy. Foreign investors help to shape their mentality and way of conducting business by introducing new managerial concepts and teaching the suppliers.

In addition to the relationship problems, we also learned about the existence and distribution of power from our survey. According to the findings, the existence of power was confirmed. Moreover, we were told that retailers were more powerful than suppliers and that they behaved aggressively. The reason for the power of retailers was the bigger number of suppliers and the limited shelf space for the abundance of goods offered by suppliers.

Generally, the analysis shows that suppliers used the informational power very often, whereas the use of expert power was moderate. It could be explained by the fact that either the suppliers were not completely aware of the effects of expert power, or they were aware of it but perceived the use of expert power would cause more costs than expected benefits. Suppliers also used reward power more often than the other power types. It could also be explained by the fact that the availability of financial resources was also very high. Coercive, legitimate, and referent power were used relatively seldomly or at least not so often as reward and informational influence strategies. Buyers also preferred to use reward and informational power more often than other influence strategies. In addition, the use of referent power was more often than in case of suppliers. It could be explained by the fact that buyers possessed a high level of image and reputation. Other power types were used not so often or moderately.

The use of the power could be connected with the availability of resources, as the analysis shows. But the availability alone was not the only factor for choosing a certain power type. Another reason, as mentioned before, could be the costliness of the chosen power types in comparison with the expected effects or benefits. According to the classification of Wilkinson (1996), power includes direct and indirect costs. Direct costs involve the costs of communicating and also the costs of keeping informed of the subject's behavior. Indirect costs include opportunity costs—the use of power in one direction may well preclude its use in another. In fact, if we are to be more specific on the nature of costs incurred through the use of influence strategies, we need to take into account other types of costs. They can include monetary (e.g., administrative costs, negotiation costs (costs of communicating the requirements), implementation (giving rewards, investing in training), surveillance (costs of keeping informed of the subject's behavior), and non-monetary costs (e.g., loss of reputation and credibility, bad image, battle of interests, negative effects on the relationship, suspicion, dislike, or unwillingness to comply in the future). Benefits could also be classified into monetary (e.g., receiving resources from punishing) and non-monetary (e.g., gaining positive image through offering information, advice, recommendation), and short-term and long-term (e.g., benefits from investing in training and consulting services, future positive effects on the relationship).

Hunt and Nevin (1974) have implicitly recognized this cost versus benefit tradeoff in withholding assistances as a form of influence. We think that the costs of coercive power outweigh the gains from cooperation. Benefits of coercive power tend to be short-term. It is generally believed that punishment does not kill the motive and only suppresses the response. So if the punishment is removed, the behavior will probably reoccur. Therefore, administering coercive power always bears a risk of reprisals from punished actors. Applying coercive power without even explaining or warning might have destructive effects on the long term relationship, since punishing reduces the economic resources of the target, and thus reduces the motivation to participate in the exchange further. In some cases, less aggressive power might be an effective way to reach compliance on a certain issue.

Legitimate, referent, expert, informational, and reward power types being known for their "soft" nature can be used to achieve cooperation among the participating supply chain actors. Some of the noncoercive power types can also be used to solve the problems of coordination. The use of reward power promotes a cooperative relationship, which eliminates the problem of aligning the interests of individual actors in the supply chain. Retailers use reward power by using discounts for a larger amount of sold goods. Reward power is effective because it can be targeted to a specific actor and to a specific behavior or performance. We posit that rewards, even though they are costly, will have a longer-lasting effect on the relationship. Also, in general, the more valuable is the reward, the longer lasting effect it will have. In general, both coercive and reward power are seen to be able to enhance predictability of actions of other members, since the existence of hierarchal elements and authority makes everyone in the network know what will happen if the rules are not observed or observed. The target of influence will either get a reward for appropriate or outstanding behavior or they will be punished or their rewards will be withdrawn from them.

Expert power is usually short- to medium-term oriented and involves low costs. Being an expert already presupposes that the expert is in possession of some kind of expertise that he can easily apply by giving expert advice. The effect of the advice is short-term oriented because expertise can be a particularly nondurable influence strategy. Once the expert advice is given, it has little or no value for consequent transactions. Expert consultations are more costly, since they may require setting up additional services or teams of workers who would be spending their time consulting and helping with the implementation of projects. However, the benefits of consultations are also higher than giving expert advice, because the expert has insight into the matters of the target and can use the results of the joint work in the future.

Setting up an information exchange might require some logistical costs as well as IT investments. Suppliers involved in business relationships with greater levels of participative decision making and joint goal setting are more likely to be committed than those in relationships characterized by lesser participation and joint planning. Participation refers to the joint expectation that both parties will share information and make joint decisions. Therefore, informational power gives more understanding into the needs and problems of the target, which can be used in the future.

Legitimate power might stem from a strong market position (characterized by a high market share and/or effective entry barriers for new competitors), which can be skillfully used to achieve cooperation and coordination goals. Legitimate power offers safeguards to a company's specific investments, because one has to take into account the legal and economic consequences of violating explicit written contracts or rules. After all, the costs of making a legal contract are quite low. However, the effectiveness of the rules and obligations stated in the contract are long lasting for both parties. Therefore, legitimate power has generally a long-term orientation.

The costs of using referent power are not very high. The benefits of using referent power are moderate, however, since they do not explicitly indicate that the task should be done, but have a suggestive character. Therefore, referent power does not have a medium-term orientation. We also posit that expected costs and benefits are the most important factors determining the choice of power for achievement of a specific goal. If the costs and benefits involved are known, then the best behavior would be to use power in such a way that there is the maximum net gain—that is, benefits minus costs. In this respect, the companies should weigh the expected costs and benefits before using a specific type of power. Realistic expectations of costs and benefits will help ensure that the right power types are applied.

We think that in order to manage strategic alliances successfully, knowledge of different types of power is essential. The examples of such differentiation could be found in the Russian agri-food business. In particular, managers should be aware of the fact that power may have different effects on coordination and cooperation depending on its source. Power can destroy a cooperative relationship or help in solving problems of coordination and aligning actions. Knowledge about these effects should be skilfully used for effective management of strategic alliances.

## ACKNOWLEDGEMENT

The authors would like to thank the German Academic Exchange Service (DAAD) for financial support of this research.

## REFERENCES

Blankertz, L. (1998). The value and practicality of deliberate sampling for heterogeneity: A critical multiplist perspective. *American Journal of Evaluation, 19*(3), 307–324.

Bourlakis, M. (2001). Future issues in supply chain management. In J. F. Eastham, S. D. Ball, & A. E. Sharples (Eds.), *Food and drink supply chain management for the hospitality and retail sectors* (pp. 297–303). Oxford, UK: Butterworth-Heinemann.

Cant, M., Strydom, C. J. W., Jooste, C. J., & du Plessis, P. J. (2009). *Marketing management* (5th ed.). Cape Town, South Africa: Juta and Company.

Cooper, M. C., Lambert, D. M., & Pagh, J. D. (1997). Supply chain management: More than a new name for logistics. *International Journal of Logistics Management, 8*(2), 1–14.

Cox, A., Ireland, P., Lonsdale, C., Sanderson, J., & Watson, G. (2002). *Supply chains, markets and power: Mapping buyer and supplier power regimes.* London, UK: Routledge.

Das, T. K., & Teng, B. (1998). Between trust and control: Developing confidence in partner cooperation in alliances. *Academy of Management Review, 23,* 491–512.

Das, T. K., & Teng, B. (2000). Instabilities of strategic alliances: An internal tensions perspective. *Organization Science, 11,* 77–101.

Das, T. K., & Teng, B. (2001). Trust, control, and risk in strategic alliances: An integrated framework. *Organization Studies, 22,* 251–283.

Das, T. K., & Teng, B. (2002). Alliance constellations: A social exchange perspective. *Academy of Management Review, 27,* 445–456.

Doz, Y. L. (1996). The evolution of cooperation in strategic alliances: Initial conditions or learning processes? *Strategic Management Journal, 17,* 55–83.

Duysters, G., Heimeriks, K. H., & Jurriens, J. A. (2004). An integrated perspective on alliance management. *Journal on Chain and Network Science, 4*(2), 83–94.

Dyer, J. H., & Singh, H. (1998). The relational view: Cooperative strategy and sources of interorganizational competitive advantage. *Academy of Management Review, 23,* 660–679.

El-Ansary, A. L., & Stern, L. W. (1972). Power measurement in the distribution channel, *Journal of Marketing Research, 9,* 47–52.

Fey, C. F. (1995). Success strategies for Russian-foreign joint ventures, *Business Horizons, 38*(6), 49–54.

Fiddis, C. (1997). *Manufacturer retailer relationships in the food and drink industry: Strategies and tactics in the battle for power.* London, UK: FT Retail and Consumer Publishing / Pearson Professional.

French, J. R. P., & Raven, B. (1959). The bases of social power. In D. Cartwright (Ed.), *Studies in social power* (pp. 150–167). Ann Arbor, MI: University of Michigan Press.

Fritsch, N. (2007). *Erfolgsfaktoren im stiftungsmanagement, erfolgsfaktorenforschung im nonprofit-sektor* [Success factors for the management of foundations, success factor research in the non-profit sector]. Wiesbaden, Germany: Gabler.

Geanakoplos, J. (1992). Common knowledge. *Journal of Economic Perspectives, 6*(4), 53–83.

Gottschalg, O., & Zollo, M. (2007). Interest alignment and competitive advantage. *Academy of Management Review, 32,* 418–433.

Granovetter, M. (1985). Economic action and social structure: The problem of embeddedness. *American Journal of Sociology, 91,* 481–510.

Gulati, R. (1995). Does familiarity breed trust? The implications of repeated ties for contractual choice in alliances. *Academy of Management Journal, 38,* 85–112.

Gulati, R., & Singh, H. (1998). The architecture of cooperation: Managing coordination costs and appropriation concerns in strategic alliances. *Administrative Science Quarterly, 43,* 781–794.

Gulati, R., & Sytch, M. (2007). Dependence asymmetry and joint dependence in interorganizational relationships: Effects of embeddedness on exchange performance. *Administrative Science Quarterly, 52*, 32–69.

Helper, S. (1991). How much has really changed between U.S. automakers and their suppliers? *Sloan Management Review, 32*(4), 15–27.

Hingley, M. K. (2005). Power to all our friends? Living with imbalance in supplier-retailer relationships. *Industrial Marketing Management, 34*, 848–858.

Hu, T-L., & Sheu, J-B. (2003). A fuzzy-based customer classification method for advanced demand-responsive logistical distribution operations, *Fuzzy Sets and Systems, 139*, 431–450.

Hu, T-L., & Sheu, J-B. (2005). Relationships of channel power, noncoercive influencing strategies, climate, and solidarity: A real case study of the Taiwanese PDA industry. *Industrial Marketing Management, 34*, 447–461.

Hunt, S. D., & Nevin, J. R. (1974). Power in a channel of distribution: Sources and consequences. *Journal of Marketing Research, 11*, 186–193.

Ireland, R. D., & Webb, J. W. (2007). A multi-theoretic perspective on trust and power in strategic supply chains. *Industrial Marketing Management, 36*, 482–497.

Kale, P., Dyer, J. H., & Singh, H. (2002). Alliance capability, stock market response and long-term alliance success: The role of the alliance function. *Strategic Management Journal, 23*, 747–767.

Kampstra, R. P., Ashayeri, J., & Gattorna, J. L. (2006). Realities of supply chain collaboration. *International Journal of Logistics Management, 17*, 312–330.

Kogut, B., & Zander, U. (1996). What firms do: Coordination, identity and learning, *Organization Science, 7*, 502–518.

Lang, T. (2003). Food industrialization and food power: Implications for food governance, *Development Policy Review, 21*, 555–568.

Medcof, J. W. (2001). Resource-based strategy and managerial power in networks of internationally dispersed technology units. *Strategic Management Journal, 22*, 999–1012.

Merkens, H. (2000). *Auswahlverfahren, sampling, fallkonstruktion* [Selection methods, sampling, case setting]. In U. Flick, E. von Kardorff, & I. Steinke (Eds.), *Qualitative forschung—Ein handbuch* [Qualitative research—A handbook]. Reinbek/Hamburg, Germany: Rowohlt Verlag.

Milgrom, P., & Roberts, J. (1992). *Economics, organization and management.* Englewood Cliffs, NJ: Prentice-Hall.

Ogbonna, E., & Wilkinson, B. (1996). Interorganizational power relations in the UK grocery industry: Contradictions and developments. *International Review of Retail Distribution and Consumer Research, 6*, 395–414.

Patton, M. Q. (1990). *Qualitative evaluation and research methods* (2nd ed.). Newbury Park, CA: Sage.

Patton, M. Q. (2002). *Qualitative research and evaluation methods* (3rd ed.). Thousand Oaks, CA: Sage.

Payan, J. M., & McFarland, R. G. (2005). Decomposing influence strategies: Argument structure and dependence as determinants of the effectiveness of influence strategies in gaining channel member compliance. *Journal of Marketing, 69*(3), 66–79.

Raven, B. H., & Kruglanski, A. W. (1970). Control and power. In P. Swingle (Ed.), *The structure of conflict* (pp. 69–109). New York, NY: Academic.

Reid, R. D., & Bojanic, D. C. (2009). *Hospitality marketing management* (5th ed.). New York, NY: Wiley.

Tretyak, O., & Sheresheva, M. (2005, September). *Russian retail chains vs. foreign retailers: Changes within the industry and supplier-retailer relationships*, Paper presented at the 21st annual IMP conference, Rotterdam, Netherlands.

Wilkinson, I. F. (1996). Distribution channel management: Power considerations. *International Journal of Physical Distribution & Logistics Management, 26*(5), 31–41.

Williamson, O. E. (1975). *Markets and hierarchies: Analysis and antitrust implications.* New York, NY: Free Press.

Yakovlev, A., & Kokorev, R. (1995). State wholesale firms in Russia amid economic reform: Changes in management and organization. *International Studies of Management & Organization, 25*(4), 59–76.

CHAPTER 13

# IMPACT OF INTERPARTNER DIVERSITY ON THE PERFORMANCE OF GLOBAL STRATEGIC ALLIANCES

Hiroshi Yasuda

## ABSTRACT

Global strategic alliances are partnerships between firms from different countries and, compared with domestic alliances, are likely to face various difficulties and instabilities due to the diversity of corporate culture and values between the partners. On the other hand, prior literature has indicated that the performance of global strategic alliances is superior to that of domestic ones, reasoning that complementary combination of diversified capabilities and knowledge may enhance the probability of innovative breakthrough. Taking these two different viewpoints into consideration, this chapter analyzes the meaning of diversity between partners from various angles and tries to clarify how the interpartner diversity impacts on the performance of global strategic alliances. For this analysis, three cases of global strategic alliances are selected from major partnerships of technology development in the semiconductor industry. Each case was studied using information obtained from an interview with the manager of each alliance project. The research clarifies that the strength of global strategic alliances lies in combining the capabilities and knowledge of partners from different countries, but the diversity of corporate culture and values adversely influences the performance of alliances. In order to achieve good performance in global strategic alliances, it is necessary to design a management structure that involves appropriate control over the partners, making use of the diversity each partner brings to the project.

**INTRODUCTION**

With the globalization of markets, optimizing activities at global level is an important requirement in corporate management. Worldwide markets are taken into consideration in planning strategies to target products and services. Manufacturing and development centers are established in countries that promise the most efficient and cost-effective operations. Strategic alliances, or management schemes for collaborative activities with partners, also operate from a global platform. It is important to select appropriate international partners for a given project and to optimize global opportunities with them. In this chapter, the term *global strategic alliances* will be used to refer to strategic alliances with partners from different countries. In these situations, the corporate cultures of each of the partners are generally different, rooted in the fundamental cultural bases of their countries. Differences in institutional systems and languages also come into play. These factors make global strategic alliances more unstable and difficult to manage than domestic alliances where partners are based in the same country.

On the other hand, there are also well-recognized advantages to global strategic alliances. As a result of the recent exceptional economic growth in emerging countries, the structure of the global market is changing dramatically. In the past, the global market has been characterized by relatively balanced activity at the global level, which was mainly initiated by advanced nations. This tendency is now shifting towards a global market initiated by newly emerging countries. As global markets diversify, they need to adapt their products and services to suit each market, and to optimize business operations across borders. In this environment, it is essential to develop corporate management so that it is flexible and can accommodate diversity. Cooperation with partners who have a variety of resources and capabilities is a more effective solution than forming partnerships with homogeneous partners. Making appropriate use of this diversity can lead to a competitive advantage, and since global strategic alliances involve partners with different business experience, expertise, and knowhow in each market, they are an ideal choice for this.

Although global strategic alliances have an advantage over domestic ones, they also experience difficulties with the diverse characteristics of their partner base. This chapter discusses the diversity between partners from a number of different viewpoints and attempts to understand how this diversity influences the performance of alliances. The chapter presents three cases of global strategic alliances and analyzes how their management and performance are influenced by interpartner diversity. The aim of this chapter is to examine the function of global strategic alliances in corporate management and to recommend ways in which these partnerships can build on the cultural diversity of their partners.

The chapter is composed of six sections, including this introduction. The next section explores prior literature that describes interpartner diversity from various viewpoints. In the third section, research subjects and methods are identified, and three cases of global strategic alliances are outlined. The fourth section studies and analyzes these cases, based on an interview with the manager of each alliance project. The fifth section evaluates how diversity between partners has influenced the performance of alliances and how such diversity is managed through the appropriate structure and framework. Finally, the last section summarizes the main points of this chapter and provides suggestions for future research.

## GLOBAL STRATEGIC ALLIANCES AND DIVERSITY IN PARTNER BASE

### Partner Attributes and Alliance Performance

A firm's decision to form an alliance with a partner critically depends upon the attributes that each firm possesses and brings to the project. Alliance literature has indicated that the most important motive for firms to form alliances is to obtain access to complementary resources (Das & Teng, 1998, 2000; Hennart, 1988; Osborn & Hagedoorn, 1997). Firms select alliance partners with resources that they can leverage and integrate to create synergy (Lin, Yang, & Demirkan, 2007). One typical example in the pharmaceutical industry would be the alliance between a biotech firm and a pharmaceutical firm, in which the biotech firm may seek the pharmaceutical firm's complementary knowledge in sales, distribution, or the Food and Drug Administration approval process, while the pharmaceutical firm in turn may seek to enhance its knowledge and capabilities in the particular therapeutic field in which the biotech firm is conducting R&D (Kumar & Park, 2012). By pooling these complementary skills and experience, the firms can produce products faster and more cheaply than either firm could alone (Deeds & Hill, 1996). Firms are more likely to choose partners with resources that are as attractive as their own, rather than weaker partners, because collaboration between firms with high-quality resources creates the mutual hostage situation that may lend stability to the relationship (Kumar, 2011).

Matching of the resource profile between partners also constitutes a key determinant of alliance performance. The concept of fit serves as an important building block in strategic management (Venkatraman, 1989), and resource fit, either complementary or supplementary, between partners is a decisive condition for the satisfactory performance of alliances. Using a large sample from the computer, steel, pharmaceutical, and petroleum industries, Lin, Yang, and Arya (2009) empirically confirm that a high degree of resource complementarity with alliance partners is positively associated with firms' performance. In addition to the match of resource profiles between partners, the match of market profiles has also been identified as a key determinant of alliance performance. Researchers have pointed out that market commonality between partners is likely to influence the alliance performance because of the potential conflict of business between partners (Bleeke & Ernst, 1991; Park & Ungson, 1997). Combining the perspectives of both markets and resources, Das and Teng (2003) submit an integrated framework that evaluates alliance performance through an analysis of partner relationships, which denotes the market commonality, resource characteristics, and resource alignments. Other factors of partner attributes have also been explored in alliance literature. In the study of the longevity of joint ventures in the electronics industry, Park and Ungson (1997) show that certain competitive relationships, such as operational overlap, direct competition, or technology transfer, are likely to cause their dissolution. Kumar and Nti (1998) argue that the difference in absorptive capacities, or abilities to appropriate knowledge from a collaborative relationship, determine the evolutionary path and outcome of the alliance. Luo (1997) also shows that the interpartner fit of absorptive capacity, product relatedness, and market power significantly influences the synergistic effect of alliance performance.

As shown above, the influence of partner attributes on the performance of alliances has been identified from various viewpoints. Considering that global strategic alliances are characterized by a high level of diversity in partner attributes, it is necessary to evaluate such interpartner diversity in order to evolve the study of alliance performance. In the following, prior literature will be reviewed, focusing on the issues of diversity in certain partner attributes such as corporate culture, values, capabilities, and knowledge.

### Diversity of Corporate Culture and Values

A country's culture influences managers' judgment and the way employees think, and it involves social norms and values. This is also reflected in corporate culture, which characterizes the way a firm behaves (Yasuda, 2011). For example, it has been noted that when a company expands into an overseas market, cultural factors of the country of origin affect its mode of entry (Kogut & Singh, 1988). Corporate culture can be defined as the values and views that have been built into the firm's operational structure and which are shared by the company's employees. It is therefore specific to each firm and different from others. However, behind each corporate culture is a broader cultural base that is specific to the country where the firm operates. Therefore, a corporate culture in the country is based on these national cultural values and is formed in response to them (Parkhe, 1991). Conflicts of national culture between firms from different countries are likely to be responsible for failures in joint ventures or M&As (mergers and acquisitions) that are implemented across countries. Since a variety of corporate cultures and values are a fundamental characteristic of global strategic alliances, there are occasions when diversity causes conflict and makes the partnership more unstable and difficult to manage than domestic alliances.

For alliances to be successful, it is important that values and norms are shared between partners; however, this is difficult in global strategic alliances, given the diversity in the cultural base. This point has been discussed from a number of different angles. For example, diversity of corporate culture and values generates inconsistency and misunderstanding between partners in terms of recognition (Lane & Beamish, 1990; Yan & Zeng, 1999), reliability (Doney, Canon, & Mullen, 1998), and finding the solution to problems (Kogut & Singh, 1998). Kumar and Andersen (2000) indicate that differences in corporate culture produce a discrepancy in each partner's understanding of the "meaning of alliance," and this can become a major cause of failure. "Meaning of alliance" indicates the degree of importance attached to the alliance, and there should be consensus on this meaning at both operational and management levels if the partnership is to succeed. They demonstrate that it is difficult to maintain this consensus in global strategic alliances, where partners tend to take different actions to solve the same problem. Moreover, a field study by Gill and Butler (2003) based on joint ventures involving Japanese, Chinese, and European firms shows that there are subtle differences in the corporate culture of each country in terms of conceptualization of trust. If partners have different views of the way the trust is established and maintained, it makes the alliance unstable and extremely difficult to manage. Furthermore, since an alliance is generally formed in order to work towards a common goal, it is important for the stability of the alliance that all partners agree on how this goal is to be achieved. Partners from different cultural backgrounds, however, are likely to differ in their understanding of how to do this.

A number of prior studies have compared joint ventures between firms with different corporate cultures and those between firms with similar corporate cultures. They have provided empirical evidence of the difficulty of managing the former type of venture in particular. For example, Harrigan (1988) evaluates the similarity between partners in a corporate culture, taking into account the size of the business and its organizational structure, and shows that joint ventures between dissimilar firms do not last as long as partnerships between similar firms. Makino and Beamish (1998) explain the cultural difference between firms using the concept of "cultural distance," and this is evaluated at both company level (whether they belong to different enterprise groups or to the same enterprise group), and at country level (whether they operate in different countries or in the same country). The study demonstrates that, at both the company and the country level, the greater the cultural distance between partners, the less time the joint ventures are likely to last. Similarly, Hennart and Zeng (2002) compare and evaluate the performance of joint ventures in terms of their duration. They demonstrate that joint ventures between two Japanese firms tend to last longer than those between Japanese and U.S. firms. This is considered to be because conflicts of ideas are more likely to occur between firms from different cultural backgrounds. In addition, Hanvanich, Miller, Richards, and Cavusgil (2003) carry out a comparative evaluation of the performance of joint ventures using an event study method based on changes of market value when their contracts are announced. They show that the performance of joint ventures between culturally different foreign firms is inferior to that of joint ventures between domestic firms that are culturally similar.

Global strategic alliances also experience communication difficulties between partners, yet communication is an essential factor in success. Sharing common knowledge, language, and recognition can make communication and learning more effective in alliances (Cassiman, Colombo, Garrone, & Veugelers, 2005). Local proximity also facilitates information exchange and produces better results (Lundvall & Johnson, 1994), and technology transfer is easier between domestic firms than between domestic and foreign firms (Bartholomew, 1997). For this reason, firms have a tendency to cooperate with local partners (Stuart & Podolny, 1996). Locational as well as cultural distance between partners can be a cause of difficulties. As mentioned above, a number of prior studies have considered differences in corporate culture and values and have indicated that diversity between partners in global strategic alliances makes management more difficult and results less satisfactory.

### Diversity of Capabilities and Knowledge

Although the prior literature introduced in the previous section highlights the difficulty of managing global strategic alliances, a different stream of research has noted better performance when partners bring diversity to the alliance. This research takes into consideration the diversity of capabilities and knowledge between partners. For example, Olk (1997) analyzes the performance of a research and development consortium and reports that it would work better if it were to adopt a global form of organization rather than one based on domestic partners. McCutchen, Swamidass, and Teng (2008) investigate examples of technical alliances in the biotech industry and also discover that global partnerships perform better and last longer than those between domestic partners. Global strategic alliances tend to be relatively heterogeneous in terms of the technology, skills, networks, and sales outlets that members bring to the partnership. Pooling these complementary capabilities can be a major factor in their success. In the study of partnerships between European firms, Garette and Dussauge (2000) conclude that, while partnerships with regional partners have defensive characteristics to reduce burdens or disperse risks, those with extraterritorial partners have offensive characteristics that aim to expand new capabilities and penetrate foreign markets. In order to obtain results that lead to competitive advantage, firms need to consider global strategic alliances that make use of foreign firms' capabilities and access to global markets.

Diversity between firms is greater in global strategic alliances than in domestic alliances because each firm is rooted in a unique regional market, and its national system influences the direction of its corporate activities. Some researchers in this field argue that the systems of a country determine the type of research and development activities that companies embark on (Bartholomew, 1997), as well as their type of processes for innovation (Frost, Birkinshaw, & Ensign, 2002). Fields of research and development activities are likely to be country-specific (Frost, 2001), and their patterns will reflect the social characteristics and institutional framework there (Bartholomew, 1997). In a comparison of U.S., German, and Japanese firms, each demonstrates unique national features in the corporate direction, including research and development activities (Pauly & Reich, 1997).

Since a company's capabilities are determined by the country or area where it is based, firms in the same country, area, or cluster tend to share similar knowledge and experience. If companies wish to improve their competitiveness, they need to extend their networks and acquire more extensive knowledge and experience (McEvily & Zaheer, 1999). Initially, companies tend to conduct a local search, where they look for new knowledge close to their existing technical or regional domains (Stuart & Podolny, 1996). When they incorporate external knowledge beyond their domain, however, they are more able to be innovative and competitive (Rosenkopf & Nerkar, 2001). In this sense, global strategic alliances give companies a competitive advantage because they can make use of capabilities and specialties from different countries and combine the technical and regional knowledge of each member company.

The above research supports the view that global strategic alliances perform better because partners have different capabilities. Other research, on the contrary, suggests that homogeneous capabilities are more likely to lead to good performance. Phene, Fladmoe-Lindquist, and Marsh (2006) note that two factors, knowledge search and knowledge transfer, contribute to the process of innovation. Although combining capabilities and knowledge can play an important role in expanding a company's knowledge base, the process of knowledge transfer can be affected by a factor known as "absorption capability." This factor, unlike "knowledge search," is enhanced if the alliance includes partner companies that are geographically close and have similarities. This is why companies tend to restrict themselves to a local search. There is considered to be an optimum distance between firms in the process of innovation because innovation involves processes of both knowledge search and knowledge transfer. Other studies also highlight the importance of homogeneity in good performance, indicating that similarities in the capabilities and knowledge of partner companies can lead to synergy effects (Dussauge & Garette, 1995). In other words, similarities improve efficiency (Folta, 1998; Garette & Dussauge, 2000), and sharing common knowledge and recognition makes learning more effective (Cassiman et al., 2005). Some research also points out the negative impact of different capabilities in terms of the transaction cost, suggesting that opportunistic behavior is more likely if information is asymmetrical because of the difference in knowledge base between partners (Folta, 1998).

## Diversity from Different Angles

As described above, prior literature on alliances has suggested that management is made more difficult by different corporate cultures and values. However, the literature also highlights the advantages of different capabilities or knowledge. This would appear to present opposing views about the impact of diversity on the performance of global strategic alliances compared to domestic ones. This means that it is necessary to approach diversity itself from different angles in order to analyze its effect on alliances. Parkhe (1991) suggests two types of diversity between partners, Type I and Type II. Type I involves diversity of management resources or capabilities and harnesses the strengths of both companies. It is beneficial to global strategic alliances because partners complement one another. Type II involves diversity of corporate cultures or strategic directions, which promotes conflict between partners and has a negative influence on the efficiency and duration of global strategic alliances. Although Type I diversity is required for the establishment and maintenance of an alliance, it will disappear over time. On the other hand, Type II diversity can be overcome by learning and adaptation. An alliance will continue if the impact of Type I is greater than the impact of Type II, but the partnership will fail if the relationship is reversed.

Tomita (2007) investigates technology alliances in the medical supplies field, examining diversity in collaborating teams from a number of different angles, such as capabilities, ways of thinking, values, and personalities. He shows that the alliance works well if capabilities and ways of thinking are heterogeneous but complementary in a team, and values and personalities are homogeneous. Diversity between partners needs to be considered from multiple angles, and it is important to exploit both homogeneity and heterogeneity.

The above has reviewed previous literature on the subject of partner diversity in global strategic alliances, which considers various factors such as corporate culture, values, capabilities, and knowledge. The research highlights a number of ways in which diversity between partners influences the performance of alliances, and different approaches to managing heterogeneity and homogeneity are also examined. Further research is expected in this field in order to explore the relationship between interpartner diversity and alliance performance. For the purpose of deepening understanding of this relationship, it will be necessary to examine detailed case studies on individual partnership and take a comprehensive look at diversity between partners. The following sections therefore develop the research subjects, examining three cases of global strategic alliances and analyzing how diversity impacts on their performance.

## RESEARCH SUBJECTS AND METHODS

### Research Subjects

The aim of this chapter is to investigate the influence of interpartner diversity on the performance of alliances by analyzing case studies empirically. As indicated in the previous section, a number of factors involving diversity influence the performance of a partnership, such as corporate culture, values, capabilities, and knowledge. Some of these factors can have a negative influence if the level of diversity is relatively high. Others can have a positive influence with more heterogeneous diversity. For example, if partners have different corporate cultures or values, the partnership may be unstable or difficult to manage so that performance never improves. On the other hand, combining complementary capabilities and knowledge should lead to the incorporation of new ways of thinking and lead to better outcomes for the partnership. The importance of merging different capabilities and management resources during the process of innovation has been highlighted by a number of researchers.

If global strategic alliances are compared with domestic ones in terms of the levels of diversity, the former would be expected to score higher because the partners are foreign companies, while the partners in the latter are domestic firms. As Hofstede (1983) shows, the importance of cultural factors varies significantly from country to country. Since corporate culture or values reflect the culture or values of the country where the firm is based, the level of diversity in corporate culture and values between foreign firms should be greater than between domestic firms. Moreover, the level of diversity in capabilities and knowledge is also greater between foreign firms because the technical domain (where R&D capabilities and knowledge dominate) or the regional domain (where marketing capabilities and knowledge dominate) also varies from country to country. The overall level of diversity between partners in global strategic alliances is therefore greater than between partners in domestic alliances.

As discussed earlier, some diversity factors are likely to have a positive impact on the performance of alliances, while others are likely to have a negative impact. If alliances are to improve their performance, they need to capitalize on the positive factors and overcome the negative ones. This requires effective alliance management. Global strategic alliances that perform well tend to be the ones that manage the diversity between partners effectively. Therefore, it is also an essential research subject to analyze and determine the key elements of such effective management.

## Research Methods

In order to deal with the above research subjects, this section selects three cases of global strategic alliances (Cases 1, 2, and 3). All three cases are major partnerships of technology development by leading firms in the semiconductor industry and have been successfully completed. Case 1 is a joint development of semiconductor memory product technologies by three companies based in the United States, Germany, and Japan. Case 2 is a joint development of semiconductor logic process technologies by eight firms from the United States, Germany, France, Korea, and Japan. Case 3 is a joint research consortium in the field of semiconductor basic technologies, in which 14 firms from the United States, Germany, France, Taiwan, Korea, Singapore, and Japan participated.

The case studies consisted of an interview with the manager of each alliance project, supplemented by an analysis of public information about each alliance and each participating firm. Levels of diversity in the participating firms as well as the impact of interpartner diversity on the performance of the alliance were analyzed using the information obtained from interviews. A face-to-face interview was conducted with each project manager at each project location, asking open-ended questions designed to encourage answers based on his/her own knowledge and views. The main interview questions included: (1) How do you evaluate the performance of your partnership project, taking into account factors such as achievement, development level, schedule, and expense? (2) How do you evaluate the level of diversity in terms of the corporate culture, values, capabilities, and knowledge of participating partners? (3) Which factors do you take into consideration in managing the alliance, and which factors do you consider important to the success of the project? All these questions were intended to contribute to the research subjects, which were to evaluate how interpartner diversity impacts on the performance of global strategic alliances and also to understand how the project is managed in order to enhance positive factors and overcome negative ones. Each case will be described in the next section.

## CASE STUDIES

### Case One

Case 1 involved a joint development of semiconductor memory product technologies in which three semiconductor firms from the United States, Germany, and Japan collaborated, and in which more than two hundred (200) engineers from the three companies worked together at the development center in the U.S. This alliance developed sophisticated and cutting-edge technologies, and the venture was widely seen as one of the most successful joint development projects in the industry. However, cooperation between the three firms did not necessarily start well. There was, at the time, no precedent for large-scale collaboration between U.S., European, and Japanese firms, and the partnership attracted considerable attention from a number of quarters, including the media. About a year after the start of the project, it clearly faced management difficulties because the U.S., European and Japanese firms had different corporate cultures and values. The three companies were trying to work out an effective management structure and precipitated a number of measures to help overcome the corporate culture barrier. These included assigning employees to the project on the basis of their cultural adaptability, holding an intercultural training course and incorporating an organizational structure that helped engineers from all three companies to work together comfortably.

However, the most effective measure in overcoming the problem was the establishment of a mechanism that ensured that top executives from each of the three companies were committed to the project. The three executives met regularly to update one another on the project. They discussed solutions to problems, and delegated responsibilities to each team through a top-down approach. This mechanism guaranteed management commitment to the project and helped to overcome many of the difficulties that had been attributed to differences in the corporate culture of three companies. According to the project manager of Case 1:

> Even if there were discrepancies in opinions and approaches in the working levels, they were discussed among top executives and immediately solved. Because engineers felt content with the good relationships among the top executives, they were not hesitant to express their views in broad-minded discussion, which they believed to be the best solution to achieve the project goals.

On the other hand, the diversity of capabilities, viewpoints, or perceptions played an important role in excellent development results. The Japanese partner, for example, would get to grips with a problem or situation thoroughly before taking action, an approach that highlighted the importance of *seeing*. On the other hand, the U.S. partner thought carefully about an issue and looked for the root of the problem. This approach focused on *thinking*. On the other hand, the German partner was good at planning and implementing an idea, a *planning*-centered approach. Finally, the *doing*, or implementation stage brought together the efforts of all three partners. In other words, by using the different approaches of all three firms in a complementary way, the "seeing–thinking–planning–doing" cycle functioned effectively and made the project successful. The project manager added, "The strengths of the three partners were perfectly complementary and they more than offset the weaknesses of other partners." This demonstrates that results improve when global strategic alliances pool the different capabilities and viewpoints of each of the partners.

## Case Two

Case 2 was a partnership of eight semiconductor firms for the joint development of semiconductor logic process technologies. It was a global strategic alliance of U.S., German, French, Japanese, and Korean firms. It was initiated as a three-partner project, but more members were added when the project achieved excellent results and attracted other companies. The project took place at the premises of one of the U.S. firms ("Firm X"), and engineers from the eight partner companies worked together in the same facility. The project has carried out successful development of advanced technologies in recent years and has remained a world leader in its field.

A notable characteristic of this alliance was that partners did not hold equal positions, and Firm X was designated a leader of the project. Ordinal decisions, such as schedule adjustment or personnel allocation, were made jointly by all partners, but only Firm X had final authority on key issues if partners could not reach an agreement. There were bound to be disagreements between partners in an alliance of eight firms from different countries, and development would have been hampered if consensus had been required for every decision. By naming Firm X a leader of the project, the alliance was able to overcome difficulties arising from differences in partners' views or policies. As the project manager of Case 2 said:

> It is important to respect the opinions of all partners as much as possible; however, if the issue is related to the policies essential to take the project forward, one responsible firm needs to take the leadership to give the direction. This is especially true in the case of alliances participated in by many firms from different countries.

The alliance also had a policy of taking on new partners where they were seen to contribute to the success of the joint project, so it was not limited to the initial group of companies. This policy meant that the number of partners increased from three at the beginning to eight at the end. New firms could join the alliance if they had proprietary capabilities or technologies that were deemed essential to the success of the project and if the existing partners did not already have these capabilities or technologies. In fact, one firm wished to join the alliance but was rejected because it was not considered to have any unique technical capabilities that could be of use to the project.

This alliance saw itself as an ecosystem in which firms with a variety of capabilities and knowledge collaborated. The most important aspect of the alliance was a mechanism where each partner contributed unique capabilities from its own domain, and these complemented the operation as a whole. In other words, the ultimate effect was a synergy of the partners' different capabilities and knowledge. Because the alliance involved firms from different countries worldwide, it was important that diversity was taken seriously. In fact, the synergistic effects of diversity have been a driving force in the successful development of innovative technologies in this project. The project manager emphasized:

> Each partner brought its proprietary technologies from its home and merged them in the project. The one partner was strong in certain technologies, while the other had superior capabilities in other technologies. Because the project picked up the best of many partners, we could achieve excellent results.

However, diversity of capabilities or knowledge does not produce synergy in itself. This requires a suitable arrangement and appropriate management. Firm X took on the role of leader to provide a central location and to act as a catalyst for creating synergy. With different corporate culture and values among firms from different countries, it was pointless to expect that everyone would think the same way. Effective management of the project depended instead on overcoming differences and coordinating views and policies. This was made possible by the fact that partners did not hold equal positions, and Firm X was designated a clear leader of the project.

## Case Three

The global strategic alliance in Case 3 was a research partnership of semiconductor basic technologies that involved 14 semiconductor firms from different countries. They included U.S., German, French, Japanese, Korean, Taiwanese, and Singaporean companies. The project was initiated and hosted by a European nonprofit organization, Firm Y, and was carried out at its premises. Firm Y had been established for the purpose of engaging in the basic research of microelectronics technologies, not running a business itself. It was financially supported by the government, which hoped to promote the regional economy by applying the results of the development to industry. To meet this expectation, a number of spinoff companies were formed from Firm Y, which have helped to activate the economy and create jobs. Moreover, Firm Y has attracted talented people with higher education to the area and is now one of the leading research and development organizations in Europe. Similar government-supported development projects for basic technologies have taken place in other countries, such as the U.S. and Japan, but this project is considered the most successful development in its field.

Firm Y itself was the most important aspect of this alliance. As an organization, its sole purpose was to manage the partnership. It was independent of partners in the alliance, and there was no shareholding relationship or exchange of personnel between Firm Y and partners. Because the partners in the project were from different countries across the world, there were bound to be differences between them in terms of corporate culture and values. There were also conflicts of interest and arguments about development methods or directions. However, decisions were always made by Firm Y, not the partners. The members of Firm Y's management team were all experts in technology development or project management and made decisions on the basis of maximizing overall project performance independently of partners' specific interests. All partners in the project had to accept the decisions made by Firm Y. This neutrality of management may not always have corresponded to some partners' wishes, but it eliminated power struggles between partners. This made it easier to concentrate on management that was in the best interests of the project as a whole. The project manager of Case 3 stated:

> If the project did not achieve good results, the financial support from the government would be reduced and the frustrated partners would leave. This was the risk borne by the management team of Firm Y. They needed to manage the project using their fair discretion, irrespective of the specific interests of each partner.

Another characteristic feature of this alliance was its openness to firms all over the world. In the case of government-supported alliances, it is usual to limit the partner members to domestic firms or to give preference to domestic firms because the project is using tax-payers' money in that country. In fact, similar alliances supported by the Japanese government only have Japanese partners, and partnerships supported by the U.S. government generally consist of partners within the U.S. However, in the case of the alliance managed by Firm Y, foreign firms were treated the same as regional firms and were free to take the results of the project back to their own countries and use them for their own purposes.

The neutrality and openness of the project convinced many of the world's leading companies to become involved in the project, and it also provided a basis for efficient management. The different capabilities, technical knowledge, and wisdom of all the partners were combined to improve performance, which in turn strengthened the commitment of partners to the project. In this way, the participation of the partners brought better results, and these results, in turn, encouraged participation. This also stabilized the management of Firm Y, which was incorporated as an independent organization. The project manager said, "It is only natural that good performance is realized if firms with various capabilities combine their efforts. This project was completely open to any qualified partners in the world and this policy led to the successful results of the project." Development of basic semiconductor technologies is a high-risk business because of its high development costs and uncertain outcomes. This burden is too heavy for each firm to bear independently, which is why there are advantages in leaving the development of basic technologies to an alliance as a noncompeting domain. Major semiconductor firms worldwide currently consider this alliance to be the appropriate focus for this type of development.

## IMPLICATIONS FOR MANAGEMENT

### Interpartner Diversity and Alliance Performance

In the interviews conducted during this research, project managers were asked to evaluate the performance of their partnerships, including the factors that had contributed to the results. All project managers agreed that, as noted in the prior literature, the enormous diversity of capabilities and knowledge between the partners were the main reasons for the superior performance of their projects. Companies from different countries had each brought their own capabilities and technical strengths to the partnership. The synergistic effects of combining these complementary resources had helped to create innovative technologies and develop novel concepts. Moreover, as shown in Case 1, the different viewpoints of each of the partners helped to establish an appropriate direction for the technology development. Partnerships may therefore work better if partners bring diversity to the project. This is the strength of global strategic alliances, and it does not tend to be a feature of collaboration between domestic partners who bring rather homogeneous capabilities and knowledge to the alliance.

However, even if the wide range of capabilities and knowledge are the main strength of global strategic alliances, they cannot be harnessed without effective management to ensure overall consensus, and there may be difficulties in terms of the diversity of corporate culture and values. In domestic alliances, partners tend to have a homogeneous corporate culture and set of values because they are based in the same country and have the same national culture. Decision-making patterns are similar, and partners communicate more easily with the same language, so management risks are minimized. In contrast, global partnerships have diverse corporate cultures and values because the partners are from a number of different countries. This can create a barrier to mutual understanding and effective communication between partners. The difference in patterns of decision making may also lead to misunderstanding or mistrust and make it more difficult to manage the alliance project.

### Structure for Managing Interpartner Diversity

All project managers also emphasized the importance of management in addressing this difficulty. To make full use of different capabilities and knowledge, they developed organizational structures that addressed the problems arising from diversity of corporate culture and values. For example, the structure of the partnership in Case 1 was intended to facilitate communication between top executives and to build relationships that could provide an immediate solution to operational problems. The partnership in Case 2 made use of a structure where one of the participating companies was the project leader, with the authority to make final decisions when partners could not agree. The structure of the partnership in Case 3 was designed so that management was independent of all partners, and the decision-making mechanisms therefore rose above partners' individual interests.

Basically, in strategic alliances, all partners control a project jointly and share its outcomes (Yoshino & Rangan, 1995). An important principle of alliance management is that there is an equal and autonomous relationship between the participants in the project. However, in the case of global strategic alliances, where diversity is a predominant factor, the project will encounter a number of management difficulties if this principle is applied. All project managers interviewed in this research noted that the alliance would not work if it were managed by partners with equal authority.

In each of Cases 1, 2 and 3, the management structure operated above the interests of individual partners, either by bringing together top executives and ensuring their commitment, by making one of the partners the project leader, or by creating a separate management organization that was independent of all the partners. It is interesting to note that, in regard to the latter case, the management structure of the alliance was characterized less by equality and more by greater control over participating partners. In other words, Case 2 was characterized by greater control than Case 1, and likewise Case 3 was characterized by greater control than Case 2. This is considered to have been due to the number of partners in the alliance: Case 1 involved three companies, Case 2 eight companies, and Case 3 fourteen. As the number of partners increases, the level of diversity between the partners gets higher. This makes the management of alliance more difficult, and then greater control over the participating partners is required. It can therefore be said that the management structure of global strategic alliances needs to be appropriately designed to meet the level of interpartner diversity if competitive advantages are to be created from such diversity.

## SUMMARY

This chapter has analyzed the relationship between alliance performance and interpartner diversity in terms of a number of factors such as corporate culture, values, capabilities, and knowledge. Three cases of global strategic alliances are selected from joint development projects in the industry and are studied through interviews with each of the project managers. In each case, the alliance includes partners from leading firms from different countries and has achieved superior performance in the development of advanced technologies. By empirically analyzing various factors of diversity between partners and their impacts on the management and performance of the alliance, the findings of this chapter can be summarized as follows.

Alliances perform better when they make appropriate use of the diversity of partners' capabilities and knowledge. It is especially important for joint technology development to combine the technical expertise, viewpoints, and perceptions of partners in a complementary way. In this sense, the strength of global strategic alliances lies in combining the diversified capabilities and knowledge of partners from different countries. This strength is limited in the case of domestic alliances, where partners tend to have rather homogeneous capabilities and viewpoints. On the other hand, the diversity of corporate culture and values makes partnerships unstable and difficult to manage, and global strategic alliances are also characterized by a high level of diversity in these corporate factors. Although these factors of diversity adversely influence the performance of alliances, this difficulty can be overcome by establishing an appropriate organizational structure for the management of alliances. If the management structure is suitable for the number of participating parties and makes appropriate use of the diversity each partner brings to the project, global partnerships will be more successful than domestic ones. With the globalization of markets, global activities in various fields play a more important role than ever. In the coming years, corporate management will need to become more actively involved in global strategic alliances and consider appropriate organizational structures for managing interpartner diversity more effectively.

Finally, it should be noted that this chapter discusses how interpartner diversity impacts on the performance of global strategic alliances, but it does not discuss the mechanisms that contribute to this impact. The chapter has demonstrated that some forms of diversity impact positively on performance, while others impact negatively. This implies that different mechanisms are at work in different aspects of diversity, and these influence the performance of alliances in a number of different ways. In order to study this mechanism, the research needs to examine in more detail the processes involved in alliance activities. It should clarify exactly how combining different capabilities leads to improved performance and how a diverse corporate culture can affect management adversely. An analysis of this mechanism should form the subject of future research. This would provide a deeper insight into the diverse elements each partner brings to the alliance.

## REFERENCES

Bartholomew, S. (1997). National systems of biotechnology innovation: Complex interdependence in the global system. *Journal of International Business Studies, 28*, 241–266.

Bleeke, J., & Ernst, D. (1991). The way to win cross-border alliances. *Harvard Business Review, 69,* 127–135.

Cassiman, B., Colombo, M. G., Garrone, P., & Veugelers, R. (2005). The impact of M&A on the R&D process: An empirical analysis of the role of technological and market relatedness. *Research Policy, 34,* 195–220.

Das, T. K., & Teng, B. (1998). Resource and risk management in the strategic alliance making process. *Journal of Management, 24,* 21–42.

Das, T. K., & Teng, B. (2000). A resource-based theory of strategic alliances. *Journal of Management, 26,* 31–61.

Das, T. K., & Teng, B. (2003). Partner analysis and alliance performance. *Scandinavian Journal of Management, 19,* 279–308.

Deeds, D. L., & Hill, C. W. L. (1996). Strategic alliances and the rate of new product development: An empirical study of entrepreneurial biotechnology firms. *Journal of Business Venturing, 11,* 41–55.

Doney, P. M., Cannon, J. P., & Mullen, M. R. (1998). Understanding the influence of national culture on the development of trust. *Academy of Management Review, 23,* 601–620.

Dussauge, P., & Garrette, B. (1995). Determinants of success in international strategic alliances: Evidence from the global aerospace industry. *Journal of International Business Studies, 26,* 505–530.

Folta, T. B. (1998). Governance and uncertainty: The tradeoff between administrative control and commitment. *Strategic Management Journal, 19,* 1007–1028.

Frost, T. (2001). The geographic sources of foreign subsidiaries innovations. *Strategic Management Journal, 22,* 101–123.

Frost, T., Birkinshaw, J., & Ensign, P. (2002). Centers of excellence in multinational corporations. *Strategic Management Journal, 23,* 997–1018.

Garette, B., & Dussauge, P. (2000). Alliances versus acquisitions: Choosing the right option. *European Management Journal, 18,* 63–69.

Gill, J., & Butler, R. (2003). Managing instability in cross-cultural alliances. *Long Range Planning, 36,* 113–134.

Hanvanich, S., Miller, S. R., Richards, M. S., & Cavusgil, T. (2003). An event study of the effects of partner and location cultural differences in joint ventures. *International Business Review, 12,* 1–16.

Harrigan, K. (1988). Strategic alliances and partner asymmetries. In F. J. Contractor & P. Lorange (Eds.), *Cooperative strategies in international business* (pp.141–158). Lexington, MA: Lexington Books.

Hennart, J. F. (1988). A transaction cost theory of equity joint ventures. *Strategic Management Journal, 9,* 361–374.

Hennart, J. F., & Zeng, M. (2002). Cross-cultural differences and joint venture longevity. *Journal of International Business Studies, 33,* 699–716.

Hofstede, G. (1983). National cultures in four dimensions: A research-based theory of cultural differences among nations. *International Studies of Management and Organization, 13,* 46–74.

Kogut, B., & Singh, H. (1988). The effect of national culture on the choice of entry mode. *Journal of International Business Studies, 19,* 411–432.

Kumar, R., & Andersen, P. H. (2000). Interfirm diversity and the management of meaning in international strategic alliances. *International Business Review, 9*, 237–252.

Kumar, R., & Nti, K. O. (1998). Differential learning and interaction in alliance dynamics: A process and outcome discrepancy model. *Organization Science, 9*, 356–367.

Kumar, S. (2011). Are joint ventures positive sum games? The relative effects of cooperative and non-cooperative behavior. *Strategic Management Journal, 32*, 32–54.

Kumar, S., & Park, J. C. (2012). Partner characteristics, information asymmetry, and the signaling efforts of joint ventures. *Managerial and Decision Economics, 33*, 127–145.

Lane, H. W., & Beamish, P. W. (1990). Cross cultural cooperative behavior in joint ventures in LDCs. *Management International Review, 30*, 87–102.

Lin, Z., Yang, H., & Arya, B. (2009). Alliance partners and firm performance: Resource complementarity and status association. *Strategic Management Journal, 30*, 921–940.

Lin, Z., Yang, H. & Demirkan, I. (2007). The performance consequences of ambidexterity in strategic alliance formations: Empirical investigation and computational theorizing. *Management Science, 53*, 1645–1658.

Lundvall, B., & Johnson, B. (1994). The learning economy. *Journal of Industry Studies, 1*, 23–42.

Luo, Y. (1997). Partner selection and venturing success: The case of joint ventures with firms in the People's Republic of China. *Organization Science, 8*, 648–662.

Makino, S., & Beamish, P.W. (1998). Performance and survival of joint ventures with non-conventional ownership structures. *Journal of International Business Studies, 29*, 797–818.

McCutchen, W. W., Swamidass, P. M., & Teng, B. (2008). Strategic alliance termination and performance: The role of task complexity, nationality, and experience. *The Journal of High Technology Management Research, 18*, 191–202.

McEvily, B., & Zaheer, A. (1999). Bridging ties: A source of firm heterogeneity in competitive capabilities. *Strategic Management Journal, 20*, 1133–1156.

Olk, P. (1997). The effect of partner differences on the performance of R&D consortia. In P. W. Beamish & J. P. Killing (Eds.), *Cooperative strategies: North American perspectives* (pp.133–159). San Francisco, CA: New Lexington Press.

Osborn, R. N., & Hagedoorn, J. (1997). The institutionalization and evolutionary dynamics of interorganizational alliances and network. *Academy of Management Journal, 40*, 261–278.

Park, S. H., & Ungson, G. R. (1997). The effect of national culture, organizational complementarity, and economic motivation on joint venture dissolution. *Academy of Management Journal, 40*, 279–307.

Parkhe, A. (1991). Interfirm diversity, organizational learning and longevity in global strategic alliances. *Journal of International Business Studies, 22*, 579–601.

Pauly, L. W., & Reich, S. (1997). National structures and multinational corporate behavior: Enduring differences in the age of globalization. *International Organization, 51*, 1–30.

Phene, N., Fladmoe-Lindquist, K., & Marsh, L. (2006). Breakthrough innovations in the U.S. biotechnology industry: The effects of technological space and geographic origin. *Strategic Management Journal, 27,* 369–388.

Rosenkopf, L., & Nerkar, A. (2001). Beyond local search: Boundary-spanning, exploration, and impact in the optical disk industry. *Strategic Management Journal, 22,* 287–306.

Stuart, T. E., & Podolny, J. M. (1996). Local search and the evolution of technological capabilities. *Strategic Management Journal, 17,* 21–38.

Tomita, K. (2007). Management of differences and similarities in strategic alliances. *Journal of Healthcare and Society, 17,* 113–123.

Venkatraman, N. (1989). The concept of fit in strategy research: Toward verbal and statistical correspondence. *Academy of Management Review, 14,* 423–444.

Yan, A., & Zeng, M. (1999). International joint venture stability: A critique of previous research, a reconceptualization, and directions for future research. *Journal of International Business Studies, 30,* 397–414.

Yasuda, H. (2011). Creation of firm's competitiveness and institution: Using the relationship between alliance and corporate culture as an example. *Aoyama Journal of Business, 46,* 75–97.

Yoshino, M. Y., & Rangan, U. S. (1995). *Strategic alliances: An entrepreneurial approach to globalization.* Cambridge, MA: Harvard Business School Press.

# ABOUT THE CONTRIBUTORS

**David Arditi** is a professor in the department of civil, architectural and environmental engineering at Illinois Institute of Technology, Chicago, IL. He is the founder and current director of the Construction Engineering and Management Program. His teaching and research focus on all aspects of construction management, engineering and support. He is the author of many papers published in professional journals and conference proceedings. He serves on the editorial board of several journals and is an active member of several professional societies. E-mail: arditi@iit.edu

**Vera Belaya** is a scientific researcher at the Institute of Farm Economics of the Thünen-Institute , Federal Research Institute for Rural Areas, Forestry and Fisheries in Braunschweig. She received her PhD from the Martin Luther University and Leibniz-Institute of Agricultural Development in Central and Eastern Europe (IAMO) in Halle (Saale). She has published over 50 articles in conference proceedings and peer reviewed journals such as *Post-Communist Economies, International Journal of Social Economics, The Marketing Review, Journal of Relationship Marketing, Journal for East European Management Studies*, and *International Business and Management*, and presented several papers at international scientific conferences. Her research areas include supply chain networks, strategic management, and supply chain management. E-mail: vera_belaya2000@yahoo.de

**Carmen Boymans** holds an MSc in strategic management from the Nijmegen School of Management at Radboud University in Nijmegen. She wrote her master's thesis about response strategies and the interaction pattern between alliance partners. She currently works as a business consultant at Atos Consulting, The Netherlands. Her areas of expertise include customer management, multichannel knowledge management and social CRM. E-mail: carmenboymans@hotmail.com

**T. K. Das** is professor of strategic management and area coordinator (strategic management and business & society) at the Zicklin School of Business, Baruch College, City University of New York. He is concurrently a member of the University's doctoral faculty. Professor Das received his PhD in organization and strategic studies from the Anderson Graduate School of Management, University of California at Los Angeles (UCLA). He also has degrees in physics, mathematics, and management, and a professional certification in banking. Prior to entering the academic life, Professor Das had extensive experience as a senior business executive. He has research interests in strategic alliances, strategy making, organizational studies, temporal studies, and executive development. Professor Das has published over a dozen books and monographs, and his research has appeared in over 45 journals, of which some of the later ones include *Academy of Management Executive, Academy of Management Review, British Journal of Management, Journal of International Management, Journal of Management, Journal of Management Studies, Organization Science, Organization Studies*, and *Strategic Management Journal*. Professor Das currently serves on the editorial boards of several academic journals, and is a former senior editor of *Organization Studies* and board member of a number of other journals. He is the founding series editor of the book series *Research in Strategic Alliances* (Information Age Publishing). E-mail: TK.Das@baruch.cuny.edu

**Gjalt de Jong** is an associate professor of strategy at the faculty of economics and business, University of Groningen. His research interests and publications include the management of strategic alliances; business ethics in transition economies; the strategy, structure, and organization of multinational enterprises; and the causes and consequences of national rules. Gjalt is responsible for the design and coordination of (under-)graduate courses in the fields of international business, international economics, and public administration. Prior to his current position, he has been affiliated as a senior management consultant to PricewaterhouseCoopers and KPMG and as such responsible for large-scale strategy and ICT programs at Dutch multinational firms in industry and the financial sector as well as for educational institutes. E-mail: g.de.jong@rug.nl

**Dries Faems** is full professor of innovation and organization at the faculty of economics and business, University of Groningen. He also is affiliated researcher at the Research Centre of Organisation Studies, Katholieke Universiteit Leuven. He has published papers in journals such as *Academy of*

*Management Journal, Organization Studies, Journal of Product Innovation Management, Journal of Management Studies, Technovation,* and *Small Business Economics.* His current research focuses on the management of internal and external innovation strategies, performance implications of alliance portfolios, and the governance of transitional governance trajectories. He also is a member of the editorial review board of the *Academy of Management Journal, Journal of Management Studies* and *Journal of Trust Research.* E-mail: d.l.m.faems@rug.nl

**Olivier Furrer** is associate professor of strategic management at the Nijmegen School of Management at Radboud University Nijmegen, The Netherlands. He previously held positions at the University of Illinois at Urbana-Champaign (U.S.), Birmingham (UK), Lausanne and Neuchâtel (Switzerland). He holds a PhD from the University of Neuchâtel. He has published in the *Journal of International Business Studies, Management International Review,* and *International Journal of Management Reviews,* among others. His current research interests are in the areas of international corporate social responsibilities and response strategies in problematic strategic alliances. E-mail: o.furrer@fm.ru.nl

**Sveinn Vidar Gudmundsson** is professor of strategic management, Toulouse Business School, France. He was senior visiting fellow, Smith School of Enterprise and the Environment, Oxford University. He earned his BSc, MBA and MSc from Florida Institute of Technology, U.S., and a PhD from Cranfield University, UK. Prior to his academic carrier, he held senior management positions in airlines and the banking sector. He has received several awards for his research and teaching. His research interests focus on strategic alliances, business performance, entrepreneurship, foresight, electronic marketplaces, low-cost strategies, intercultural management, and decision making and learning through interactive teams. E-mail: s.gudmundsson@esc-toulouse.fr

**Jon H. Hanf** is professor for international wine business at Geisenheim University and the coordinator of the bachelor program IWW. He has studied economics in Stuttgart Hohenheim. He wrote his dissertation on network management at the Justus-Liebig-University Giessen. Afterwards he was working as a research group leader at the Leibniz Institute for Agricultural Development in Central and Eastern Europe. He has published over 100 articles in books, conference proceedings, and peer reviewed journals such as *Agribusiness: An International Journal, Food Economics, International Food and Agribusiness Management Review,* and *Journal on Chain and Network Science.* His research interests include marketing, consumer behavior, strategic management, and supply chain management. E-mail: jon.hanf@hs-rm.de

**Pamela R. Haunschild** holds the Jack R. Crosby Regents Chair in Business at the McCombs School of Business, University of Texas at Austin, and also holds IC2's Cynthia Hendrick Kozmetsky Fellow position. Professor Haunschild earned her PhD in organizational behavior and theory from the Graduate School of Industrial Administration at Carnegie Mellon University. Earlier, she was an assistant professor at Stanford University's Graduate School of Business. Her research involves studying organizational (and interorganizational) learning processes, especially how and under what circumstances organizations learn from their "errors" or "mistakes." Professor Haunschild is also interested in issues related to networks and corporate governance as well as how governance decisions are affected by network information and influence. Her publications appear in journals such as *Administrative Science Quarterly* and *Organization Science*. Her awards include a Fulbright Distinguished Chair in Corporate Governance, best paper award from the Academy of Management, Louis R. Pondy Award for best paper based on a dissertation, and the McCombs Research Excellence Award. She has served on several editorial boards and as an ad hoc reviewer for several premier management journals. In 2005–2006 she was the chair of the organization and management theory division of the Academy of Management. E-mail: pamela.haunschild@mccombs.utexas.edu

**Michael Hitt** is a distinguished professor of management at Texas A&M University and holds the Joe B. Foster Chair in Business Leadership. He received his PhD from the University of Colorado. Dr. Hitt has coauthored or co-edited 26 books and authored or coauthored many journal articles. A recent article in the *Journal of Management* listed him as one of the ten most cited authors in management over a 25-year period. Additionally, the *Times Higher Education* in 2010 listed him among the top scholars in economics, finance, and management based on the number of articles with a high citation rate on the Web of Science. He has served on the editorial review boards of multiple journals and is a former editor of the *Academy of Management Journal* and the *Strategic Entrepreneurship Journal*. He is a fellow in the Academy of Management and in the Strategic Management Society, a research fellow in the National Entrepreneurship Consortium and received an honorary doctorate from the Universidad Carlos III de Madrid. He is a former president of the Academy of Management, a former president of the Strategic Management Society, and a member of the Academy of Management Journals' Hall of Fame. He received awards for the best article published in the *Academy of Management Executive* (1999), *Academy of Management Journal* (2000), and the *Journal of Management* (2006). He received the Irwin Outstanding Educator Award and the Distinguished Service Award from the Academy of Management and the Falcone Distinguished Entrepreneurship Scholar Award from Syracuse University. E-mail: mhitt@mays.tamu.edu

**Morten Jakobsen** is an associate professor of management accounting. He has a PhD and an MSc degree. His research areas are management accounting and governmentality, management accounting and interorganizational relations, and managerial practices concerning performance measures. E-mail: mja@asb.dk

**Annabelle Jaouen** is professor of entrepreneurship at Groupe Sup de Co Montpellier Business School, France. She is specialized in small and very small business strategies, and she teaches entrepreneurship and project management. She is the author (or coauthor) of six books on the subject and regularly advises entrepreneurs on their projects of creation or development. Her research concerns types of entrepreneurs, territorialized cooperative strategies, alliances and networks, human resources management, and information systems in very small business. Her research has been published in French and international peer-reviewed journals, such as *International Journal of Entrepreneurship and Small Business, Journal of Small Business and Entrepreneurship, Revue Française de Gestion, Revue Internationale PME, Revue Sciences de Gestion, International Journal of Business and Globalisation*, among others. E-mail: a.jaouen@supco-montpellier.fr

**Pieter Kamminga** is assistant professor at the Open University of the Netherlands. He teaches and conducts research in the field of management accounting and management control. His research focuses on the control of interfirm relationships and on the dynamics in these relationships. He defended a doctoral dissertation on management control of joint ventures (2003). He had publications on this topic in *Accounting, Organizations and Society* (2007) and in the *European Management Journal* (2006). In addition, he contributed to the books *Accounting in Networks* (Routledge, 2010) and *International Management Accounting and Control* (McGraw-Hill, 2010). E-mail: pieter.kamminga@ou.nl

**Saleema Kauser** is a lecturer in the organization studies group at Manchester Business School (MBS). She earned her first degree in psychology from the University of London. She holds a master's degree in information systems and technology from Cass Business School, an MBA from Aston Business School, and a PhD from the Warwick Business School, University of Warwick. She has been lecturing for over 10 years on strategic and organizational management issues. E-mail: saleema.kauser@mbs.ac.uk

**Poonam Khanna** is an assistant professor at the W. P. Carey School of Business, Arizona State University, and a Kauffman Foundation Dissertation

Fellow. She earned her PhD in strategic management from the University of Texas at Austin. Her research interests include interorganizational networks, informal network ties between top executives and the implications of those ties for CEO and board effectiveness and firm performance, and corporate governance. Her research has been published in journals such as *Administrative Science Quarterly* and *Academy of Management Journal*, and she has been a finalist for the distinguished paper award from the BPS Division of the Academy of Management. She serves as an ad hoc reviewer for the *Academy of Management Journal*, *Academy of Management Review*, and *Strategic Management Journal*, among other leading management journals. E-mail: poonam.khanna@asu.edu

**Rosalinde Klein Woolthuis** is assistant professor at the faculty of economics and business administration at the VU University Amsterdam, and consultant at TNO Innovation and Environment. She has published papers in journals such as *Organization Studies*, *Technovation*, and *Technological Forecasting & Social Change*. Her research focuses on the diffusion of sustainable innovations and practices, thereby changing existing business models and entire industries. She is a consultant to national and international governmental bodies on how sustainable innovation can be promoted through measures such as stimulating entrepreneurship and modernizing rules and regulations. E-mail: rkleinwoolthuis@feweb.vu.nl

**Dovev Lavie** is an associate professor at the Technion, a Sloan Industry Studies Fellow, and a recipient of the SMS Emerging Scholar Award, the INFORMS TMS best dissertation award, and the Academy of Management Newman Award for best paper based on a dissertation. He earned his PhD at the Wharton School and served as an assistant professor at the University of Texas at Austin. Focusing on strategic management, his research interests include value creation and appropriation in alliance networks, relational capabilities and performance implications of alliance portfolios, as well as applications of the resource-based view in interconnected technology-intensive industries. His work has been published in the *Academy of Management Journal*, *Academy of Management Review*, *Strategic Management Journal*, *Organization Science*, among other leading journals. He currently serves as an Associate Editor of the *Academy of Management Journal* and is on the editorial boards of the *Strategic Management Journal* and *Organization Science*. E-mail: dlavie@ie.technion.ac.il

**Christian Lechner** is professor of strategic management and entrepreneurship, and head of the Research Center for Entrepreneurship and Growth Strategies at Toulouse Business School. He has a diploma in Italian and international business studies from University of Florence, Italy; German diploma in business administration from Ludwig-Maximilians-University,

Munich, Germany; MBA from University of Georgia, U.S.; and a PhD in business administration, University of Regensburg, Germany. He has spent periods as visiting professor at the University of Regensburg, Germany; Rutgers University, U.S.; Libera Università di Bolzano, Italy; ESSEC Barcelona, Spain; and WHU Germany. His research interests cover entrepreneurship, regional and small firm networks, high-tech clusters, strategic networks, cooperative competition, and growth strategies. E-mail: c.lechner@esc-toulouse.fr

**Olivier Meier** is professor and research director at the University of Paris East/IRG, France. He holds a master in strategy and marketing (Paris Dauphine Université) and a PhD in management (UPEC/ IRG), and a HDR (Habilitation à Diriger des Recherches). Dr. Meier has taught corporate strategy and international strategy in various master, full-time and executive MBA, and executive education programs. He is a visiting Professor at European Center Research–Harvard Business School (HBS). His research concerns the strategic management of mergers and acquisitions, with a particular emphasis on the relationships between innovation and external growth and integration policies. He has contributed to several books (18) and academic journals such as *Growth and Change*, *Journal of Small Business and Entrepreneurship*, *Systèmes d'information et Management* (SIM), *Management International*, *Finance Contrôle Stratégie*, *Gestion des Ressources Humaines*, *Revue Française de Gestion*, and *Revue International de Psychosociologie*. Dr. Meier has been involved in teaching in executive programs in large international firms. Corporate clients have included Bouygues Telecom, EADS, SAFRAN, EDF, GDF Suez, E. Leclerc, PSA Peugeot Citroën, and Schneider Electric. E-mail: olmeier@yahoo.fr

**Audrey Missonier** is professor of strategic management at Groupe Sup de Co Montpellier Business School, France. She focuses her research activities on strategy, mergers, acquisitions, and alliances. She has published papers in peer-reviewed journals: *Journal of Small Business and Entrepreneurship*, *Corporate Governance*, *Systèmes d'information et Management* (SIM), *Finance, Contrôle, Stratégie*. She has presented the results of her research in international conferences. She has edited three books and contributed chapters to 12 books. She serves as a project manager for mergers and is an invited speaker at conferences for practitioners. She advises entrepreneurs on their projects of alliances. E-mail: a.missonier@supco-montpellier.fr

**Bart Nooteboom** is emeritus professor of innovation policy. He is the author of 11 books and some 300 articles on small business, entrepreneurship, innovation and diffusion, innovation policy, transaction cost theory, interfirm relations, trust, networks, and organizational learning. He is a member of the Royal Netherlands Academy of Arts and Sciences. He was awarded the Kapp prize for his work on organizational learning, the Gunnar Myrdal prize for his book on trust and the Schumpeter prize for his book on a cognitive theory of the firm. His most recent book (2012) is a philosophy book on humanism. In 1988–1990 he was member of a government committee on technology policy. In 2006–2007 he was a member of the (Dutch) Scientific Council for Government Policy (WRR) where he supervised the production of an advisory report to the Dutch government on innovation policy. E-mail: b.nooteboom@uvt.nl

**Anne Norheim-Hansen** pursues a joint doctoral degree in management at SKEMA Business School (knowledge, technology, and organization (KTO) PhD in management) and IAE Aix-en-Provence, Aix-Marseille Université (Doctorat en Sciences de Gestion), and teaches at SKEMA Business School. In her dissertation, she examines the role of firms' proactive environmental strategies in determining firm-specific and joint competitive advantages in the different phases of strategic alliances. Other research interests include intercluster and firm–NGO alliances, reputational interdependencies in networks, and strategic environmental management. She holds an MA degree in public communication and public relations from the University of Westminster, and a BBA from Zicklin School of Business, Baruch College, City University of New York. Before initiating a career in academia, she worked as a consultant and freelance journalist, writing on a broad range of business related topics. Earlier professional experiences include in-house positions in the media and telecommunication industries. E-mail: anne.norheimhansen@skema.edu

**Beliz Ozorhon** is an assistant professor of construction management in the department of civil engineering at Bogazici University, Turkey. Her research initiatives focus on innovation management, international joint ventures, strategic decision making, performance management, and knowledge management. Her recent projects investigate the sustainability issues in built environment, innovative project delivery and integration in construction, and investment decision making. She has published many papers in leading journals and international conference proceedings. E-mail: beliz.ozorhon@boun.edu.tr

**Robert E. Spekman** is the Tayloe Murphy Professor of Business Administration at the University of Virginia's Darden Graduate School of Business. He is a recognized authority on business-to-business marketing strategy, channels of distribution design, and the implementation of go-to-market strategies. Professor Spekman is also well known for his research and corporate consultancy work in strategic alliances, partnerships, and supply chain management. In 2004, he was named a fellow to the Institute for the Study of Business Markets at the Pennsylvania State University's Smeal School of

Business. Professor Spekman has worked with many of the Fortune 100 as well as with a number of non-U.S.-based global firms. The author of more than 100 articles and papers, he has also written/edited eight books and monographs. His book, *Alliance Competency*, was published by John Wiley in 2000, and his most recent book, *The Extended Enterprise*, was published by Prentice Hall/Financial Times in 2003. E-mail: Spekmanr@virginia.edu

**Brian Tjemkes** is an associate professor in the department of management and organization of the faculty of economics and business administration at VU University Amsterdam, The Netherlands. He received his PhD in business administration from Radboud University Nijmegen, The Netherlands. His dissertation focused on the relationships among value creation, value appropriation, and alliance performance. He has published in the *Journal of Management Studies*, *Management Decision*, and *Journal of International Management*, among others. His research interests include the management and performance of strategic alliances. E-mail: b.v.tjemkes@vu.nl

**Marit Ubachs** studied at the Nijmegen School of Management of the Radboud University, Nijmegen, The Netherlands. In 2011 she received a master of science degree in international management and strategy. She is researcher for several international projects on corporate social responsibility, foreign direct investment, and strategic alliances. Currently she holds a position as management consultant in the sustainable commercial sector. E-mail: m.ubachs@ibc.nl

**Jeltje van der Meer-Kooistra** is a professor of financial management at the University of Groningen. She was appointed as professor in 1998. Until 2010 she was director of the Management Accounting Research Institute and director of the BSc and MSc accountancy and controlling. Her research focuses on the management and control of intrafirm and interfirm relationships. Her current research projects are directed to the governance of product development projects, the role of learning processes in the development of interfirm control, dynamics in joint venture relationships, and the control of intrafirm transactions. She is a member of the editorial board of *Management Accounting Research* and a Dutch scientific journal. She was a guest editor of a special issue of *Management Accounting Research* (2006) on the theme of management control of interfirm transactional relationships. She has published her work in journals such as *Accounting, Organizations and Society*, *Management Accounting Research*, *Accounting, Auditing & Accountability Journal*, *Advances in Management Accounting*, *Journal of Organizational Change Management*, *Journal of Accounting and Organizational Change*, and *International Transfer Pricing Journal*. She co-edited the book *International Management Accounting and Control* (McGraw-Hill, 2010) and contributed book chapters in *Accounting in Networks* (Routledge, 2010) and *Researching*

*Strategic Alliances: Emerging Perspectives* (Information Age Publishing, 2010). E-mail: j.van.der.meer-kooistra@rug.nl

**Hans van Kranenburg** is professor of corporate strategy at Radboud University Nijmegen, the Netherlands. He has been a visiting scholar at National Opinion Research Center affiliated with the University of Chicago and visiting professor at Jönköping International Business School. He received his BA (agricultural economics) from the University of Exeter and his MA (econometrics) from Tilburg University (the Netherlands). His PhD in econometrics/industrial economics is from the Maastricht University. His research interests cover market and nonmarket strategies, industry dynamics, industrial organization, international business, (strategic) behavior of firms, and information and communications industries. E-mail: h.vankranenburg@fm.ru.nl

**Pepijn Vos** is a researcher and consultant in the field of managing strategic alliances, co-creation and innovation at the Netherlands Organization for Applied Scientific Research (TNO). He holds a BSc in food technology management from the University of Applied Science HAS in Den Bosch and a MSc in business administration from Radboud University in Nijmegen. E-mail: pepijn.vos@tno.nl

**Hiroshi Yasuda** is a professor in the School of Business, Aoyama Gakuin University in Tokyo, Japan. His main research interest exists in the analysis of strategic alliances, especially in the context of competitive strategies and management of technologies. He graduated from the University of Tokyo in applied physics and received his Master of Science degree in management from Sloan School of Management at Massachusetts Institute of Technology, and PhD in industrial engineering and management from Tokyo Institute of Technology. E-mail: yasuda@busi.aoyama.ac.jp

# INDEX

## A

Abolafia, M., 159
Absorptive capabilities, 286
Absorptive capacities, 8, 282
Acomplementary, 102–103, 108–109, 111–112, 114–117, 120–125
Adolfs, K., 99, 100
Aggressive voice as response strategy, 100–101, 107, 109, 113–114, 116–121
Ahmed, M., 227
Ahuja, G., 77, 80, 83, 88, 229
Aiman-Smith, L., 79, 85
Aldrich, H. E., 191, 202
Ali, M. Y., 241
Alliance bench depth, 19
Alliance competence, 3
Alliance competence, antecedents of, 10–16
Alliance competence, building at firm level, 18–20
Alliance competence, implications for managers, 20–22
Alliance competencies, teachable and unteachable, 16–18
Alliance constellations, 133
Alliance duration, 136, 140
Alliance failure, 187
Alliance formation and corporate reputation, 82–83
Alliance formation, 73–75, 79–85, 87–88
Alliance governance, roles of third parties, 57
Alliance know-how, 18
Alliance learning, 8, 19
Alliance management roles and responsibilities, 15
Alliance mindset, 19
Alliance performance, 28–31, 33, 39, 41–45, 47–51
Alliance performance, high versus low, 20
Alliance performance, indices of alliance processes and infrastructure, 21–22
Alliance process and structure, 18
Alliance processes, 98–99, 125, 129–130, 132–133
Alliance relationships, 188–190, 201–202, 204
Alliance tensions and proprietary assets, 139–141
Alliance tensions, 139–140
Alliance-specific investments as exchange variable, 100, 107, 112–113, 123

Allouche, J., 79, 81
Ambec, S., 74, 78, 79
Anand, B., 18
Anand, J., 9
Andersen, P. H., 283
Anderson, E., 203
Anderson, J. C., 133, 189–191, 193, 195, 203
Ang, S. H., 81
Anticomplementary, 102–103, 109, 113–114, 116–117, 119–121, 123–125, 130
Aragón-Correa, J. A., 74, 75, 76, 77, 78, 81, 84
Arditi, D., 233–253
Arend, R. J., 82
Argyres, N. S., 170
Ariño, A., 58, 98–99, 104, 106, 128, 166, 169, 181
Arya, B., 74, 282
Ashayeri, J., 258
Ashkanasy, N. M., 49, 52, 54
Assael, H., 193
Asymmetrical power distribution, 260
Attractive alternatives as exchange variable, 100, 107, 116, 119, 123
Aulakh, P. S., 31, 80, 87, 195
Axelrod, R. M., 4

## B

Bachmann, R., 62, 69–70, 217
Baden-Fuller, C., 6
Bae, J., 74, 80–81, 83, 86, 88
Baier, A. C., 228
Bakås, O., 86
Baker, W. E., 57, 63
Ball, D. F., 28
Ball, S. D., 275
Bandyopadhyay, S. P., 85
Banerjee, S. B., 78
Banks, J. C., 191
Bargaining power, 220
Barkema, H.G., 240, 247
Barker, K., 78, 79
Barnes, J., 136

Barnett, M. L., 79, 82
Barney, J. B., 5, 29, 75–78, 81, 83–84
Baron, J., 157
Bartholomew, S., 284–285
Bauer, T. N., 79, 85
Baum, J. A. C., 71, 137
Beal, B. D., 137
Beamish, P. W., 151, 169–170, 183, 188–193, 201, 203, 208, 235, 238–240, 242, 246–247, 283–284, 298
Becerra, M., 55
Beckman, C. M., 80
Beguin, J. P., 190–191, 193
Behavioral capabilities, 7
Behrens, D., 58
Belaya, V., 255–278
Bell, J. H. J., 240
Bello, D. C., 123
Benassi, M., 143
Berchicci, L., 74, 76–77, 79, 81
Berg, J., 61
Berger, P., 159
Berry, M. A., 78
Berry, T., 227
Bertels, S., 79, 82
Bijlsma-Frankema, K., 57, 64–65
Bing, L., 235, 238, 239, 242–243
Birgonul, M. T., 238, 248
Birkinshaw, J., 285
Blankertz, L., 261
Bleackley, M., 191, 201
Bleeke, J., 56, 188, 282
Blodgett, L. L., 188, 242
Blumberg, B., 63
Bodwell, C., 78
Boeker, W., 2
Bojanic, D. C., 258
Bollen, K. A., 243
Bolstad, A., 86
Borgatti, S. P., 138
Borys, B., 192
Bouchikhi, H., 98, 122, 134
Boulian, P. V., 195
Bourdieu, P., 157
Bourlakis, M., 260
Bowditch, J. L., 35
Bowles, S., 62

Boyd, R., 62
Boymans, C., 97–130
Brady, A., 75, 79, 81–82
Broadfoot, L. E., 49
Bronson, J., 192
Brouthers, K., 247
Brouthers, L., 247
Brown, L. T., 241, 247
Browne, M. W., 100
Buckley, P. J., 83, 188, 191, 193, 203, 234, 236–237, 247
Bunker, B. B., 64–65, 70
Buono, A. F., 35
Burchell, G., 216, 230
Burks, A. W., 218
Burt, R. S., 59, 66, 132, 134–138, 141, 145, 157, 228
Butler, J. E., 76
Butler, R. J., 188, 283

## C

Cable, D. M., 79, 85
Cacioppe, R., 78
Cadden, T., 213
Cadogan, J. W., 236, 246
Caldwell, D. F., 29
Camerer, C., 228
Cameron, K. S., 40
Cannon, J. P., 283
Cant, M., 258
Cardinal, L. B., 106
Carnevale, P. J., 151
Carr, A., 5
Carson, R. C., 101, 102
Carter, P., 212, 217
Carter, S. M., 81, 82
Cartwright, D., 276
Cartwright, S., 34, 39
Cassiman, B., 284, 286
Casson, M. C., 191, 234, 236–237
Cavusgil, S. T., 31, 80, 87, 284
Central organization, 133, 136
Chan, Y. K., 74, 78–79, 81
Charness, G., 56–57, 60–61
Chatman, J., 29

Chen, C. C., 241, 247
Chen, H., 5, 189–190, 192
Chen, M., 240
Chen, T.-Y., 5
Chen, Y. M., 58
Chew, D. A. S., 238, 239
Chi, P. S. K., 240
Child, J., 28, 81, 188, 190, 202
Choi, B., 85
Choi, C. B., 242
Choi, J., 241, 247
Chu, W., 85
Chung, S., 80, 83
Churchill, G. A., 194
Circumplex approach, 97–126
Closure, 132, 135–137
Cobo-Reyes, R., 56–57, 60–61
Cognitive distance, 57, 60, 64
Cohen, G., 85, 86
Cohen, W. M., 8, 60, 88
Cohesive ties, 137–138
Coleman, J. S., 132, 134, 136–137
Colombo, M. G., 284, 286
Commitment, 187, 189–196, 198–199, 201–204, 236–237, 240–241, 245–248
Communication, 187, 189–196, 199, 201–204, 237, 241–242, 245–249
Competence trust, 229
Competency defined, 6–8
Complementary assets, 141–142
Complementary capabilities, 285
Complementary principle, 97–98, 102–105, 108–126, 130
Complementary resources, 281
Complex web, 132
Conflict resolution, 191–193, 201–202, 237–238, 241, 245, 247
Conflict, 187–199, 201–204
Considerate voice as response strategy, 100–101, 107–109, 111–114, 116–121, 124
Constantin, M. J., 98, 101, 102, 104, 115, 124
Constellations, 133
Consultation-based control pattern, 171, 179–180

Content-based control mechanisms, 168, 171–172, 177
Content-based control pattern, 170, 172, 177, 179–180
Context-based control mechanisms, 168, 171–173
Context-based control pattern, 168, 171
Contextual fit, 239–240, 244
Contractor, F. J., 169, 183, 188, 205, 207, 234, 250, 297
Contracts, 56–59, 61, 67–68
Contractual trust, 229
Control complexity, 170–173
Control, 149, 151, 153, 155
Cook, K. S., 145
Cool, K., 75, 81, 83–84
Cooper, C. D., 65
Cooper, C. L., 34, 39
Cooper, M. C., 258
Cooperation versus competition, 135–136
Cooperation, 237–238, 241, 245–248
Coordination, 187, 189–197, 201, 204.
Corporate culture, 283, 288–289
Corporate reputation and alliance formation, 82–83
Corporate reputation, 75, 79, 82, 85
Corporate social responsibility (CSR), 75, 87
Correspondence, rule of, 97, 102, 104, 108–124
Corsten, D., 10
Costa, L. A., 86
Cox, A., 257
Coyne, J., 28
Creative voice as response strategy, 100–101, 107–108, 110, 112, 114, 116, 119
Cropper, S., 90
Cross-level embeddedness, 132
Cuganesan, S., 227
Cui, C. C., 28
Cullen, J., 192, 227
Culpan, R., 206
Cultural differences, 192, 201
Cultural distance, 57, 63–64, 284
Cultural fit, 27–28, 47, 49, 236, 240–242, 244
Cultural misunderstandings, 192, 201–202, 204
Cultural proximity, 150, 158–160
Cummings, J. L., 80, 87
Cummings, L. L., 25
Currall, S. C., 165–166, 169–171, 239
Cyert, R. M., 8

## D

Dacin, M. T., 75, 80, 87–88, 137
Daft, R., 195
Dahlgren, G., 214, 217
Dai, Y., 79, 82, 85
Dale, B. G., 227
Damanpour, F., 241, 247
Dang, T., 189
Das, T. K., 14, 28, 56, 74, 76, 83–84, 87–88, 98, 122, 125, 130, 132–135, 140, 146, 150–151, 169–170, 185, 188–193, 201, 203, 214, 217, 238, 258–259, 281–282
Datta, D. K., 34
de Boer, E. R., 133
de Boer, L., 212
de Jong, B., 55–71
De la Torre, J., 98, 166, 181
de Man, A.-P., 29, 56
De Rond, M., 98, 122, 134, 208
De Vries, H., 104
Deakin, S, 58
Dean, M., 215–217
Deeds, D. L., 281
Deephouse, D. L., 82, 85
Dekker, H. C., 214, 217
Deleuze, G., 217
Delgado-García, J. B., 79, 82
Delios, A., 169, 235
deMan, A., 11
Demirkhan, I., 281
Destructive relationship termination, role of third parties, 57
Deutsch, M., 192, 201
Devlin, G., 191, 201

Dickhaut, J., 61
Dierickx, I., 75, 81, 83, 84
Dikmen, I., 238, 248
DiMaggio, P., 157
Dineen, B. R., 65
Ding, D. Z., 188, 189, 190, 191, 193
Dirks, K. T., 57, 63, 65
Disciplinary power, 216–217
Disciplining process, 223
Distrust during negotiations, 63
Diversity of capabilities, 284–286, 294
Diversity of corporate culture, 282–284, 286, 294
Diversity of knowledge, 284–286
Diversity of values, 282–284
Dollinger, M. J., 80–82, 84–85, 87
Doney, P. M., 283
Dooley, K., 105
Douglas, T. J., 78, 79
Dowell, G., 74–79, 81
Dowling, G. R., 81, 85
Doz, Y. L., 98, 132–134, 188, 236–238, 258
Draulans, J., 11
Druckman, D., 152
du Plessis, P. J., 258
Duan, J., 236, 246
Duijsters, G., 236
Dunlop, A., 227
Dunn, S. C., 243
Dussauge, P., 285–286
Dutton, J. E., 137
Duysters, G., 29, 56–57, 60, 258
Dyadic relations, 132, 139
Dyer, J. H., 11, 28, 30, 35, 49–50, 76, 85, 258
Dynamic capabilities, 9
Dynamic evolution of JV relationship, 163–166, 168–170, 172, 174, 181–182

E

Eastham J. F., 275
Ebers, M., 212
Ebers, M., 90

Eccles, R., 146
Echambadi, R., 31, 80, 87
Economic satisfaction as exchange variable, 100, 107, 123
Ecosystem, 291
Eisenhardt, K. M., 74, 76, 82–83, 88, 105–106
El-Ansary, A. L., 257
Embeddedness theory, 137–138
Emerson, R. M., 133
Ensign, P., 285
Environmental capabilities, 74, 76–77, 79, 81, 84, 87
Environmental credibility, 73, 75, 81, 84, 86
Environmental performance, 77, 79, 81
Environmental reputation and reputational spillovers, 84–86
Environmental reputation and resource-richness, 83–84
Environmental reputation, 73, 75, 79, 81–84, 86–88
Eriksson, K., 189
Ernst, D., 56, 188, 282
Evans, J., 240
Everett, M. G., 138
Exchange variables, 100, 104, 106–107, 121, 123–125, 128
Exclusive dyads, 142
Exit propensity as response strategy, 100–101, 107, 122
External transaction networks, 137, 143

F

Fabrigar, L. R., 100
Faems, D., 55–71, 99, 104–105
Falkus, S., 49
Fan, W. W., 238–239
Fang, L., 123
Fang, T., 158
Fann, K. T., 218
Faulkner, D. O., 208
Faulkner, D., 28, 81, 188, 190, 202
Faust, K., 138
Fehr, E., 56–58, 60–62

Ferguson, T. D., 85
Ferguson, W. I., 85
Ferrin, D. L., 57, 63, 65
Fey, C. F., 188–189, 201, 238–239, 259
Fichman, M., 171
Fiddis, C., 260
Fiegenbaum, A., 85–86
Financial situation of the Joint Venture (JV), 166, 172–173, 182
Firm-specific value, 131
Fischbacher, U., 56–58, 60–62
Fisher, R., 14
Fladmoe-Lindquist, K., 286
Flick, U., 277
Folta, T. B., 286
Fombrun, C. J., 82, 84–85
Forbes, T. M., 28
Forbes, T., III, 12
Foreign direct investments, 256–257
Forster, N., 78
Foucault, M., 211, 214–217
Fouts, P. A., 77, 79
Fowler, S. J., 77
Fox, M., 78
Fragale, A. R., 104
Frankort, H. T. W., 132, 135
Fréchet, M., 158–159
French, J. R. P., 256, 258, 260
Freytag, P. V., 213
Fridh, C., 158
Friedman, T. L., 2
Friedman, W. G., 190, 191, 193
Fritsch, N., 261
Frost, T., 285
Fuente-Sabaté, J. M., 79, 82, 85
Fulk, J., 56
Funder, D. C., 99, 104
Furrer, O., 97–130

## G

Gachter, S., 62
Gallarotti, G. M., 78–79
Gambetta, D., 62
Ganesh, U., 247
Gardberg, N. A., 82
Garette, B., 285–286
Gargiulo, M., 7, 74, 80–81, 83, 86, 88, 137–138, 143, 229
Garrone, P., 284, 286
Gartenfeld, M. E., 151
Gaski, J. F., 61
Gatewood, R. D., 82, 84–85
Gattorna, J. L., 258
Geanakoplos, J., 258
Geringer, J. M., 80, 167, 188–189, 235–236, 240, 242, 247
Germain, R., 192–193, 201
Geyskens, J., 189
Ghemewhat, P., 203
Ghoshal, S., 61
Gill, J., 188, 283
Gilsing, V., 57, 60
Gintis, H., 62
Glaister, K. W., 83, 188, 191, 193, 203, 234, 247
Glick, W. H., 106
Global market, 280, 285
Global strategic alliances, 280, 282, 288
Goldberg, A. I., 85–86
Golden, P. A., 80–82, 84–85, 87
Gomes-Casseres, B., 132–134, 240
Gordon, C., 214–217, 230
Gottschalg, O., 258
Governmental apparatuses, 217, 222
Governmentality, 214–217, 224
Gowan, M. A., 82, 84–85
Graham, J. L., 158
Granovetter, M. S., 4–5, 31, 64, 132, 134, 136–138, 141, 157, 258
Grant, R., 8, 76
Graves, S. B., 78
Gray, B., 188–189, 238, 242
Green credence, 75, 87
Greening, D. W., 85
Gregory, M. J., 6
Greve, H. R., 75, 80, 87–88
Gudmand-Høyer, M., 215
Gudmundsson, S. V., 131–147
Gulati R., 258
Gulati, R. 7, 38, 58, 82–83, 135, 137–138, 151, 188, 191, 212, 214, 217, 229, 258, 260

Gulbro, R., 151
Gunhan, S., 239
Gurnani, H., 98, 122
Guthrie, J. P., 240
Gutman, H., 230

## H

Habib, G. M., 191
Hagedoorn, J., 132, 135, 138, 188, 281
Haig, B. D., 218
Håkansson, H., 133, 185, 227
Hald, K. S., 227
Hall, R., 81, 84–85
Hambrick, D., 189
Hamel, G., 6, 132–134, 165–166, 169–170, 188
Handfield R. B., 189, 195, 203
Hanf, J. H., 255–278
Hansson, J., 214, 217
Hanvanich, S., 284
Hargadon, A. B., 60
Harrigan, K. R., 151, 165–166, 169, 174, 188, 240, 247, 284
Hart, S. L., 74–79, 81, 84
Hartman, C. L., 77
Hastings, M., 81, 83
Haunschild, P. R., 27–54, 80
Hebert, L., 167, 189, 238, 242, 247
Hedberg, B., 214, 217
Heene, A., 6, 23–24
Heide, J., 5
Heimeriks, K. H., 258
Hellriegel, D., 158, 236
Helper, S., 260
Henderson, L., 98, 101–102, 104, 115, 124
Hennart, J. F., 166, 173–174, 188, 240, 281, 284
Herbert, L., 188
Herbig, P., 151
Hergert, M., 193, 203
Hierarchical relationship, 163–164
Hill, C. W. L., 281
Hill, R. C., 158, 236
Hillebrand, B., 57–58, 61

Hillenbrand, C., 79
Hills, H. L., 104
Hingley, M. K., 261
Hirsch, B., 82
Hirschman, A. O., 61
Hitt, M. A., 80
Hoang, H., 86
Hoetker, G., 74, 81
Hofstede, G., 7, 240–242, 288
Holm, D. B., 189
Holmberg, S. R., 80, 87
Holmes, M. E., 105
Homans, G., 4
Hon, A. H. Y., 82
Hoon-Halbauer, S. K., 192
Hope, C., 77
Hopmann, P. T., 152
Horizontal relationship, 163–164
Horowitz, L. M., 98, 101–102, 104, 115, 124
Houston, M. B., 85–86
Howells, J., 66
Hu, M., 189–190, 192
Hu, T-L., 257
Huber, G. P., 8, 195, 213
Huberman, A. M., 106, 128, 154–155
Huemer, L., 55
Hughes, J., 202
Humphreys, P., 213
Hunt, S. D., 2, 14, 61, 74, 189, 273
Hutton, P., 230
Huxham, C., 90
Hybels, R. C., 86

## I

Inkpen, A. C., 10, 151, 165–166, 169–171, 237, 239
Institutional environment, 170, 173, 175–177, 182
Interdependence, 187, 189–197, 201
International construction, 233–234, 236, 243, 248
International strategic alliances, 187–189, 191–193, 195, 197, 199, 201–204

Interorganizational negotiation, 151–152
Interorganizational relationships, 203
Interpartner diversity and alliance performance, 294
Interpartner relations, 236–243
Interpersonal networks, 149–150, 157
Interpersonal relationships, 187
Interpersonal theory, 97–99, 101–102, 104, 114–115, 124–127, 129–130
Ireland, P., 257
Ireland, R. D., 258
Isabella, L. A., 2, 10, 12, 14, 15, 17, 18, 28
Isomorphic acomplementary, 102–103, 108–109, 112, 114–117, 120–121, 123–125
Ittner, C. D., 213
Iyer, E. S., 78

## J

Jablin, F. M., 207
Jackson, N., 212, 217
Jain, C. S., 191, 201–202
Jakobsen, M., 211–232
Janger, A. R., 234
Janssens, M., 99, 104–105
Jaouen, A., 149–162
Jaworski, B. J., 34
Jemison, D. B., 192
Jermier, J. M., 79, 82
Jimenez, N., 56–57, 60–61
Johanson, J., 133, 189, 239
John, G., 203
Johnson, B., 284
Johnson, H. T., 174
Johnson, J., 191–192
Joint problem solving, 192, 201, 203–204
Joint Venture (JV) control, 163–168, 170–173, 177–178, 180–183
Joint Venture (JV) dynamics, 165, 168–169, 171, 174, 181
Joint Venture (JV) management, 171–173
Joint Venture (JV) parties, 170–171, 174, 180, 182
Joint Venture (JV) performance, 172–173
Jolly, D., 9
Jooste, C. J., 258
Judge, W. Q., 78–79
Jurriens, J. A., 258

## K

Kachra, A., 246
Kale, P., 2, 8, 10–11, 18–19, 28, 31, 35, 50, 80, 83, 165, 169–170, 188, 258
Kamauff, K., 19
Kamminga, P. E., 163–185
Kampstra, R. P., 258
Kao, J. L., 85
Kaplan, R. S., 174
Kashyap, R. K., 78
Katsikeas, C. S., 123
Katz, R., 57, 64
Kauser, S., 187–209
Keown, S., 20
Key individuals, 166, 171–172, 182
Khamseh, H., 9
Khanna, P., 27–54
Khanna, T., 18, 38, 135, 191
Khodyakov, D., 228
Kiesler, D. J., 98, 101–102, 115, 124
Kiessling, T. S., 6
Killing, J. P., 166, 172, 183, 188, 190–191, 193, 201, 208, 234, 236, 238, 240–242, 298
Kilmartin, C. T., 104
Kim, D. J., 240
Kim, P. H., 65
King, A., 74, 76–77, 79, 81
Klassen, R. D., 77
Klein Woolthuis, R., 55–71
Klein, B., 85
Knez, M., 138
Knowledge search, 286
Knowledge transfer as a competency, 9–10
Knowledge transfer, 286

Knowledge-based view of the firm, 8
Koch, P. T., 192
Kogut, B., 2, 8, 164, 188, 195, 240–241, 258, 283
Kohli, A. K., 34
Kokorev, R., 259
Kotabe, M., 195
Kozan, M. K., 192
Krackhardt, D., 58
Kramer, R. M., 70
Kraus, K., 185
Kruglanski, A. W., 256, 260
Kumar, N., 189, 195, 203, 217
Kumar, R., 14, 151, 169–170, 188–193, 201, 203, 282–283
Kumar, S., 173, 176, 281
Kwok, H. C. A., 235

## L

Labro, E., 212
Lafferty, B. A., 79, 82
Lambe, C. J., 2, 14, 74
Lambert, D. M., 258
Lane, C., 68–70
Lane, H. W., 188, 190–193, 201, 240, 283
Lane, P. J., 64
Lang, T., 260
Lange, D., 79, 82, 85
Langfield-Smith, K., 214, 217, 228
Lanier, K., 104
Lanoie, P., 74, 78, 79
Larcker, D. F., 213
Laroche, P., 79, 81
Larson, A., 63
Lasbordes, V., 157
Lasserre, P., 241
Lautenschlager, G. J., 82, 84–85
Lavie, D., 27–54, 74, 76, 85–86
Lazzarini, S. G., 132–134, 139
Learning as a competency, 8–9
Learning, 166, 169–170, 174, 176–177, 181–182
Leary, T., 101–102
Lechner, C., 131–147

Lee, D. Y., 189
Lee, K., 80, 83
Lee, P. M., 79, 82, 85
Lee, R., 227
Leffler, K. B., 85
Leinhardt, S., 147
Lengel, R., 195
Leonard-Barton, D., 105
Leong, C. H. Y., 240
Lester, R. H., 83–85
Leung, K., 192
Levinthal, D. A., 8, 60, 88, 171
Levitas, E., 80
Lewicki, R. J., 64–65, 70
Lewis, J. W., 35
Lewis, M. A., 6
Lewis, J. D., 190–193
Li, J., 189
Li, P. P., 57, 64
Li, X., 240
Lin, N., 145
Lin, X., 192–193, 201
Lin, Z., 74, 281–282
Lind, J., 185, 227
Local proximity, 284
Local search, 285, 286
Locke, K. D., 99, 104
Lock-in, 135, 142, 144
Lomi, A., 132, 137, 141
Long, C. P., 106
Long-term orientation, 135, 140
Lonsdale, Ch., 257
Lorange, P., 169, 183, 188, 205, 207, 234, 250, 297
Lorenzoni, G., 6
Louch, H., 157
Low, P. S., 240
Lu, L., 192
Lubatkin, M., 64
Luckmann, T., 159
Lui, S. S., 29, 82
Lundvall, B., 284
Lunnan, R., 55
Luo, Y., 98, 122, 106, 181, 236–237, 239, 243, 246, 282

## M

Macaulay, S., 228
MacAvoy, T. C., 2, 10, 12, 14–15, 17–18, 28
MacKenzie, D., 159
Macneil, R. I., 4
Madhok, A., 29, 31, 39, 99, 104–105, 189, 191
Mahoney, J. T., 76
Makhija, M. V., 247
Makino, S., 235, 284
Management structure of alliances, 295
Managerial competence, 7
Managing conflict, 188–189, 192
Managing interpartner diversity, structure for, 294–295
Mandel, N. J., 138
Maravelias, C., 229
March, J. G., 8
Margolis, J. D., 79
Market pressures for environmental capability ambitions, 78–79
Markey, P. M., 99, 104
Marks, M. L., 151
Marsh, L., 286
Martin, I., 230
Mavondo, F. T., 235, 240
Mayer, K. J., 81, 85, 170
Mayer, R. C., 56–57, 62, 64–65, 67
McCabe, K., 61
McCutchen, W. W., 285
McEvily, B., 38, 58, 141, 285
McFarland, R. G., 257
McIvor, R., 213
Mead, R., 240
Meaning of alliance, 283
Medcof, J. W., 260
Meier, O., 149–162
Mellewigt, T., 58, 74, 81
Merchant, H., 240
Merchant, K. A., 173, 176
Merkens, H., 261
Mesquita, L. F., 56, 62
Meyer, C. W., 104
Meyer, M., 82
Michalisin, M. D., 76, 78
Miles, A. M., 154–155
Miles, M. B., 106, 128
Milgrom, P., 85, 258
Miller, C. C., 106
Miller, P., 230
Miller, S. R., 284
Millo, Y., 159
Mirvis, P. H., 151
Mismatch of Joint Venture (JV) control, 168, 170–171, 179–180, 182
Missonier, A. 149–162
Mitsuhashi, H., 75, 80, 87–88
Mjoen, H., 242
Mockler, R. J, 151
Moen, Ø., 86
Mohr, J., 10, 74, 189–190, 192, 194–195, 201, 203, 237, 241, 247
Möllering, G., 57, 62, 67
Monckza, R. M., 189, 195, 203
Money, K., 79
Monge, P. R., 56
Moon, J., 74
Moorman, C., 2
Moran, P., 61, 137
Morgan, R. M., 189
Morlacchi, P., 212
Morosini, P., 240
Morris, B., 236, 246
Morris, D., 193, 203
Mouritsen, J., 212, 227
Mowday, R. T., 195
Mullen, M. R., 283
Multilateral alliances (MLAs), 132–134, 138–143
Multilevel embeddedness, 132, 142–143
Multiplexity, 132
Muthusamy, S., 5
Mutual agreement, 151, 159
Mutual trust, 27, 29–32, 35–39, 41, 43–45, 47–49
Myhr, N., 19

## N

Nagar, V., 213
Narus, J. A., 189–191, 193, 195, 203

National culture fit, 241
Natural termination of Joint Venture (JV) relationship, 164–168, 180–181, 183
Natural-resource-based view (NRBV), 73–77, 79, 82, 84, 87
Neglect as response strategy, 100–101, 107–108, 111–113, 116–121, 124
Negotiation, 149–152, 154–159
Nelson, B. N., 104
Nelson, R., 29, 33
Nerkar, A., 285
Network view of the firm, 4
Neuijen, B., 241–242
Neuijen, B., 7
Nevin, J. R., 61, 189, 203, 273
Newman, W. H., 165–166, 169, 174
Ngo, H. Y., 29, 82
Nidumolu, R., 78
Nohria, N., 38, 135, 146, 191
Non-redundant ties, 141
Noorderhaven, N. G., 132–134
Noordeweir, T. G., 203
Nooteboom, B., 55–71
Norheim-Hansen, A., 73–96
Nti, K. O., 188, 191, 282
Nunnally, J. C., 194
Nyaw, M. K., 246

## O

O'Grady, S., 240
Obstfeld, D., 56–57, 59, 64, 66–67
Ogbonna, E., 260
Ohayv, D., 7, 241–242
Oliver, A. L., 212
Oliver, C., 74, 85
Olk, P., 285
Olson, L. B., 195
Olve, N., 214, 217
Operating routines, 27–30, 33, 47–51
Operations management system, 222
Opportunism as response strategy, 100–101, 107, 110–111, 114
Opportunistic behavior, 150, 170, 182
O'Reilly, C. A., 29

Orford, J., 104
Organizational culture fit, 241–242
Organizational differences between partners, 28–30, 32–35, 38–42, 44–46, 48–51
Organizational differences, dimensions of, 32–35
Organizational differences, internal task routines, 37–38
Organizational differences, management style, 35–36
Organizational differences, marketing routines, 38
Organizational differences, recognition of, 38–39
Organizational differences, responsiveness, 36–37
Organizational fit, 233–234, 236, 238–240, 244–246, 248–249
Oriani, R., 9
Orlitzky, M., 79, 81
Osborne, R. N., 281
Overembeddedness, 132, 138, 143
Oxley, J. E., 87
Ozer, D. J., 99, 104
Ozorhon, B., 233–253

## P

Padula, G., 49
Pagh, J. D., 258
Pajunen, K., 123
Pan, Y., 240
Pandian, J. R., 76
Parent companies, 163–176, 178, 180–183
Park, J. C., 281
Park, S. H., 188, 238, 240–241, 247, 282
Parkhe, A., 49, 169, 188, 234, 236, 238, 241–242, 246–247, 283, 286
Parmigiani, A., 74–75, 81
Partner attractiveness, 73, 75, 79–83, 86, 88
Partner attractiveness, and alliance formation, 80

Partner attractiveness, and environmental reputation, 81–82
Partner attributes and alliance performance, 281–282
Partner selection, 75, 80, 86, 234–236, 248
Partner variety, 141, 144
Partnership attributes, 188–190, 196–197, 201–203
Partnerships, 190, 192, 202–203
Patience as response strategy, 100–101, 107–114, 116–117, 119–120, 122, 124
Patton, M. Q., 261
Pauly, L. W., 285
Payan, J. M., 257
Pays-to-be-green (PTBG), 79, 87
Pedersen, V., 86
Peirce, C. S., 218
Peloza, J., 79, 82
Penrose, E. T., 75
Perlmutter, H., 28, 31, 165, 169–170, 188
Perrone, V., 38, 58
Peteraf, M. A., 76
Peterson K. T., 189, 195, 203
Peterson, M. F., 52, 54
Peterson, R. B., 201
Petkova, A. P., 85
Phases of the alliance life cycle, 11–12
Phene, N., 286
Phillips, D. J., 80
Pisano, G., 76, 78
Podolny, J. M., 138, 157, 284, 285
Polanyi, K., 137
Polonsky, M. J., 77
Poole, M. S., 105
Poppo, L., 58
Porter, L. W., 195, 207
Porter, M. E., 76, 79, 203, 206
Portes, A., 146
Positional embeddedness, 7
Pothukuchi V., 241, 247
Power as a management tool, 257–259
Power, 255–260, 264–265, 269, 271, 273–275
Prahalad, C. K., 6, 78
Priem, R. L., 76

Proactive environmental strategies, 73, 75–78, 87
Proprietary transaction partners, 138
Prospective partners, 73, 75, 79–82, 84, 86–87
Pruitt, D. G., 151
Putnam, L. L., 207

## Q

Quality of partner relations, operationalization, 237–238
Quevedo-Puente, E., 79, 82, 85
Quinn, R. E., 40

## R

Raffnsøe, S., 215
Ragatz G. L., 189, 195, 203
Rahman, N., 150
Rajan, M. V., 213
Randall, D. M., 195
Rangan, U. S., 135, 295
Rangaswami, M. R., 78
Raven, B. H., 256, 258, 260
Rawlinson, R. A., 203
Reciprocity, rule of, 97, 102, 104, 108–110, 112–112, 114–119, 121–124
Reich, S., 285
Reid, D., 75, 87–88
Reid, R. D., 258
Relational commitment, 27, 30–32, 36–39, 41, 43–45, 47–49
Relational complexity, 132
Relational embeddedness, 27, 29, 31–32, 41, 43–45, 49
Relational governance, impact of third parties, 62–66
Relational intensity, 143
Relational mechanisms, 27, 29–33, 35–39, 41–47, 49
Relational norms, 158–159
Relationship dynamics, 189–190, 202
Remer, S., 236

Reputation, 57, 59–61, 65, 67
Reputational dimensions, 81–82
Reputational spillovers and environmental reputation, 84–86
Reputational spillovers, 73, 83–88
Resource complementarity, 282, 294
Resource dependency, 5–6
Resource profiles, 73, 80, 82, 87
Resource-based view (RBV), 5, 75–77, 82
Resource-richness and environmental reputation, 83–84
Resource-richness, 73, 83–84, 86–87
Resources, 149, 151, 153, 157
Response strategy, 97–126
Reuer, J. J., 11, 58, 82, 85–86
Rhoades, D., 140
Richards, M. S., 284
Richardson, G., 132
Richey, R. G., 6
Rigidity versus flexibility, 135–136
Rindova, V. P., 85
Ring, P. S., 4, 31, 63, 75, 87–88, 90, 99, 104, 106, 128, 181
Rivera-Santos, M., 74–75, 81
Roberts, J., 85, 258
Roberts, K. H., 207
Roberts, P. W., 81, 85
Robson, M. J., 123
Rodriguez, C. M., 34, 42
Roehl, T., 166, 173–174
Rondinelli, D. A., 78
Roos, J., 169
Rose, N., 217
Rosenberg, M., 146
Rosenkopf, L., 49, 58, 285
Rothaermel, F., 2
Rousseau, D., 228
Rowley, T., 58
Royer, S., 82
Ruefli, T. W., 81–82
Rugman, A. M., 78, 241, 247
Rühli, E., 152
Rule, E., 20
Russian agri-food business, 255–257, 259–264, 269–272
Russo, M. V., 77, 79

Ruth, J. A., 85
Rynes, S. L., 79, 81

## S

Sadler, P., 99, 104
Saebi, T., 21
Sahay, A., 195
Sakano, T., 192
Sako, M., 170, 214, 228
Salancik, G. R., 141
Sampson, R. C., 87
Sanchez, R., 6, 23–24
Sanders, G., 7, 241–242
Sanderson, J., 257
Saorín-Iborra, M. C., 157
Sarkar, M. B., 31, 80, 87
Saxton, T., 30, 80–82, 84–85, 87
Schaan, J. C., 188
Schaetzlein, R., 236
Scheer, L. K., 189, 195, 203
Schmidt, F. L., 79, 81
Schmidt, S., 152
Schoonhoven, C. B., 74, 76, 82–83, 88
Schreiner, M., 10
Schultzberg, S., 158
Seabright, M. A., 171
Seaker, R. F., 243
Seal, W., 227
Semiconductor industry, 288
Semimorphic acomplementary, 102–103, 108, 111, 114, 116–117, 120, 122–125
Seth, A. A., 173, 176
Sever, J. M., 82, 85
Shah, P. P., 57, 63
Shah, R. H., 75, 80, 82–83, 87–88
Shane, S., 85, 240
Shanley, M., 82, 84–85
Sharma, S., 74, 75, 76, 77, 78, 79, 81, 84
Sharples A. E., 275
Shaw, V., 188, 189, 201
Shenkar, O., 98, 122, 237–241, 246–247
Sheresheva, M., 259
Sheu, J-B., 257
Shimada, J. Y., 201

Short-term versus long-term, 135–136
Shrivastava, P., 78
Shuen, A., 76, 78
Sim, A. B., 241
Simiar, F., 192
Simmel, G., 67
Simonin, B. L., 11, 85
Simons, R. H., 82
Simpson, M., 78–79
Singh, H., 2, 8, 11, 18–19, 28, 30–31, 35, 49–50, 76, 80, 83, 85, 165, 169–170, 188, 240–241, 258, 283
Singh, J. V., 71
Singsuwan, K., 195
Sitkin, S., 57, 64–65, 106, 228
Skitmore, M., 235
Smith, D., 214, 217, 228
Smith, K. G., 240
Social capital, 157, 159
Social construction, 159
Social exchange theory, 4–5
Social network theory, 136–137
Social network, 150, 155, 157, 160
Social satisfaction as exchange variable, 100, 107, 117, 120, 123
Song, M. R., 85
Song, X. M., 192, 201
Spekman, R. E., 1–25, 28, 74, 189–190, 192, 194–195, 201, 203, 237, 241, 247
Spender, J.-C., 174
Sridharan, G., 236, 240
Stafford, E. R., 77
Stahl, G. K., 29
Stanwick, P. A., 77, 79
Stanwick, S. D., 77, 79
Staw, B. W., 25
Steenkamp, J. E. M., 189, 195, 203
Steers, R. M., 195
Steinke, I., 277
Stephens, K. J., 56
Stern, L. W., 257
Stinchfield, B. T., 76, 78
Strategic center, 6
Strategic fit, 28, 42, 44–47, 49–51, 236, 239–240, 244–246, 248
Strategic motives, 166–169, 174, 177, 180–183
Strauss, A., 152
Strengthened Joint Venture (JV) relationship, 164, 166, 172, 174
Strickland, D., 104
Stringfellow, A., 192, 201
Strong, S. R., 104
Structural characteristics, 233–234, 237, 242–245, 247–249
Structural embeddedness, 138
Structural governance, impact of third parties, 58–62
Structural holes, 132, 135–143
Strydom, C. J. W., 258
Stuart, T. E., 284–285
Stuart, T. E., 86
Sullivan, H. S., 102
Surroca, J., 81
Swamidass, P. M., 285
Swaminathan, V., 2, 75, 80, 82–83, 87–88
Swingle, P., 278
System supplier, 219
Sytch, M., 260

# T

Tallman, H., 242
Tallman, S. B., 7, 28–29, 39, 81
Tatoglu, E., 234
Taylor, N., 78–79
Technological and market developments, 174
Teece, D. J., 76, 78
Teng, B., 28, 56, 74, 76, 83–84, 87–88, 98, 122, 125, 132–135, 140, 151, 188–189, 191, 214, 217, 238, 258–259, 281–282, 285
Tensions perspective, 134–136
Tertius, two roles, 59
Thaning, M., 215
Then, D., 235
Third parties in alliance governance, 55–69
Thomas, H., 6, 23–24

Thompson, M., 239
Thrane, S., 212, 227
Tiedens, L. Z., 104
Tiong, R. L. K., 235, 238–239, 242–243
Tjemkes, B., 97–130
Tomita, K., 286
Tomkins, C., 214, 217
Tomlinson, E. C., 56–57, 62, 64–65, 67
Tomlinson, J. W. C., 188, 239
Tracey, T. J., 104, 106
Transaction cost economics, 4
Tretyak, O., 259
Tribó, J. A., 81
Trick, M. A., 146
Trilateral governance, 59
Trust repair, 65
Trust transfer, 63
Trust, 149, 151, 157, 168, 170–172, 176, 179–182, 187, 189–196, 199, 201–204, 225, 236–237, 238–239, 241, 243, 245–246, 283
Trust, blind, 64
Trust, myopia and groupthink, 57, 63–64
Trust-building process, 62–63
Trustworthy relationship, 164, 168, 171, 181
Tsui, A., 189
Turan, B., 98, 101–102, 104, 115, 124
Turban, D. B., 85
Turkish Contractors Association (TCA), 243
Turkish contractors, 234, 243
Turner, R. H., 146
Tushman, M. L., 57–58, 64
Tyler, T. R., 70
Types of power, 256–258, 275

## U

Ubachs, M., 97–130
Ulgen Aydinlik, A., 99–100
Ulijn, J., 236
Uncertainty, 164, 168, 172–173, 175–177, 181

Ungson, G. R., 188, 238, 240–241, 247, 282
Unique resources, 135–136, 140, 142
Ury, W., 14
Uzzi, B., 30–31, 49, 137, 143, 228–229

## V

Vachon, S., 77
Vahlne, J. E., 239
Valdez, M. E., 82, 85–86
Valentino, D., 6
Van de Ven, A. H., 4, 31, 63, 105–106, 181, 190
van den Oord, A., 57, 60
Van der Linde, C., 79
Van der Meer-Kooistra, J., 163–185, 214, 217
Van der Stede, W. A., 173, 176
Van Haverbeke, W., 57, 60
van Kranenburg, H., 131–147
Van Looy, B., 99, 104, 105
Vanhaverbeke, W., 132, 133–134
Vasconcelos, L., 86
Vassolo, R. S., 9
Ventresca, M. J., 137
Verbeke, A., 78, 241, 247
Vermeulen, F., 240, 247
Veugelers, R., 284, 286
Visser, P. S., 100
Voigt, A., 29
Volberda, H., 11
von Kardorff, E., 277
Vos, P., 97–130
Vosselman, E. G. J., 168, 214, 217
Vredenburg, H., 74–79, 81, 84

## W

Waddock, S. A., 78, 81
Waldersee, R. W., 82
Walker, G., 190
Walker, K., 79, 82, 85
Waller, M. A., 243

Walsh, J. P., 79
Watson, G., 257
Weak ties, 137
Weakened Joint Venture (JV) relationship, 163–164, 166–167, 170, 178
Webb, J. W., 258
Weber, Y., 28, 40
Weibel, A., 57, 64–65
Weiner, B., 65
Weiss, J., 202
Weitz, B., 203
Wernerfelt, B., 5, 76–77
Whetten, D., 133
White, M., 5
Wiggins, J. S., 101
Wight, A., 81
Wilderon, C. P. M., 52, 54
Wilkinson, B., 260
Wilkinson, F., 58
Wilkinson, G., 227
Wilkinson, I. F., 273
Wilkinson, I., 213
Williamson, I. O., 85
Williamson, O. E., 4, 58, 67, 174, 258
Wilson, K. R., 98, 101–102, 104, 115, 124
Winship, C., 138
Winter, S. G., 8, 29, 33
Wolff, K. H., 71
Wolpert, J. D., 60
Wright, R. W., 191
Wu, W., 191

## X

Xie, J., 192, 201
Xin, K., 189

## Y

Yakovlev, A., 259
Yan, A., 164, 166, 169–170, 173, 188–189, 236, 238, 242, 246, 283
Yang, H., 74, 281–282
Yasuda, H., 279–299
Yeung, B., 78
Yin, R. K., 105, 128
Yoshino, M. Y., 135, 295
Young, L., 213
Yu, T., 83–85

## Z

Zaheer, A., 38, 58, 141, 285
Zaman, M., 235
Zand, D. E., 61
Zander, U., 8, 258
Zeira, Y., 237–238, 247
Zeng, M., 164, 166, 173, 240, 283–284
Zenger, T., 58
Zietlow, D. S., 166, 173–174
Zollo, M., 11, 258
Zolotsev, P., 98, 101–102, 104, 115, 124
Zucker, L. G., 7, 170